EMBODYING CHARISMA

Emerging often suddenly and unpredictably, living Sufi saints practising in India, Pakistan and Bangladesh are today shaping and reshaping a sacred landscape. By extending new Sufi brotherhoods and focused regional cults, they embody a lived sacred reality.

This collection of essays from many of the subject's leading researchers argues that the power of Sufi ritual derives not from beliefs as a set of abstracted ideas but rather from rituals as transformative and embodied aesthetic practices and ritual processes, Sufi cults reconstitute the sacred as a concrete emotional and as a dissenting tradition, they embody politically potent postcolonial counter-narrative. The book therefore challenges previous opposites, up until now used as a tool for analysis, such as magic versus religion, ritual versus mystical belief, body versus mind and syncretic practice versus Islamic orthodoxy, by highlighting the connections between Sufi cosmologies, ethical ideas and bodily ritual practices.

With its wide-ranging historical analysis as well as its contemporary research, this collection of case studies is an essential addition to courses on ritual and religion in sociology, anthropology and Islamic or South Asian studies. Its ethnographically rich and vividly written narratives reveal the important contributions that the analysis of Sufism can make to a wider theory of religious movements and charismatic ritual in the context of late twentieth-century modernity and postcoloniality.

Pnina Werbner is Reader in Social Anthropology at Keele University. She has published on Sufism as a transnational cult and has a growing reputation among Islamic scholars for her work on the political imaginaries of British Islam. **Helene Basu** teaches Social Anthropology at the Institut für Ethnologie in Berlin. She has studied spirit possession cults and living goddesses in Gujarat, India, and in Sindh.

EMBODYING CHARISMA

Modernity, locality and the performance of emotion in Sufi cults

Edited by
Pnina Werbner and Helene Basu

London and New York

First published 1998
by Routledge
11 New Fetter Lane, London EC4P 4EE

Simultaneously published in the USA and Canada
by Routledge
29 West 35th Street, New York, NY 10001

© 1998 Selection and editorial matter Pnina Werbner and Helene Basu;
individual chapters, the contributors

Typeset in Baskerville by RefineCatch Limited, Bungay, Suffolk
Printed and bound in Great Britain by
Biddles Ltd, Guildford and King's Lynn

All rights reserved. No part of this book may be reprinted or
reproduced or utilised in any form or by any electronic,
mechanical, or other means, now known or hereafter
invented, including photocopying and recording, or in any
information storage or retrieval system, without permission in
writing from the publishers.

British Library Cataloguing in Publication Data
A catalogue record for this book is available from the British Library

Library of Congress Cataloguing in Publication Data
Embodying charisma: modernity, locality, and the performance of emotion
in Sufi cults / [edited by] Pnina Werbner and Helene Basu.
p.   cm.
Includes bibliographical references and index.
1. Sufism – 20th century.   I. Werbner, Pnina.   II. Basu, Helene.
BP189.23.E45   1998
297.4′09′049 – dc21   97–37918
CIP

ISBN 0–415–15099–X (hbk)
ISBN 0–415–15100–7 (pbk)

CONTENTS

List of illustrations   viii
List of contributors   ix

PART 1
Introduction   1

1 **The embodiment of charisma**   3
PNINA WERBNER AND HELENE BASU

PART 2
Embodying locality

2 **The hardware of sanctity: anthropomorphic objects in Bangladeshi Sufism**   31
SAMUEL LANDELL MILLS

3 **A 'festival of flags': Hindu–Muslim devotion and the sacralising of localism at the shrine of Nagore-e-Sharif in Tamil Nadu**   55
S.A.A. SAHEB

4 **'The saint who disappeared': saints of the wilderness in Pakistani village shrines**   77
LUKAS WERTH

PART 3
The performance of emotion

5 *Langar*: pilgrimage, sacred exchange and perpetual sacrifice in a Sufi saint's lodge   95
PNINA WERBNER

6 Hierarchy and emotion: love, joy and sorrow in a cult of black saints in Gujarat, India   117
HELENE BASU

7 The *majzub* Mama Ji Sarkar: 'a friend of God moves from one house to another'   140
JÜRGEN WASIM FREMBGEN

8 A *majzub* and his mother: the place of sainthood in a family's emotional memory   160
KATHERINE P. EWING

PART 4
Charisma and modernity

9 The literary critique of Islamic popular religion in the guise of traditional mysticism, or the abused woman   187
JAMAL MALIK

10 Prophets and *pir*s: charismatic Islam in the Middle East and South Asia   209
CHARLES LINDHOLM

Name index   234
Subject index   238

ILLUSTRATIONS

Plates

3.1	The lodge at Nagore-e-Sharif during the annual festival of the saint	57
3.2	The erection of the flagpoles on one of the five minarets, built by the Maratha ruler Pratap Simha, Tanjavur, Tamil Nadu	64
3.3	The illuminated chariot ready to carry the sacred flags in procession	66
3.4	The devotees are blessed by the 'ritual saint' (*pir*) through *theertam*, sandalwood paste, lemon, rose petals and amulets	67
3.5	Carrying the sandalwood paste with which the saint's lineal descendant will anoint the tomb of the saint. The illuminated chariot of the procession is seen in the background	69
5.1	Cooking pots and wood piled high in anticipation of the '*urs* at Ghamkol Sharif	101
5.2	A pilgrim leads his sacrificial goat for the *langar*	102
5.3	Distributing the *langar* to the pilgrims	106
7.1	The *majzub* Mama Ji Sarkar	141
7.2	The living saint Mama Ji Sarkar in his *darbar* in Rawalpindi, to the left of his attendant 'Abdul Rashid	147
7.3	The painter and devotee Sayyid Ishrat	149
7.4	The veneration of the dead saint in the *astan* in Rawalpindi; the *majzub* is depicted in a painting by Sayyid Ishrat	152
7.5	The devotee Sain 'Abdul Majid, residing in the village of Nurpur Shahan	154
8.1	Rabi'a, mother of a *majzub*	164
8.2	Sa'in Sahib	174
8.3	A *mela* at the family shrine	179
9.1	The shrine of Shâh Daulah	193

ILLUSTRATIONS

Figures

3.1	Travels of Sahul Hameed Nagore Andavar in India, Asia and Europe	59
3.2	Ground plan of the sacred complex of Nagore-e-Sharif	71
5.1	The structure of sacrificial giving	103
5.2	Sacrifice and offering in the context of migration	104
9.1	Rano's mystical path	198

Table

3.1	The types of sacred performances conducted at the Nagapatnam and Nagore sacred centres during the Kanduri festival of the Saint Sahul Hameed Nagore Andavar	63

CONTRIBUTORS

Helene Basu teaches Social Anthropology at the Institut für Ethnologie, Free University of Berlin. Her monograph *Habshi Slaves, Sidi Faqirs: A Muslim Cult in Western India* (Das Arabische Buch, Berlin 1995, in German) is on a black Muslim Sidi saints' cult in Gujarat, India, and she has published several articles on the cult. She is currently studying female renunciation and shakti 'living goddesses' among the Charan caste, with special emphasis on women's participation in neo-Hindu movements and nationalist politics in Western India.

Katherine P. Ewing is Associate Professor of Cultural Anthropology at Duke University, Durham, North Carolina. She received her PhD in Anthropology from the University of Chicago and has done fieldwork in Pakistan and Turkey. She has also received psychoanalytic training at the Chicago Institute for Psychoanalysis. She has published numerous articles on Sufism in Pakistan, is the editor of *Shari'at and Ambiguity in South Asian Islam*, and is the author of *Arguing Sainthood: Modernity, Psychoanalysis and Islam* (Duke University Press, Durham NC 1997).

Jürgen Wasim Frembgen is Head of the Oriental Department of the State Museum of Anthropology, Munich, and Lecturer in Religion at the University of Munich. He has conducted extensive research on popular Islam, material culture, ethnohistory and tourism in Karakorum, Kohistan, the North-West Frontier Province and Punjab, as well as in North India and Rajasthan. His publications include ten books and numerous articles, most recently *Darwische, Gelebter Sufismus* (Cologne 1993), *Derwiche und Zuckerbacker* (Munich 1996), and an edited volume, *Rosenduft un Sabelglanz* (Munich 1996).

Samuel Landell Mills is an anthropologist who wrote his doctoral thesis at the London School of Economics. He has also held a British Academy post-doctoral research fellowship at Cambridge University. Having done fieldwork in Bangladesh on Sufi saints and Islamic fundamentalism, he has recently been working with the Baul tradition of West Bengal. He has published several articles, and his forthcoming book, *The Face of God*, is a study of Sufi and fundamentalist movements in Bangladesh.

CONTRIBUTORS

Charles Lindholm is a member of the University Professors' Program and of the Anthropology Department at Boston University. He did his fieldwork in Swat, Northern Pakistan, and recently published a book of essays based on that research entitled *Frontier Perspectives: Essays in Comparative Anthropology* (Oxford University Press, Karachi 1996). His most recent book is *The Islamic Middle East: An Historical Anthropology* (Blackwell, Oxford 1996). His present research is on cross-cultural notions of the self and agency, and on the ramifications of egalitarian ideologies. He has also written extensively on various forms of idealisation, and is the author of *Charisma* (Blackwell, Oxford 1990).

Jamal Malik obtained his doctorate from the South Asia Institute, University of Heidelberg (1988), and his Habilitation in Islamic Studies from Bamberg University (1994). He teaches at the universities of Bamberg and Bonn. He is author of *Colonialization of Islam* (Manohar, New Delhi 1997) and *Islamic Scholarly Tradition in North India* (Brill, Leiden 1997, in German), as well as numerous academic articles on mysticism, Islamicisation, urban societies and traditional institutions.

S.A.A. Saheb is a senior researcher in the Social Anthropological Survey of India, Southern Regional Centre, Mysore. He has been a member of the New York Academy of Sciences since 1994. His doctoral thesis was on the shrine sacred complex of Nagore-e-Sharif and he has published extensively in journals and academic collections. He has also organised several museum exhibitions on tribal life in South India and has conducted research on communities in Andra Pradesh, Karnataka and Tamilnadu.

Pnina Werbner is Reader in Social Anthropology at Keele University and Research Administrator of the International Centre for Contemporary Cultural Research (ICCCR) at the Universities of Manchester and Keele. Her publications include *The Migration Process: Capital, Gifts and Offerings among British Pakistanis* (Berg, Oxford 1990), *Economy and Culture in Pakistan: Migrants and Cities in a Muslim Society*, co-edited with Hastings Donnan (Macmillan, London 1991), *Debating Cultural Hybridity* and *The Politics of Multiculturalism in the New Europe*, both co-edited with Tariq Modood (Zed Books, London 1997). Her forthcoming book, *Diaspora and Millennium*, is on the political imaginaries of British Pakistanis. Her fieldwork on Sufi transnational cults was conducted in Britain and Pakistan.

Lukas Werth is a lecturer in Social Anthropology at the Free University of Berlin. His first fieldwork was on a peripatetic society in South India, and he has published a monograph, *Von Gottinnen und ihren Menschen: die Vagri, sine Wandernde Gesellschaft Sudindiens* (Das Arabische Buch, Berlin 1996), on this research. He is presently conducting research in Pakistan on contemporary Sufism in its social context and has written a number of articles on this theme.

Part 1

INTRODUCTION

1

THE EMBODIMENT OF CHARISMA

Pnina Werbner and Helene Basu

Sufi saint cults: embodying the sacred

In South Asia living Sufi saints emerge periodically to shape and reshape a sacred landscape; in embodying the sacred as a lived reality they create and extend new Sufi brotherhoods (*tariqa*) and focused regional cults and pilgrimage centres, a vast network of individual supplicants and devotional communities generated through voluntaristic loyalties which extend beyond local, regional and even international boundaries. It is this continued vitality of Sufism as a living, embodied, postcolonial reality which this book interrogates. For alongside living saints are their mythical predecessors, believed to be alive from beyond the grave. Throughout South Asia, shrines of Sufi saints appear juxtaposed to other complex, postmodern and postcolonial realities: in rural and urban contexts, in the wilderness, besides modern bank buildings or railway stations, opposite mosques or skyscrapers. While some shrines dominate small towns or a vast hinterland, others find their place among hundreds of similar structures in the metropolitan cities of Bombay, Karachi or Dacca.

In South Asia great reformist, living saints have continued to emerge in Bangladesh and Pakistan, as Landell Mills and Werbner show in Chapters 2 and 5. They exist alongside caste-based regional cults of black African saints in Gujarat, discussed by Basu in Chapter 6; famous shrines, such as the shrine of Nagore-e-Sharif in Tamil Nadu, which Saheb shows are the focus of a major transnational cult encompassing both Hindus and Muslims (Chapter 3); and countless living, 'mad', divinely intoxicated *majzubs*, analysed here by Frembgen in Chapter 7 and Ewing in Chapter 8. There are the unnamed shrines to unknown saints which mediate between communities in rural Pakistan, Werth discloses in Chapter 4, while shrine practices have been the target of critical literary reformist texts (Chapter 9, by Malik). Despite reform movements, the continued vitality of Sufism in Islamic South Asia is evident, and is considered by Charles Lindholm (Chapter 10) in the context of a sweeping historical comparison between Sufism in South Asia and the Middle East.

In studying Sufi saint cults as living, contemporary modes of organising the sacred we seek to expose false dichotomies applied to the *description*, and hence also theorisation, of Sufi cults throughout the Islamic heartland and its peripheries. Such dichotomies deny the embodied nature of ritual and religious belief and practice by positing a series of spurious separations: between magic and religion (the one supposedly instrumental, the other ethical); between ritual and belief (the one aesthetic and symbolic, the other cognitive); between folk and official or normative religion; between syncretic practice and Islamic orthodoxy. These separations have been imposed upon different facets of what is, we argue here, a single, total, symbolic reality. Indeed, even the conjunction of Sufism with saints' cults is unusual. On the one side, Sufism is glossed as an elaborate and coherent neo-Platonic theosophy of mystical realities: Sufis in this construction were historically renowned mystics and ascetics, now long dead, whose writings and poetry today inspire mostly middle-class or elite urban circles, seeking 'new' religious experiences (Gilsenan 1982: 244–246). On the other side are the cults of saints or marabouts whose tombs are the focus of magical, superstitious 'folk' (North Africa) or ('Hinduised') 'syncretic' (South Asia) practices by the ignorant (eclectic, tolerant) masses. The shrine's magicality is grounded in heterodox beliefs regarding the divine powers of the saints, who are thought to be able to intercede for the living in their search for personal boons (fertility, worldly success, health) by granting them saintly *baraka*, divine blessing. Such saints, unlike Sufis, are described as miracle makers whose deeds are publicised through sacred hagiographies.

Despite Trimingham's classical study of Sufi saints and their cult organisation, which spelled out clearly the generative connections between saints, cults and *tariqa* (Trimingham 1971), a third scholarly discursive disjunction is also prevalent, especially in studies of the Islamic heartland. This scholarly discourse, best exemplified in anthropology by the work of Clifford Geertz and Ernest Gellner (Geertz 1968; Gellner 1981; for a critique see Baldick 1989: 155–156), severs Sufism from its organisational underpinnings: neither Sufi mysticism nor folk superstition is conceived to be related empirically or theoretically to the organisation of Sufi orders or *zikr* (meditation) circles; these in turn are often not related to the focused organisation of regional cults around specific saints' tombs or newly emergent living saints (but see Eickelman 1976; Gilsenan 1973, 1982; Lings 1961). To add further to this conceptual fragmentation is the fact that rural saintly lineages are not regarded as linked either to Sufism, to saints' cults, to revivalist Sufi religious movements (Evans-Pritchard 1949; Vikor 1995; Clancey-Smith 1988) or even, as Baldick argues, to Islamic scholarship (1989: 156). Saintly lineages are simply 'there', at most mediating as peacemakers between warring tribes (Barth 1959; Gellner 1969).

One of the advantages of studying Sufi cults as contemporary, viable and generative symbolic and ethical movements is that this enables us to explore the connections between Sufi cosmologies, ethical ideas, bodily ritual practices and organisational forms, which have been lost in earlier historical and anthropological studies. By exposing the falsity of former discursive separations, we hope to reveal the enormous contribution which the study of Sufi cults can make to a theory of charismatic ritual and religious movements in the context of late twentieth-century modernity and postcoloniality. Our close-grained, finely observed studies allow us to demonstrate the 'complex interweavings of knowledge and acting' (Davis 1991: xii); the fact that, as Davis argues about Hindu rituals, ritual serves to illuminate and objectify philosophical categories and topics, while philosophy illuminates the purposes and strategies of ritual; they are two modalities of a 'unitary power of consciousness' (ibid.: xi).

Reifying belief

Clearly, the opposition posited by anthropologists and orientalists between folk (syncretic) magic and official Islam draws on indigenous Islamic reformist discourses critical of the practices at saints' tombs, as Jamal Malik shows in his chapter on reformist literary texts. The new realist Urdu writing highlighted the secretive authoritarianism and dark, rapacious sexuality of the guardians of saints' shrines. Yet despite their modernist thrust, these *avant-garde* writers continued to draw on allegories of divine, mystical illumination. Sufi *pir*s (saints) are ambivalent, liminal figures, Werth and Ewing argue in Chapters 4 and 8. Not only do they claim exaggerated powers (Chapter 10, by Lindholm), but they are associated with chicanery and greed in the popular mind (Sherani 1991). Yet they continue to epitomise a human promise and ethical power beyond the ordinary.

This ambivalence reflects the fact that contemporary Sufism is a contested tradition, as indeed are all the different Islamic streams in South Asia (Metcalf 1982; Werbner 1996a; Ahmad 1991). In response to attacks by rivals, adherents of these various approaches have been compelled to create discursive defences of their 'beliefs', which thus emerge as increasingly reified and remote from the practices that underpin them. In this respect, the study of Islamic ritual as embodied and transformative poses a challenge to anthropology, more used to studying ritual in small-scale, preliterate societies. In these, practice and belief appear closely intertwined, grounded in ethical premises which remain largely implicit or mythically articulated. 'Belief' in this context can only be extrapolated from ritual action itself, or deciphered from fragmentary exegetic commentaries. By contrast, for students of Islam the written religious corpus and hermeneutical traditions of a world religion seem overwhelming.

Yet a major strand in the anthropology of religion, even concerning preliterate societies, has repeatedly detached 'belief' (in witchcraft, in spirits, in the ancestors) from ritual action, and reconstructed it as disembodied and abstract. This intellectualist strand, which continued to grapple with Frazerian, Tylorian or Lévy-Bruhlian questions of the relation between magic and rationality (see Tambiah 1990), transmuted the sited, embodied ethics of ritual practice into ideological constructs. The same legacy affected even Durkheimian anthropology, where ritual was often reconceptualised as an (ideological) template 'cementing' the social order, a stultifying tendency of some Marxist approaches (e.g. Bloch

1986). Even Mary Douglas's groundbreaking work on the body as a metaphor for society and cosmos (1966), in stressing the *parallels* between the body social and the body as microcosm, ultimately privileged the ideological over embodied practice.

Nevertheless, it was Douglas's critique of the false dichotomy between magic and religion which was crucial in moving the debate forward. Against prior evolutionist approaches, she demonstrated that magic and religion were equally grounded in classificatory oppositions between purity and pollution, good and evil, the permitted and the forbidden, the powerfully beneficial and the dangerous, community and strangerhood (Douglas 1966). In this respect the anthropological contribution to theories of embodiment is widely recognised (Turner 1991; Shilling 1993).

The bodies of saints are enormously powerful. Sufism postulates precisely the same analogical relation identified by Douglas between body and cosmos (Nicholson 1978: 121) and between a denial of embodied desire (*nafs*) and the acquisition of true knowledge, gained by the detached, eternal, rational 'soul' (*ruh*). It is the soul that, through ascetic work on the body, a progressive purification of its hidden 'lights' that parallels the transcendental journey towards the Prophet and God, can deny carnal desire, greed and selfishness and gain cosmic knowledge of eternal realities. This knowledge creates a double movement: the death of the desiring soul, the *nafs*, brings about the eternalisation of the body after death, while the soul retains its living agency; and the ethical subjectivity of the journeying *faqir* is transformed into a source of infinite love. He is now the conduit of divine giving, blessing the world, with the powerful capacity to change and order both nature and human society; to overcome evil spirits and demonic possession; to heal and pacify.

But this Sufi theory of charisma and the elaborate cosmology it has generated are not necessarily articulated explicitly either by saints or by their devotees. The Sufi theory remains an implicit, embodied form of charismatic knowledge. It is manifested, as our case studies show, in the ritual capacity of saints to imbue their concrete surroundings with their sacred persona (Chapter 2, by Landell Mills) and extend their spiritual dominion through infinite giving (Chapter 5, by Werbner), creating moral spaces of intimate love and amity (Chapter 7, by Frembgen), sacralising urban neighbourhoods through ritual processions and sacred exchanges (Chapter 3, by Saheb), protecting strangers (Chapter 4, by Werth), exorcising demonic spirits and enacting an alternative ethical order (Chapter 6, by Basu). It is equally evident in the antinomian privileges granted saints (Chapter 8, by Ewing) and their powers over ordinary people (Chapter 9, by Malik).

The challenge in the study of Sufi saints and their cults is how to incorporate the Cartesian dualism between body and mind/soul, which devotees presume to be a fundamental truth of human existence, into a higher-order theory which discloses how, in reality, the emotional and ethical premises of Sufism are inscribed in ways that negate such a dualism.

The anthropological study of ritual embodiment

The elements of mythical thought, Lévi-Strauss has argued, 'lie halfway between percepts and concepts' (1966: 18). This embodied quality of objects/persons explains the power of signifying practices to reproduce the social order, even in the face of disruptive external forces. As an embodied phenomenon culture is inscriptive, beyond words, a habitus and hexus (Bourdieu 1977, 1984). So too, modernity's 'civilising' mission is imposed through disciplining practices (Elias 1983; Foucault 1979; see also Shilling 1993). Time and memory are themselves inscribed in the performance of ritual and commemoration ceremonials (Connerton 1989). It is this dimension of embodiment that is particularly evident in Sufi cults, which, as Landell Mills shows (Chapter 2), both anticipate the future and re-enact their own realities in cyclical time.

In contemporary theory, the most important contributions to our understanding of ritual as an embodied, ethical and experiential practice have come from three key anthropological approaches: the processual, grounded in the work of Durkheim and of van Gennep on liminality in rites of passage; the aesthetic, inspired by French phenomenologists and poststructuralists; and the substantive, building on Mauss's insights into the symbolic embodiment of subjects through objects.

Undoubtedly, Victor Turner's study of the Ndembu ritual process has been foundational in revealing the rootedness of ethical ideas in the body and body substances, manipulated and worked upon to achieve a social, emotional and moral transformation of a liminal subject (Turner 1967). In recognising the emotional underpinnings of the normative, Turner followed Durkheim in attempting to explain the felt force of sociality. Adopting a more structuralist approach, Richard Werbner (1989) has shown that substantive flows between persons, and between persons and places, are morally incorporative, thus underlining the power of ritual to create ethical spaces which counter the alienation and enstrangement produced by modernity. This incorporative capacity is an important feature of Sufi cults. In South Asian anthropology, the focus on personhood as constituted by bodily flows and exchanges of substances has been inspired by the work of McKim Marriott in particular (Marriott 1976), and extended to Sufi cults by Richard Kurin (e.g. Kurin 1983, 1984). The tension between embodied ideas about purity/pollution and creative fertility in South Asia is an important subject, considered here by Helene Basu (Chapter 2).

While building upon Turner's insights, anthropologists have also drawn upon aesthetic and phenomenological theories to consider experiential transformations of subjectivity (Fernandez 1982; Kapferer 1983; Boddy 1989; Devisch 1993). In the present volume, Ewing and Frembgen (Chapters 8 and 7) probe the subjectivities elicited in interactions with living saints which go beyond explicit cultural construction. Emotions, anthropologists have proposed, rather than being explicitly articulated, are embodied in gesture and performance. The Balinese cockfight may be interpreted as an 'alternative' cultural text, enacting a forbidden, officially denied, aesthetic experience of violence (Geertz 1973). Sufism, we show, creates its own alternative texts – utopian experiential imaginaries of other, possible world orders. Through such imaginings it also contributes to 'shaping a communal moral consciousness' (Waardenburg 1979: 348).

Discussions of the constructedness of emotion suggest that emotions may be grasped as discursive performances embedded in ongoing power struggles (Abu-Lughod 1986; Abu-Lughod and Lutz 1990). Hence studies of resistance in anthropology have drawn on Gramscian and Foucauldian notions of embodied difference (Comaroff 1985; Boddy 1989) to argue that disadvantaged groups such as women or the urban poor can re-form the world from their own perspective. Through mimesis and play the disadvantaged appropriate the power of colonists and dominant classes and make it their own (Taussig 1993; Stoller 1995). Sufism too often occupies, as many of the contributors here argue, such a resistive space.

In all these studies the *power* of ritual is seen to derive not from belief as a set of abstracted ideas but from ritual as a complex set of transformative, embodied, negotiated ethical and aesthetic practices and the experiences which their enactment generates. Ritual performances must be interpreted as embedded in quotidian ontologies, often implicit and inarticulate, even if particular ritual events or symbolic complexes are set apart spatially and temporally. In this sense one has to disagree with Asad's genealogical account of anthropological studies of ritual which, he argues, almost universally have tended to divorce symbolic analysis from 'pragmatics' (Asad 1993: Ch. 4).[1] While it is true that the stress on 'belief' and 'communication' has often led anthropologists into blind alleys, the main thrust has been towards more holistic approaches, ones which explore the connections between ethical, cognitive, aesthetic and organisational features of symbolic systems.

Embodied emotions

Sufism has often been represented as a realm of Islamic emotional discourse opposed to the 'cold' and 'technical' constructions put forward by theologians and judicial scholars (Schimmel 1975: 130–148, 287 *passim*; Rahman 1979). The core of classical Sufi mysticism consists of divine love (*ishq*, *muhabbat*) conceptualised as inner experiences of growth and realisation in the relationship between individual worshippers and a saint. The few studies dealing with emotions in the context of saints' cults have so far been confined to a consideration of saint and disciple, focusing upon the conceived mystical content of dyadic relationships (cf. Nanda and Talib 1989; Pinto 1989, 1995). In the present collection Sam Landell Mills, arguing against the Durkheimian view of symbols as collective representations, suggests that saint–disciple relations can indeed be interpreted as a model for all human dialogical interaction.

Yet several of the authors in this volume go beyond the stress on dyadic relations to examine constructions and experiences of emotion generated amongst followers themselves and the organisations these create (Frembgen, Ewing, Basu, Werbner).

If emotions are embedded in implicit local ontologies, these are often crystallised in liminal phases and figures. A common thread running through all the chapters is the elaboration of liminality at shrines as sacred localities, and of charismatic saints as threshold persons mediating between two distinct symbolic orders. The liminal has been analysed as a transgressive moment that enables actors to play upon or probe beneath the limits of conventional social understandings (Turner 1967). Such moments may also, Handelman proposes, resonate in some societies with ideas about the 'unpredictable play of forces in flux', denying the boundaries that divide 'paranatural and human realms' (Handelman 1990: 63 and *passim*) and revealing the limits of human understanding. Yet the unboundedness of experience, the sense of the 'inchoate' beneath the conventional which phenomenologists evoke, is ultimately knowable only in its embodied forms. We may speculate upon, but cannot reach, the biologically 'unspeakable'. This is, of course, the problem with suggestions, such as those by Csordas (1990) or Shilling (1997), that the study of embodiment needs to look beyond nature–culture or social–biological dualisms in order to recover the pre- or unsocialised dimensions of emotion and sensuality – to escape from a 'sociological imperialism' that reduces the complexity of human experience (Shilling 1997).[2] Although providing a salutary reminder of our embodied nature, both writers cannot cope with the fact that – beyond philosphical reflections – the moment of the emotionally expressive is also the moment of dialogical and social communication, that is, the moment of the cultural. Even if the expressive does not exhaust human understanding and experience, one can only study human feelings or perceptions through their cultural and social articulations. The interest of Sufism is not in the unbounded mystical experience or biological transcendence it invokes, but in the tension it embodies between the conventional and the emotionally expressive. This is an important theme, addressed here.

Several chapters deal with a category of transitional ritual figures neglected until recently: the *majzub* and *mastan* – those drunk on divine love, the rebels and madmen of medieval Sufism (Eaton 1978; Digby 1984). In Islamic discourses, *majzub* represent the Other of orthoprax Sufism categorised as *ba-shar*, outside and beyond the reach of the Law (cf. Ewing 1984, 1988; Frembgen 1993; Gaborieau 1986). Both Katherine Ewing and Jürgen Frembgen here explore the processes of constructing a *majzub*, though they approach this subject from slightly different angles. Whereas Frembgen concentrates upon followers' experiences of a living *majzub*, Ewing focuses upon the narrative experiences of the mother of a *majzub*. A prominent feature of *majzub*s is that they are mad. Their 'madness', however, is understood as a positive sign of proximity to God and absorption in love, a feature also of the intoxicated Sidi *mastan* analysed here by Basu.

In Ewing's analysis, the death of the *majzub* marks the point in his mother's narrative when he is recognised as a true saint. Death means perfection. Over a series of interviews, Ewing recaptures how a son is transformed from a troublesome and subversive young man into a recognised charismatic. Death is critical in this process, mediating the transformations of identity leading to sainthood.

Ewing's study thus reveals how a holistic approach can elicit complex, shifting ethical and emotional perspectives. On the one hand, the bereaved mother mythologises her son as the saint he became, drawing on familiar tropes about the lives of saints; but on the other hand, she reveals the maternal anxieties she felt for him as a wayward and often vulnerable person for whom she was responsible. Ewing uses these narratives to argue, as she has elsewhere, against South Asianist ethnocultural interpretations of personhood that stress their cultural incommensurability with Western notions. Beyond cultural differences, she argues, there are also shared assumptions, rooted in the present instance in maternal concerns for the health and happiness of children. These can only be revealed, however, by listening to alternative, less formalised narratives. There is sadness and a sense of guilt at the death of a son, even as there is pride in his canonisation.

One fascinating question rarely addressed in studies of Sufism is the sense of loss Sufi devotees experience when their saint dies. From a cosmological perspective, the saint remains present and alive in the grave and, indeed, as Jürgen Frembgen shows here in his study of Mama Ji Sarkar, an urban *majzub* in Rawalpindi, the death of their beloved saint is conceptualised by disciples precisely in these terms. Yet the *physical* loss of the saint cannot be denied. Even as a very old man, barely speaking and functioning, he was an embodied presence in their lives, cared for, washed and fed by his disciples, the focus of intense sociality. Although in the grave his power has remained and is increasingly institutionalised by the disciples, as the absence of a felt presence his death is experienced as a personal loss, and Frembgen draws on aesthetic theories of ritual in anthropology to conceptualise this transition which cannot be culturally articulated.

The living stillness of Mama Ji Sarkar is in some ways reminiscent of the living stillness of the *pir* of Atroshi studied here by Landell Mills. In his otherworldliness, the *majzub* subsisted just before his death in a condition of 'living death': even the bodily functions that render ordinary human beings impure were seen in his case to be particularly pure; he had hardly any excretions and they did not smell. He had attained physical purity even before death.

The power of emotion to heal and exorcise evil is the basis for the saints' cult in Gujarat studied here by Helene Basu. Believed to be descendants of the Abyssinian companion of the Prophet who was said to be the latter's most devoted follower, the *Sidi* guardians of the shrine centre trace their ancestry and that of their saints to Africa. Rather than a single charismatic saint, the cult centre consists of a triad of saints, differentiated by gender and seniority, who mythologically are said to have defeated dangerous 'Hindu' demonic forces. Between them the three saints embody cosmogonic forces of heating and cooling, of anger, love and rationality. Basu shows how the Sidis' perceived command of the full emotional spectrum of human passions, from love to anger, symbolised as a hot–cold continuum, enables them to transcend their lowly caste status and invert hierarchical definitions of purity and pollution. These place their cult below those of *Sayyid* saints who claim descent from the Prophet. Through the manipulation of embodied symbols of heat and coolness, male and female, the *Sidi* empower a cosmogonic world order of fertility, joy and divine madness which they themselves privilege beyond static cosmic definitions of hierarchical order. This counter-hegemonic definition places the cult ambiguously within the broader regional network of saints' cults in Gujarat.

Acts of generosity and giving embody emotions, as Pnina Werbner argues here in her analysis of the *langar* (the communal distribution of food at a religious lodge or celebration) as a form of 'perpetual sacrifice'. The *langar* is the core institution of Sufi shrines, a locus of sacred exchange which extends the social and spatial ambit of the lodge. Pilgrims arrive at the lodge carrying offerings of grain and livestock for the *langar*, and are fed by it. People give out of love (*muhabbat*), expecting merit and grace in return. The saint's generosity, granted by Allah, makes possible this substantive sharing of substance and nurture.

Sacred peripherality

Most anthropological studies of ritual have focused on bounded, small-scale communities, albeit now embedded in larger national collectivities and subject to external cultural influences and the reifications of print capitalism or reform scholarship. The 'movement' or 'journey' these studies have analysed is between different subjective conditions, roles and spaces within a local congregation; in initiation rites, sacrifices or curative rituals, or the imaginative travels of local shamans and healers (see Tsing 1993). An important feature of such journeys, anthropologists have shown, is the overcoming of ordeals, sometimes (as in some initiation rites) actual, physical ordeals; at other times in the form of symbolic encounters with dangerous demons or ritual clowns (Kapferer 1983; Werbner 1989) or by crossing dangerous thresholds – as between the domestic and the wild. These encounters, as Basu too shows, are mythologically critical; they move the ritual forward and transform the condition of performers and spaces of community. Such movement is also effected through sacred exchanges across thresholds which exorcise pollution and radiate purity, a subject we discuss more fully below.

It was, once again, Victor Turner's study of pilgrimage as sacred peripherality, 'the centre out there', which opened up a whole new set of questions regarding ritual journeys as transformative movements, this time across vast distances (Turner 1974: Ch. 5). Turner conceptualised pilgrimage centres as alternative loci of value within feudal-type societies. Like the rites of passage of tribal societies, he argued, the ritual movement in pilgrimage culminated in a liminal moment of 'communitas' which was anti-structural and anti-hierarchical, releasing an egalitarian sociality and amity. Pilgrimage centres thus embodied an alternative ethical order, one uncircumscribed by territorially defined relations of power and authority.

In the face of a host of critiques levelled against this argument (Sallnow 1987; Eade and Sallnow 1991; and for India see Fuller 1993: 212–213), it seems more accurate to say that sacred pilgrimage creates not 'anti'-structure but 'counter'-structure. Nevertheless, Turner's key point, that pilgrimage centres and the cults generated around them produce sacred geographies where alternative, non-temporal and non-administrative ethical orders are ritually embodied, still seems valid. In this spirit, regional cults were conceived to create spatially alternative focal organisations to those centred on bounded, territorially based states or administrative units, and to be inclusive rather than exclusive, tending to cross ethnic and national boundaries and incorporate diverse populations around a single sacred centre (Werbner 1989: Ch. 7).

One way local Islam manifests itself is through the symbolic use of space. The Sufi notion of *wilayat* refers to spiritual dominions controlled by famous saints, but these also have an organised temporal, spatial and social realisation. Shrines thus represent important landmarks in the sacred geography of Islam in South Asia. Symbolically, their spatial ordering often mirrors the sacred pilgrimage centres of Islam in Mecca and Madina. In the present volume Werbner analyses the symbolic connections between local shrine sacrifices and the *hajj* (the pilgrimage to Mecca). The 'counter-structural' movement in pilgrimage, she shows, is also a movement of subjective purification, a return to a state of pristine ethical purity.

At the same time, the organisation of a shrine's space is embedded in place and community. This is reflected even at the most local level, in the countless shrines to unknown saints found on the outskirts of Punjabi villages. Against the unique biographies of named saints, these anonymous shrines, Lukas Werth discloses here, call for explanation. Situated at the threshold of human civilisation, on the margins between the village community and the wilderness, their anonymity is a key feature, he suggests, of their placement as mediators between the dangerous forces of nature and cultural continuity. The ambivalence of such saints' positioning, betwixt and between, is also the source of their power, and is embodied in the sacred groves of trees and springs surrounding the shrines, symbols of continuity and life which may also be the abode of dangerous *jinn*s and other malevolent spirits. A possible (unspoken) implication of the myths told to Werth about these nameless, unknown saints might be that they are manifestations of Khizr, the wayfaring saint and guardian of strangers. Werth shows that the shrines can be understood as standing for a broader and more inclusive ethical vision, beyond the little community: as guarantors of safe passage for stranger-travellers in the wilderness, they create connections between villages, across the wild spaces that separate them.

The association of death and power in social constructions of sanctity is further underscored here by Sam Landell Mills in his study of living saints in Bangladesh. Examining the social production of saints through interactions between a *pir* and his followers, Landell Mills draws attention to the creation of an iconic image of the living *pir* through contrasting images of stillness and action. The stillness of the saint is like the immobility of the tomb, while the projection of his power depends upon a blend of action and stillness. This is achieved through the organisation of space into objectified structures perceived as an extension of the saintliness of the *pir*. A living *pir* thus reverses the image of the dead saint and anticipates his own death: the living *pir* of Atroshi embodies the tomb, while the lodge he has built and all its objects are transformed into anthropomorphic extensions of his persona, to survive his physical death.

Another facet of localised sacred power is invoked by implicit allusions to royal courts, a common feature of saint worship (Eaton 1982, 1984; Gilmartin 1984; Metcalf 1984). The *dargah* of Sahul Hameed in Tamil Nadu, studied here by Saheb, is modelled upon the ideal of the Mughal emperor Akbar, who, in the Indian historical imagination, represents the tolerant Muslim ruler *par excellence*. Royal splendour is invoked during the annual *'urs* celebration by the symbolism of flags and the firing of cannons. As a powerful emperor incorporates the subjects of his state, so the *pir* of Nagore-e-Sharif, Sahul Hameed, extends the ambit of his embodied persona to the congregations of his followers or subjects throughout his spiritual (*wilayat*) and geographical domain, which includes Muslim and Hindu occupational groups and devotees from as far afield as Singapore and Sri Lanka.

Hence, a further feature of pilgrimage centres highlighted here, and one particularly evident in South Asia, is their role as sites of sacred exchange. This is true of the great pilgrimage centre of Mecca or Benares (see, for example, Parry 1989). It is equally true at lesser pilgrimage centres. Supplicants arrive with offerings or objects to be sacralised and return home carrying with them a bit of the sacred centre. Sacred exchanges of this type, as Richard Werbner has argued more generally (1989), generate movements of exorcism and purification, on the one hand, and connections between distant places, on the other. The waters of the Ganges (Gold 1988) or of *ab-e Zamzam* (the spring at Mecca), the earth of Mwali or of Karbala, gowns, amulets and other accoutrements crystallise embodied connections between a sacred centre and its extended peripheries (on the resulting trade in 'charismatic' amulets see Tambiah 1984: Ch. 22). The connection is metonymic as well as metaphoric. Indeed, the whole study of ritual embodiment, and of charisma as sacred embodiment, necessarily hinges on an understanding of symbolic movement as effecting both a metonymic and a metaphoric transformation. Meaning is substantively inscribed by creating contiguities and connections, while inscription is rendered meaningful.

Cults of saints create realms of anti/counter-structure by reversals of quotidian logic. The 'saint who disappeared' described here by Werth is an absent presence. In the *hajj* a reversal of time is achieved, Werbner suggests, by reversing the Islamic myth of Ismail's expulsion into the desert and his subsequent immolation. The charismatic body, as Frembgen shows here, exudes pure polluting substances. Similar inversions underscore the hierarchy of the *Sidi* cult (Chapter 6, by Basu): the *majzub* or *mastan* is not bound by conventions; instead, he is struck by divine madness, embodying emotional knowledge beyond learned wisdom. This knowledge is marked by movement and ecstacy rather than by stillness. Within a regional context, the *mastan* are the rebels in a respectable establishment of *Sayyid* Sufi shrines. When participating in the rituals of these shrines, they enact a carnivaleque anti-structure.

Charisma and modernity

Perhaps it is this anti-structural emphasis that accounts for the continued vigour of saint cults in Muslim South Asia. Their vitality nevertheless needs to be considered against the backdrop of the more general debate about the decline of charisma in the context of modernity. Interrogating Weber's notion of charisma, Eisenstadt proposes that he was centrally concerned with 'the problems and predicaments of human freedom, creativity, and personal responsibility in social life in general and in modern society in particular' (Eisenstadt 1968: xv); and it was in relation to the problem of individual freedom and creativity that Weber's notion of charisma as antithetical to routine and rationalised institutional orders was formulated (ibid.: xviii–xix). The disenchantment of the world, the hallmark of modernity, was, in Weber's view, the product of increasing rationalisation, of the growing reach of bureaucratic structures of domination, which he typified as permanent, routinised, recurrent, systematic, methodical, calculating, ordered, procedural and rule bound (Weber 1948: 245 *passim*). By contrast, he saw charismatic domination as highly personalised, intense, expressive and *irrational*, as well as being innovative and creative. The source of charisma was a perception of the unique, extraordinary, supernatural or heroic qualities of the charismatic leader. Leadership was thus based on voluntaristic recognition and authority constituted by inner restraint and personal responsibility rather than external, rule-bound discipline.

The question of the possibility of attaining personal freedom and ethical subjectivity against modernity's pervasive, imposed disciplines has been revived in discussions of new social movements. In his last works, Michel Foucault examines the way erotic self-denial and self-imposed asceticism, much like that practised by Sufi saints, operated within an 'economy of desire' among the Ancient Greeks, to enable the 'individual to fashion himself as a subject of ethical conduct' (Foucault 1992: 251). Although there are echoes here of the exemplary autonomy Dumont attributes to the world renouncer (Dumont 1957), Foucault's primary contribution to our understanding of saintly charisma lies in the connection he draws between self-mastery, truth and love: 'The one who is better versed in love will also be the master of truth; and it will be his role to teach the loved one how to triumph over his desires and become "stronger than himself"' (Foucault 1992: 241). The fashioning of the self is interpreted by Foucault as a precondition both of true knowledge and of lasting, other-oriented bonds of love and friendship (ibid.: 201). Elsewhere he implies that aesthetic self-fashioning enables the individual to achieve critical distance from a taken-for-granted order, and hence the possibility of dissent (Foucault 1983: 211; for a discussion of this view and its limits in relation to Sufi cults see Werbner 1995: 134–135).

A further insight into the dynamics of Sufi sainthood may be derived from Edward Shils's critical re-evaluation of Weber's theory (Shils 1965). Rather than stressing the antithesis between charisma and bureaucratic or patrimonial domination, Shils argues that institutionalised charisma 'permeates' all walks of life. The source of charisma is the 'contact through inspiration, embodiment or perception, with the vital force which underlies man's existence', a force located at the centre of society (ibid.: 201). The defining features of charisma are intensity, embodied centrality (of values or institutions) and the capacity for ordering. This capacity for ordering and cultivating, for taming the wilderness, is also the hallmark of Sufi saints in South Asia, as Werbner has argued (1996b) and as Werth and Landell Mills highlight in the present volume.

In a fine essay building on Shils's insights, Clifford Geertz interrogates the sacred centrality of sovereign power and its symbolic, ordering capacities. Through royal progresses and processions, he shows, sovereigns mark out their territories 'as almost physical parts of them' (Geertz 1983: 125), allegorically shaping their dominion according to some cosmic, 'exemplary and mimetic' plan (ibid.: 134). Even in the context of modernity, he argues, political authority retains its charismatic aura.

There is, however, something intrinsically problematic in this siting of charisma at the centre and equating of it with state power and its routinised extensions. For the citizens of postcolonial societies, it is often the *opposition* between a morally grounded charisma and the rationalised authority of the state which more accurately reflects, we believe, the experiential reality of modernity. What needs thus to be theorised is the nature of charismatic (saintly) *dissent and opposition* to the bureaucratic domination of the state. At most we might extend Geertz's view to argue that embodied resistance to the centre's values draws on the same fund of charismatic symbols which the centre attempts to appropriate for itself. Sufi lodges, we show (Landell Mills, Saheb), are often shaped architecturally like Mughal courts, the lodge (*dargah* = court) replicating imperial courts, just as the latter in the past replicated charismatic saints' modes of eliciting allegiance (Cohn 1983).

But beyond these mimetic borrowings, the Weberian opposition still holds true, with a difference. In South Asia Sufis have appropriated the sacred symbols of a tolerant, all-encompassing, inclusive Islam. As Werbner, for example, argues here, the capitalist, commodity economy is converted at a saint's lodge into a good-faith, moral economy through altruistic giving to the communal *langar*; indeed, the sites of saints' lodges, many of the contributors demonstrate, are set apart as spaces of expressive amity and emotional good will. The state and its politicians, by contrast, are seen as menacing, corrupt, greedy and unfeeling. They are not truly 'rational' in the Weberian sense since they bend the rules to their selfish interests; but they use the instruments of patriarchal and bureaucratic power to achieve their goals. Theirs is a charisma of unbridled power. By contrast the saint's charisma – and his achievement of subjective autonomy and freedom – is the product of his perceived (and projected) self-denial and self-mastery, of love and generosity. Writing about the network of hermitage centres and subcentres in the forests of Thailand, Tambiah describes them as a 'formidable system of charismatic influence and presence' countracting both ecclesiastical authority and the 'political authority with its patrimonial-bureaucratic attributes and weaknesses' (Tambiah 1984: 334).

Hence the charismatic power of saints' tombs is experienced by followers as an extension of the ambience of divinely inspired love, *not* the power of the state. The processions to and from the shrine of Nagore-e-Sharif, analysed here in great detail and with great subtlety by S.A.A. Saheb, stamp the saint's charisma on the neighbourhoods and *mohallas* (wards) in the vicinity of the shrine through an elaborate ritual of sacred exchange. Tambiah speaks of the 'sedimentation of power in objects – and of the sedimentation of charisma in gifts' (ibid.: 339 *passim*). At Nagore-e-Sharif, the processors move back and forth to the lodge over an extended period of several weeks. They carry with them sacred icons and flags to be revitalised at the lodge, coming from as far away as Singapore and Sri Lanka. The embodiment of Sufi Islamic values through this processing, Saheb shows, includes both Hindus and Muslims, and many different castes and organised associations. Sacred peripherality, to return to Turner, is an intrinsic feature of charisma, and all the more so if the state is perceived to be divorced from the core values of the society.

To what extent do Sufi cults embody distinctively South Asian *hierarchical* values? In what measure are Hindu influences and borrowings the key to understanding South Asian saints' cults and their continued viability? In his contribution to the present volume, Charles Lindholm asks himself why, whereas Sufism has been peripheralised in the Middle East, in South Asia it has remained a vital institution. One possible reason, he suggests, is that South Asian Muslims share with Hindus notions of hierarchical order which support the belief in transcendentally inspired individuals. By contrast, the individual egalitarianism and progressive rationalisation of Middle Eastern societies make charismatic saints an anachronism. Lindholm's argument here tends to support one kind of interpretation of Weber's theory which stresses, *contra* Shils or Geertz, that 'in the modern world, with its cumulative rationality and machine technology', personal charisma has no place (Wilson 1975: ix). At most it remains a 'romantic idea' or faith (ibid.: x).

Beyond the thorny question as to whether one can typify the two societies as 'hierarchical' or 'egalitarian' in any absolutist sense, Lindholm himself argues here and elsewhere that the alienation, fragmentation, materialism and solipsism of modernity 'push individuals toward immersion in a charismatic group' (Lindholm 1990: 82). The idea of excessive rationalisation invading the 'life world' and denying expressive forms of identity underlies much of the theorising on new social movements (Habermas 1987: 395; Melucci 1997). Nor has charismatic leadership *per se* vanished from the Middle East: as Lindholm himself reports, along with popular movements of resistance to the power of the state (Lindholm 1996: 163), in Egypt the lure of charisma has resurfaced in the form of Islamist movements which 'have also been driven to idealisation of charismatic leaders and Sufic organisation', while condemning 'all formal authority as immoral imposition' (ibid.: 206, 207).

The view that Sufism has been entirely marginalised in the Middle East has, moreover, itself been challenged. Denying this trend, Julian Baldick reports that in 1982 there were six million members of Sufi brotherhoods in Egypt, representing a third of the male population, united through a Supreme Council recognised by the state, and having powerful legislative, judicial and executive functions (Baldick 1989: 159). The impression that Sufism in North Africa is no longer viable may stem largely from a dearth of detailed contemporary research on living saints; it may, however, be the case, as Lindholm suggests here, that political repression by successive colonial and postcolonial regimes has turned charismatic leaders towards more violent agendas. Certainly it is striking that in modern Israel Jewish immigrants coming from North Africa have revived a sacred landscape of saints' shrines and cults, along with all the theosophical premises these embody (Weingrod 1990).

In one sense, then, in highlighting the continued vitality of Sufism in South Asia, this book also constitutes a challenge to Middle East scholars to probe more deeply into the embodiments of Sufi charismatic authority and organisation in the Middle East and North Africa today. This is also the importance of wide-ranging, comparative analyses such as those by Lindholm which raise new questions about the limits of concepts and their application in different contexts. Through such comparisons, the distinctive features of South Asian Sufism, the product of its historical co-existence with 'Hindu' beliefs and practices, might be better comprehended.

The debate about syncretism

The study of Sufism has until recently mainly been the domain of orientalists and historians. From the perspective of orientalists, contemporary shrine cults predominantly appear as *degradations* of classical Sufism into 'decadence' characterised by superstition and magical practices (see Lindholm, this volume; Ahmad 1969). Historians, on the other hand, have for long emphasised the syncretism of saint worship or popular Islam, depicting it as part of a process of 'indigenisation' of Islam and rendering saint worship as basically a Hindu institution (Misra 1964; Moini 1989; Mujeeb 1967; Schwerin 1981; Sen 1985). Implicitly or explicitly, this perspective has also informed several of the more recent anthropological studies of Muslim practices associated with shrines and saints (cf. Buddenberg 1993; Currie 1989; Einzmann 1988; Fruzzetti 1981).

The theory of saint cults as being, in effect, incompletely veiled Hindu institutions has been most vigorously proposed by the sociologist Imtiaz Ahmad (1981). Ahmad distinguishes between three distinct levels of Muslim practice: (1) 'the beliefs and practices that are traditionally described as belonging to formal or scriptural Islam' (1981: 12); (2) customs glossed as being Islamic (ibid.: 13); and (3) 'practical religion', containing 'a large number of non-philosophical elements such as supernatural theories of disease causation, propitiation of Muslim saints and, occasionally at least, deities of the Hindu pantheon, or other crude phenomena such as spirit possession, evil eye, etc.' (ibid.). These different levels of Indian Islam co-exist, he argues, and are integrated at the local level.

In a key respect Ahmad's view meshes with Geertz's theorisation of Islam as plural and embedded in taken-for-granted, historically and culturally specific locales (Geertz 1968). The debate about Islam, one or many, is a perennial one (see, for example, Al-Azmeh 1993; Launay 1992). Arguing against the pluralist interpretation of South Asian Islam, Francis Robinson proposes that the exemplary life of the Prophet constitutes a unifying template of practice and belief, progressively adopted by Muslims in India and worldwide (Robinson 1983).

For both Ahmad and Robinson, however, 'Islamisation' refers exclusively to Islamic orthodoxy at the cost of plurality, thus overlooking the diversity of views represented by Islamic scholars, theologians, Sufis and holy men as well as the historically contingent and shifting nature of internal Muslim debates over questions of correct practice. As Richard Eaton has shown, there never was a uniform agreement upon the definition of 'orthodoxy'. Sufism in medieval Bijapur was represented by different 'types': warrior Sufis, literati, reformers and rebels (called *majzub*) who accepted, challenged and disputed each other's religious positions (Eaton 1978: 243ff). Variously interacting with both Muslim powerholders and the local population, they mediated Islamic concepts of power, value and knowledge. Moreover, nowhere was conversion a sudden event. Rather than being forced (see Schwerin 1981), it evolved over many centuries (Eaton 1978, 1982, 1984, 1993). In a recent work, Eaton rejects not only the interpretation of the regional cult of *Satya pir* as syncretic, but the general notion of Bengali folk-religion as constituting a synthesis of Islam and Hinduism (1993: 280).

Present constructions of syncretic folk-religion are based – Eaton maintains – upon the projection of contemporary religious categories, which gained prominence in the nineteenth and twentieth centuries, onto a premodern Indian past, thus postulating 'the more or less timeless existence of two separate and self-contained communities in Bengal, adhering to two separate and self-contained religious systems, "Hinduism" and "Islam"' (ibid.). Instead of imagining two neatly distinct and bounded groups, he suggests we look at 'a single undifferentiated mass of Bengali villagers' unsystematically picking and choosing 'from an array of reputed instruments – a holy man here, a holy river there – in order to tap superhuman power' (1993: 281).

A key feature of the process of Islamisation involves a 'displacement' of local superhuman agencies by Islamic ones (ibid. 282). Hence, the structure of the sixteenth-century Bengali epic *Nabi-Bamsa* ('Family of the Prophet') resembles that of an eighth-century Arabian text (ibid.: 285): in both, local deities are represented as forerunners of Biblical prophets culminating in the Prophet

Muhammad. Both texts are divided into two parts, the first on the predecessors of the Prophet, the second on his own life (ibid.: 286). The author attempts to situate the holy Prophet, Eaton argues, within a Bengali context: Adam is said to have been created by a Bengali goddess, and the four vedas are seen as preceding revelations made by God to different 'great persons' of whom Muhammad was the last (ibid.: 289).

Still, this cannot be regarded as syncretism, he proposes, because the basic conceptions underlying the narrative mediate Islamic notions, especially of time (linear Islamic versus cyclical Hindu) and the singularity of prophethood in contrast to Hindu concepts of reincarnation and rebirth (ibid.: 289). Moreover, the Hindu social order of pre-Islamic times is depicted as the realm and creation of the fallen angel Iblis or Satan (ibid.: 290). 'In short', Eaton concludes:

> far from describing Islamic superhuman agencies in Indian terms, the *Nabi-Bamsa* does just the opposite: while Brahmans are portrayed as the unwitting teachers of a body of texts deliberately corrupted by Iblis, the rest of the Hindu social order is portrayed as descended from Cain, the misguided son of Adam and Eve. It was only from Adam and Eve's son, Shish, that a 'rightly guided' community, the Muslim *umma*, would descend.
>
> (ibid.: 290)

Such transformations indicate that Islam had come to be regarded in its own right, representing a cosmology distinct from the indigenous one.

We have quoted Richard Eaton extensively in order to clarify the proposition that Islamisation processes occur in the form of embodied ideas not reducible to the effects of Muslim reformists' missionary zeal. In contrast to Ahmad's theory of the 'indigenisation of Islam' we have to recognise the reverse process of an 'Islamisation of the indigenous'. Moreover, Islamisation in terms of a 'purification of local cosmologies' is not confined to the encounter with modernity but represents a concrete manifestation of the very rise of Islam under different geographical and cultural conditions (Eaton 1993: 284). In contemporary South Asia, Islamisation processes are influenced by the mutual hostilities, antagonisms and wars between Hindus and Muslims. Since Partition, and in the face of Hindu nationalist religious discourses and communal violence which culminated in the destruction of the mosque in Ayodhya, religion, as Peter van der Veer shows, has become more intensely politicised than ever, shaping theories of both syncretism and anti-syncretism (van der Veer 1994a). As elsewhere, the politics of syncretism in South Asia defines religious 'purity' and 'hybridity' in political terms (Stewart and Shaw 1994).

Van der Veer criticises Nandy's view (1990), aligned with that of Ahmad, that while orthodox fundamentalist ideas promote communalism, syncretic 'folk-religion' promotes communal harmony. Although Muslim shrines attract both Muslim and Hindu worshippers, he claims, they do so for different reasons:

whereas for Muslim followers a spiritual relationship to the *pir* is of central importance, Hindus see the *dargah* mainly as a healing domain specialising in the cure of demonic illnesses. Consequently, Muslims and Hindus are clearly divided by different degrees of participation and non-participation in rituals defined as Islamic, such as prayers in the mosque (van der Veer 1994a: 207; 1994b). Yet against this view is a counter-reality, described by Basu and Saheb in the present volume, in which Muslim shrines do often create islands of Hindu and Muslim communal harmony.

According to van der Veer, for Hindus:

> Muslims appear to be close to the world of spirits and thus are able to master that world. In that sense they appear to be close to untouchables, who also can be specialists in exorcism. Thus there seems to be an incorporation of saint worship as a lower, impure practice in a Hindu worldview.
>
> (van der Veer 1994b: 207)

Kakar too notes that the majority of possessed Hindus he encountered were afflicted by Muslim spirits; from a Hindu point of view, he suggests, Muslims not only are seen as impure but represent the alien and the demonic, understood as a reification of the unconsciously abjected (Kakar 1982, 1992). The mere presence of Hindus at Muslim shrines, therefore, cannot be taken as a sign of a common, syncretic practice of folk-religion. Rather, the different meanings and values associated with visits to Muslim shrines must be carefully delineated.

Such studies seem to confirm that the encounter of Hindus and Muslims at shrines of saints exemplifies what Dumont long ago wrote about Hindu–Muslim relationships in general: 'we are faced with a *reunion* of men *divided* into two groups, who devalorize each other's values and who are nevertheless associated' (Dumont 1980: 211; emphasis in the original). The majority of individual Hindu supplicants both at Nagore-e-Sharif and at the shrine of Bava Gor in Gujarat are, Saheb and Basu indicate here, women suffering afflictions of spirit possession. However, the shrine in Gujarat reveals a kind of mirror reversal of the Hindu construction of a demonic Muslim image. Here it is Hindus who are seen to instantiate the demonic by embodying evil spirits when seeking treatment. Moreover, the shrine narrative represents the Muslim saints as victorious destroyers of local Hindu deities represented as demons. Rather than Hinduism encompassing an impure Islam, it is Islam which is constructed as infinitely superior and more powerful, subjugating immoral, alien forces. So too the most important saint in India, Mu'in al-din Chishti of Ajmer, is said to have conquered a 'Dev' (god) at whose former temple the shrine is now situated (Currie 1989: 66ff).

Against van der Veer it may be argued that Hindus and Muslims do, in fact, still join together at shrines in amity. This inclusive aspect of local Islam is stressed here by Saheb as the 'universalist' dimension of the cult of Nagore-e-Sharif in Tamil Nadu. The various communities participate as equals in the processions to the shrine centre, but Hindus construct the saint as a diety, while for Muslims he was/is an extraordinary man. Clearly, the charismatic power embodied by a Sufi shrine is crucially dependent on the cosmological ideas actors bring to bear on the saint's image.

Evidently, Muslims do not perceive the presence of Hindus at shrines as indicative of non-Islamic practices. On the contrary, the symbolic repertoires of regional saints' cults in South Asia reinforce beliefs in the universalism of Islam. The Sufi fable of world renunciation is shared by shrines throughout India, Pakistan and Bangladesh (see Werbner 1995). Although each specific cult is deeply embedded in and shapes a local environment, all address similar ontological themes related to death, place and embodiment through which sanctity and sainthood are constructed. To argue that these practices are marginal to the 'true' Islam represented by the mosque and the *'ulama* (religious scholars or officials) is to misrecognise the centrality of eschatological ideas about redemption and salvation to Islam in general (Werbner 1996a). As Jamal Malik demonstrates here in his subtle interpretation of a modern Urdu short story, written as a critique of the practices at saints' shrines, reformist ideas and arguments are 'still bound up with norms and symbols which are rooted in a long tradition'. Thus, although the progressive writer Ahmad Nadim is highly critical of the traditional order, the narrative structure he deploys in his texts follows a pattern similar to that underlying mystical Sufi discourses. According to Malik, modernist reformist values are influenced by a common symbolic framework. It is this multifaceted framework that is the subject of this book.

In interrogating the processes that sustain the devotion to Muslim saints and their tombs, our cases, seen together, examine the social interactions between place, person and society that endow Sufi morality with its continued vitality. The social construction of sainthood by saints, and their perception by followers and devotees, combine to create an alternative universe of ethical meanings. Hence, whereas charisma is usually taken for granted as a magical attribute, the contributors to this book interrogate the fabrications of charisma as they extend to concepts of the body, emotion, morality and sacred topography. In different ethnographic contexts, in Pakistan, India and Bangladesh, charisma (*baraka, karamat*) is revealed as an embodied quality of exemplary persons who creates spaces of potential freedom. This, it seems to us, helps explains the vitality of Sufism both as a mystical philosophy and as a utopian imaginary of an alternative social order.

Acknowledgements

This book is the result of a workshop on 'Muslim Shrines in South Asia' convened by the editors at the Thirteenth European Conference of Modern South Asian Studies at Toulouse in August 1994. In addition to the contributors to the present volume who participated in the workshop, Sylvia Vatuk and Claudia Liebeskind also helped make the workshop a success. Jamal Malik advised on Urdu meanings and transliterations and his invaluable assistance is gratefully acknowledged.

Notes

1 While Asad has argued convincingly against Foucault's representation of a 'microcosm of solitude' in the case of Christian monks (Asad 1993: 112), the case of Muslim saints appears to fit better Foucault's rendition of asceticism among the Ancient Greeks.
2 It is noteworthy that Shilling advocates a return to Durkheim's theory of emotional effervescence in order to go beyond simplistic theories of cultural construction, without acknowledging the major contributions made by anthropologists such as Turner or Douglas to the study of embodiment, which draw upon this Durkheimian legacy. See Sharma (1996) on embodiment as an attempt to go beyond Cartesian dualisms, and the difficulties she perceives in reaching towards an alternative mode of theorisation.

References

Abu-Lughod, Lila (1986) *Veiled Sentiments: Honour and Poetry in a Bedouin Society*, Berkeley and Los Angeles: University of California Press.
Abu-Lughod, Lila and Catherine A. Lutz (1990) 'Introduction: Emotion, Discourse and the Politics of Everyday Life', in Catherine A. Lutz and Lila Abu-Lughod (eds) *Language and the Politics of Emotion*, Cambridge: Cambridge University Press, pp. 1–23.
Ahmad, Aziz (1969) *An Intellectual History of Islam in India*, Edinburgh: Edinburgh University Press.
Ahmad, Imtiaz (1981) 'Introduction', in Imtiaz Ahmad (ed.) *Ritual and Religion among Muslims in India*, Delhi: Manohar, pp. 1–20.
Ahmad, Mumtaz (1991) 'The Jamaat-i-Islami and the Tablighi Jamaat of South Asia', in Martin Marty and Scott Appleby (eds) *Fundamentalism Observed*, Chicago: University of Chicago Press, pp. 457–530.
Al-Azmeh, Aziz (1993) *Islams and Modernities*, London: Virago.
Asad, Talal (1993) *Genealogies of Religion: Discipline and Reasons of Power in Christianity and Islam*, Baltimore and London: Johns Hopkins University Press.
Baldick, Julian (1989) *Mystical Islam: An Introduction to Sufism*, London: I.B. Tauris.
Barth, Fredrik (1959) *Political Leadership among the Swat Pathans*, London: Athlone Press.
Bloch, Maurice (1986) *From Blessing to Violence: History and Ideology in the Circumcision Ritual of the Merina of Madagascar*, Cambridge: Cambridge University Press.
Boddy, Janice (1989) *Wombs and Alien Spirits: Women, Men, and the Zar Cult in Northern Sudan*, Madison: University of Wisconsin Press.
Bourdieu, Pierre (1977) *Outline of a Theory of Practice*, trans. Richard Nice, Cambridge: Cambridge University Press.
Bourdieu, Pierre (1984) *Distinction: A Social Critique of the Judgement of Taste*, trans. Richard Nice, London: Routledge and Kegan Paul.
Buddenberg, Doris (1993) 'Islamabad: Schreine im islamischen Kulturraum. Soziale Funktionen für Hoch- und Volksreligion', in Stephanie Zingel-Avé Lallemant and Wolfgang-Peter Zingel (eds) *Contemporary German Contributions to the History and Culture of Pakistan*, Bonn: Schriftenreihe des Deutsch-Pakistanischen Formus, vol. 10.
Clancey-Smith, Julia (1988) 'Saints, Mahdis, and Arms: Religion and Resistance in Nineteenth-Century North Africa', in Edmund Burke and Ira Lapidus (eds) *Islam, Politics, and Social Movements*, Berkeley: University of California Press, pp. 60–80.
Cohn, Bernard S. (1983) 'Representing Authority in Victorian India', in Eric Hobsbawm

and Terence Ranger (eds) *The Invention of Tradition*, Cambridge: Cambridge University Press, pp. 165–210.

Comaroff, Jean (1985) *Body of Power, Spirit of Resistance*, Chicago: Chicago University Press.

Connerton, Paul (1989) *How Societies Remember*, Cambridge: Cambridge University Press.

Csordas, Thomas J. (1990) 'Embodiment as a Paradigm for Anthropology', *Ethos* 18: 5–47.

Currie, P.M. (1989) *The Shrine and Cult of Mu'in al-din Chishti of Ajmer*, Delhi: Oxford University Press.

Davis, Richard H. (1991) *Ritual in an Oscillating Universe: Worshipping Shiva in Medieval India*, Princeton NJ: Princeton University Press.

Devisch, Rene (1993) *Weaving the Threads of Life: The Khita Gyn-Eco-Logical Healing Cult among the Yaka*, Chicago and London: University of Chicago Press.

Digby, Simon (1984) 'Qalandars and Related Groups: Elements of Social Deviance in the Religious Life of the Delhi Sultanate of the Thirteenth and Fourteenth Centuries', in Yonathan Friedman (ed.) *Islam in Asia*, Jerusalem: Magnus Press, vol. 1, pp. 60–108.

Douglas, Mary (1966) *Purity and Danger: An Analysis of Concepts of Pollution and Taboo*, London: Routledge and Kegan Paul.

Dumont, Louis (1957) 'World Renunciation in Indian Religions', *Contributions to Indian Sociology* 1: 3–62.

Dumont, Louis (1980) [1966] *Homo Hierarchicus: The Caste System and its Implication*, Chicago: University of Chicago Press.

Eade, John and Michael J. Sallnow (1991) 'Introduction', in John Eade and Michael J. Sallnow (eds) *Contesting the Sacred: The Anthropology of Christian Pilgrimage*, London: Routledge, pp. 1–29.

Eaton, Richard M. (1978) *Sufis of Bijapur, 1300–1700*, Princeton, NJ: Princeton University Press.

Eaton, Richard M. (1982) 'Court of Men, Court of God: Local Perceptions of the Shrine of Baba Farid, Pakpattan, Punjab', *Contributions to Asian Studies* XVII: 44–46.

Eaton, Richard M. (1984) 'The Political and Religious Authority of the Shrine of Baba Farid', in Barbara Daly Metcalf (ed.) *Moral Conduct and Authority: The Place of Adab in South Asian Islam*, Berkeley: University of California Press, pp. 333–356.

Eaton, Richard M. (1993) *The Rise of Islam and the Bengal Frontier, 1204–1760*, Berkeley: University of California Press.

Eickelman, Dale (1976) *Moroccan Islam: Tradition and Society in a Pilgrimage Centre*, Austin: University of Texas Press.

Einzmann, Harald (1988) 'Ziarat und Pir-e-Muridi: Golra, Sharif, Nurpur Shahan und Pir Baba', in Einzmann *Drei muslimische Wallfahrtsstätten in Nordpakistan*, Stuttgart: Franz Steiner Verlag.

Eisenstadt, S.N. (1968) *Max Weber on Charisma and Institution Building: Selected Papers*, Chicago: University of Chicago Press.

Elias, Norbert (1983) *The Court Society*, Oxford: Blackwell.

Evans-Pritchard, E.E. (1949) *The Sanusi of Cyrenaica*, Oxford: Clarendon Press.

Ewing, Katherine (1983) 'The Politics of Sufism: Redefining Saints of Pakistan', *Journal of Asian Studies* XLII, 2: 251–268.

Ewing, Katherine (1984) 'Malangs of the Punjab: Intoxication or *Adab* as the Path to God?', in Barbara Daly Metcalf (ed.) *Moral Conduct and Authority: The Place of Adab in South Asian Islam*, Berkeley: University of California Press, pp. 357–371.

Ewing, Katherine P. (ed.) (1988) *Shari'at and Ambiguity in South Asian Islam*, Berkeley: University of California Press.

Fernandez, J.W. (1982) *Bwiti: An Ethnography of the Religious Imagination in Africa*, Princeton, NJ: Princeton University Press.

Foucault, Michel (1979) *Discipline and Punish: The Birth of the Prison*, London: Penguin.

Foucault, Michel (1983) 'The Subject and Power', in H. Dreyfus and Paul Rabinow (eds) *Beyond Structuralism and Hermeneutics*, Chicago: University of Chicago Press, pp. 208–226.

Foucault, Michel (1992) [1984] *The Uses of Pleasure: The History of Sexuality Vol. 2*, London: Penguin.

Frembgen, Jürgen W. (1993) *Derwische: Gelebter Sufismus. Wandernde Mysticker und Asketen im islamischen Orient*, Cologne: DuMont Verlag.

Fruzzetti, Lina M. (1981) 'Muslim Rituals: The Household Rites vs. the Public Festivals in Rural India', in Imtiaz Ahmad (ed.) *Ritual and Religion amongst Muslims in India*, Delhi: Manohar, pp. 91–112.

Fuller, Chris (1993) *The Camphor Flame: Popular Hinduism and Society in India*, Princeton NJ: Princeton University Press.

Gaborieau, Marc (1986) 'Les ordres mystiques dans le sous-continet indien', in A. Popovic and G. Veinstein (eds), *Les ordres mystiques dans l'Islam*, Paris: Editions de l'Ecole es Hautes Etudes en Sciences Sociales, pp. 105–134.

Geertz, Clifford (1968) *Islam Observed: Religious Development in Morocco and Indonesia*, New Haven CT: Yale University Press.

Geertz, Clifford (1973) *The Interpretation of Cultures*, London: Hutchinson.

Geertz, Clifford (1983) 'Centers, Kings, and Charisma: Reflections on the Symbolics of Power', in Geertz *Local Knowledge*, London: Fontana Press, pp. 121–146.

Gellner, Ernest (1969) *Saints of the Atlas*, London: Weidenfeld and Nicolson.

Gellner, Ernest (1981) *Muslim Society*, Cambridge: Cambridge University Press.

Gilmartin, David (1984) 'Shrines, Succession and Sources of Moral Authority', in Barbara Daly Metcalf (ed.) *Moral Conduct and Authority: The Place of Adab in South Asian Islam*, Berkeley: University of California Press, pp. 221–240.

Gilsenan, Michael (1973) *Saint and Sufi in Modern Egypt: An Essay in Comparative Religion*, Oxford: Clarendon Press.

Gilsenan, Michael (1982) *Recognizing Islam*, New York: Pantheon.

Gold, Ann G. (1988) *Fruitful Journeys: The Ways of Rajasthani Pilgrims*, Berkeley: University of California Press.

Habermas, Jürgen (1987) *The Theory of Communicative Action: The Critique of Functionalist Reason* Vol. 2, Oxford: Blackwell.

Handelman, Don (1990) *Models and Mirrors: Towards an Anthropology of Public Events*, Cambridge: Cambridge University Press.

Kakar, Sudhir (1982) *Mystics, Shamans and Doctors: A Psychological Inquiry into India and its Healing Traditions*, Delhi: Oxford University Press.

Kakar, Sudhir (1992) 'Some Unconscious Aspects of Ethnic Violence in India', in Veena Das (ed.) *Mirrors of Violence: Communities, Riots and Survivors in South Asia*, New Delhi: Oxford University Press, pp. 135–145.

Kapferer, Bruce (1983) *A Celebration of Demons: Exorcism and the Aesthetics of Healing in Sri Lanka*, Bloomington: Indiana University Press.

Kurin, Richard (1983) 'The Structure of Blessedness in a Moslem Shrine in Pakistan', *Middle Eastern Studies* 19: 312–325.

Kurin, Richard (1984) 'Morality, Personhood and the Exemplary Life: Popular Conceptions of Muslims in Paradise', in Barbara Daly Metcalf (ed.) *Moral Conduct and*

Authority: The Place of Adab in South Asian Islam, Berkeley: University of California Press, pp. 196–220.

Launay, Robert (1992) *Beyond the Stream: Islam and Society in a West African Town*, Berkeley: University of California Press.

Lévi-Strauss, Claude (1966) [1962] *The Savage Mind*, London: Weidenfeld and Nicolson.

Lindholm, Charles (1990) *Charisma*, Oxford: Blackwell.

Lindholm, Charles (1996) *The Islamic Middle East: An Historical Anthropology*, Oxford: Blackwell.

Lings, Martin (1961) *A Muslim Saint of the 20th Century*, London: Allen and Unwin.

Marriott, McKim (1976) 'Hindu Transactions: Diversity without Dualism', in Bruce Kapferer (ed.) *Transaction and Meaning: Directions in the Anthropology of Exchange and Symbolic Behaviour*, Philadelphia: ISHI, pp. 109–142.

Melucci, Alberto (1997) 'Identity and Difference in a Globalised World', in Pnina Werbner and Tariq Modood (eds) *Debating Cultural Hybridity: Multi-Cultural Identities and the Politics of Anti-Racism*, London: Zed Books, pp. 58–69.

Metcalf, Barbara Daly (1982) *Islamic Revival in British India: Deoband, 1860–1900*, Princeton NJ: Princeton University Press.

Metcalf, Barbara Daly (1984) 'Introduction', in Barbara Daly Metcalf (ed.) *Moral Conduct and Authority: The Place of adab in South Asian Islam*, Berkeley: University of California Press, pp. 1–20.

Misra, Satish C. (1964) *Muslim Communities in Gujarat*, Bombay: Asia Publishing House.

Moini, S.L.H. (1989) 'Rituals and Customary Practices at the Dargah of Ajmer', in Christian W. Troll (ed.) *Muslim Shrines in India*, Delhi: Oxford University Press, pp. 60–75.

Mujeeb, Mohammad (1967) *The Indian Muslims*, London: George Allen and Unwin.

Nanda, Bikram N. and Mohammad Talib (1989) 'Soul of the Soulless: An Analysis of Pir–Murid Relationships in Sufi Discourse', in Christian W. Troll (ed.) *Muslim Shrines in India*, Delhi: Oxford University Press, pp. 125–144.

Nandy, Ashis (1990) 'The Politics of Secularism and the Recovery of Religious Tolerance', in Veena Das (ed.) *Mirrors of Violence*, Delhi: Oxford University Press, pp. 69–93.

Nicholson, Reynold A. (1978) [1921] *Studies in Islamic Mysticism*, Cambridge: Cambridge University Press.

Parry, Jonathan (1989) 'On the Moral Perils of Exchange', in Jonathan Parry and Maurice Bloch (eds) *Money and the Morality of Exchange*, Cambridge: Cambridge University Press, pp. 64–93.

Pinto, Desiderio (1989) 'The Mystery of the Nizamuddin Dargah: The Accounts of Pilgrims', in Christian W. Troll (ed.) *Muslim Shrines in India*, Delhi: Oxford University Press.

Pinto, Desiderio (1995) *Piri–Muridi Relationship: A Study of the Nizzamuddin Darga*, Delhi: Manohar, pp. 112–124.

Rahman, Fazlur (1979) *Islam*, Chicago: University of Chicago Press.

Robinson, Francis (1983) 'Islam and Muslim Society in South Asia', *Contributions to Indian Sociology* n.s. 17, 2: 185–203.

Sallnow, Michael J. (1987) *Pilgrims of the Andes: Regional Cults in Cusco*, Washington DC: Smithsonian Institution Press.

Schimmel, Annemarie (1975) *Mystical Dimensions of Islam*, Chapel Hill: University of North Carolina Press.

Schwerin, Kerrin Gräfin (1981) 'Saint Worship in Indian Islam: The Legend of the Martyr Salar Masud Ghazi', in Imtiaz Ahmad (ed.) *Ritual and Religion among Muslims in India*, Delhi: Manohar, pp. 143–161

Sen, Dinesh Chandra (1985) [1920] *The Folk Literature of Bengal*, Delhi: B.R. Publishing House.

Sharma, Ursula (1996) 'Bringing the Body Back into the (Social) Action: Techniques of the Body and the (Cultural) Imagination', *Social Anthropology* 4, 3: 251–264.

Sherani, Saifur Rahman (1991) 'Ulema and Pir in the Politics of Pakistan', in Hastings Donnan and Pnina Werbner (eds), *Economy and Culture in Pakistan: Migrants and Cities in a Muslim Society*, London: Macmillan, pp. 216–246.

Shilling, Chris (1993) *The Body and Social Theory*, London: Sage.

Shilling, Chris (1997) 'Emotions, Embodiment and the Sensation of Society', *Sociological Review* 45, 2: 195–219.

Shils, Edward A. (1965) 'Charisma, Order and Status', *American Sociological Review* 30: 199–213.

Stewart, Charles and Rosalind Shaw (eds) (1994) *Syncretism/Anti-Syncretism*, London: Routledge.

Stoller, Paul (1995) *Embodying Colonial Memories: Spirit Possession, Power and the Hauka in West Africa*, New York: Routledge.

Tambiah, Stanley (1984) *The Buddhist Saints of the Forest and the Cult of Amulets: A Study in Charisma, Hagiography, Sectarianism, and Millennial Buddhism*, Cambridge: Cambridge University Press.

Tambiah, Stanley J. (1990) *Magic, Science, Religion, and the Scope of Rationality*, Cambridge: Cambridge University Press.

Taussig, Michael (1993) *Mimesis and Alterity: A Particular History of the Senses*, New York: Routledge.

Trimingham, J.S. (1971) *The Sufi Orders in Islam*, Oxford: Oxford University Press.

Tsing, Anna L. (1993) *In the Realm of the Diamond Queen*, Princeton NJ: Princeton University Press.

Turner, Bryan S. (1991) 'Recent Developments in the Theory of the Body', in Mike Featherstone, Mike Hepworth and Bryan S. Turner (eds) *The Body: Social Process and Cultural Theory*, London: Sage, pp. 1–35.

Turner, Victor (1967) *The Forest of Symbols: Aspects of Ndembu Ritual*, Ithaca NY: Cornell University Press.

Turner, Victor (1974) *Dramas, Fields, and Metaphors: Symbolic Action in Human Society*, Ithaca NY: Cornell University Press.

van der Veer, Peter (1992) 'Playing or Praying: A Sufi Saint's day in Surat', *Journal of Asian Studies* 51, no 3: 545–564.

van der Veer, Peter (1994a) *Religious Nationalism: Hindus and Muslims in India*, Berkeley: University of California Press.

van der Veer, Peter (1994b) 'Syncretism, Multiculturalism and the Discourse of Tolerance', in Charles Stewart and Rosalind Shaw (eds) *Syncretism/Anti-Syncretism*, London: Routledge, pp. 196–211.

Vikor, Knut S. (1995) *Sufi and Scholar on the Edge of the Desert: Muhammad b. Ali al-Sanusi and his Brotherhood*, London: Hurst.

Waardenburg, J.D.J. (1979) 'Official and Popular Religion as a Problem in Islamic Studies', in P.H. Vrijhof and J.D.J. Waardenburg (eds) *Official and Popular Religion: Analysis of a Theme for Religious Studies*, The Hague: Mouton, pp. 340–386.

Weber, Max (1948) *From Max Weber: Essays in Sociology*, trans., eds and intro. H.H. Gerth and C. Wright Mills, London: Routledge and Kegan Paul.

Weingrod, Alex (1990) *The Saint of Beersheba*, Albany NY: State University of New York Press.

Werbner, Pnina (1995) 'Powerful Knowledge in a Global Sufi Cult: Reflections on the Poetics of Travelling Theories', in Wendy James (ed.) *The Pursuit of Certainty: Religious and Cultural Formulations*, London and New York: Routledge, pp. 134–160.

Werbner, Pnina (1996a) 'The Making of Muslim Dissent: Hybridized Discourses, Lay Preachers, and Radical Rhetoric among British Pakistanis', *American Ethnologist* 23, 1: 102–122.

Werbner, Pnina (1996b) 'Stamping the Earth with the Name of Allah: *Zikr* and the Sacralizing of Space among British Muslims', *Cultural Anthropology* 11, 3: 309–338.

Werbner, Richard (1989) *Ritual Passage, Sacred Journey: The Processs and Organization of Religious Movement*, Washington DC: Smithsonian Institution Press.

Wilson, Bryan R (1975) *The Noble Savages: The Primitive Origins of Charisma*, Berkeley: University of California Press.

Part 2

EMBODYING LOCALITY

2

THE HARDWARE OF SANCTITY
Anthropomorphic objects in Bangladeshi Sufism

Samuel Landell Mills

The cast of characters

Pir of Atroshi	The most popular (and unpopular) living *Pir* (saint) in Bangladesh
Saddar Uddin Chisti	A small-time heterodox holy man in Old Dhaka
Mujibur Rahman Chisti	A peripatetic *pir* with many rich clients and bases in Dhaka and Bogra
Pir of Sayedabad	A *pir* with an ostentatious *darbar* (court) based in Dhaka, who heals but does not accept disciples
Nazimuddin	A small-time *pir* who specialises in healing

Their places

Atroshi	A 'holy court' (*darbar sharif*) in Faridpur district
Modaleb Shah's Mazar	A small tomb-shrine (*dargah*) in Old Dhaka
Maishbandar	A village of saintly tombs in Chittagong district

Introduction: the sources of charisma

This chapter explores the relationship in Bangladesh between the identity of Muslim holy men (or the living and dead saintly figures connected to the Sufi tradition known as '*pir*s'), and the spaces and objects with which they are almost invariably associated. Whilst saintly tombs, for instance, have an obvious commemorative function, is it possible to tease out the dynamics which make the attribution of a saintly identity to material objects so effective?

The sanctity of *pir*s derives not from some imagined essence of Sufism or Islam, nor from the mere appropriation of a holy name, but from the structured use by *pir*s and devotees of a whole range of paraphernalia, associated with the saintly body, through which their relationship is conducted and into which their collaboration can be sublimated. The association with material objects underpins and reproduces the sanctity of living *pir*s, as a diverse category and as individuals, by both focusing and multiplying their presence. This allows both routinised and miraculous attributions of saintly identity, since it is characteristic of South Asian Sufi saints that they connect the living and the dead, the seen and the unseen, the divine and the mundane, the locality and the wider world, the real and the ideal. In ideal terms, their personalities are mirrored, voided and given over to the Other; first, in devotion to their own preceptors, to the Prophet and to God; second, in that the extinction of their selfish passions places them at the disposal of their devotees.

Devotees believe that the spiritual mastery achieved by the *pir* irradiates his body with blessedness, and that this spreads to the persons and objects with which he comes in contact. These objects extend the physical presence of the *pir*, and provide solid matter for the construction of his sanctity. The devotional imagining of a *pir*'s capacity to animate otherwise inert objects, often downplayed as a peripheral ramification of his spiritual power, is the crux of his 'saintly' performance. And these saintly vehicles are anthropomorphised; they are attributed with almost human capacities to interact.

To carry this further, the notion of a transcendent power itself rests upon an anthropomorphism.[1] It represents the suffusion of one order of experience, that of a person manipulating the solid universe, with a subtlety borrowed from the complex interplay of sameness and otherness in encounters between two persons. I suggest that the thinkability of a limitless source of blessing (and this is true not only of South Asian Muslim but of many other religious cosmologies) is based on an extrapolation from the experience of a relative difference in the subtlety of interpersonal and person–object relations.

Such an approach returns to Mary Douglas's long-standing observation that the predecessors of modern anthropology separated magic and religion because of their social evolutionist premises, and because of the theological righteousness of early comparative religionists such as Robertson Smith (Douglas 1966:13–19). As Douglas also suggests, Durkheim's influential vision of the sacred attributed its 'contagious' quality to the fictive, abstract nature of religious entities as collective 'ideas awakened by the experience of society . . . [and] projected outwards', and hence without a 'fixed material point of reference' (1966: 21). This implies that however sanctity is mediated, represented or objectified, it is social relations which invest objects of totemic affiliation with power. In this chapter I wish to suggest that the empowerment of sacred objects which from a Durkheimian perspective is seen to stem from the experience of collective psychology may in reality be derived from a more intimate experience, that of dyadic intercommunication with its moments of mutual incorporation.

Of course, the devaluation of the specific qualities of objects was also enshrined in structuralism, with its emphasis on the arbitrary nature of the signifier. Poststructuralists such as Bourdieu have subsequently attempted to rescue agency through a theoretical stress on the contested features of signifiers and their manipulation in systems of distinction (Bourdieu 1984). In his latter work, Foucault too moved towards a stress on agency and resistance (Foucault 1983, 1984: 388). In studies of religious culture, this new emphasis on the performance and embodiment of culture has made holy persons seem freshly significant as foci of mediation between religious idealism and the world. Moreover the anthropocentrism underpinning religious practice may, it has been suggested, have a deep cognitive basis (Boyer 1996). Without doubt, many religions revolve around exemplary figures or some kinds of anthropomorphic representation of natural forces (Guthrie 1993).

Sufism in general, and popular Sufism in Bangladesh in particular, places the human exemplar at the centre of sanctity (as the pathway to God, sometimes even as God himself), and continually reimagines his presence through the use of material objects. Paradoxically, because of this equation between person and object, the more personal and parochial the exemplar is, the more his universality is demonstrated. From this perspective Bangladeshi Sufism can be seen to denote a range of practices which explore the position of the human Other as the foremost of the perceptual objects and instruments through which we organise our worlds. The Face of the Other, in Levinas's terms (1987), is ever present but also elusive, implicit in whatever we think and experience but never quite crystallising as promised. Sufism can therefore be both accessible and appealing (an ideal instrument of conversion) and elitist and esoteric. In fact, that very diversity of Sufi or *pir* identity, objectively correlated in the hardware of sanctity, is essential to its reproduction as a cultural institution.

Embodying the sacred

Writing about *pir*s, in Bangladesh at least, is like rotating a crystal ball that continuously reveals new aspects. This is due not only to their, or my own, prolixity but also to the sheer generativity of their image; a human embodiment of the sacred. The corporeal overflow of divine blessing yields miraculous signs. *Pir*s may visit devotees in dreams, rescue people in distress, appear everywhere, read people's minds and bodies, grant disciples miraculous experiences. The disciple who submits to a *pir*, in approximating the ideal of complete malleability, becomes another tentacle through which he acts. Any voiding of the agency of that disciple is patterned on the egolessness of his or her *pir*. The chain of deference leads through the *pir* to the Prophet and to God.

As a *pir* acts through people so he must act through objects. *Pir*s work both miraculously and routinely through tombs, buildings, trees, food or just about any object which can be somehow identified with them. Whilst the spiritual authority of a *pir* is for those who are allowed to become disciples, his spiritual power is more freely available. The manipulation of that power by devotees is ideologically disguised as reverence for his attributes, which the disciple will learn to recognise in an inexhaustible variety of miraculous signs. Sharing belief in and experience of such extraordinary events underpins every devotee's reverence for the objects and places which a *pir* has created or consecrated by dint of his 'spiritual power' (*adhartik shakti*).

That devotion is rewarded by such 'mediations' is a corollary of the *pirs*' personal elusiveness, of their presence in the world as a kind of inner absence. Conversely, on leaving the world, the institutions they bequeath express their post-mortem absence as a kind of active 'presence'.

The flux of identity between *pir* and devotee suggests infinite possible resolutions, and miracles are permutations of these. Like pilgrimage destinations, *pirs*' miracles and *pirs* themselves materialise the transcendent to offer a worldly meeting point with a sanctity which is reworked by devotional journeying and effort. *Pir* devotion brings together and conflates the most mutable and fluid experience, that of eyeball-to-eyeball interaction, and the infinitely less subtle encounter with the inert, whether soil, stone or corpse. Into the limits of the latter are compressed the volatility and vitality of the former.

Living *pir*s

In Bangladesh, there is a wide variety of people who are termed '*pir*'. Some teach in Islamic schools (*madrasah*) and only take disciples within that realm, some are tantric *faqirs* who do not have a wide following. I am primarily concerned here with living *pir*s who invite public recognition and create or inherit sacred sites by spiritual or filial succession. Living *pir*s are not regulated or recognised by any higher authority, and depend for social recognition on their own ability to recruit a body of disciples, devotees and supplicants.

The contemporary *pir*s of Atroshi, Maishbandar or Sayedabad are exemplars of the many Sufi subtraditions in contemporary Bangladesh, but they are primarily their own men, manipulating *pir* identity in individual ways. At the same time, they are implicitly invoking a whole tradition built upon veneration of dead saints, many of whom are enshrined in thousands of tombs scattered all over Bangladesh. *Pir*s in South Asia have always been associated with territory claimed for Islam, which they were depicted as controlling in hierarchical delegation from God (Gaborieau 1989; Haq 1975; Roy 1983). The greater the stature of the saint the greater the area controlled. When told of my intention to study *pir*s in their country, many Bangladeshi people politely asked whether I had visited the famous tombs of Shah Jahlal in Sylhet or Baizid Bustami in Chittagong, both saints mytho-historically associated with the Islamisation of Bengal.[2]

In a sense, the archetypal image of a *pir* may be that of the entombed saint, but such an image is continually revalidated in the living practice of putative successors to the saintly tradition and their adherents.[3] As *pir*s are not part of an ecclesiastic structure, the process of being and becoming a *pir* is fluctuating and ambiguous. Therefore, a *pir*'s standing depends on individual initiative, entrepreneurial flair and organisational virtuosity, quite apart from spiritual attainment itself. *Pir* practice anticipates the creation of establishments which will retroactively affirm the *pir*'s lifetime sanctity. Almost always, this involves post-mortem struggles between the families of a *pir* and his unrelated devotees for control over his identity and name, and the benefits they bring. Both sides must compete to transcendentalise the not-so-departed soul.

In Bangladesh, there is a distinction between the lodges inhabited by *pir*s, popularly known as *darbar*, or 'courts', where a living descendant of the founding *pir* is in control and which are therefore entitled to remain in the private sector, and *dargah* (a legal category), where a tomb exists but the caretakers (*khadem*) who run it are no longer of the same bloodline. At this point the place of burial becomes subject to government regulation. In recent years the government has been attempting to extend its grip upon the *mazar* (a generic term for saintly tombs) in Bangladesh, in order to regulate their activities, appropriate their income and ensure that their influence is not subversive. Although both *darbar* and *dargah* can be legitimate recipients of endowments (*waqf*), which legally require government administration and scrutiny, endowments to living saints do not become *waqf*, and thus many lodges can remain free of government interference in their administrative and financial affairs. One complaint I often heard against *pir*s was that they paid no income tax on the huge income which they derived from pilgrims and supplicants.

As living *pir*s are theoretically 'dead in life', having mastered their lower selves, so entombed *pir*s transcend death to remain as active presences in the world. In practical terms, the spiritual power of a dead *pir* is accessible to devotees through the material objects and structures with which he has come to be identified. The idiosyncratic presence of the *pir*, immersed in the divine, flows through tombs, buildings, land, furniture, food, amulets; all are described by the adjectival noun *tabarok* (full of blessing). It is the material qualities of these objects that makes their anthropomorphisation the key to the revelation of spiritual power.

*Pir*s, by imitation, inherit the institutions of their predecessors. A living *pir* who attracts sufficient patronage can develop an institutional framework where his spiritual authority is unquestionable, enabling him to approximate those *pir*s of renown whose sanctity has been consummated by death. Less successful *pir*s may selectively imitate, or may emphasise their apprenticeship or service to, a more established *pir*. Either way, the association between the tomb and the ideal *pir* lends symmetry to diverse *pir* cults, whilst successful enshrinement affirms the saintliness of particular personalities.

A living *pir* and his devotees progressively sublimate his public persona in the objective structures constructed around him, so that they can be taken as extensions of him. By establishing a personified arena where his presence may be felt, these structures institutionalise and routinise his saintliness. The hardware of sanctity, then, enables *pir*s and their devotees to elaborate and sustain an image, that of a miraculous agency ever poised at the brink of temporal intervention.

What gives Sufism its distinct flavour is its mortuary symbolism and its permanent dwelling in the charismatic moment. In South Asia especially, Sufi saints are always the miraculous signifiers of their religious tradition. Their divine absorption prefigures the eventual return of all creation to the Creator. *Pir*s therefore linger in a personalised *avant*-armageddon liminality. This is reminiscent of the suspension of time by Hindu Aghori renouncers described by Parry (1982). Such a state of suspension has structural parallels with millenarist religious phenomena in many other non-Muslim and non-South Asian cultural contexts, where the anticipation of a 'triumphal re-entry' into the world by transcendent forces, ritually bifurcated by the elaboration of their negative alter (the wicked world), is marked by an abandonment of ordinary productive activities (Bloch 1986). Islam shares the millennialism of Judaeo-Christianity: Allah, whose presence is signified by language, adopts a routinised place hovering on the edge of visual reciprocity, so that the anticipated moment of 'seeing the face of God' is modelled anthropomorphically. Sufism, by privileging the tomb, not only brings this sense of anticipation to a pitch of intensity, but also gives it a concrete focus and grants it perpetuity. It imagines the divine as both absent and present, as real as life and more real besides.

The appearances of spiritual power

Many Sufi shrines in Bangladesh are centred on tombs, with ritual items or markings that characterise and demarcate the sanctified domain in which *pirs* are experienced. Such objects, particularly the architectural structures of Sufi shrines, have a rhetorical quality. They help regenerate and focus a religious discourse, emboldening it through the apparent proof they offer of the temporal consequence of transcendent ideals.

The material culture at Sufi centres in Bangladesh provides a set of props enabling the continuous renewal of the saintly standing of a particular *pir* or *pir* lineage. Famous Sufi establishments in Bangladesh, such as Atroshi and Maishbandar, might be described as religious theme parks, given the atmosphere of other-worldliness their constituent paraphernalia is organised to evoke. Solid expression in commemorative objects not only focuses the concepts of sanctity and spiritual power which *pirs* command, but also lends specificity to each individual *pir* and generates new experiences of contact with that sanctity.

In the courts of living *pirs*, a particularly tomb-like sanctity is evoked through the combination of intimacy and formality in the interactions of *pirs* with devotees. This is paralleled by the dynamic contrast of stillness and action through which many *pirs* work: the entire structure of a dead *pir*'s shrine evokes a body at rest, infused with the latent capacity to act, whilst the behaviour of living *pirs* often verges on the still and iconic. Not all *pirs* behave in a restrained fashion, but all partake of an image of the *pir* as 'spiritually powerful', capable of acting in unseen ways, and therefore can enjoy a kind of authority distinct from that of the scripturally learned (*'ulama*) who form a worldly class of ritual specialists, or that of politicians who are seen as primarily pragmatic and self-interested. Each *pir* must blend action and stillness, the visible and the unseen, into an image of power itself. (This may imply an idealised vision or critique of more worldly power and of the prevailing social conditions which it objectifies and sometimes influences.) *Pir*s must provide their clients with clues, or cues, from which they themselves must infer sanctity. It is both the inner (*antorik*) devotional work of the disciple to realise the spiritual capacity of the *pir* and his outer (*bajjik*) duty to help reproduce the appearances of sanctity by following the decorum that the *pir*–disciple bond entails.

The ideal *pir* welcomes all, especially the poor, the sick and the mentally anguished. However, in a moralistic and conservative society, an image of decorous comportment is associated with social status. The most successful living *pir*s attract many apparently well-balanced and successful people, and so, at least, devotees feel as though their self-interest is not threatened by going to a *pir*: they may even feel that such visits give them both wholeness and a new set of opportunities. Devotees, like their *pir*s, pursue the art of appearances, observing the decorum of the Sufi realm in spite of their pressing personal requirements. Their worldly and spiritual needs can be neatly elided by the rhetoric of 'blessing' (*doa*), which addresses both. The consciously 'religious' sentiments which *pir*s invoke in their followers certainly pivot upon some measure of self-transcendence, or identification with a larger entity. Hence, *pir*s both mirror and focus their devotees' own efforts to strike a balance between self-assertion and self-abnegation. Although living *pir*s are obliged to act in order to become established, their actions must seem effortless, altruistic and God-gifted. How is this distinction between worldly and spiritual endeavour embodied by *pir*s? In other words, how do they occupy and manage that contradiction?

The usual pattern is as follows: first, a domain is established where the authority of the resident *pir* is uncontested and uncontestable. This demands the routinisation and control of a court culture by *pir*s or by their successors. But most *pir*s' establishments are set on a path of expansion. *Pir*s are forever looking to expand their material and institutional framework as they attract more customers. Because such worldly growth has to be kept consonant with the other-worldly image of the *pir*s, the space and the objects with which a *pir* is associated must be seen to be kept within the ambit of his personal authority and identity. As the worldly signs of his saintly stature proliferate, so the 'spiritual' stature of a *pir* itself grows to match them and to anticipate even greater manifestations of his power. When a *pir* moves from being of local interest to becoming a regional, national or international attraction, his putative spiritual power and his accoutrements increase in tandem. The more a *pir*'s identity becomes sublimated in and through his environment, the easier it is for devotees to experience him as simultaneously close and distant, as man and superman, and to feel that they must strive to earn his blessing. Thus, the notion of spiritual power which *pir*s and their clientele manipulate is itself dependent on the ability to create domains of spiritual authority, which are materially constituted and identified with each *pir*.

The single-minded devotion of the ideal disciple is a kind of 'choice of no choice'. Most frequently, this attitude is materially enshrined in a space or arena of non-contradiction, where a particular *pir*'s authority is consensually accepted and where some degree of respectful behaviour is compulsory. Devotional activity continually redefines these social and physical spaces as exemplary centres. Even the most instrumental supplication to an entombed, invisible *pir* consists of the acknowledgement of authority in return for a benevolent exercise of power. How, then, does the *pir*'s authority contribute to, and interweave with, the disciples' experience of his spiritual power?

In the particular case of the cult centred on Muhammad Hashmatullah, the *pir* of Atroshi, the most successful living *pir* in Bangladesh, the death of the *pir* is continually anticipated as the consummation of his sanctity. The *pir* occupies a site of over one hundred acres in rural Faridpur district, about a hundred miles from Dhaka. The site, known as the *Bishwa Zaker Manzil*,[4] is in a constant state of transformation through a never-ceasing series of construction and earthworks. Architecturally, the place is unremarkable except for the mosque, which has been taking shape gradually since the late 1980s. While the *pir* is alive his centrality to the work in progress seems far more compelling than the appearance of the establishment itself.

The *pir* of Atroshi has lived continuously in the same place for the last forty years, following a command from his own *pir* to establish himself there. Arriving as an anonymous *maulana* (learned man), he slowly built up the site, and his identification with it is complete. Nothing is allowed to happen there without the *pir*'s authorisation, and disciples claim that everything that does occur there is by the power of the *pir*. As the scale of the establishment has increased so too has the reputed spiritual stature of the *pir*, who is now revered by his disciples as a *wali mukammel*, a perfected friend of God. People who are hostile to the *pir* assert that he is trapped in Atroshi by various jinns which he controls within the *darbar* area but which would destroy him if he left. The place is famous as a pilgrimage centre for hundreds of thousands (claimed as millions) of devotees. The *pir* was also visited regularly by President Ershad during his time in office. As a result of the patronage of the president's followers, there was a big increase in visitors and income to the *darbar*, and the *pir* became famous throughout Bangladesh. Yet because of the sheer size of his following, the *pir* is available to disciples only within a rigid framework of etiquette rules, albeit one which bears the imprint of his personality and which allows him some room for idiosyncratic manoeuvre.

The *pir* gives *darshan* (appearance) three times a day, and the disciples who have come to petition him are managed in such a way as to prevent their becoming too burdensome, clinging or obstructive to others waiting behind them. The *darbar* is structured, in effect, as a series of frames around the person of the *pir* or, more exactly, around the experience of seeing and being seen by the *pir*. Disciples spend the time away from the *pir* striving to remember his face, in parallel with their *jikir*, the repetition of the divine name. Sometimes this devotional labour is rewarded with a dream vision in which something may be communicated.[5] A crucial idea is that the disciple is transparent to the *pir*, so that the brief ocular encounter with him is a very highly charged experience, in which the disciple sees himself as being absolutely known. The disciple, conversely, has to struggle to know the *pir*, as a means of pursuing material and spiritual blessing. This necessitates the disciple's spiritual submission and also devotional labour. He will 'know' the *pir* through the atmosphere, the rituals, the words and the accoutrements which surround him and which therefore become part of the saintly identity. The more material an object associated with the *pir*, the more specifically a disciple can fasten his attachment upon it and suffuse it with adoration. The *pir*'s establishment, that which he has 'given', is treated with reverence. In this way, a death-transcending personality is constructed during his lifetime.

The site which is absolutely identified with the *pir* is markedly discontinuous from the locality surrounding it. It runs according to a fixed pattern in which everything has to be instigated by the *pir* and can be changed arbitrarily only by him and by nobody else. This includes prayer times, eating and all practical work. Disciples' devotional labour is utterly identified with the *pir* and is seen as his own devotional labour to his preceptor, from whom he receives instructions beyond the grave. Eventually, when the octogenarian *pir* dies, the institution will be able to function according to the pattern which he has already established. His devotional labour will be eternalised, having been detached from his physical person even in his lifetime. Moreover the contrast between seeing the *pir* as an ordinary living person and as a one-man powerhouse of divine blessing, on which the complex attitudes of devotion are elaborated, will reach a necessary resolution at his death: his post-mortem personhood (his interactive, accessible, saintly personality) will be an index of his power, whereas his pre-mortem material power and authority are symptoms of his extraordinary personality. Hence death will represent the consummation of his sanctity and this will be celebrated at his *'urus* (ritual commemoration of the day of his death).

Theoretically, the spiritual power which the *pir* possesses is unlimited, in the sense that disciples should not have the impertinence to imagine its limitations. Devotional activity centres power in the *darbar* (space-wise) and reinvigorates it at the annual *'urus* (time-wise). The ritual structures which focus the power in exemplary spaces and moments also survive the mortal demise of the *pir* and celebrate his incorporation into the chain of divinely illuminated souls, united with God, through which direct experience of divine blessing can be obtained.

In fact, tombs are where the different and sometimes conflicting aspects of *pir* identity in general can be momentarily reconciled. The Islamic saints of Bangladesh vary enormously in their attributes, and sometimes it is only through the use of the tomb symbol that some commonality and shared meaning in the *pir* category is evoked. For example, Shah Jahlal is revered for his preaching and warrior exploits (Haq 1975: 147), Lallon Shah for his tantric expertise, his ecumenical spirit and his music, and the (living) *pir* of Sayedabad for his bestowal of fertility. The reverence shown for each of these figures and attributes implicitly reaffirms and sometimes influences the reverence shown for the others. The tradition is thereby susceptible to renegotiation, renewal and change. For example, the *pir* of Sayedabad declares that he does not 'make disciples', which is indicative of an 'orthodox' attitude of disapproval of the *pir–murid* (disciple) relationship. In itself it is likely to strengthen the influence of the orthodox conception of *pirs* in neo-Sufi discourse, which downplays their supernatural powers and instead depicts both living and historic *pir*s as pious men whom God may favour, but who have no esoteric power to call their own.

Intimacy with a living *pir* implies discrimination concerning his habits of communication, but these intimacies do not encroach upon the formality of a *pir*–disciple relationship, which is premised on the hierarchical devotion of the disciple. Bachu, a disciple of Atroshi, told me something which suggested how this is experienced: 'I have seen *Huzur* most days for the last twenty years. Any other person you see for a while then you get tired of them, but with him, never!' Similarly, people who venerate a deceased *pir* may develop a relationship with him as an active and idiosyncratic power in their lives. In both cases, there is an interplay of formality and intimacy, of distance and familiarity, which keeps the sacred identity alive. The holy identity is reconstituted by, and experienced through, the tension between these modes of interaction. Distance and familiarity are both present within individual practice and, at the same time, bifurcated as characterising the difference between intimate and occasional visitors to a *pir*.

The dynamic of conflicting, or complimentary, attitudes between *pir*s and disciples itself depends on the particular kind of presence which is held to be characteristic of a *pir*. The association with a tomb often endows the *pir* with certain qualities resembling those of a material object; unshakeable, complete, silent, immemorial and unquestionable. These strengthen the image of encounters with the *pir* as interactions with an outward shell, a self whose own proclivities have been subordinated to an inner realisation of Islam and which thus radiates transformation. The tripartite structure of a popular *pir*'s identity – an inner self which forms a sanctum sanctorum into which the privileged few may have an insight, an outer appearance which devotees may reverentially harness, and a world of effects (miraculous experiences) – is reflected in the structure of the places saints in Bangladesh occupy before and after death.

Atroshi, centred on a living incumbent, exemplifies this kind of structure and also shows that the more the separation of each of these interdependent levels is accentuated, the more intense the experience of them becomes. The iconic presence of a living *pir* is a point of balance between his inner spiritual identity and his miraculous effects, just as *darshan* itself is where *pir* and disciple belong to each other, where the disciple may grasp the feet of his preceptor but may only feel himself scanned by his eyes. The Atroshi site phases from the *pir*'s private abode, where he is only elusively present to almost all his assembled devotees, to the audience chambers, where he presents himself to his people, to the buildings, the earthworks, fields and so on, which are the indices of his power but whose identification with the *pir* is part of the devotional work of the disciple. *Pir* and place share a joint existence in the memories of them which are taken away and dreamt about, meditated upon, prayed to and imitated, and which are the object of subsequent pilgrimages. The annual *urus* ritual brings this all together as a kind of miraculous testimony to the attraction of a saint. At this point also the fragmentation of the *pir*'s identity into the private worlds of his disciples is redeemed.

In Atroshi, the kind of interaction which the disciples have with the body of the *pir* is almost as formulaic and limited as their future interactions with his tomb will be. This means that the living person is treated as a far less dynamic subject/object than he actually is; the compression of normal human interactivity beneath a routine, predictable surface of appearances parallels the bifurcation in the mind and practice of the believer between the simultaneous intimacy and unknowability of a *pir*.

The iconicity of a *pir* is thus bound up with materiality, as the hardware of sanctity manifesting the reality of saintliness. It is the platform or medium enabling the performance of ritualised, exemplary respect behaviour towards the *pir* through which his saintliness can be realised and routinised. When a *pir* is entombed, the material dimension takes centre stage. At the same time the activation of a devotional attitude within delineated spaces becomes the means by which the intimate, iconistic and miraculous aspects of a *pir*'s identity are realised. Devotion, itself a compound of different emotions and attitudes, is always focused by a material boundedness which can be saturated with spiritual content. This is as true of major shrines as it is of the less prominent ones.

For example, the tomb of Modaleb Shah in Old Dhaka is an unremarkable brick structure with a corrugated roof, found down an alleyway backing onto the Buriganga river. Stepping through its main door one reaches a kind of yard. Beyond it is a small brick room where food is cooked and some *khadem* sleep on rush mats. The *pir* is represented by the tomb edifice which exists within its own enclosure, accessible only to male visitors. The devotee enters this enclosure individually and prostrates himself before the tomb. By contrast, the wider enclosure of the *darbar* is an area of public ritual and celebration where music is made, food is consumed, and the congregational side of the *pir*'s spiritual identity is manifested. At the time of *'urus* the *dargah* overflows onto the surrounding streets, and a kind of imagined universality is celebrated, even though there are many in the locality who disapprove of such revelry.

In Atroshi, the *'urus* ritual identifies the *pir*, the discipleship and the place in order to rehearse an ideal image of 'Muslim Bangla', uncompromised by economic, political and cultural subordination to the West and to India (Landell Mills 1994). It obtains its own particular layering of history and meaning, as does each separate *'urus* ritual for Sufi saints in Bangladesh, but the death-day celebration is the crucial ritual of almost every *pir* cult I witnessed, not least for economic reasons.

I suggest that the association with a memorial object in fact enables a living *pir*, such as the *pir* of Atroshi, to present himself in a rather tomb-like fashion. In effect he is offering very limited information about himself to the disciples in the anticipation that devotees will be able to fill in the gaps themselves. Disciples in Atroshi, having observed the regimen of the *pir* over forty years (or, rather, knowing that the same regimen has been observed for over forty years), come to acquire a certain complicity in the regimen of the *pir*'s behaviour, just as he too shares their complicity by constantly reaffirming their conception of him. Yet during his lifetime there is always the dangerous possibility that the *pir* could depart radically from his habitual lifestyle, that he could desanctify himself, and disenchant the relationship with his disciples. Of course, he does not do this: ritual is allowed to leave intention obscure.

The deliberate visualisation which disciples inculcate and the visions which they are given in return are facilitated by the *pir*'s iconic behaviour and the accompanying contrast between the simplicity of his appearance and the unseen forces which are supposedly swirling invisibly around and within him. Whether in dreams, day-visions, conversations or miraculous appearances, devotees effectively take away and activate the iconic image of a *pir*, a man whose imagined mastery over his base nature supplies an inviting space in which their own needs and desires can find response, and where their minds can find repose.

I suggest that this is possible not only because they want and expect it to happen, and not only because there is a gap between what the disciples actually see when they encounter a *pir* and what they hope for, but also because the incomplete information afforded by the restrained behaviour and the sublimated interactivity of the *pir* provides the image of a person on the verge of action. Devotees are offered a set of unfinished scripts which they must complete by themselves. And, as disciples often reminded me, the actual intervention of the remembered holy man is conditioned by the devoutness of the rememberer. Moreover, for the real disciple, devotion is its own reward. The tomb and the court and all the people and objects within them are extensions of the person of the *pir*, and good disciples will attribute their own collective and individual action to that of the *pir*.

The subject/object of identity

*Pir*s are extraordinary channels of divine blessing, through which people aspire to be reconstituted. A living *pir* strives to become a very particular kind of object of devotion; an embodied subject who can reach out to encompass the subjectivity of his disciples. Devotees must reach through the solidity of a *pir* to grasp his ethereal inner subjectivity, imagined as a suffusion of divine blessing. To this end, the disciple is invited to appropriate the image of the *pir* and, through an act of self-abnegation, make an instrument of it. A *pir* represents the proximity of the human to the divine and vividly contrasts the infinity of the creator to the finitude of the created. The mystical approach to God asserts the possibility of direct experience of the divine, through the person of the *pir*. Given that *pir*s are most often encountered in a highly structured setting, their own qualities as subjects/objects of perception are in dynamic contrast to the orchestrated material environment which surrounds and ultimately comes to represent them.

The iconic presentation of a living *pir* provides the devotional object *par excellence*, as the particular reverence shown by disciples who wish for the 'dust of his feet' (*choronduli*) demonstrates. Reverence for the physical person of a *pir* is itself exemplary, as the correlative respect for words, rituals, buildings, animals or anything else associated with him draws its performative models from actual or imagined interactions with him. When one disciple of Atroshi commented to another on the spiritual attainment of the *pir*'s eldest son, he speculated that the son's sleepless appearance was due to his being rewarded with dream visitations by the *pir* in which he clutched the *pir*'s feet the whole night (*O shara ratre kotombushi pae*). This would be the definitive attainment through meditation on the *pir*'s remembered countenance. Whilst he is a medium to higher blessings, the *pir* himself is never transcended by the disciple.

Just as a *pir*'s subjectivity is elusive, so his iconic self comes to include all of the encompassed devotees and accoutrements that surround him. In identifying with the *pir* the disciple projects a mirror reflecting his own subjectivity onto that of the *pir*. In imagining that he is seen by the *pir*, he can deepen his cognisance of being seen by God. The impact of seeing one's *pir* is intensified for the disciple because, in seeing and envisaging the *pir*, one is remembering the entire ensemble of the *pir*'s presentation of self, and attributing to the *pir* a power to act on the self which is, in truth, a collaborative achievement. It seems that the hardware of sanctity is organised to amplify the dyadic communication or flow between disciple and preceptor, to extrapolate from that subtle interplay of specularities (the constant reframing that human interaction requires by comparison with other experiences with the world) a sense of infinite possibility deriving from the dissolution of the disciple's own subjectivity. The reflecting surface of the *pir*, routinised by his own 'embodiment' in non-human objects and renewed by his performance through them, provides a specular image that can allow the disciple to access such emotions as his or her own.

Lawrence Babb (1986, 1987) suggests that Hindu holy men enable devotees to experience a transcendental wholeness by being 'known'. Eck (1985) describes the all-seeing eye as being at the centre of Hindu temples, and this can be applied to the structure of the *darbar/mazar* complex.[6] Other identifiably Hindu idioms proliferate in the devotional culture surrounding *pir*s. The giving of food to the *pir* which is subsequently consumed as *tabarok* seems to echo *prasad* (food offered is a deity in Hinduism). However, these idioms are used self-consciously by *pir*s such as Atroshi to convey 'Islamic' messages. The centrality of mortuary symbolism to *pir* identity was outlined above, and tombs are a Muslim symbol. Bangladeshi *pir*s represent an image of indigenous culture and personhood subordinated by the reality of divine power, of Bengal made Islamic. *Pir*s endeavour to provide a persuasive, incarnate vision of a notion of spiritual hierarchy, which may be informed by 'Hindu' sentiment and style, but is premised upon the remembrance of Allah. For many devotees of *pir*s, their preceptor is the iconic focus of that remembrance.

Within their own realms, *pir*s enact imitations of their own *pir*s and, by extension, of the Prophet. It is only through the channel of the saintly person, encountered in an environment that projects his being as limitless, that the exemplary disciple will approach the divine. *Pir*s tend to actualise their extraordinary identity by occupying separate spaces. *Pir* culture in Bangladesh is certainly not unitary, but enterprises associated with *pir*s are mutually referential. One immediate example of this during my research period in Bangladesh was the extent to which the *pir*s and supplicants of Maishbandar, Sayedabad, Sarshina, Char Monai or Narinda were very much aware of, and concerned about, the activities of Atroshi and, in varying degrees, of each other.

Postcolonial refractions of place and person

Whilst *darbar* and *mazar* provide centres of *pir* culture, these are characteristically all-encompassing when one is within them and almost invisible when outside. When 'moving around' (a pejorative term for feckless young men) in Dhaka, for example, one encounters public expressions of state power everywhere, from uniformed policemen and new roads to urban landscaping, hiding makeshift slums from view. Equally public are the signs of the affluence of the wealthy: imported cars and clothes, palatial residences in the new 'model' suburbs. The symbolic domination of foreign commerce and culture is visible in shop hoardings and billboards which equate the good life with consumption. The very names of shops echo the language of the departed imperial power. Islam too is visible and audible, in people's clothes, in mosques and minarets, and in the sound of the *azzan* (call to prayer) rippling across the city. These kinds of power are partly reproduced through their ubiquitousness, but the realm of *pir*s is less visible and is concentrated in certain specific locations. Whilst Islamists[7] seek to bring the unrealised order of Islam into the world, *pir*s are impresarios of a hidden reality of divine power in the present.

Obviously, the resistance to the right of Islamic leaders to wield worldly authority must be seen in historical context, particularly in relation to the recent history of Bangladeshi secularism. There is a major difference in the rootedness of different Islamic traditions in Bangladesh. On the one hand, the Islamist perspective portrays Islam as transcending history and demanding realisation. By contrast, even if some Bangladeshi *pir*s participate in Islamist movements, both their own embodiment and the material and ritual structures which *pir*s bequeath enfold layers of history; interactions between extra-territorial Islam and local religious practice, colonialism, modernity and cultural ethnicity. The aesthetic of Bangladeshi *pir*s' domains is one engendered by the ongoing construction of *pir*s, Sufism and Islam as transcending mundane realities, as well as Hinduism, Christianity, rational secularist modernity, and *pir*-debunking political Islam. There is a historical depth to Sufism as a source of postcolonial identity.

For example, the design of the tombs and *darbar* at Maishbandar is clearly inspired by Mughal architecture. Apart from its obvious function in demarcating the *darbar* area as a special space distinct from the surrounding countryside, another implicit meaning embodied in its structure is that, in spite of the perceived British interruption of the temporal dominion of Islamic rulers in

Bengal,[8] the ideals of Islam are still sovereign. Islam has divine sanction as compared to the fragmentary paganism of the Hindus or Christians, or the contemporary atheism of the Western powers. The enshrinement in the tomb, and its bright decoration, suggest the vitality of the saint as opposed to the sterility of scripturalist Islam, of the living exemplar as opposed to the *mullah* (scholar learned in scripture). As a self-consciously Islamic building, antithetical to colonialism and modernity, it suggests that the Sufi tradition offers a more enduring truth.

The devotees of Maishbandari *pir*s revere one of their entombed saints as *gausul azam* (the final saint), or *zamaner wali* (the saint of the epoch), and thus as sovereign in relation to other Sufi saintly figures. The most recent large tomb, that of Zia ul Haque who died in 1989, is in the form of a huge concrete *shapla*, the national flower of Bangladesh, which celebrates the ecumenical values of Bangladeshi secularism and of Maishbandari Sufism.

Saintly tombs convey such meanings, in part, by their implicit references to Sufi shrines elsewhere, which commemorate the same ideas of spiritual hierarchy. Just as the continuity of nomenclature used throughout the Muslim world itself plays a strong role in helping the faithful to essentialise their religion (Al-Azmeh 1993: 51), so the construction of saintly tombs throughout the Muslim world provides an 'objective correlative' around which concepts of saintly power can coalesce.

The aesthetics of devotion

While grand buildings may be evocative just by themselves, material relations are rendered meaningful (or interactive) by the adoption of certain physical attitudes in relation to objects as parts of an encompassing whole. The requisite physical attitudes, or body techniques, are those of submission and supplication. Respect is offered to a *pir*'s tomb as if to a living master. When attending the *urus* of Korosani Baba in Sylhet in 1989, I was ushered into the tomb room and was invited to touch my forehead to the eastern end of the tomb, where the feet of the *pir* were pointing respectfully away from Mecca. At the tomb of Modaleb Shah, a heterodox *pir*, in Faridabad, Dhaka, there is an emphasis on inversion. All of the dead *pir*'s Hindu disciples were commanded to wear *lungi* (the Muslim lower garment), and the Muslims were instructed to don *dhoti* (the Hindu lower garment), reversing their normal dress codes. One of the old devotees who had been sitting at the tomb for ten years, ever since the *pir* died, keeps a small red trident, as carried by Siva. On nearing his tomb the devotees enter complete prostration, as to God in orthodox prayer.

In Atroshi, at the time of the '*urus* of the *pir*'s own preceptor, thousands of disciples of the *pir* of Atroshi cry when he takes to the specially constructed stage. This sweep of emotion is enabled by the preceding devotional labour (*khidmat*), whether physical, clerical, economic or mental, of the disciples under the aegis of the *pir*. The appearance of effortless power in the context of the holy court is therefore the fruition and embodiment by the *pir* of complex histories of devotional labour.[9]

In fact, the summoning forth of intense physical responses to a tomb is due to the metonymic extension of the tomb to the person of the *pir*, and vice versa. This in turn is contingent upon the demarcation of the area since, whether living or dead, the tomb or court space is especially identified with the *pir* and thought to be saturated with his 'presence'. Hence entry into that space denotes entry into proximity with the *pir*. For example, at the time of the annual *urus*, the Atroshi *pir* is maximally identified with his court. This is also a moment when it is believed that his saintly predecessor and all the other saints gather over the *darbar*. In a similar fashion, the idea of an unwavering presence of the dead saint at his tomb is, on closer inspection, contingent upon moments of greater intensity of ritualised remembrance by people who attend the tomb.

An example: at the *mazar* of Modaleb Shah on Thursday nights, the music starts at eight and continues for three or four hours. All of the songs are *murshidi gan*, the songs of the spiritual guides, including some written by Lallon Faqir. Initially, men sit around in groups conferring. After a while the musicians ask Saddar Uddin Chisti, a neighbourhood *pir* with whom I am sitting, to come and sit near them so that they can play in a more inspired way. He is a well-known and highly regarded visitor to the tomb, especially since his unorthodox teachings resemble those of the dead saint. The proceedings in the women's section are already considerably more intense than in the male devotees' section, but some men are already beginning to dance. They move as if running on the spot, letting their upper body and head rock backwards and forwards. Their hands are held together in front of their chests and then thrown forwards to the tomb and brought back again to the chest, as if scooping blessing into the heart and hurling devotion back out. Saddar Uddin has ceased being the observer he was when seated beside me and now sits with the musicians very quietly with his eyes downcast. People sense that there is something coming. Suddenly he gets to his feet and starts to jump up and down. People shout; 'He has come to life', 'He has become hot' (*zinda hoye geche, gorom hoye geche*). Galvanised by the charismatic old man, everybody dances. The fat man who has been dancing all the while starts pointing to everyone around him and shouting (in English for my benefit) 'God! God! God!' The ageing headmaster of the local primary school is kneeling before Saddar Uddin with his arms outstretched towards him. At eleven, the music and dancing stop abruptly and people disperse.

On a functional level, it seems that there have to be peak moments of presence objectified by devotees in order to maintain the notion of the 'active' tomb. It also seems that these are moments when the living not only can revitalise the image of the tomb but are remade in its image. The manner in which Saddar Uddin behaved at the tomb was entirely uncharacteristic of his usual practice as a *pir*, with its stress on written and verbal *tafsir* (interpretation of the Qur'an), albeit highly unorthodox. By dancing at the tomb, Saddar Uddin Chisti, man of letters, was operating in a far less 'distinguished' fashion. The tomb was being used to reaffirm an ecstatic, emotional sanctity buried along with that of the entombed *pir*. And to dance at the tomb was to revalidate those other practices which emphasise Saddar Uddin's personal uniqueness, rather than the generic tomb-like impersonality of the holy man.

The use of material objects as extensions of *pir*s in Bangladesh is often achieved by mimicking other material and symbolic expressions of both 'religious' and 'worldly' power, whether kingly, ascetic, technological, juridical or even Islamic, inasmuch as Islam is sometimes seen to be a foreign exotic force.

In Atroshi, the domination of the *pir* over his *darbar* evokes the Prophet as the unique individual in whom the political and spiritual leadership of the *umma* were combined. Given that the impossibility of ordinary mortals assuming both these aspects of leadership is virtually inscribed in Sunni Islam (Combs-Schilling 1989: 87), we can say that *pir*s and their disciples (self-interest notwithstanding) marshal their spaces and objects in order to commemorate, by imaginative imitation, some of the attributes of the Prophet. Among reform Muslims, of course, *pir*s and their devotees often provoke controversy because they appear to assume a position which transgresses the uniqueness of the Prophet or of divinity itself. Even so, Sufi flirtation with the uniqueness of the Prophet seems to me to reaffirm his singularity. This is because mimesis does not so much usurp the Prophet's position as implicitly acknowledge that there is no unmediated experience of God (Katz 1983: 4). Without human exemplars the transcendental has neither salience nor identity.

It is embodiment in performance and practice that gives the 'nominal' unity of Islam its 'essence'. Whether in the mystical pursuit of extinction in the Sufi guide, or in decorous observance of the *Sunna* (body of traditional Islamic law), Muslims participate in an ongoing fragmentary reproduction of the person of the Prophet. Without the figure of the Prophet thus remembered, there is no unipolar Islam and no *umma*. As his person encompasses the quarrelsome interpretations it generates, so the eternally refigured identity of the Prophet is made all the more transcendent and unattainable.[10]

Moreover, in Bangladesh at least, the Prophet's singular fusion of spiritual and temporal authority cannot be surpassed by his imitators, because their 'spiritual' authority demands a materially enshrined separation from the hurly-burly of routine politics. Much as the hardware of sanctity demarcate boundaries that *pir*s' *doa* can overflow, these also describe the temporal limitations of their power. Their energised boundedness points to the imminent reality of the hereafter wherein the divinity, whose veil they twitch, manifests its all-encompassing sovereignty.

*Pir*s and their plans

The sanctity on which *pir*s and their clients draw is not fixed. Each incarnation of blessedness and each encounter with it redefine its limits. Other-worldly saintliness is counterpointed by the need or desire to attract new devotees and to project values and interests in the wider social domain.

The havens which *pir*s create are often springboards to further expansion.

Quite apart from the need to materialise a sacred centre, the symbolic capital which *pir*s amass often inspires more worldly undertakings. For example, the Atroshi *pir*, having constructed a mosque on the scale of the Taj Mahal which will be his enduring monument, and having nearly completed a 600-bed hospital, has also entered the textile business, building a spinning mill and importing Chinese machinery to compete with the influx of Indian produce. Less successful, however, was the *pir*'s direct attempt to enter politics.

The *pir* of Atroshi affiliates himself to the Naqshbandi-Mujaddidiya Tariqa, which has a history of involvement in politics in north India, Pakistan and Afghanistan. In Bengal, the Tariqa spread eastward into contemporary Bangladesh from Furfura in Calcutta. Its offshoots have included many politically involved *pir*s. Atroshi's own preceptor, the *pir* of Eneyetpur, was an active supporter of the Muslim League, whilst the *pir* of Sharshina was, like Atroshi, connected to the pro-Pakistan side in the war which led to Bangladeshi independence. The growth of the Atroshi *pir*'s stature during Ershad's regime (1982–1990), led first to his forming a *songarton*, or association, in 1986, and then a political party (the Zaker Party) in 1989. Despite an expensive campaign in the 1991 election, the party won no seats. While it is possible that the Zaker movement overestimated its own strength, it seems likely that we are concerned with a disjunction: although people might credit the *pir* with spiritual authority, they were less ready to grant political power to his family and their henchmen. The *pir* himself seemed to foster this ambiguity by declaring that the party, which he suddenly called into existence one day in his normal pre-dawn address, was not a political party in the ordinary sense. It was only there, he said, to defend Islam from external threats, a coded language for Indian (post-secular 'Hindu') domination. Such a demand to enter politics might also have been due to the internal pressure within the discipleship itself; many 'disciples' of the *pir* were opportunists seeking to tap into the connections of the *darbar* to members of the governing regime. Although Ershad was uneasy about the political aspirations of the *pir*'s family, he could have called an election before his fall, which would have been boycotted by other opposition parties, and would have provided an entree to a co-opted Zaker Party to the lucrative arena of politics. As it is, the party did not succeed in the democratic atmosphere which briefly prevailed following Ershad's overthrow.

Perhaps because his *tariqa* was traditionally concerned with rallying the Muslims of the region against a Hindu threat, the *pir* of Atroshi has aimed at recruiting as many disciples as possible. Disciples who bring in new people to the *tariqa* are given high status, as well as the straightforward respect which is due to those who are *tariqater boro*, senior within the brotherhood. One enhances one's position as a disciple by recruiting new disciples, thus becoming a relative insider, or by contributing one's money and labour. In seeking to expand their human and material resource base as much as possible, *pir*s must develop their organisation and institutional trappings. As they acquire wealth, some of it is reinvested in development of their resources. In fact, apart from motives of personal aggrandisement, there is an implicit imperative to expand embedded within the *pir* identity. If one is a *pir* then one is moved to act by larger forces, in accordance with destiny. The Atroshi *pir*, as he must, credits his own preceptor with the inspiration for his actions; it is not for himself that he is operating.

Popularity allows *pir*s to supply the worldly accoutrements that their putative spiritual stature warrants. However, their imagined inner being, their iconic surface and their devotees' miraculous experience of them all grow in tandem. The acquisition of worldly impedimenta is inevitably taken as a sign of hitherto undisclosed spiritual pre-eminence, unveiling new horizons of possible worldly development. More people then have miraculous experiences associated with the *pir*. It seems unlikely that the *pir* of Atroshi would be as easily attributed with the spiritual powers he is purported to possess without the symbolic and material edifices that are taking shape around him. Similarly, he may be able to persuade others to invest themselves in a somewhat distant vision of the construction of a spiritual city on the strength of his achievement to date.

There is an ideal vision of a 'true *pir*' who is too deeply absorbed in quiet contemplation to become famous. As one famous orthodox *'alim* (person learned in the scripture) said to me, implicitly criticising all those who make it their business to be known to the public as *pir*s, 'Those who are friends of God keep quiet about it [*jara oli'allah tara chupchap thake*].' I heard of one man, a businessman in the commercial Motijheel district, who used to visit a small number of 'friends' with no suggestion that he was 'making disciples'. As the son of one of them told me somewhat jokingly, 'My father was very angry because he was always an atheist, but he escaped from a plane crash, and as he was running from the wreck he kept seeing that man before him.' While people may imagine 'hidden masters', or even know *pir*s who operate in a very discreet fashion, these are only comprehensible as the unseen counterparts of a more visible phenomenon. Nevertheless, the suggestion of a spiritual hierarchy without material referents is an important aspect of *pir* identity. It is often asserted that *pir*s amass wealth not for themselves but for their disciples, who are pleased to see their preceptor so honoured. Indeed the Atroshi *pir* is reputed to live an ascetic life, in spite of the wealth that his *darbar* brings in. Disciples often claim, erroneously but compellingly, that Atroshi was a wilderness when he arrived there with little to his name. This reiterates a narrative associated with many other *pir*s in South Asia (Werbner 1995, 1996).

The trajectory of worldly development undertaken by any *pir* is in a sense the exploration of a contradiction between the need to be not only active and accessible, but also quietist and aloof.[11] Often described as 'living scriptures' (*kitab*), *pir*s are products and prisoners of the imperative to make palpable the simultaneous presence and invisibility of divine blessing. Moreover, through their explorations, *pir*s relocate and reproduce this tension.

Although there are doubtless exceptions, the present analysis has highlighted the fact that *pir*s generally need to be associated with a space. Almost all *pir*s of substance have a seat of power, or a place on the map where they can be located, which is saturated with their presence, and entry to which is meant to connote movement to a more transcendent state of existence. *Darbars* are part of the necessary compromise between accessibility and remoteness. This enables *pirs* not only to stay in business but also to effect the transformations their customers desire of them.

The plans for expansion in Atroshi are a means of eliciting donations of labour and wealth. It may be the case that the success of Atroshi has influenced the way that other *pirs* in Bangladesh conduct their affairs. Certainly I encountered several *pirs* who aspired towards the creation of centres like Atroshi. For example, the *pir* of Sayedabad and *pir* Mujibur Rahman Chisti both have existing *darbars*, all of which are a prelude to greater things, if their devotees can only keep the faith and keep the offerings rolling in.

Certain kinds of construction activities, such as building mosques and *madrasahs*, are regarded as meritorious acts. For the *pir* of Atroshi the mosque which is presently under construction at his lodge is his final work, as well as being the greatest task he has undertaken. To the visitor, Atroshi always seems more like a building site than a sacred place, with the construction work in progress there. Makeshift elements are juxtaposed with concrete formations. The mosque presently represents the most permanent structure which the *pir* will bequeath, and signals his service to the wider *umma*. At the same time its ostentation ensures that his name will be remembered. Since the mosque will be identified with its patron, the tenor of the undertaking could perhaps be best described as 'conspicuous humility'.

Conclusion

In popular Sufi tradition in Bangladesh, as elsewhere, the veneration of *pirs* makes embodiment crucial to sanctity. *Pirs* embody a divine order, poised at the brink of the world, punctuating mundane lives with miraculous interventions. The part-human, part-divine image of these saintly figures is realised by their association with physical materials regarded as extensions of their person. Just as *pirs* are venerated as conduits to an otherwise unreachable essence, so the attributes of *pirs* are treated as interactive extensions of their authors' powerful personalities. These objective extensions create spaces where spiritual authority and temporal power can be conjoined. The devotee imagines, celebrates and sometimes experiences the boundless nature of the *pir*'s insight into his physical, mental and moral condition. On this basis, the devotee collaborates with others to recreate the *pir*'s sanctity. The identity of a *pir* is a product of interaction. The *pir*'s embodiment represents the social relations which create him as a holy man. (Eccentric, stray *faqirs* partly anticipate this, even if public recognition does not arise.) The extension of this embodiment to metonymically connected objects, whether spoken words, rituals, small gifts, buildings or even territory, is anticipated by much contemporary *pir* practice.

Pirs 'remember' God and offer exemplary help to others to do likewise. The unfolding career of a living *pir* ideally constitutes the creation of the saintly identity of a dead *pir*. It gradually confers a power which is infinite and inexhaustible, an unlimited good. This is achieved through the effective suffusion of inanimate objects with anthropomorphic qualities.

Since *pir*s and their followers must work to accomplish this, saintly endeavour seems a kind of worldly pursuit. Saints are entrepreneurs with individual goals which are as much social and transformative as 'transcendental'. Much of their work is designed to make a lasting impression and thereby to influence the world. As individuals, they not only follow culturally predicted schemes but renegotiate them. Their uniquely individual identities are assets which are indispensable to their aspirations; they are not merely the by-product of challenging a conservative, holistic social order, as Dumont has suggested for the Hindu 'world renouncer' (Dumont 1957). In short, *pir*s need the world as a stage.

Waghorne (1994) has suggested that the 'vital surfaces' of objects (and of holy persons like South Asian divine kings or *pir*s) have been neglected by religious studies and by anthropology as a result of the Victorian bowdlerisation of sanctity and the concomitant devaluation of magic. Against the notion that the essence of spirituality is other-worldly and beyond ordinary materiality, perception or intention, Waghorne suggests that 'the spiritual is coterminous with the very outwardness that the nineteenth century scholar assumed must give way to some inner truth' (1994: 258). The very point of the sacred or the divine is its suspension in time and space; in other words, its material extensions.

Such a devaluation of magic, in favour of a 'universal' religious experience, is also consonant with the devaluation of popular religion by Muslim scripturalist elites. The logocentric bias of the latter regards Sufism as degenerate, a view endorsed by some orientalist scholars seeking the 'essence' of the religion in its scriptural past, just as clerics find a perfect Islam in the Qur'an and Hadiths. Both types of scholar devalue local practice in favour of the 'great tradition'. Against that, I have argued here, Sufi traditions represent a diverse set of practices, the Islamic identity of which has repeatedly been interrogated partly because the notions of spiritual knowledge as power that they purvey seem to be less exclusively Muslim than those of unassailable Islamicity, the Qur'an, the Hadiths and the Prophet himself.

Throughout both the Muslim world and Muslim history, the continuity of Islamic culture is manifest in enduring nomenclature and narratives and in the foregrounded figure of the Prophet. The celebration of Muhammad has an anchoring effect because his remembered corporeal presence provides the exemplary channel and ground for the reception and transmission of the divine word. It is upon his unsurpassable uniqueness that the religion hinges. While Sufis situate themselves within this Muslim history as adherents of Islam as universal religion, by combining in themselves human and divine inspiration they flirt with and thereby re-emphasise the boundaries that hedge the Prophet as a singular figure. As this implies, Sufism and Islam share the paradox of asserting their identity through inclusive practices (pilgrimage, ecstasy, prayer, fasting, congregationalism) which newcomers can learn because they are universal kinds of technique, while that universality potentially subverts claims to singularity embodied in the unique figure of the Prophet, leaving an ambiguity and transgressive potential which Sufism can both contain and exploit.

Sufism and Islam renew themselves as real presences in the world by the work of continuous remembering and reminding. This kind of 'embodiment' can be metonymically extended to any transference that occurs between their discourse of self-proclamation and the otherwise silent arenas within which the work of devotion can unfold. The conflations of meaning and stature, first in bodies and second in inanimate objects, is one of the keys to saintly identity. Sufi Islam requires the corporeal (and by extension the anthropomorphic 'hardware') to describe divinely inspired spiritual immanence. At the same time, it evokes the transcendence of the divine by attempting the impossible: to fix what cannot be pinned down, to surpass what cannot be surpassed, and to do this by the cry of separation from what cannot, in this life, be rejoined.

Acknowledgement

The writing of this chapter was enabled by a three-year British Academy fellowship on Islam in contemporary Bangladesh.

Notes

1 I use the term 'anthropomorphism' to refer to the attribution of a non-human object with human intentionality. Pascal Boyer (1996) has suggested that anthropomorphism, or 'magical' animistic thinking, is a matter of cognitive predisposition, although most definitely not a throwback to a 'primitive' childhood inability to distinguish persons and things. My intention here is only to illustrate that the surface 'performance' of a *pir* implicates the qualities and potential both of material objects and of persons as icons. I do not suggest that 'anthropomorphism' is a psychological process in its own right, but suggest that the circularity between holy persons and miraculous animations (Babb 1986; Gilsenan 1982) reflects the privileged position of *dyadic* intercommunication in human experience.
2 The most authoritative recent account of the Islamisation of Bengal is by Richard Eaton (1993), who demystifies some of the mythical associations between *pir*s and territory by explaining the conversion of Bengali Muslims as connected to the eastward spread of rice cultivation on the 'Bengal frontier'.
3 I would go as far as to say that 'saint' could only be used as a translation of '*pir*' when the *pir* concerned is a dead person whose sanctity is less contested than that of the often controversial living *pir*s.
4 *Bishwa* means either world or universal. *Zaker* is a term for someone who remembers God, or performs *jikir*, and is used to refer to a disciple of Atroshi. *Manzil* is a non-vernacular term meaning a house or a way-station.
5 Ewing (1980) has described the importance of dream communication between Pakistani *pir*s and their disciples. The idea of the *pir* as a divinely sanctioned 'true' image, as opposed to a 'false' one conjured up by the self or by the devil, is also relevant to the use of the *pir*'s visage as a focus of meditation. There was no special group of disciples to whom these kinds of practice or experience were restricted. They were not

written about in the cult literature and were suggested quietly to newcomers by more experienced devotees.

6 Eck (1985) describes the all-seeing eye as being at the centre of Hindu temples, and as characterising the interactivity of divine statues. On the other hand, there are notable Muslim precedents. The Atroshi *pir*'s practice of *darshan* seems also to borrow from that of Mughal emperors, as described by Cohn (1987), and by extension of the Nawabs.

7 By 'Islamist' I mean principally those such as the political party Jama'at-e Islami, who seek a top-down assertion of Islamic rule, and those who seek a bottom-up reconversion of the society and focus on the virtue of the individual, like the proselytising organisation Tabliq Jama'at. Both organisations derive in certain respects from Sufism but are antagonistic towards *pir*s, who stray from their 'orthodox' interpretations of Islam.

8 Whether Mughal or local, rulers were always upper-class, Urdu-speaking (*ashraf*) Muslims rather than indigenous (*ajlaf/bangalee*) Muslims.

9 As part of the specific customs that constitute the culture of particular tombs and courts, there are very often gendered regimens in dealing with entombed and living *pir*s. Women, thought to be impure, are often not permitted to approach them directly. There is much more to be said about *pir*s as exemplars of values which also shape notions of masculinity, and insufficient space here.

10 Many Sufi groups in Bangladesh maintain the belief that the Prophet is constituted of light (*nur*), was the first creation of God, and had intercessionary powers. In Chittagong district, for example, those who maintain this belief characterise themselves as 'Sunni', respectful of the Prophet, against those they call 'Wahabi', whose belief that the Prophet was, like other men, made of clay (*mathi toyri*) is seen as impudent (*be-adab*). The accusation that, for example, *pir*s should not be petitioned to intercede is a coded assertion of the 'Wahabi' agenda. From the 'Sunni' point of view, though, the Prophet encompasses his imitators, who are expressing their love and devotion.

11 This is a recurrent dilemma in ascetic traditions. The equivalent dilemma for peripatetic Buddhist *arahant* (forest saints marginal to the Buddhist monastic orders) is described by Tambiah (1987:119–120).

References

Al-Azmeh, Aziz (1993) *Islams and Modernities*, London: Verso.

Babb, Lawrence A. (1986) *Redemptive Encounters: Three Modern Styles in Hindu tradition*, Berkeley: University of California Press, pp. 168–186.

Babb, Lawrence A. (1987) 'Sathya Sai Baba's Saintly Play'. in J.S. Hawley (ed.) *Saints and Virtues*, Berkeley: University of California Press.

Bloch, Maurice (1986) *From Blessing to Violence: History and Ideology in the Circumcision Ritual of the Merina of Madagascar*, Cambridge: Cambridge University Press.

Bloch, Maurice (1992) *Prey into Hunter: The Politics of Religious Experience*, Cambridge: Cambridge University Press.

Bourdieu, Pierre (1984) *Distinction: A Social Critique of the Judgement of Taste*, trans. Richard Nice, London: Routledge and Kegan Paul.

Boyer, Pascal (1996) 'What Makes Anthropomorphism Natural: Intuitive Ontology and Cultural Representations', *Journal of the Royal Anthropological Institute* n.s. 2: 83–97.

Cohn, Bernard S. (1987) *An Anthropologist Among the Historians and Other Essays*, Oxford: Oxford University Press.

Combs-Schilling, M.E. (1989) *Sacred Performances: Islam, Sexuality and Sacrifice*, New York: Columbia University Press.
Douglas, Mary (1966) *Purity and Danger: An Analysis of Concepts of Pollution and Taboo*, London: Routledge and Kegan Paul.
Dumont, Louis (1957) 'World Renunciation in Indian Religions', *Contributions to Indian Sociology* 1: 3–62.
Eaton, Richard M. (1993) *The Rise of Islam and the Bengal Frontier, 1204–1760*, Berkeley: University of California Press.
Eck, Diane L. (1985) [1981] *Darsan*, Chamberburg: Anima Books.
Ewing, P. Katherine (1980) 'The *Pir* or Sufi Saint in Pakistani Islam', PhD thesis, Department of Anthropology, University of Chicago.
Foucault, Michel (1983) 'The Subject and Power', in H. Dreyfus and Paul Rabinow (eds) *Beyond Structuralism and Hermeneutics*, Chicago: Chicago University Press, pp. 208–226.
Foucault, Michel (1984) *The Foucault Reader*, ed. Paul Rabinow, London: Penguin.
Gaborieau, Marc (1989) 'Pouvoirs et autorité des Sufis dans l'Himalaya', in V. Bouillier and G. Toffin (eds) *Priesthood, Power and Authority in the Himalayas*, Purusartha 12, Editions de L'Ecole des Hautes Etudes en Sciences Sociales, Paris: Collections Parusartha.
Gilsenan, Michael (1982) *Recognizing Islam*, London: Croom Helm.
Guthrie, Stewart (1993) *Faces in the Clouds: A New Theory of Religion*, Oxford: Oxford University Press.
Haq, Muhammad Enamul (1975) *A History of Sufism in Bengal*, Dacca: Asiatic Society of Bangladesh.
Jeffrey, Patricia (1981) 'Creating a Scene: The Disruption of Ceremonial in a Sufi Shrine', in Imtiaz Ahmad (ed.) *Ritual and Religion among Muslims in India*, New Delhi: Manohar, pp. 162–194.
Katz, Stephen T. (1983) *Mysticism and Religious Traditions*, Oxford: Oxford University Press.
Landell Mills, Sam (1994) 'The Atroshi Urus', *Journal of Social Studies* 63: 83–106.
Levinas, Emannuel (1987) *Collected Philosophical Papers*, trans. A. Lingis, Dordrecht: Martinus Nijhoff.
Parry, Jonathan (1982) 'Sacrificial Death and the Necrophagous Ascetic', in Maurice Bloch and Jonathan Parry (eds) *Death and the Regeneration of Life*, Cambridge: Cambridge University Press, pp. 74–110.
Roy, Asim (1983) *The Islamic Syncretistic tradition in Bengal*, Dhaka: Academic Publishers.
Tambiah, Stanley J. (1987) 'The Buddhist Arahant: Classical Paradigm and Modern Buddhist Manifestations', in John Stratton Hawley (ed.) *Saints and Virtues*, Berkeley: University of California Press, pp. 111–126.
Waghorne, Joanne Punzo (1994) *The Raja's Magic Clothes: Revisioning Kingship and Divinity in England's India*, Philadelphia: University of Pennsylvania Press.
Werbner, Pnina (1995) 'Powerful Knowledge in a Global Sufi Cult: Reflections on the Poetics of Travelling Theories', in Wendy James (ed.) *The Pursuit of Certainty: Religious and Cultural Formulations*, London and New York: Routledge, pp. 134–160.
Werbner, Pnina (1996) 'Stamping the Earth with the Name of Allah: *Zikr* and the Sacralising of Space among British Muslims', *Cultural Anthropology* 11, 3: 309–338.

3

A 'FESTIVAL OF FLAGS'

Hindu–Muslim devotion and the sacralising of localism at the shrine of Nagore-e-Sharif in Tamil Nadu

S.A.A. Saheb

Introduction: Sufi tolerance

The liberal attitude of Sufism and its tolerance of other religions have made its shrines centres of inter-religious cooperation. The *pir–murid* (master–disciple) relationship is an open one, and hence Sufi lodges in South Asia are places of worship for communities of both Muslims and Hindus. The 'shrine' of a Sufi saint is a place where he has preached and breathed his last, and the tomb built after his death is venerated as a sacred place. Yet it is often the case that members of Hindu and Muslim communities refer to these departed Sufis by different names. Hence, for example, the saint of Kanifnath, whose shrine is located at the village of Mahdhi in Parthardi Taluka, Ahmad Nagar, District of Maharastra, is regarded as a Hindu saint, Navnath, and worship at his shrine is conducted by a *pujari* (Hindu priest). The Muslims call the same saint 'Shah Ramzan Moti-Sarwar' (*kanobaba*) and their prayers are performed with the help of a *mujawar* (Muslim ritual expert).

It is possible, then, for a Sufi saint to stand as a common saint for Hindus as well as Muslims, and his lodge may become a shared religious centre which maintains local communal amity among the members of different faiths living in a single locality (Hulbe *et al.* 1994), and even beyond it. Further instances of this potentiality are recorded in south India. The Tinthin village shrine, for example, located in Gulbarga District, Karnataka, combines the physical structures of Sufi shrines with local cultural traditions (Abdi 1993). Some shrines have sacred plants (Malhotra and Basak 1984: 45) or sacred groves (Gadgil and Vartak 1976: 152), while many are purified with water in a way reminiscent of the pouring of libation water on idols by Hindus (Bhaumik 1993: 10). At Nagore, the Sufi saint Sahul Hameed Nagore Andavar, the subject of the present chapter, is worshipped by Hindus as a presiding god. Sufi saints' shrines were recorded in the earlier gazetteers as *pallis* (mosques), but the term, in fact, denotes a *dargah* (court, shrine) of a Sufi saint. Even today, the Tamils refer to the *dargah* of a Sufi as a *palli*. Hence, the records grant the sacred merit of a mosque to a *dargah*, to be regarded as a religious place of prayer for orthodox Muslims (Hemingway 1906: 809; Shariff 1921: 121). Yet *dargahs* are places of veneration for all religious faiths. They not only fuse architectural styles and motifs, but create a fusion of local customary rituals as well. The practice of offering flowers, sweetmeats and food, the conduct of worship, the playing of musical instruments, although disapproved of by Islam reformists, are all practices shared by Muslims with Hindus in local traditions.

It might seem that Hindu devotees' involvement and participation in a shrine's activities legitimise 'Hindu' practices in the *dargah*'s sacred performances. Yet the origin and current provenance of various customs is not so clearly identifiable. What is clear is that such cultural fusions, vividly evident in the performance of the great Kanduri festival of the saint of Nagore, are modes of incorporating and sacralising an inter-religious community and its spaces, joined in celebrating the anniversary of the saint's death.

The legend of the Sufi saint

The first Sufi religious order to arrive on Indian soil was the Chishti, founded by Khawaja Garib Nawaz during the sultanate period of the twelfth century. Subsequently, the Qadiriya order was introduced into the Indian subcontinent by Mohammad Ghouse Gwalior, the spiritual guide of Syed Sahul Hameed Nagore Andavar of Tamil Nadu, south India, whose commemorative rituals are analysed here.

It is said that the parents of the saint of Nagore, Syed Hassan Kuthos and Bibi Fatima, migrated from Baghdad during the rule of Sultan Feroz Shah Thugluk of Delhi, and settled in the small town of Manikpur in the Pratapgarh District of Uttar Pradesh. The saint was a true *Sayyid*, who claimed direct descent in the thirteenth generation from the Prophet of Islam, and in the fifth generation from Sayyid Abdul Qadir Jilani of Baghdad. He was also related to this saint, founder of the Qadiriya order, by a spiritual genealogy (*silsila*, 'chain') of Sufi masters and disciples.

The hagiological literature reports that Sahul Hameed came into the 'material' world through 'the divine message of Allah to his parents'. He performed miracles (*karāmāt*)[1] even while still a foetus in his mother's womb. He was said to have been born on a Friday and to have been named Sahul Hameed by God's messenger, Khidr.

Sahul Hameed received his Islamic education at Gwalior in Uttar Pradesh under the guidance of Hazarat Mohammad Ghouse. After completing his education, he declined a proposal of marriage and decided to remain celibate and to spend his life in the service of Allah. He left home to preach this message, first performing the pilgrimage to Mecca. On his way to Mecca he met a couple,

Plate 3.1 The lodge at Nagore-e-Sharif during the annual festival of the saint

Mufti Nooruddin and Bibi Zohara, and, endowed with divine power, blessed them with a son of great spiritual excellence who would become his disciple. It was thus that he received his spiritual son, Yusef Saheb, whom he is said to have fostered with great affection. Along with his foster son and several followers, he returned to Mecca and from there continued his travels throughout South West Asia and Europe (see Figure 3.1).

The saint and his spiritual team then began retracing their footsteps eastwards, visiting the Maldives and Sri Lanka before arriving finally at Nagore, a sacred town located in the Qaide Millat District of Tamil Nadu, south India, where the saint settled in AH 940 (AD 1533–1534) (Quddusi 1991: 2).

Nagore is situated nine kilometres from the district headquarters by the banks of the river Vettar, on the coast, at the confluence of the Bay of Bengal (Rahim 1971). In the early nineteenth century, the port of Nagore played a prominent role in the import–export business (ibid.), far exceeding that of its neighbouring town, Nagapatnam. In due course, however, Nagore lost its economic significance as a port, but it continued to flourish as the abode of the holy saint, Sahul Hameed Nagore Andavar.

The period of the saint Sahul Hameed

The compiled records of Nagore Kaifiat deal with data collected from elderly people around 1817, and issued by the kings Chandra Sekhara and Jai Konda Chollan of the Tanjore region. Sayyid (AH 1346: 25–60) and Qadir Hussain (1957) basically agree that the saint reached and settled at Nagore in AH 940 (AD 1533–1534) or AD 1532 and lived until approximately AD 1600. The reported dates of the saint's birth on 10 November AD 1504. (AH 910) and his death on 10 November AD 1570. (AH 978) all place him in the sixteenth century (Quddusi 1991: 2; Hussain 1985: 133; Chandrasekharan 1817; Qadhiri 1980: 4). Tradition and historical records mention that he came to Nagore during the period of the then Maratha king, Achutappa Nayaka. According to legend, the saint cured the king's illness and in return the monarch endowed him with land as an offering of gratitude. The Hindu sage Sivananda (1966: 41–42), while praising the healing powers of the saint, described Sahul Hameed as 'Nagore Andavar'. Since then the Nagore saint is locally known by this name,[2] by which he will henceforth be referred to here.

The saint Nagore Andavar led a simple and pious life. The hagiological literature suggests that he was a strict adherent of the *Shari'at*, the religious legal canons of Islam. The saint gained increasing popularity through his miracles, performed for the many supplicants who beat a path to his door. Local people, both Muslim and Hindus, became his devotees and treated his lodge as a pilgrimage centre.

The Nagore Andavar predicted his death by conveying to his son, Yusef Saheb, that he was about to leave this mundane world of appearances. The saint revealed to him also how to conduct the funeral rites and funerary prayers, and indicated

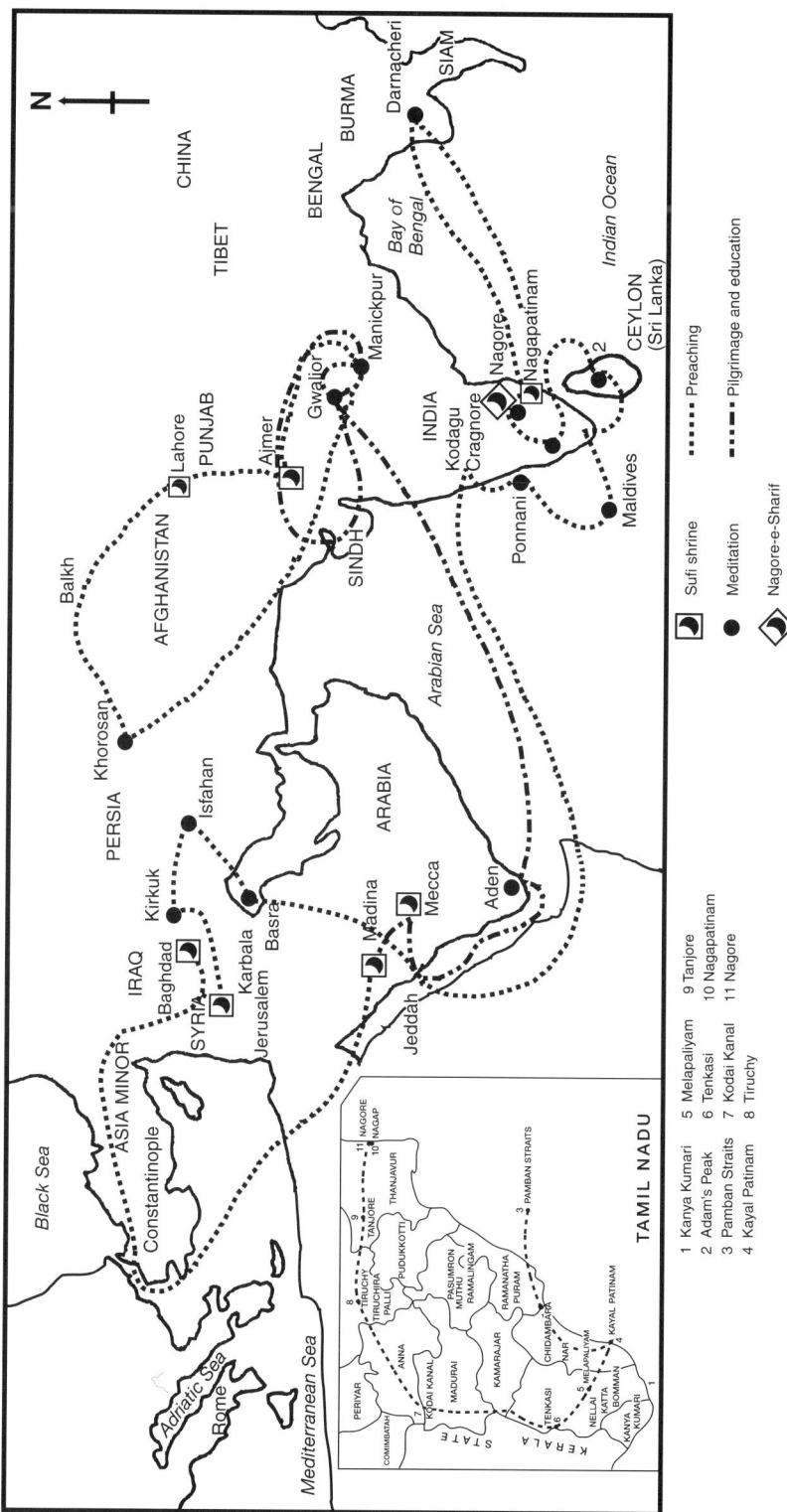

Figure 3.1 Travels of Sahul Hameed Nagore Andavar in India, South West Asia and Europe
Source: "The Divine Light of Nagore" (English) by Hasan Sahib Qadhiri, S.A.S. "Aftha Be Nagore" (Urdu) by Mohammad Yusuf Sahib, M.S.

the place of his desired burial. He advised the son to visit his grave on the third day after his death and to greet him. He is said to have told his son that 'if [he] were to get a reply from the saint's tomb, [he] should continue his stay at Nagore; otherwise [he] could leave the place and was permitted to go wherever he liked'. On the 10th of Jamathul Akhir AH 978 (10 November AD 1570) (Quddusi 1991: 2), the saint's soul departed to the next world. His funeral ceremonies and rituals were duly conducted by his son according to his father's instructions. Yusef Saheb visited the grave on the third day, conveyed his greetings and got a reply from his father's grave. He decided to stay at Nagore for the rest of his life. A mausoleum was constructed over the grave and people began venerating the site of burial. Thus, the pilgrimage to Nagore Andavar's tomb was first initiated by his son, Yusef Saheb. From then until the present day, the tradition of pilgrimage to Nagore-e-Sharif has been perpetuated by his followers and devotees in the region, throughout the Indian subcontinent and beyond it, in Singapore and Sri Lanka.

Even after the death of the saint Nagore Andavar, his miraculous powers did not disappear. As soon as his tomb was consecrated, prayers there in the name of God and the saint brought devotees relief from pain and cure from personal afflictions. The saint's son too had immense faith in his father's transcendant powers and used to advise supplicants to share in this faith and pray at the tomb with devotion.

Among devotees the prevalent, strongly held belief is that a pilgrimage to a sacred centre brings religious merit on the Day of Judgement. This is attributed to a verse by the Prophet himself and is echoed by the sayings of saints in the area. The pilgrimage to Mecca is obligatory for those Muslims who can afford the journey. It is believed that every step taken in the direction of pilgrimage to Mecca washes out a mortal sin (Hughes 1975: 136). The Muslim poor who cannot afford the trip to Mecca perform pilgrimage instead to local saints' tombs, believing that their visits convey the same merit as that of the *hajj* (enjoined pilgrimage to Mecca). Thus the saint Gesudaraj of Gulbarga, Karnataka, says that 'When, for good reason, people were unable to make the pilgrimage to Mecca, a visit once in their lives to his mausoleum [tomb] would convey the same merit' (Shariff 1921: 131). The statement of the saint Sultanul Arfin of Baudan, Calcutta, also supports such a view. He advises people to perform a pilgrimage to his grave, saying that 'Needy people should visit my grave for three days, and if their desires are not fulfilled, then they may demolish my grave on the fourth' (Raja 1967: 21). These sayings highlight the fact that Sufi saints possess the power to bring about not only material blessings but also the same religious merit endowed by the pilgrimage to Mecca. There are popular beliefs among the Muslims of north India that 'seven pilgrimages to Ajmer are equal to performing the *hajj*' (Moini 1989: 241).

There is a similar kind of tradition among the Tamil-speaking Muslims of south India: 'Those who cannot afford to pay their visit to Mecca, seven visits to the shrine of Nagore-e-Sharif conveys the same merit as the *hajj*' (Rahim 1971: 21).

More (1993: 91) has a different opinion, that people visit Sufi shrines like Nagore and Muthupet to wash away their sins. The earlier hagiological writings and the popular beliefs support the view that pilgrimage to Sufi saints' shrines earns religious merit as well as material benefit. Such beliefs endow Sufi cults with continued vitality among the local populace of India wherever such shrines exist.

The great Kanduri festival of Sahul Hameed Nagore Andavar

The pilgrims to the tomb of Nagore Andavar come to attend the annual *'urs* of the saint. The *'urs* is celebrated in commemoration of the anniversary of the saint's death, and pilgrims participate in the rituals and witness the rites. The observances of such anniversaries of Sufi saints in the Deccan and northern India often develop unique indigenous traditions. In south India and Sri Lanka (for a case study of a village festival in Sri Lanka, see de Munck 1994: 273) the annual festivals are known as 'Kanduri' by the Tamil-speaking Muslims. It is stated that the word 'Kanduri' is derived from the Persian word for tablecloth. In Indonesia, the same word denotes a feast or a commemorative meal (Cyril 1978: 540). The *New Royal Persian–English Dictionary* (Moini 1932: 336) states that 'Kanduri' means a feast or ceremony observed in honour of holy personages. The *Tamil Lexicon and Jubilee Tamil Dictionary* (Moini 1935: 716) specifically explains that 'Kanduri' is the festival held at Nagore in honour of the holy saint Meera Saheb, which is a local name for the saint Sahul Hameed Nagore Andavar (ibid.: 718). In some places the ritual is referred to as the *jande*[3] (flags) festival. Thus the *Gyarmi ke Jande* festival is celebrated in commemoration of the Sufi saint Sayyid Abdul Qadir Jilani of Baghdad. The anniversary of the saint Sahul Hameed's death is also called the *Qadir Wali ke Jande* festival.

The flags used during the festivals of Qadir Wali of Nagore and the saint Sayyid Abdul Qadir Jilani of Baghdad are *lal* (saffron) and *hara* (green) respectively. Traditionally, these flags are taken in procession from the devotee's house and after processing the streets, they are hoisted on a tree known as *Jande ka Jahad*. The south Indian Muslims observe these flag-festival rituals not only during the occasion of the anniversary of the saint's death but also at the commencement of any auspicious occasion, such as *khatna* (circumcision) for boys and the marriage ceremony of either boys or girls. It is believed that the flag rituals give the merit of *ziarat*[4] (visitation) to the *dargah* of Nagore, and obtain the direct blessings of the saint himself. The analysis of the colour of the flags and the motives behind them shows that the devotees offer green flags for success in any adventurous acts and for prosperity, the saffron flags as an offering to the saint. Hence, the devotees who are unable to attend the flag festival at Nagore can perform the same festival at their respective native places by way of offering *fatiha*[5] in a manner similar to that at the Nagore *dargah*. This tradition is observed throughout south India and outside the country, in Singapore and Sri Lanka. In these localities flag rituals provide different spaces, which are, in turn, linked to the Nagore sacred shrine complex. Thus, the shrine complex revitalises the wider social world in time and space through the flag festival of the saint. The devotees who are unable to attend the flag festival at Nagore can send offerings in either cash or kind through the pilgrims who do attend it. Nowadays, the *dargah* management has adopted a new method: they invite the devotees to offer donations to the *dargah* trust bank account and, in return, they send *tabarruk* (sanctified food) to the devotees after the completion of the flag festival of the saint. This is one instance of sacred exchange, a key transaction explained fully below. Historically, the flag festival may have been borrowed from local Hindu customary celebrations, although the use of flags is common in Islam too. This may explain the local solidarity of the mixed faiths of the region, and their joint participation in the flag festival of the saint. The two versions related to the history of the flags are as follows.

The first version, recorded in the Tanjore District Records (Hemingway 1906), states that flags were symbolically associated with the royal Maratha kings of Tanjore, and were introduced by devotees of the saint of Nagore as a sign of victory and prosperity. A tall flagpost, richly decorated and elaborately installed on the minarets of the *dargah*, would mean a rich and prosperous *dargah* commanding royal patronage. In this sense the flag is a sign of pomp and pride. The Nagore Andavar is the greatest of the region's kings and the *dargah* is his palace. Another version told by the *dargah* management and descendants of the saint claimed that the flags are the symbolic representation of Ali (the Prophet's son-in-law), who died in the holy war (jihad) against the unbelievers, while preaching the message of Allah. Hence, the flags are embroidered with the Zulfikar emblem of the Prophet's nephew, Ali,[6] (two swords and one shield), which confirms that the *dargah* is intended to bring the message of Allah and that the descendants are the true preachers of the message of God. These multivocal associations explain why one can observe a mixture of faiths under the combined shadow of the flags at the festival of the saint of Nagore.

The main attraction of the anniversary of the saint's death is, indeed, this hoisting and carrying of the flags in procession, in an unselfconscious fusion of Hindu as well as Islamic rituals. The Islamic rites include recitation of Qur'anic verses and observance of the *fatiha* ritual, whereas the procession with its models and floats is reminiscent of other Hindu processions in Tamil Nadu.

The Kanduri festival of the Nagore Andavar lasts fourteen days, starting from the first day of Jamathul Akhir, the sixth month of the Muslim calendar year (see Table 3.1). Just before its commencement, the flagpoles are erected on the five minarets of the shrine (Nagore-e-Sharif). Four flags (*kodi* in Tamil) are received from the Nagapatnam Muslim *jama'at*. They are traditionally sent from Singapore by devotees of the Nagore Andavar, while the fifth flag is donated by the descendants of the then Maratha kings of Tanjore. After the *fatiha* ritual has been performed, the five flags are carried on the back of the *dargah* elephant to Nagore-e-Sharif. Later, the flags are displayed in the Mera Palli (mosque) at

Table 3.1 The types of sacred performances conducted at the Nagapatnam and Nagore sacred centres during the Kanduri festival of the saint Sahul Hameed Nagore Andavar

Day and Month as per Muslim calendar	Time and place	Types of sacred performance
26th Jamathul Avval AH 1413	2.00 p.m. Nagore	Erection of flagpoles on the five minarets of the Nagore Andavar's *dargah*
30th Jamathul Avval AH 1413	11.00 a.m. Nagapatnam	Reception of *kodi*. Installation of the *iradam* (car) in the *usimaram* (chariot) for flags procession.
30th Jamathul Avval AH 1413	8.30 p.m. Nagapatnam	Display of fireworks at the *iradam* place
1st Jamathul Akhir AH 1413	8.30 a.m. Nagore	Reception of Faqir *jama'a*s
1st Jamathul Akhir AH 1413	12.00 p.m. Nagapatnam Nagore	Procession of *kodi*
1st Jamathul Akhir AH 1413	8.30 p.m. Nagore	*Thuvaja rohanam* (flag-hoisting ceremony)
8th Jamathul Akhir AH 1413	8.30 p.m. Nagore	*Vana vedeke* (display of fireworks)
9th Jamathul Akhir AH 1413	8.00 a.m. Nagapatnam	Installation of *sandana koodu* in the *usimaram*
9th Jamathul Akhir AH 1413	10.00 p.m. Nagore	Installation of *pir*[6] (Nagore Andavar's disciple's fasting ceremony)
10th Jamathul Akhir AH 1413	7.00 p.m. Nagore	Reception of Nagore Andavar's *rowla sharif* (tomb chamber, sanctum sanctorum) *chadar*
10th Jamathul Akhir AH 1413	8.30 p.m. Nagapatnam Nagore	Procession of *sandana koodu*
11th Jamathul Akhir AH 1413	4.30 a.m. Nagore	Anointment of *rowla sharif* with *sandanam* (sandalwood paste)
12th Jamathul Akhir AH 1413	5.00 p.m. Nagore & Chilladi	*Pir* proceeds to seashore to break his fast
14th Jamathul Akhir AH 1413	8.30 p.m. Nagore	*Thuvaja avarohanam* (flag-lowering ceremony)

Nagapatnam. On the flags, as well as the Zulfikar emblem, are embroidered the words '*Ya Nagore! Murade Hassil*' ('Oh! Lord Nagore! My vows are fulfilled'). The flags are also imprinted with sandalwood paste palm prints of the devotees' hands. Devotees who desire to hoist the flag on the *dargah* Minaret have to pay a fee (*kanikai*) of Rs 1000 as a gift to the *dargah* office. Such devotee flags are hoisted daily on the big minaret, at 6 p.m.

The special attraction of the saint Nagore Andavar's Kanduri is the presence of the Faqir (mendicant priests) *jama'a*s, disciples of the saint. It is said that the saint has 404 disciples as his followers in his 'spiritual' team. All these are divided into four groups, each of which consists of one hundred members along with a headman. The four groups are the Banwa, Malang, Mondal and Jalali. Since the

Plate 3.2 The erection of the flagpoles on one of the five minarets, built by the Maratha ruler Pratap Simha, Tanjavur, Tamil Nadu

tomb of the saint Nagore Andavar was first erected, these saintly followers have visited the fair annually, to pay their homage to their spiritual master. In due course, the local mendicant priest association, the Rafai *jama'a*, was added to the earlier four mendicant groups of Yusef Saheb. Thus, at present, five mendicant groups attend the saint's Kanduri festival and observe his rituals.

The first mendicant group welcomed to the Kanduri festival by the *dargah* management is the Banwa *jama'a*, which arrives at 8 a.m. Members of this group are honoured with garlands, the cannon (*thop*) is fired and the musical pipes are played, marking respect for the arrivals, who now get their heads tonsured. This is the reason why local people refer to them as *mutte faqir* (tonsured mendicant priests). They claim higher social status than the other four mendicant groups. The next group to arrive, at 12 p.m., are the Malang *jama'a*. Usually, members of this groups grow their hair long. Hence they are called by the people *jhata faqir* (long-haired mendicant priests). The third group are the Mondal *faqir*, who enter the *dargah* precincts at 3 p.m. They are distinguished by the custom of playing the *danka* (drum) while going out to preach Islam – a custom which gives them their other name, the Danka Faqir *jama'a*. The fourth group arriving at the shrine are the Jalali Faqir, who carry along with them a *kombu* (horn) and so are known as the Kombu Faqir *jama'a*. The fifth group is the Rafai *jama'a*. They play with the *guruj* (mace) during the festival in order to entertain the public, and hence have been given the title of Guruj Faqir *jama'a*. These five *jama'a*s are welcomed to the saint's Kanduri festival by the *dargah* management and perform *chilla* (forty days' meditation) at Nagore-e-Sharif. The main duty of the five *jama'a*s is to conduct the rituals at the saint's anniversary fair and to perform *ziarat* in the evening, during their stay on the *dargah* premises.

Ritual processing: sacralising locality

On the first day of the month of Jamathul Akhir, which opens the Kanduri festival proper, the five minaret flags are taken out for procession. (For a case study of processions, communal identity and locality, see Freitag 1989; Werbner 1996.) The procession starts at midday at Nagapatnam town, from the Meerapalli mosque. It sets off after first performing the *fatiha* ritual, and moves through the streets of Nagapatnam, bringing the residential areas of the town into contact with the sacred emblems of the *dargah*. The procession consists of five big models or floats, conceived of as offerings: a big chariot (*peria ratham*), a small chariot (*chinna ratham*), a model of Mohammad Ghouse's ship (*testa*), a model of Mohammad Gwalior's ship and the model palanquin (*pallaq*) offered by the merchant caste.

Once the procession reaches the shrine, its flags are hoisted on the five minarets of the *dargah*. The first flag to be hoisted is placed on the *Talamattu Manora* minaret, located towards the head of the saint's shrine complex. This is the flag carried by the big chariot model, the expenses of which are borne by the Nagapatnam Muslim *jama'at*. The second minaret flag, carried by the model palanquin, is hoisted on the *Sahib* minaret of the *dargah*. This model is paid for by the Hindu merchant group and this explains its name, the *Chettiar* palanquin. The *Muthubaq* minaret, which is the third one located on the north side of the *dargah*, receives the flag carried by the model of Mohammad Ghouse's ship. The float itself is funded by individual contributions made by the devotees of the locality. The fourth, *Ottu* minaret receives the flag carried by devotees residing in Singapore. The fifth minaret flag is carried by the model of Mohammad Gwalior's ship. The procession of these five flags, borne by the five models, is preceded by individual devotees' models, which include small ships (*cuppal*), boats (*padagai*), ship engines, minarets (*manora*), flower palanquins (*poopallaq*) and model fish (*minu*), all of which belong to the local area. These models are driven by the devotees, to represent the fulfilment of their vows to the Nagore Andavar. After the procession the models are kept at home, imbued by the power of their sacred contact with the shrine, and they are used again only at the saint's next annual festival. The tradition of carrying these personal and familial models annually to the shrine is perpetuated from

Plate 3.3 The illuminated chariot ready to carry the sacred flags in procession

generation to generation by the descendants of the devotees. The flag procession is followed by an aloe-wood cart (*ud-vandi*) which releases the smoke of the aloe wood, according to tradition a mode of worship of the Nagore Andavar flags, which may also be conceived of as a way of sanctifying the residential areas of the locality. At the back of the flag procession, Western musical bands (*sanai*) and double-reed pipes (*nadaswaram*) are played, representing the 'Hindu' part of the festival.

The procession commences from the Meera Palli mosque and passes through Abhiram Ammal Sannadi Street, Neela Dathchayani Ammam West Street, East Street, North Street, Nethaji Road and Hospital Road, traversing the town of Nagapatnam. From there the procession proceeds to the town of Nagore through streets such as Kunjali Mericar Street, Miya Street, Pandha Saliar Street, Theru Palli Street and Sayyadu Palli Street, until it finally reaches the illuminated west gate of the *dargah*, *Alankara Vasil*. The five flags are received with great honour by the *dargah* management and hoisted on the five minarets at 8.30 p.m., after the performance of the *fatiha* prayer. This ritual is known as *thuvaja rohanam* (flag hoisting). It is performed with great devotion and immense shows of faith, and is witnessed by tens of thousands of pilgrims from different parts of the region and beyond it. The ritual is honoured by the firing of the *dargah* cannon. The flags remain flying on the minarets for fourteen days until the completion of the Kanduri festival.

As happens with many festivals, the entertainment programme includes a display of fireworks. This takes place a week after the flag-hoisting ritual, on the eighth day of the month of Jamathul Akhir, starting at 8.30 p.m. and lasting for two hours. The display of fireworks is a joyful occasion for all those attending the festival.

The following day, on the 9th Jamathul Akhir, the Nagapatnam *jama'at* assembles at the shed for the 'sandalwood paste anointment', carried by the *koodu*. First, as in all the rites, the *fatiha* is said, and the arrangements are made for bringing out the chariot in procession.

That evening the ceremonial installation of the ritual saint takes place. At 10 p.m., a disciple from the Malang Faqir *jama'a* is selected to be 'saint' (*pir*) in a ritual which is referred to as 'the installation of the *pir*'. It is performed at the place where the funerary prayers over the saint's body were originally offered (*janaze ke namaz*), by members of the Malang Faqir *jama'a*, whose founder was one of the saint's original disciples who followed him during his travels as he preached the divine message of Allah. In the evening all *dargah* trustees, the *khalifa* (spiritual

Plate 3.4 The devotees are blessed by the 'ritual saint' (*pir*) through *theertam*, sandalwood paste, lemon, rose petals and amulets

successor) of the *dargah*, members of the five Faqir *jama'a*s and the rest of the pilgrims assemble near the ritual saint, *pir mandapam*. The *fatiha* is conducted and the *pir*'s toes are tied with a fine thread. It is believed that the thread should remain in this position for three days. The ritual saint, during this period, observes meditation (*zikr*), constantly reciting the names of God. During this, he throws lemons to the crowds. There is a popular belief that a lemon thrown by the *pir* has miraculous powers; the pilgrims believe that these lemons are auspicious, and will bring good luck to anyone who catches them, since all their desires will be fulfilled by the Nagore Andavar. The womenfolk especially believe that if a barren woman catches a lemon, it means that she will be blessed with offspring. So people stand before the *pir* day and night, in the hope of catching a lemon. They do not mind burning in the scorching heat of the sun or being soaked by the rain. Their sole desire is to catch one of the lemons and with it the blessings of the Nagore Andavar.

Reception of Nagore Andavar's rowla sharif chadar (shawl)

In earlier days, the *chadar* of Nagore Andavar's *rowla sharif* used to be presented by the then Maratha kings of Tanjore. Later, Palaniandi Pillai, a devotee of Nagore Andavar, requested the Maratha king to allow him to present the shawl to the saint. Since then the tradition has been upheld by the descendants of the Palaniandi Pillai. On the morning of the day following the installation of the ritual saint, at 7 p.m., the *dargah* trustees and the descendant of the saint's son, Yusef Saheb, visit the family of Palaniandi Pillai's descendants, Karthikeyan, to receive the shawl. The shawl is displayed for viewing in the central hall of the house. After performing the *fatiha* the shawl is carried on the back of the *dargah* elephant. Later on, the shawl is spread on the saint's tomb after being anointed with sandalwood paste.

That evening, at 8.30 p.m., the chariot containing *sandanam* is pulled by the pilgrims, preceded by the aloe-wood cart, from Nagapatnam town to Nagore. No models of the devotees are carried during this procession, but the procession includes a variety of musical instruments like drums (*tappu*), a troupe of horns, the double-reed *nadaswaram*s played in Hindu temples and a three-piece Western band, making it much like a fair (*mela*). The chariot, while being pulled, stops at different intervals. Wherever it does so, the devotees, including Hindus, offer *fatiha* to it by inviting the Muslims accompanying it into their houses. They also offer the chariot pullers tea, coffee and snacks, honour them with towels (*thundu*), and distribute *prasadam* (sweetmeats) to the pilgrims following the procession. What is effected by these acts is a fusing of public and domestic spaces through sacred exchange, in which offerings and food mediate between the spaces of houses, the public spaces of the city and the shrine.

The procession first moves through Nagapatnam and from there to Nagore, to bestow the blessings of the Andavar on the people of the area. Finally, at 4.30

Plate 3.5 Carrying the sandalwood paste with which the saint's lineal descendant will anoint the tomb of the saint. The illuminated chariot of the procession is seen in the background

a.m., the chariot reaches the south gate of the *dargah*. The two pots of *sandanam* which have been carried through the town in procession are received by the saint's descendants, who take them inside the sanctum sanctorum of the *dargah*, where they are used to anoint the *rowla sharif* of the saint early the next morning. This ritual act is performed by the spiritual successor (*khalifa*) of the *dargah*, who first utters the *fatiha* and recites the spiritual genealogy of the saint. Following the prayers and ritual smearing, the shawl, imbued symbolically and metonymically with the spaces of the towns through which the sandalwood paste chariot has moved, is spread over the saint's tomb. After the anointment ritual, the *dargah* gates are opened to the pilgrims and public.

Two days later, on the 12th of Jamathul Akhir at 5 p.m., the *dargah khalifa*, along with the trustees and five Faqir *jama'a*s, assemble around the *pir mandapam*. After saying the *fatiha*, the knots on the ritual saint's toes are untied. Along with the headman (*sarguru*) of the Malang *jama'a* and the devotees, the released *pir* then moves towards the seashore, to break his fast (*roza*). He proceeds to the *chilladi dargah*, where, according to tradition, the saint Nagore Andavar had performed meditation for forty days. Here the *fatiha* ritual prayer is conducted and the water in a shallow pit is sipped ritually. People believe that the water in this excavated pit at this moment is sweet, whereas at other times it is salty. This transformation reflects the miraculous powers of the saint and his power over nature. Finally, the ritual saint visits the seashore and pays tribute to the ocean God *Khizr*, before returning to the *dargah*.

The revitalising power of the *dargah*

We see here how a series of movements between the town and the shrine culminate in a movement beyond 'culture', to a site which symbolises the rejuvenating power of 'nature' and the control of the saint over the powers of life and fertility. Having linked the *dargah* to a wider social world and its immediate locality, the shrine complex itself is now revitalised by a movement back and forth into nature. During this series of movements different ritual substances are juxtaposed: the hot fire of the fireworks is counteracted by the coolness of the lemons, of the sandalwood paste and finally, of the sweet water and the sea. The fragrance of the aloe and sandalwood permeates the social universe surrounding the *dargah* and reaches out towards God above. So too, perhaps, do the flags, flying above the models and minarets.

If we analyse the shrine complex as a whole, we can see that the sanctum is a constellation of the five elements that are basic to the entire universe (for the design of the shrine complex, see Figure 3.2). In this context, it is apt to quote Rao (1979: 84): 'the foundation of the temple is made to represent Earth (*prithvi*), the walls of the sanctum [are] water (*ap*) and the tower over it fire (*tejas*); the finial (*kalasa*) of the tower stands for air (*vayu*) and above it is the formless ether (*akasa*)'. In the present context of the Sufi shrine, the foundation of the sacred complex of the *dargah* represents earth (*jameen*), the walls of the rowla sharif symbolise water (*pani*) and the minarets within the *dargah* complex represent fire (*aug*), while the *kalasa* (dome) of the minarets stands for air (*hava*). Thus the *dargah* sacred complex confirms the interrelated phenomena of five basic elements of the universe. And fire being the active element that fuses the others, the minarets which carry the flags become an important limb in the *dargah*. Its sacred complex thus demonstrates the constellation of human and divine currents; matter (flags) moves up and the spirit (blessings of the saint) flows down. The devotee who stands in front of the tomb is expected to partake in this transaction. The emanations that proceed from the tomb of the saint must be picked up by the faith in the devotee's heart. Devotion is the transformer. The rituals conducted within the shrine involve these ideas, and attempt to facilitate this transformation along the horizontal axis of tomb, saint and devotee. The devotee represents active matter and the tomb of the saint, passive spirit. The two are brought together in the creative act of worship.

On the evening of the 14th of Jamathul Akhir, two days after the procession to the sea, the flags from the five minarets are lowered. Before that, the *fatiha* is said amidst the gathering of *dargah* trustees, *dargah khalifa* and the five Faqir *jama'a*s. This ritual is known as *thuvaja avarohanam* (the flag-lowering ritual). That night the Qur'an is read along with the *silsila* of the saint. This marks the completion of the saint's annual Kanduri festival, attended by vast numbers of disciples and local people, which has lasted in total fourteen days. Through the festival, localism is inscribed in the *dargah*, while the sanctity of the *dargah* is carried to the towns in its immediate vicinity, affording them spiritual blessing and protection.

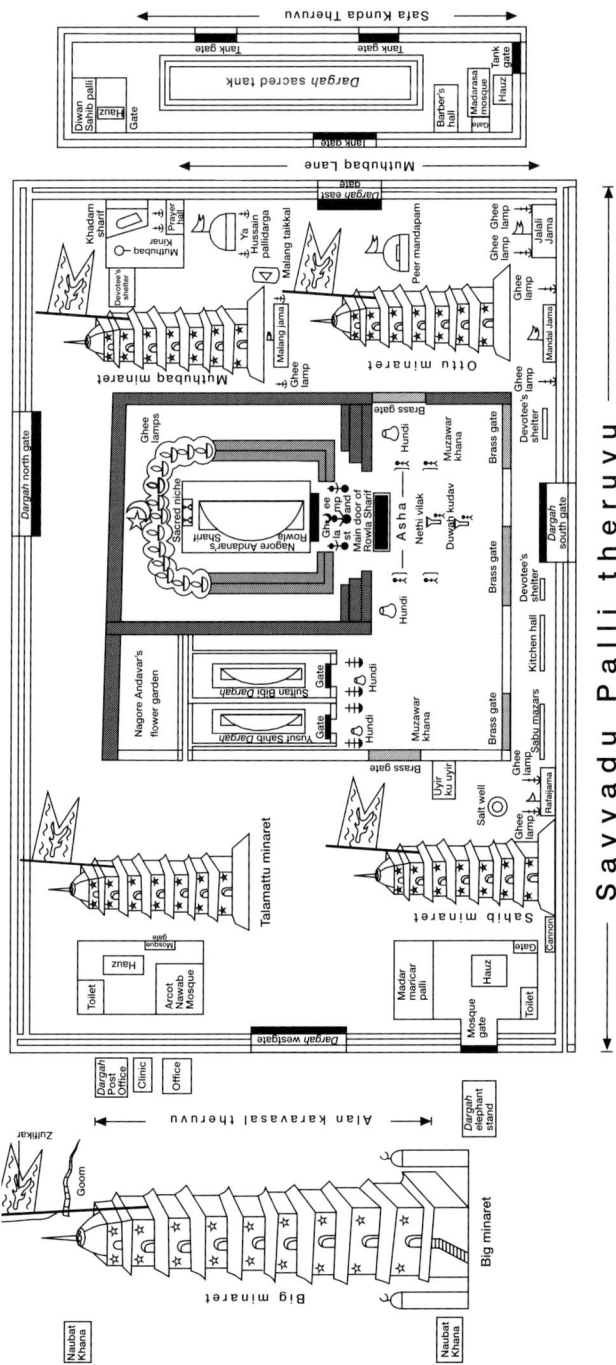

Figure 3.2 Ground plan of the sacred complex of Nagore-e-Sharif[7]

The flags, the models and the chariots are carefully preserved to become once again, the following year, the ritual bearers of the shrine's sanctity.

Although this annual festival is of great importance, it should be noted that daily and weekly rituals are also held at the *dargah*. The daily ones, such as cleaning the tomb and adorning it with flowers, lighting the lamps and offering *fatiha*, are performed by the religious custodians of the *dargah*. Thursday (*Jumerat*) has special significance, as it does in most Sufi lodges. People believe that prayers performed on that day are answered by the saint. The *dargah* is kept open daily for one hour, after the morning and evening prayers; on Thursdays it remains open from afternoon to evening.

The healing powers of the shrine

Supplicants visit the shrine in search of help for a wide variety of afflictions: physical illness, mental disturbances and a range of personal problems, from a sense of disgust with life to the suffering and hardships of poverty. Supplicants seek cures for barrenness and infertility, success in examinations or job promotions, and victory in civil or criminal court cases. It is believed that the saint's intercessionary prayers can bring success in love and, indeed, can damage the property and life of rivals in love; they can resolve marital conflict and bring about the return home of a lost child, or the reform of a wayward husband or son. Thus every wish, right or wrong, good or bad, moral or otherwise is placed before the saint. Supplicants sit before his tomb for hours at a time until they feel that their prayers are heard by him.

The supplicant fulfilling a vow at the shrine often experiences an epileptic fit – his limbs are distorted, his face drawn in agony, his eyes first bulge ferociously, then, at intervals, close in serenity, his throat is choked with emotion, and his whole body perspires profusely. This ecstasy is understood as a tribute either in fulfilment of a vow or in submission of requests to the saint. Among the regular supplicants are included not only Muslims, but Hindus and Christians as well.

The huge crowds and the fusion of a single Hindu and Muslim brotherhood at the Kanduri festival reflect the feeling that the saint has the power to solve any problem. In the eyes of supplicants and devotees, he possesses a higher spiritual rank than ordinary human beings. The sanctity maintained in the *dargah*, and the aggregation of people of different faiths and classes, itself embodies this sacredness of the saint. Although saint shrines differ from locality to locality and from one region to another, in all, objects embodying the sanctity of the saint emerge over time. For example, at the tomb of Khawaja Garib Nawaz, *chaddar*s are offered before the saint and used to cover his tomb. Some shrines tie threads to the strings of the *dargah* gate. After the fulfilment of the vow these threads are offered before the saint along with *nazarana* (a tributary gift). At the *dargah* of Sahul Hameed Nagore Andavar, however, the devotees, as we have seen, offer flags in the name of the saint. This special form of offering is a feature of worship at saints' shrines throughout south India, and particularly in Tamil Nadu. The flag offerings are made during the annual death ceremony of the saint. In addition, devotees also make food offerings, which consist of puffed-up dried sugar mixed with wheat (*malida*), along with an offering of flowers of a special variety of *chemeli*. These offerings are given to the descendants of the saint, the *mujawar* (the 'protectors' of the *dargah*).

After the *fatiha* has been recited, a little quantity of the offering is taken by a *mujawar*, and the rest is returned to the devotees for distribution among their friends and relatives. This sanctified offering is known as *tabarruk* and is a further instance of the sacred exchange effected with God via the saint. (For a case study of sacred exchange, ritual organisation and the path to local eminence, see Werbner 1989.) The thick layers of soot (*masi*) available in the sacred niches of the sanctum sanctorum are also taken by the devotees as a proof of the living memory of the saint. The *ghee* (sanctified butter) available in the sacred niche lamps is touched and smeared on the face and hands as a token of blessings from the saint. The high praise for the saint's mystical powers, the veneration by offering flags and lighting *ghee* lamps at his tomb by local people (particularly Hindus), and the acceptance of all these customs by Muslims show the importance of the *dargah* as a great Muslim shrine and yet at the same time as a universal one.

The shrine of Nagore Andavar is known for its efficacy in exorcising *jinn*s. It is widely believed that mental illness is the evil act of evil *jinn*s, rather than being due to psychological stress. The cure for affliction is for the patient to visit the tomb and pray until he or she finds relief. If necessary, he or she may stay there for months at a time. Thus, the poor, who cannot afford more costly biomedical treatments, depend upon the supernatural treatment of the saint, available free to almost any supplicant.

Conclusion: pilgrimage and sacred exchange

In front of the saint's tomb there is an iron chain hanging from the roof. It is believed that this iron chain has miraculous powers. The tradition relates that it was given by the very first human couple, Adam and Eve, to the saint, when he visited Adam's peak during his preaching in Sri Lanka. The inscriptions at Adam's peak witness this fact (Qadhiri 1980: 17). The devotees, after their *ziarat*, and having offered *fatiha* at the saint's tomb, bring water from the sacred tank of the *dargah* (*safa kunda*) and touch the iron chain with this sacred water, before carrying the water home. This water is consumed during any illness and its divine powers, it is believed, will cure any disease. The water is thought to have the same effect as that of the *zamzam* (sacred spring) water in Mecca. All these discourses and miracles are known to the devotees of the saint through dreams (*basharat*).

Sufi saints are believed to have immense power. Undoubtedly, support for Sufi cults comes from the lower classes and castes of Muslim society. Yet, despite the wholesale rejection by Muslim reformists of the rites at the saints' tombs, many pious Muslims respect the asceticism of saints and their simple way of life, devoted to the propagation of Islam. In the present case, it is widely agreed that the Sufi saint Sahul Hameed Nagore Andavar, the most pious of men during his lifetime, possesses the supernatural powers of healing the possessed, fulfilling heartfelt desires, providing solace for unhappy souls, blessing the barren and granting an infinite variety of requests made by supplicants. These saintly miracles revitalise the faith in the saint's soul as a living presence which continues to rescue the needy and the distressed. Though the people who come to the *dargah* may belong to different castes and different religious faiths, their destination is one: the saint, with his power to intercede between the living and God. They derive faith from their concrete relation to the *dargah* and its guardians rather than from a direct relation to a distant and metaphysical God.

Notes

1 *Karāmāt* refers to the powers possessed by the Sufi saint (*wali*) through which human needs are satisfied. Due to these miraculous powers, saints are thought to be nearer to God, and to work as intermediaries between humanity and God. The miracles performed by the prophets are known as *mujizat*.
2 In Tamil vernacular, Andavar means 'God'. The Sufi saint Sahul Hameed of Nagore-e-Sharif is called Nagore Andavar because of his high degree of spiritual excellence and his power to fulfil the material needs and vows of devotees. He was honoured with this title in 1966 by the Hindu sage Shivananda for his remarkable miraculous acts. Since then, the saint of Nagore is referred to as Nagore Andavar by the local people.
3 *Jande* are the *dargah* flags, carrying the Zulfikar emblem (see Plate 3.1, p. 57), which are ceremonially hoisted on a tall and imposing wooden pillar called *thuvaja-stambha* (flagstaff), although it is not clear in the textual accounts where the terms derive from, probably because this was a later innovation. The Sanskrit word used for the flag (*thuvaja*, and in Tamil *kodi*), strictly means 'that which is raised'. It therefore has connotations of hope, desire (especially erotic desire, which can be physically expressed as erection, and the Sanskrit expression is frequently employed in that context), pride, arrogance and will – whatever raises a man to a higher level of understanding and activity is a flag of the festival of the saint. The flag in the traditional context means a resolve to exert and a will to succeed. Hoisting the flag suggests setting out to conquer. The devotee coming into the *dargah* would have to resolve to conquer his own base nature, and set out on a war with his own mean disposition. A look at the flagstaff would be a reminder for him in this regard.
4 *Ziarat* is, traditionally, a visit to the tomb of the Prophet at Madina, Saudi Arabia. The place of ziarat is called *ziaratgarh* or *dargah*, which also refers to the Sufi saint's residence or burial place. The burial place of an ordinary person is referred to as *qabar* (grave); for high dignitaries such as *'ulama* (Islamic scholars) the word *mazar* (grave) is used. Thus at the regional level there is a distinct style of usage of words for the graves of Muslims in south India.
5 *Fatiha* indicates a single recitation of the *Sura fatiha* (the first verse of the holy text) and three times of the *Sura Iklas*, a chapter that occurs in the daily prayer and reads thus: 'He is God, the One and Only God, the Eternal, Absolute. He begetteth not, nor is He begotten, and there is none like unto Him.' Usually this ritual is conducted by Muslims before making an offering in the name of Allah and to Sufi saints at the beginning of auspicious occasions as a mark of respect to God or saints.
6 *Pir* literally means a spiritual mentor, one who initiates the novices into the spiritual line

of Sufism. He is called *shaikh* or *murshid*. But in the present study the word *pir* denotes the disciple of the saint Sahul Hameed Nagore Andavar who attends to the traditional Kanduri festival of the saint. He performs as a 'ritual saint' and symbolises the spiritual exercises of the saint of Nagore.

7 Key to terms used in Figure 3.2:
Naubat Khana = a room where musical instruments are played.
Zulfikar = the emblem of two swords and one shield, the title of Hazarat Ali's sword.
Goom = millipeede.
Alankara Vasil Theruvu = the illuminated gate of the street.
Hauz = water tank.
Arcot Nawab mosque = Arcot Nawab's mosque.
Madar Maraicar palli = Madar Maricar's mosque.
palli = mosque.
Talamattu minaret = Saint's head-side minaret.
Sahib minaret = minaret built in the name of the saint, Nagore Andavar.
Uyir Ku Uyir = releasing of the pigeon.
Sabu mazars = saint's descendants' tombs.
Mujawar Khana = a place meant for the *dargah* custodians.
Yusef Sahib *dargah* = saint's son's tomb.
Sultan bibi *dargah* = Saint's daughter-in-law's tomb.
Hundi = gift collection box.
Duwam Kudavu = a container used to burn aloe-wood.
Nethi Vilak = lamp used to light the purified butter.
Asha = saint's walking stick.
Ghee lamps = lamps used to light the purified butter.
Ottu minaret = bricks minaret.
Muthubaq minaret = Saint's leg-side minaret.
Mandal jama'a = Mandal mendicant *faqir* group.
Julali Jama'a = Jalali mendicant *faqir* group.
Pir mantapam = a place used for the '*Pir* installation ritual'.
Malang Taikkal = Malang mendicant *faqir* tombs.
Ya Hussain palli *dargah* = mosque built in the name of the Prophet's grandson.
Muthubaq Kinar = saint's leg-side well.
Khadam Sharif = Saint's footprints.
Diwan Saheb Palli = Diwan Saheb's mosque.
Madarasa Mosque = Arabic school mosque.
Malang Jama'a = Malang mendicant *faqir* group.
Rafai Jama'a = Rafai mendicant *faqir* group.
Theravu = street.
Madar = surname.

References

Abdi, S.N.M. (1993) 'On the Sufi Trail', *Illustrated Weekly of India*, 5–11 June: 16–18.
Bhaumik, S.N. (1993) 'A Holy Mix', *India Today*, 7 November: 10.
Chandrasekharan, T (1817) ' Nagore Kaifiayat: A Descriptive Catalogue: Marathi Modi Manuscripts', D, Nos. 107 and 108, Madras: Government Oriental Manuscript Library.

Cyril, G. (1978) *The Concise Encyclopedia of Islam*, London: Stancey International.
de Munck, Victor C. (1994) 'Sufi, Reformist and National Models of Identity: The History of a Muslim Village Festival in Sri Lanka', *Contributions to Indian Sociology* n.s. 28, 2: 273–293.
Freitag, Sandria B. (1989) *Collective Action and Community: Public Arenas and the Emergence of Communalism in North India*, Berkeley: University of California Press.
Gadgil, M. and V.D. Vartak (1976) 'The Sacred Groves of the Western Ghats in India', *Economic Botany*, 30: 152–160.
Gibb, H.A.R. and J.H. Karmers (1981) *Shorter Encyclopedia of Islam*, Karachi: South Asia Publishers.
Hemingway, F.R. (1906) *Madras District Gazetter Records*, Tanjore: Government Press Madras.
Hughes, T.P. (1975) *Notes on Muhammadanism*, Delhi: Idarah-I-Adabiyat-I-Delhi.
Hulbe, S.K., T. Vetshere and S.B. Khomme (1994) 'The Sacred Complex at Madhi', *Man in India* 55: 237–253.
Hussain, S.S. (1963–1964) *Annual Report on Indian Epigraphy*, No. D-161–163, Nagpur: Archaeological Survey of India.
Hussain, M.M.A. (1985) *Karunaik kadal Ajmer Haja Nayagam*. Madras: Three Em Publications.
Malhotra, K.C. and S. Sah (1993) 'Association of Pomegranate (Punica Granatum) with the Sacred Complex at Madhi, Maharastra', *Man in India* 73, 4: 395–400.
Malhotra, K.C. and J. Basak (1984) 'A Note on the Cultural Ecology of Husbanded Plants', *South Asian Anthropologist*, 5, 1: 45–47.
Moini, S.L.H. (1932) *The New Royal Persian English Dictionary*, Vol. 1, Madras: Madras University.
Moini, S.L.H. (1935) *The Tamil Lexicon and Jubilee Tamil Dictionary*, Vol. 2, Part I, Madras: Madras University.
Moini, S.L.H. (1989) 'Rituals and Customary Practices at the *Dargah* of Ajmer', in W. Troll Christian (ed.) *Muslim Shrines in India*, Delhi: Oxford University Press, pp. 60–75.
More, J.B.P.L. (1993) 'Tamil Muslims and Non-Brahmin Atheists – 1925–1940', *Contributions to Indian Sociology* n.s. 27, 1: 83–104.
Qadhiri, S.H.S (1980) 'The divine light of Nagore'. Dargah Sharif/Nagore S.K.
Qadir Hussain, K. (1957) 'The South Indian Musalmans', *Madras Christian College Magazine* 30: 365–369.
Quddusi, M.I. (1991) 'A Bilingual Inscription of Pratap Singh from Nagore (Tamil Nadu)', Paper presented at the 17th Annual Epigraphical Congress, Tanjore.
Rahim, M.A. (1971) *History of Nagapatnam and its Surroundings from the 16th Century*, Madras: Madras University.
Raja, M. (1967) 'The Mazar Worship in Budaun', *Journal of Social Research* 10, 2: 27–36.
Rao, S. (1979) *The Temple: Its Meaning and Symbolism*, Bangalore: Theosophical Society
Sayyid, M. (AH 1346) 'Manquibul Majid Fi Manaquib Sah-al Hamid (Arabic)', trans. S.M. Hussain Alam as 'Sawanth Hayati Hadrat Quadriwali', Madras: (AH 1379).
Shariff, J. (1921) *Islam in India: The customs of the Musalmans of India*, trans. G.A. Herklots (1975), London: Curzon Press.
Sivananda, V. (1966) 'Release the Pigeon: Avert Death', *Animal Citizen*, Madras Animal Welfare Board.
Werbner, Pnina (1996) 'Stamping the Earth with the Name of Allah: *Zikr* and the Sacralizing of Space among British Muslims', *Cultural Anthropology* 11, 3: 309–338.
Werbner, Richard (1989) *Ritual Passage, Sacred Journey: The Process and Organization of Religious Movement*, Washington DC: Smithsonian Institution Press.

4

'THE SAINT WHO DISAPPEARED'

Saints of the wilderness in Pakistani village shrines

Lukas Werth

Introduction

In the mountains dividing the plains of the Punjab from the slightly elevated plateau of the Potwar, the salt range, lies the village Rajpur, inhabited mainly by the *Bahadar*.[1] Rajputs who live there regard it as the place of their origin. Inside that village, just beside the mosque, stands a small, green-painted tomb in which the graves of a man and his wife are found, who lived in Rajpur about sixty years ago. They belonged to a subcaste of the *Sayyid*, the descendants of the Prophet, and are regarded by the people of the village as saints or *pir*s. The tomb is their shrine (*ziarat, khanqah*), and their relatives still visit the village from time to time. Local people have just completed a small lodge beside the shrine for their stay when visiting the village.

The green tomb is located right at the centre of the village.[2] More to the periphery, at a place associated with one of the three major descent groups in the village, another shrine is found which is hardly more than a heap of rough stones, integrated into a wall separating a plot from the public street (*gali*). A small, old, rugged tree grows beside the wall, and on a stone plate set in it stand some old bottles and tin oil lamps; signs that the shrine is worshipped by women on Thursdays. A series of smooth stones has been placed on the wall: people rub them over their limbs when they feel physical pain. The shrine is the burial place of a mendicant woman (*faqirni*) who died in Rajpur; nobody knows her name, where she came from, or what she had achieved. She is, however, regarded as a member of the *Sayyid* caste, which is the common reason given why a shrine was made for her.

A third shrine lies just outside the village, hidden in a small grove. It is a rectangular compound about six metres by six, surrounded by a wall about a metre high; the small gate leading into the compound is never locked. There are two graves inside it, and several more can be discerned below the shrubs and trees which are allowed to grow freely outside. One shrub growing inside the compound is adorned with pieces of cloth, testimonies to the vows of the worshipping women who come here to pray. Plenty of old oil bottles are scattered around. This shrine probably plays the most central role in the social life of the village. No wood, not even dead branches or twigs, is ever taken from the dense grove, except when preparing a sacrificial meal for the *pir* right there on the spot, although firewood in that mountainous area has to be gathered from far away, an arduous task, and the thick trunks of the trees growing around the shrine could be profitably sold. The people of Rajpur say that the *pir* does not want wood to be collected from his grove, and when a woman once tried to defy this interdiction, she was harassed by him during the night, and had to return all the wood the next morning. The name of the *pir* buried here is not known, nor where he came from. But every Thursday the women of the village go to his grave, burn lights, and pray in his name.

These are the shrines of Rajpur. There are others nearby, quite a number in one hamlet (*dhog*) of the village, used when people live temporarily or permanently by their fields. Some are constructed in very much the same way as the shrine inside the grove near the village and are even bigger than it, others are mere shrubs of which people say that they are shrines (*khanqah*). All the villages around have similar shrines, and these exist alongside bigger shrines in the area. In fact, the sight of small shrines is ubiquitous in the Pakistani landscape.

The shrines are the visible expression of a tradition which is shared with Christianity and some forms of Judaism: the veneration of holy persons, known as saints. Islamic shrines function, of course, in their own way. Without an institutionalized church, but in a cultural environment which places much emphasis on the principle of descent as a means of determining and positioning persons, the shrines are often powerful centres of regional influence and political factors of considerable importance, managed under the guardianship of descendants of the deceased saint (*pir*) who once lived there. These descendants are *pir*s in their own right; they participate in the charisma of their ancestors and may acquire new fame, and, once they die, they too will be worshipped. If these *pir*s handle the authority which has been passed down to them skillfully and astutely, they may enhance their power, even gaining considerable influence in national politics.[3] The visible expression of this power is a magnificently decorated mausoleum and the flock of people who come there daily but especially at the time of the '*urs*, the annual celebration of the death of the *pir*, which is conceived of as the moment of his union with God. Like other villagers, the people of Rajpur too visit these great regional shrines.

However, the small shrines at Rajpur and elsewhere are visited only by local people, not by pilgrims, and normally no big annual celebrations take place there. Known descendants exist only for the saint whose tomb marks the centre of the village. They live some thirty miles away, and although when they visit they are treated with considerable respect, they are themselves poor people. There are no business interests of any importance involved in the maintenance of this shrine, and none at all in the other shrines. Nevertheless, people take care of the places. The two graves of the shrine in the grove are always adorned by a beautifully decorated shawl (*dupatta*), oil lamps are lit by women on Thursdays, and people come when they have requests or sorrows in the same way as they do on visits to the bigger shrines.

There are shrines of all sizes in Pakistan, and the small ones exist in people's consciousness in the very same way as do the big ones. Religious activities are to a considerable extent connected with the shrines, and their omnipresence shows that they must have an important place in the local culture. Islam in Pakistan, as elsewhere in the Muslim world, cannot be explained only by its Five Pillars, but rests also essentially on local traditions. Shrines are a part of those traditions in which the universal principles of Islam find the application they seem to need. In this chapter I shall concentrate on these small shrines of seemingly only local importance – or not even that – like the ones at Rajpur. Here, there are no economic or political interests involved, and no elaborate interactions take place. How, then, are all these small shrines used, and why are they there? My hope is to find some tentative answers to the question: 'What, if anything, is a shrine in Pakistan?'[4]

In order to achieve this aim I begin by interrogating the identity associated with the notion of the saint, or *pir*, and the people's attitude towards their saints. This will lead us towards some observations about how the sacred is conceived in Pakistan. Second, I explore what role the shrines themselves play in the social life of villagers, the activities in which they play a part, and their location in the eyes of the worshippers.

The *pir*

It may be appropriate to start the argument with a very general observation: in Judaism, Christianity and Islam a succession of extraordinary human beings hold central positions. The mythologies of the three 'religions of the book' tell of a sequence of persons who make up a sacred history (Eliade 1986: 116ff; Peters 1982: 194ff). God is a singularity in these religions which humans – not only humankind – interact with. Hence the dialogue between God and humans lies at the core of these religions, and it is through prophets or saints that communication with God is achieved. Social reality is seen to be mediated by agents conceived as human, although the ultimate guarantee of their knowledge is a distant god. Even though it is believed, of course, to be God Himself who gives meaning to the universe, it is thus human contact which endows reality with meaning.

Death frees the potentialities of saints: in a religion where people's real destination is conceived to be reached only after death, to be where God is situated likens the saints to God in their transcendence of death. What they did in life is regarded merely as a preliminary endeavour, a preparation to this end – although there is a difference in the Islamic concept where more emphasis is placed on living saints, and we have to be aware of this also when dealing with the graves of unknown *pir*s. Even here, as we shall see, the emphasis is placed on their continuing presence. In both cases, however, the link to the world beyond the grave is in the locality itself: in the relics of Christian saints or the graves of Muslim *pir*s. These define a particular point in space associated with a saint, and hence sacralized. Such sacred points attract worshippers, who travel on pilgrimage (if they cover longer distances) through space in order to reach out to God. But since God is everywhere, it is the plurality of saints that makes this ubiquitous God concrete. It turns the macrocosm into an extension of the microcosm by attaching it to a certain locality. And as the invisible becomes a graspable entity in a particular locality, so too the purpose of praying also becomes specifically defined. People often pray to the *pir*s at their shrines because of concrete problems: disease, childlessness and other afflictions.

The Sufi legacy in Islam has traditionally been used in several ways to concretize religion, particularly to localize an abstract pattern of worship. This may happen even against the intention of those persons who become saints, as in the case of Ibn Taimiya who, in his lifetime, violently attacked the cult of saints, and whose tomb in Damascus became a centre of veneration after his death (Denny 1988: 76–77).

In Pakistan the *pir*s normally, but by no means always, belong to the caste of the *Sayyid*s, the descendants of Muhammad. In the local consciousness of the people, the *Sayyid* are closely associated with sainthood. The expression *pira-di qaumzat*, 'the caste of the *pir*', is often used as an alternative to *sayyida-di qaum*, 'the caste of the *Sayyid*'. The meaning remains the same in both cases, with no discernible shift. I first heard the expression used with reference to the dominant caste of a neighbouring village. The *Sayyid*s qualify unequivocally as the highest Muslim caste in South Asia, to an extent that they may be compared with the Hindu brahmins. Such parallels should, however, not be carried too far. The concept of caste is also important in Muslim South Asia, but it has been transformed in many respects. Thus the high status of the *Sayyid*s is due not to their exclusive right to conduct religious services (they are not priests), but to their participation in the sacredness of Muhammad, and therefore of God. But, I was told, they will live at a specially reserved place in paradise, and they are a category qualified to act as mediators between God and humans. In that sense, the ideology of the caste system is refracted in Muslim ideas: a category of Islamic holiness is represented as a caste (*qaum, zat*), which means a distinct quality or species.[5]

This is one reason why it is not necessary in Pakistan to know the name or even the life of the *pir* of a small shrine: the fact that he is supposed to belong to a holy category is sufficient to qualify him to be prayed to, even though the personality of the saint has been almost effaced and is of very limited importance. But still the fact remains that it is human graves which are the point of veneration, and by no means the grave of every *Sayyid* becomes a shrine. We shall come back to this point, but first we have to take a closer look at the *pir*s of the shrines of Rajpur.

Rajpur *pir*s

Once the people of Rajpur wanted to have a saint (*pir*) in their village, and they called a man from a family of *Sayyid*s living in the area. They gave food, money, and fields to him, all of their own free will; the *pir* never asked for anything. After his death the people made the green tomb inside the village for him, in which his adorned grave alongside that of his wife still remain. Some men told me that the wife was of their own caste, given by them to the *pir* because he requested a wife. However, the old, blind *hafiz*[6] living in the village denied this, and maintained that she too was a *Sayyid*. He had known her personally; she had lived much longer than her husband, taught the Qur'an to the blind-born child (as she did to the other children), and gave him the permission (*ijazat*) to heal people by breathing holy verses upon them (*dam dena*). *Pir*s are able to heal people in this manner, and they may grant this power to other people if they consider them worthy of it. A common reason to blow (*dam*) on somebody (often a woman or child) is to rid them of an affliction by an evil force. A shadow (*saya*) might have fallen on a woman, or a *churel* or *bala* (witch-like creatures) might have seen her, or a *jinn* might have slipped inside her. These accidents happen most of all under trees, and in the *jangal*.[7] There one has to be careful. The *pir* and his wife healed people from these afflictions, but also from others: once a great disease broke out in Rajpur. First the rats fell dead from the roofs, and then the people developed lumps under their armpits, and died.[8] But the *pir* and his wife saved the village by praying for whole nights one sura (*ya'sin*) from the Qur'an. In a similar way they once also saved the cattle of the village from an epidemic. Other shrines of the same family of *pir*s are found in the area; in one neighbouring village there is a shrine of the father's brother's son of the *pir* in Rajpur. The members of this family are, however, Shi'a, whereas the majority of the population of Rajpur are Sunni Muslims. Only the *biradari* (local kin group) of one service caste (*kammi*), the shoemaker (*mochi*), are also Shi'a, and they have now somewhat taken over the care of the shrine, sponsoring a celebration there at Moharram to which they invite other people. The small shrine of the mendicant woman is not regularly used as a place of worship at all, but sometimes, on a Thursday, a woman will come, pray, and light an oil lamp there. When women pass by the shrine, some of them bow down in front of it and say a short prayer. And if someone is afflicted with aches and pains, he or she may also rub his or her limbs with one of the smooth, round pebbles lying at the shrine.

The saint who disappeared

The *pir* of the grove outside the village is also called *pir ghaib* ('the saint who disappeared'). The name derives from a story which is told about him: once a bald-headed bridegroom was marrying a one-eyed bride. When the marriage procession (Urdu *barat*, Punjabi *janj*) was standing at the place of the shrine, people ridiculed them, at which point the whole marriage party, including the bridal couple, disappeared. The graves around the shrine are those of the marriage party. Therefore, I was told, the man must have been a *pir*. In another, diluted version of the story, the *pir* had come to Rajpur to find a wife, but the people disrespected him (*besti dena*), and he suddenly vanished when walking over the place of the shrine.

No other stories are known about that *pir*'s life, but he sometimes appears to people in their dreams, and he is seen occasionally in the shape of a lion near his shrine. On Thursday nights, people say, a light may be seen coming to Rajpur from another shrine at a neighbouring village, also located outside the village amidst the trees, and it moves on from there to a third shrine at a nearby hamlet in the wilderness, located just like the first two, near a *dhog* of Rajpur.

In Rajpur, this is the only one of the three shrines which lies outside the village boundaries, but it is the most frequented one. If the people of the village have troubles, they are most likely to go there. It is here that the women of the village read prayers every Thursday, and burn oil lights. When they have wishes, they knot pieces of cloth and hang them on the shrub by the grave as tokens of a vow, and when their requests are fulfilled, they hang a new piece of cloth on the same shrub. If they are very grateful, they bring a whole shawl and spread it on the grave. If that gets old, it is hung on the shrub along with the other pieces of cloth. People also leave money at the shrine, and it is said that once, when a *mochan* (woman of the shoemaker caste) had taken away money from there, she was afflicted with many troubles until she brought the money back.

Once, during my fieldwork, the winter rains were late, and in the salt range where there is no irrigation, if the rain does not fall, it means that the crops will wither in the fields. Faced with this prospect, the people of Rajpur decided to appeal to the *pir ghaib*. Some men gathered money from every family, and right in front of the shrine they prepared one big pot of spiced rice, and one of sweet rice. To light the fire for this, they were permitted to use the wood lying around the shrine. Over time, more people arrived, and some went to pray at the shrine. They took care that the whole Qur'an was recited aloud. The women came in separate groups, and also prayed at the shrine. Once the Qur'an had been read completely, the congregation ate the rice right in front of the shrine. The men who had prayed at the shrine, and prepared the food, included not only peasants from the village, but also men working in cities or serving in the army, who were spending some time in their natal home.

People also go to supplicate at this shrine before marriages, to pray that nothing will disrupt the celebrations; and after them, if all went well. During a marriage, when the bridegroom makes his round through the village on a horse, he and the friends who accompany him leave the others behind for a while, and go to pray at the shrine – as they do at the shrine in the centre of the village. So too, when the bride is carried on a litter through the village (Punjabi *doli uthana*), bride and bridegroom go to the shrine together, and the shawl (*dupatta*) of the bride is tied to the bridegroom's turban in front of the grave. This is done only there, not at the village shrine.

Saints and wilderness

It is said that *pir ghaib* in the grove does not want a house to be built for him. I was told that when the people once tried to build a proper tomb with a roof over the grave, it broke down, and he appeared before somebody in a dream and said he did not want a 'closed' shrine for himself. Another name for him which is sometimes evoked is that of *sava jangal wala pir*, 'the green saint of the *jangal*'. The colour green is regarded as holy in Islam, but the association with the *jangal* is made plain here. His shrine is clearly outside the borders of the village, and he came once upon a time from beyond the village and is often thought to have been a *faqir* (beggar or ascetic). He sometimes appears as a lion, and he also takes care that nobody carries away the wood which grows around his shrine. All this points to the shrine's association with the area outside the settlement, the wilderness.

Trees, in particular, and the space around them are regarded in Pakistan as populated with *jinn*s, who are mostly thought to be evil or hostile towards humans. If a human being, particularly a woman, walks below a tree, she is in danger of being possessed by a *jinn*. It is often said that a woman who urinates under a tree, thereby accidently killing the child of a *jinn*, gets possessed by the dead *jinn*'s enraged father. Or a shadow (*saya*) may fall from under trees on her, the notion of a 'shadow' here referring to an evil influence which makes people weak or sick, without the explicit interference of a *jinn* or a similar spiritual being. There are also female *bala* or *churel* who are thought to be ugly and naked, with long loose hair covering their body, feet, and, according to some people, with breasts pointing backwards. They, too, are associated with trees. One woman told me she had once seen a witch sitting at night in the tree inside her courtyard. But mostly they appear in the *jangal*, where they may afflict humans. One man told me that he had once, when hunting, seen a *churel* who had hair down to the floor, and her body was so long that her head was up in the sky. Of another man it is said that he once went out to steal goats, and when he found one at a certain lonely place, and loaded it on his shoulders, its legs grew longer and longer. When they were touching the ground, he threw the goat (which had turned out to be a *bala*) into the pond in front of the village where he had arrived in the meanwhile, and she called after him: 'If you did not have an axe with you, I would have done to you that which you do to goats [namely, slit your throat].' *Bala/churel* are, so I was told, afraid of iron.

These creatures belong to the *jangal*, and their characteristics are clearly anti-cultural: the nakedness, the long, loose hair, the transposition and reversal of body parts, their fear of iron. They also live in trees, which is where they appear even inside the borders of a human settlement. Trees, the characteristic of the *jangal* and the wilderness, generally are places where people are particularly in danger of being afflicted by evil forces. Not only witch-like spirits, but other creatures which attack human beings under trees, are met mostly outside human settlements, in the *jangal*. Trees, therefore, are associated with the opposite of human culture, with the wilderness, and hence with danger.

And they are associated with many shrines. The grove outside Rajpur is left growing only because it belongs to the shrine which is inside it, and the people usually emphasize the fact that no wood should be taken from there. The same is true at other shrines, like the one near a *dhog* of Rajpur. There the shrine itself has the form of an open platform which lies within a large, walled compound about fifteen by thirty metres long in which many trees grow. The real name and life of that *pir* too are not known; he is known as *pir Geru*. The following tale is told about him: once somebody cut the branches of the trees of the *faqir* (as he is also often called), and a servant asked him: 'What sort of *faqir* are you, if you allow people to do such things?' The *pir* answered: 'Just wait a little.' That night the man who had cut the branches had an arrow shot into his heart, and he died.

In the vicinity, well hidden inside a watered tree plantation, another shrine is to be found, a low wall marking a compound of approximately four by four metres, in which the small grave of a child can be seen. Nothing is known about this child, often referred to as a *masum badshah* (lit. 'innocent king/prince', a common term for child saints), besides the fact that it is thought to have been the grandson of the *pir Geru* in the larger grave.

Other places near the same hamlet, designated by the people as shrines, are only marked by trees without any further signs, and in the area there are further shrines near villages with small groves around them. In the majority of the shrines there is at least one big, old tree growing in the compound of a shrine. There is a rugged old tree at the green tomb inside Rajpur, but its association with the shrine is not clear. Just beside the small shrine of the mendicant woman, however, are two small but relatively ancient trees belonging to the shrine. Thus, there is an association between trees and shrines, and most of all shrines which lie outside the borders of villages, and which do not have a mausoleum with a roof. These shrines seem to have a clear association with the wilderness. The light which people in Rajpur report to have seen on Thursdays moving between different shrines in the area connects such shrines which lie outside villages, within groves. In this symbolic interconnection, the shrines map a sacred geography.

Another aspect, which should at least be mentioned, is the association of shrines with springs or wells if located outside village borders. Those too are places where humans are likely to notice *jinn*s or to be molested by them, and one Rajpur story tells of a *musalli* (low service caste with ceremonial duties at marriage) who came back from a marriage where he had acted as a drummer, carrying his instrument. He was taken by *jinn*s by the village spring where people draw water for their own marriage, and where he used to play his drum, and was only later released. A locally well-known spring near Kallar Kahar is also associated with a shrine: the spring of Baba Farid. This famous saint (see Eaton 1984) is reputed to have met village girls who were carrying water near the lake of Kallar Kahar. When he asked for a drink, to quench his thirst, they teased him and said: 'The water is bitter.' Three times he repeated his request, with the same answer, at which point he turned the lake's sweet waters bitter (its waters are salty). Then he disappeared into the mountain above, to a lonely place whence nowadays his spring emerges, flowing with sweet water containing healing powers. He is said to have vanished into a cave near the top of the mountain, above the spring, where there is also a small shrine, accessible only after some half-hour's climb. Other shrines too are associated with springs, like that of *pir Kara* at the foot of the salt range. This saint, whose shrine is managed by his living relatives, is thought to have miraculously produced the spring by beating on the ground with his staff when he arrived in the area. This spring also flows with sweet water, whereas the streamlets nearby are all salty.

These shrines all have the power of healing, often of physical pain, and of bringing fertility to barren women. The real names of the saints are usually not known, and only one or two episodes, if any, are told about their lives. But they are regularly visited by local people, and their graves are nearly always decorated with beautifully adorned shawls. It may be concluded, then, that their connection with the wilderness, as opposed to the dwelling places of humans, is in itself significant for their position. The connection of shrines with wilderness here does not seem to be unique. Many of South Asia's shrines, large or small, seem to rely at least in one of their dimensions on the same symbolism (see for example Werbner 1996). They are, or were originally, built outside settlements, in areas conceived as *jangal*. Trees are a prominent symbol marking such areas, but not an exclusive one, since the word *jangal* in both Punjabi as and Urdu refers to uncultivated places in general, as explained earlier.

Liminality embodied

Large shrines are connected with the names of their saints, and with their individual biographies. In the case of the village shrines described here, by contrast, the stories of their *pir*s carry no individuating features, and, in particular, give no clear moral reasons as to why the figures in question should be venerated as saints – with the exception of the *pir* of the green tomb at Rajpur, of course, to whom we shall return shortly. The mythic narratives about the saints of the small, open shrines describe stereotypical supernatural events which show the power of the *pir*. In the case of *pir ghaib* the narrative uses the culturally important theme of honour and shame, and points out also in another way the marginality of the saint: he is bald-headed, and has a one-eyed bride. Unknown saints typically come from outside the village and are mendicants, and/or otherwise people outside the normal order. Another story which I was told by a young man from Faizlabad illustrates this: for three years he had seen on his way to school a young man sitting by the roadside. What he ate appeared to other people to be white worms, but for him it was rice. One day seven men kidnapped a good and honest girl who was alone at home. When they passed by the young man, the girl cried for help. He just waved his hand, and the seven fell unconscious. After the girl had gone home, her brothers came, prostrated themselves in front of him, and touched his feet. He disappeared on the spot, and just there his family erected a shrine for him.

Beyond the moral dimensions of the young man's act, the story is concerned with his strange behaviour, which seems to show him positioned outside and beyond society. It is that externality which enables him to perform a miracle, and his final disappearance qualifies him to become a saint. His story, however, also reports an individual, moral act, and thus refers to a hagiographic tradition of individual saints, belonging to various Sufi orders, who wander through the wilderness, acting against conventions. Such narratives represent the mystical dimensions of Islam as existing outside the social order. The same pattern is also evident in the symbolism of the village shrines. But these no longer focus on the historical dimensions of mystical philosophy in relation to the personal achievements of individual saints. The centre of gravity has shifted from the unique character of persons to what is *shared* by them, symbolized by their graves – although even this material feature may highlight conspicuous absence rather than presence: in a village in another district of the Potwar I found a shrine which was, I was told, only a *baithak* of a *pir*, which means a place where he used to sit, without a grave. It was not known where this *pir* had come from, his name or the time he lived in. But it was said that he did not have a grave because he disappeared alive after sitting at his place for a long time without motion, talking to *jinn*s. Here the *disappearance* of the saint has become a central aspect, emphasizing his continual presence: we must remember that all the shrines are thought of as places where the saint's power continues to work. And although this shrine was inside the village, the theme of coming from the outside here corresponds with the saint's disappearance.[9]

The association with wilderness and the outside points to a mythological reversal: shrines belong to a liminal space and are thus imbued with a sacred liminality. A typical feature of large shrines is the gatherings of pilgrims in amity and communitas, to use Turner's expression (see Turner 1974). This is surely not absent from the village shrines, but the dominant feature of boundary shrines fits more precisely the term 'liminality': they mark the threshold with the wilderness beyond the village.

Wilderness in South Asia has always been both the abode of the gods, and, as elsewhere, the place of danger and power. Their liminal positioning enables shrines to act as markers and mediators of opposed cultural categories: they define the place of humans in opposition to a sacred space prior to it. 'Wilderness' refers not simply to 'nature' in the Western sense; it is the realm of danger, where humans may be caught by *jinn*s or *churel*s, but it is also the realm of saints who sustain, nurture and protect the villages. The people of the villages are dependent on the shrines outside, and go there to state their fears, whether personal or communal – like the danger of drought. Women – and men – supplicate for the wellbeing of relatives or for children.

The regular worshipping of *pir ghaib* thus ensures the continuity of the village community. The saint also communicates with his people: apart from appearing as a lion or even as a living man, he appears to people in dreams to tell them his wishes, or, for example, that his grave is not well cared for. His 'people' is the village community of Rajpur; only those who have a home there turn to him, including those, of which there are many, who live and work in cities, but keep up the links with their kin and the village, and may return there after their retirement. Thus I once met an elderly man who hailed from Rajpur, but lived and worked in Rawalpindi (he repaired television and video recorders), and had come to Rajpur to marry his son there. He told me of his *pir* who belonged to the order of the Naqshbandiyya, of the exercises of *zikr* (meditation) he had learned from him, and of the bond between his *pir*'s and his own soul, which made him feel his *pir*'s wishes. Other *pir*s also demanded his attention and devotion in this way from their graves, and in Rajpur it was *pir ghaib* who addressed him and demanded *zikr* when the man passed by.

The picture invoked by this man, who belonged to an urban, lower middle class of smaller shop owners and businessmen and was a devoted follower of his *pir*, was of a multitude of *pir*s graded at different spiritual levels, with the Prophet at the top, but each being relevant in his own context in which he could be evoked. In this picture, which I found quite common among followers (*murid*s) of *pir*s in Pakistan, the shrine of *pir ghaib* is given its own, locally confined significance within a wider network. He is addressed solely by the people of Rajpur, but other villagers in the area have similar shrines to which only they turn. Yet there is a connection, we saw, drawn between these villages when a light is seen moving on Thursday evenings from shrine to shrine. Through the shrines a sacred topography linking small village communities within an area, across the dangerous spaces between villages, is revealed.

The green tomb inside Rajpur is not, of course, associated with wilderness as such. It is younger than the shrine in the grove; it was erected within living memory. It might therefore be seen as a modern development which came into existence under the influence of cities. But this would in any case be no more than half of the truth. The *Sayyid* caste, which is held to be the caste of *pir*s, has served a traditional role within the population of the area for generations. In one of the neighbouring villages *Sayyid*s (of another subcaste) constitute the dominant caste, and in another neighbouring village – inhabited mainly by *Awan* (a landowning caste) – a tomb was built for a father's brother's son of the *pir* of Rajpur. The *Bahadur* of Rajpur, who call themselves 'Rajput', being addressed by other castes with the honorary title 'Raja', and who claim to be of very high caste, told me unambiguously that one generation ago they would sit on the floor in the presence of a *Sayyid*, letting him alone sit on a *charpai* (a South Asian bed).

It may well be that the reason given for the *pir*'s move to the village, in response to the wishes of the people of Rajpur, is an invented myth which emerged later, but it marks a long-established, realistic and pervasive desire in the area for a guardian saint. The arrival of a *pir* surely helped to enhance the status of the village and met a religious demand. And even if his shrine lies inside the village and he is not associated with the wilderness as such, his personality is construed as expressing a sacred liminality: he has come from outside, having been localized, according to some accounts, by marriage to a woman from the local *biradari*, but he never asked for any payment for his services. Everything was given to him with the people's free will. He did not care for material possessions, and his character was described as *mast*: an out-of-this-world state of mind, hinting at madness and religious frenzy (on *mast* see also Basu, Frembgen and Ewing in this volume). It is reported that he twice sat for two months at the place where his shrine now is, and read the Qur'an and *namaz* (the daily prayers) day and night. It was said that he had drawn a circle around himself, and outside the *jinn*s and *bhut*s (evil spirits or demons) were sitting and speaking, but he gave them no answer. These acts attributed to him are more famous in the village than his power of healing the bubonic plague, a tale which was told to me only by the blind *hafiz*, and they point out his liminality *vis-à-vis* the realm of *jinn*s.

Here too we find, therefore, factors of localization as acts in the life of the *pir*. The emphasis, more than in the other cases, is on the *pir* as a unique individual, but it nevertheless identifies him with a key social category – his caste – and a liminal existence, which is again the main feature of the small shrine of the mendicant woman in Rajpur, despite this shrine's location within the village limits. Both shrines, however, figure far less importantly in the attention of the villagers than the shrine of the *pir ghaib* in the grove. That shrine is probably the oldest one in Rajpur, but its importance may also be due to the fact that it most convincingly embodies a cultural paradox.

Conclusion: the liminal ethics of marginal shrines

There are at least two principal ways to approach a phenomenon like Sufism and Islamic shrines: first, it may be described as a historical phenomenon, as a history of people and ideas.[10] But one may also try to work out the distinct quality of symbols and institutions, and the features associated with their development. These two approaches need not be contradictory, but one may prove more powerfully explanatory in certain contexts.

The small shrines at the village of Rajpur cannot be understood if analyzed historically. They are stripped of almost all specific, differentiating attributes apart from their spatial location and putative *Sayyid* connections. Their veneration hardly invokes individual ideas or personal strategies for the accumulation of power or prestige. In this respect they are different from the famous, large shrines of Pakistan, the life of whose devotees, particularly the most devoted *murid*s, may be considerably influenced by the authority of their *pir*. Nothing of this holds true for the small shrines, yet they are symbolic complexes which seem to be immensely important for local people. The small shrines as well as the large ones provide points of orientation. Both draw meaning from their liminal placement, and serve to sacralize and domesticate space: they not only transform the map of South Asia into an Islamic domain, but also localize and concretize sacredness in a way which has already been hinted at; they link the Islamic macrocosm to a local microcosm.[11] As in the Sinai desert, where saintly shrines are widespread according to Emanuel Marx, their significance also derives from their connections with social groups (tribes) and areas, and their liminal sitings (Marx 1977: 46–48).

We must not forget also that the village shrines analysed here are only one part of the much larger complex of saints' cults in Islam and in Pakistan, and that they exist alongside a multitude of small Hindu shrines and temples. The anonymous *pir* shrines in the villages usually present aspects of the wider complex in a condensed form, and one topic which has been shown to be repeatedly stressed in narratives about the shrines is that of sacred liminality, expressed in the figure of the stranger appearing from the wilderness, who is yet a focus of communal life. The position of the saints is thus emphasized as belonging to the outside as well as being relevant for the inside: saints give the spaces between the villages a moral dimension and, by appearing as strangers appealing for hospitality, define ethical relations between villages and regions.[12] Thus, we find that even the small village shrines play a similar role to that of the larger shrines ruled by named, living *pir*s. By constituting centres of pilgrimage and drawing their following from different areas and social contexts, those larger shrines break up the confinements, separations and divisions of Pakistani society, whereas the small shrines, constituted only by an unnamed *pir*'s grave, apart from being associated with localities, also define relations between them – as embodied by the light seen moving in the night between shrines of different localities.

We have seen, however, that the 'outside' – that which is beyond the boundary, signified by symbols of the wilderness, by trees, and by springs – is ambivalent: it also stands for malevolent beings which afflict humans who come into contact with them. Perhaps it is not too far-fetched to suggest that these 'abstract' saints and the malevolent beings afflicting human beings are construed along parallel lines.[13] In Pakistan saints are often seen as liminal, dangerous and unpredictable figures. It is perhaps this ambivalence that the shrines on the margins embody. At the same time, as Basu also shows (this volume), it is only saints with their special powers who are able to control the dangers of the *jangal* for the sake of human sociality.

Notes

1. The names 'Rajpur' and '*bahadur*' are pseudonyms.
2. In this chapter I shall use the ethnographic present.
3. I will not go into details concerning the succession of authority at shrines, which is an important topic in its own right, about which I am preparing a paper, but see Eaton (1984).
4. Islam in Pakistan is, of course, part of a broader South Asian pattern.
5. Lindholm (1986: 72) shows, however, that the relation between caste ideology and Islam is difficult to determine, that it may be at least partly one of opposition and negation, and that endogamous groups with different status are common in the Islamic world (ibid.: 65).
6. A *hafiz* is a man who knows the whole Qur'an by heart.
7. The term in Urdu and Punjabi refers not only to forest, but also to wilderness.
8. That is the description of the epidemic given to me, which seems to fit the bubonic plague.

9 I could not find in this case expressive allusions to Khidr, who is often called Zinda *pir* in Punjab, because he also is thought to have disappeared alive (see Schimmel 1975: 202).
10 Barth (1987) rightfully presses the point that this approach has been neglected in symbolic anthropology. He is not even concerned with an area with a discernible historical record, but maintains that rituals of initiation in New Guinea can only be understood if the thoughts and ideas of the men in charge of them are taken into account.
11 In Pakistan many of the most famous shrines tell of the original Islamization of the country, and some of the smaller ones also echo this theme, like the shrine of Kallar Kahar, which tells of Muslim Sufis killed by Hindus (see Schimmel 1980: 97).
12 This interpretation was suggested to me by Pnina Werbner; Marx (1977) also suggests that the saints of south Sinai link the rights of outsiders to those owning the region the saint is associated with.
13 Such a view, although surely not shared by the people of Pakistan, is not without parallels: Dinzelbacher (1995) shows that Christian saints in the late Middle Ages and early modern times, particularly charismatic women, articulated themselves with a systematically ambivalent pattern of signs, which were basically the same as those looked for in witches (like ecstasy or possession, miracles or magic, bride of Christ or mistress of the devil, and so on). Saints were often accused of being witches, a tendency which became stronger with the beginnings of the witch hunt in the sixteenth century. Dinzelbacher describes convincingly how similar in fact were the symbols which construed the sacred communitas of the saints, and the dangerous liminality of the witches.

References

Barth, Fredrik (1987) *Cosmologies in the Making: A Generative Approach to Cultural Variation in Inner New Guinea*, Cambridge: Cambridge University Press.

Denny, Frederick M. (1988) 'Prophet and Wali: Sainthood in Islam', in Richard Kieckhefer and George D. Bond (eds) *Sainthood: Its Manifestations in World Religions*, Berkeley: University of California Press.

Dinzelbacher, Peter (1995) *Heilige oder Hexen? Schicksale auffälliger Frauen in Mittelalter und Frühneuzeit*, Zürich: Artemis and Winkler.

Eaton, Richard M. (1984) 'The Political and Religious Authority of the Shrine of Baba Farid', in Barbara Daly Metcalf (ed.) *Moral Conduct and Authority: The Place of Adab in South Asian Islam*, Berkeley: University of California Press, pp. 333–356.

Eliade, Mircea (1986) *Kosmos und Geschichte: der Mythos der ewigen Wiederkehr*, Frankfurt am Main: Suhrkamp (French original: *Le mythe de l'éternel retour: Archétypes et répétition*, Paris: Editions Gallimard, 1949).

Lindholm, Charles (1986) 'Caste in Islam and the Problem of Deviant Systems: A Critique of Recent Theory', *Contributions to Indian Sociology* n.s. 20: 61–73.

Marx, Emanuel (1977) 'Communal and Individual Pilgrimage: The Region of Saints' Tombs in South Sinai', in Richard P. Werbner (ed.) *Regional Cults*, London: Academic Press.

Peters, F.E. (1982) *Children of Abraham*, Princeton NJ: Princeton University Press.

Schimmel, Annemarie (1975) *Mystical Dimensions of Islam*, Chapel Hill: University of North Carolina Press.

Schimmel, Annemarie (1980) *Islam in the Indian Subcontinent*, Leiden and Cologne: E.J. Brill.

Turner, Victor (1974) *Dramas, Fields, and Metaphors: Symbolic Action in Human Society*, Ithaca NY: Cornell University Press.

Werbner, Pnina (1996) 'Stamping the Earth with the Name of Allah: Zikr and the Sacralizing of Space among British Muslims', *Cultural Anthropology* 11, 3: 309–338.

Part 3

THE PERFORMANCE OF EMOTION

5

LANGAR

Pilgrimage, sacred exchange and perpetual sacrifice in a Sufi saint's lodge

Pnina Werbner

Introduction: pilgrimage and sacred exchange

An important feature of pilgrimages, it has been argued, is that the symbolic transformations pilgrims undergo effect a sacred exchange between two symbolic worlds, and mediate the contradictions between those worlds (see R. Werbner 1989: 261–262, 296). During pilgrimage, pilgrims shed their mundane persona, often through metonymic giving to the poor or at a sacred site, while they return bearing symbolic substances imbued with the sacred power of the ritual centre. Hence, for example, Huichal Indians in Mexico go on annual pilgrimage to their sacred centre of Wirikuta in order to return reborn and bearing with them the peyote needed to revitalise their world (Meyerhoff 1974). In the Kalanga cult of the high god of Mwali, the 'hot' ash of the old year is rubbed on the back of a female klipspringer buck, which is released into the mountains where the rain washes off the ash, bringing coolness. Paralleling this act, Kalanga adepts of the cult bring back from the oracle centre the dust they roll in when 'tied' in possession by Mwali. The dust is only washed off when they reach their natal homesteads, bringing coolness, fertility and prosperity to the earth (Werbner 1989).

A focus on sacred exchange in pilgrimage reveals the limitations of theories which stress merely the experiential dimensions of pilgrimage. Of these theories, that of Victor Turner on pilgrimage as 'anti-structure' and 'communitas' powerfully captures an important dimension of the pilgrimage experience, while glossing over the fact that pilgrimage is a highly structured process of metonymic (and not just metaphoric) transformation. The view proposed here is that pilgrimage is both 'anti-structure' and 'counter-structure'. The counter-structural features of pilgrimage refer to the fact that pilgrims expect to undergo not only a spiritual renewal but a renewal of personhood through contact with the sacred, and a renewal of community through the bearing of what has been in contact with the sacred centre home into the structured, mundane world. These transformations of personhood and home often require a highly structured and elaborate series of symbolic acts. Some of these acts may be in the form of transactions with ritually designated persons. Hence in Benares, as Parry (1994) has shown, pilgrims must unload their 'sins' in the form of gifts to brahmins before they can purify themselves.

This type of interested exchange leads Eade and Sallnow to describe metonymic exchanges effected at pilgrimage centres as 'self-interested exchanges between human beings and the divine' (1991: 24). 'This market ideology', they argue, 'embraces both the miracle and the sacrificial discourses' (ibid.). Although, they recognise, 'lay helpers are enjoined to set an example in self-sacrifice to other pilgrims by giving freely of their time and labour [in the spirit of the "pure" gift] ... For a strongly salvatory religion ... it is questionable whether the notion of purely disinterested giving can be anything other than a fiction' (ibid.: 25). Hence, Eade and Sallnow refer to this type of sacred exchange frequently associated with pilgrimage as 'sacred commerce' (ibid.).

In the spirit of this interpretation, studies of Islamic pilgrimage have repeatedly stressed the intercessionary role of the saint who mediates between supplicants and God. Pilgrims make offerings at a saint's tomb in the name of the saint in order to return imbued with the saint's charisma or *baraka*, containing the curative powers and blessing they desire. This type of sacred exchange seems on the surface to be relatively simple, and has been explained as modelled upon supplicants' everyday experiences of secular power as being based on patronage (Eickelman 1976).

Sacrifice more generally has also often been conceived of in relatively simple terms as a sacred exchange between humans and god with the victim acting as mediator (Hubert and Mauss 1964). Recent research has, however, begun to explore the extreme complexity of the symbolic transformations involved in animal sacrifice as analysed in particular cultural settings (see de Heusch 1985; R. Werbner 1989: Ch. 3; also Werbner 1990: Ch. 5).

But reduction of processes of sacred exchange in pilgrimage to mere interested reciprocity, however disguised, obscures the highly structured and complex set of symbolic operations which bring about the desired transformation, both in the moral persona of a pilgrim and in his or her acquisition of the desired sacred substances to be taken back on the journey home. Within this process, animal sacrifice is a key moment which has to be set in relation to other symbolic acts.

The present chapter argues that the *langar* (the communal distribution of food at a religious lodge or celebration) at a Sufi saint's lodge may be regarded as a form of perpetual sacrifice which is a key symbolic moment of metonymic exchange during pilgrimage to the lodge. As such, it structures both the routine organisation of the lodge and the wider organisation of the Sufi regional cult focused upon it. In its generative organising capacity, it also structures gender relations and makes women integral to the process whereby God's blessing is objectified at the lodge.

My interpretation of the acts of sacrificial service, and the act of sharing in a sacrificial meal at the lodge, stresses the need to unmask a self-interested discourse in order to reveal the central experience of altruism and humanism which energises Sufism. My argument thus reverses a common sociological tendency to seek material interests beneath the surface of apparent altruism. In Sufism, a discourse of market relations and patronage is used by supplicants to 'explain' their relation to the saint, alive or dead. Given an occidental tendency to seek self-interested motives behind apparently altruistic facades, this Sufi allegory of interested exchange may easily be accepted at face value, as a 'true' explanation of supplicants' motives. Similarly, the occasional unmasking of individual saints as exploitative charlatans or sexually promiscuous seducers of innocent female supplicants, is seen as proof of the manipulative nature of Sufism.

To comprehend fully the Sufi *langar*, however, it needs to be understood in the context of other forms of Islamic sacrifice, on the one hand, and in relation to the other sacred exchanges accompanying it – of voluntary service, ritual substances, social identification and powerful blessing – on the other.

For Muslims the *hajj* enjoined pilgrimage to Mecca is the ultimate pretext for all sacred exchanges during pilgrimage. My research on the *hajj* was conducted in Manchester through discussions with returning *hajji*s, who, in telling me of their journey in minute detail, relived the experience of the *hajj* while reflecting, at my request, on its significance.

Seen as sacred journeys, the counter-structure of the *hajj* and *umra* (see below) rituals achieves the desired symbolic transformation in the person of the pilgrim through a series of significant alternations and reversals in time. Starting from Mina on the eighth day of the month of *hajj*, the pilgrims are moved back in time on the ninth day at the valley of Arafat, which is both the beginning and end of time (the birthplace of Adam and the site of the final Day of Judgement). The sacrifice of the *eid*, commemorating the binding of Ismail, is followed on the tenth day by the encounter with the devils which lead to the binding of Ismail. This reversal of the original time sequence of the sacred Qur'anic (and Biblical) narratives is not accidental, in my view, but part of the process through which the pilgrim gradually sheds her or his sins and becomes as pure and innocent (*masum*) as a newborn infant. The pilgrim starts this symbolic journey dressed in two white sheets, likened to the shrouds of the dead; that is, at the end of life. After the sacrifice commemorating the binding of Ismail his or her head is shaved or clipped and he or she is reborn as a new person.

The *hajj* ritual is highly elaborate. From the valley of Arafat, where the pilgrims spend a day in the baking sun, they move to the valley of Muzdaliffah, where they spend the night and where they collect forty-nine tiny pebbles. Returning to Mina for the second time on the tenth day, the day of *hajj*, they cast one lot of seven pebbles onto a single pillar, that of Aqaba. They then perform the *qurbáni* sacrifice of the Eid and eat of the meat. Finally, they shave their heads or clip their hair (in the case of women). Once they have completed the sacrificial meal, they can put on their normal clothes and all taboos are lifted, except the prohibition on sexual intercourse.

On the eleventh day of the *hajj*, following the sacrifice, the pilgrims move to Mecca to perform the Meccan ritual. This ritual, also performed on its own throughout the year and known then as *umra*, highlights the time reversal of the narrative even more clearly. The movement during *umra* is from *tawaf*, the circumbulation of the house of God which is believed to have been rebuilt by Ibrahim (Abraham) and Ismail *after* their reunification. In the second phase, the pilgrim moves to the sacred spring, the *zamzam*, which Hajara (Hagar) discovered had sprung from the heel of Ismail as he lay wailing in the sand; here the pilgrim washes and drink the water. The final stage of the *umra* is *sai*, the running back and forth between the two hills of Saf and Marwa, which recalls Hajara's agonised running in search of water for her baby boy. The movement is thus backwards from death towards purity like that of a baby.

Having completed the Meccan episode, the pilgrims then return to Mina once more for a final stoning – this time of all three devils. Altogether in these post-Meccan stonings, the pilgrims cast forty-two pebbles, fourteen at each of the pillars (seven times three, on each of two days). The pilgrims start from the pillar farthest from Mecca and end with the Aqaba pillar, which is the nearest. In the original narrative, Ibraham (some say Ismail) encountered these three devils *before* the binding of Ismail. During *hajj* and *umra* the multiple stonings of the devils (except for the first stoning) occur *after* the sacrifice, reversing the original narrative. Finally, the pilgrims return to Mecca for another re-enactment of the Meccan ritual.

The *hajj* is thus a moral allegory which can only be understood in relation to its sacred pretext. The sequence of acts, moreover, brings about a series of identifications with exemplary persons. The key identifications elicited are two: with Ibraham and the ordeal he faced in having to sacrifice his son, and with Hajara, his wife, and the ordeal she faced in wandering with her son in the desert, with no water to quench his thirst. The mythic narratives of these two exemplary persons are structurally identical. In both, a parent is asked to sacrifice his or her child for the sake of God without losing faith in God. In both, God intervenes miraculously at the final moment to save the child from certain death. The pilgrims enact this dual ordeal during the *hajj* and *umra*.

Islamic traditions stress the voluntarism of these ordeals: Ismail knew in advance, pilgrims told me, that God had ordered Ibrahim to sacrifice him and told his father to obey God's command. Hajara too accepted the edict of God. Hence one pilgrim explained:

> Mina is where Ibrahim sacrificed Ismail. The pillars are the places where the devil tried to stop him. The first devil was small, the second medium and the third large. Ismail said to Ibrahim: 'Tie my legs and put my face away [from you] so that the affection [you feel for me] won't stop you [from fulfilling God's will].'

She explained about Ibrahim's ordeals that 'Whomever Allah likes most he tests more than others.' Hence Hajara was sent into the desert in order that water be found and the Kaaba, the shrine housing the sacred black stone in Mecca, rebuilt.

The identification with a woman is significant. Hence, a woman pilgrim who had just returned from *hajj* explained to me that the story of Ismail and Hajara was very important to her as a woman. When she was there and performing *sai*, she said, she reflected on what an effort Hajara as a mother had made for her son. Just as all the pilgrims, both male and female, identify with Ibrahim, a male, so too they all identify with Hajara, a female.

The Meccan pilgrimage creates other key identifications. Pilgrims invariably explain that they perform the *hajj* in this particular order because this is the way the Prophet performed it; they are merely retracing his footsteps. When they visit Arafat, one pilgrim told me, they stand where Adam stood on Jabal (Mount) Rehemat to ask God for forgiveness:

> In Arafat Adam asked in the name of the *kalimah* for forgiveness, so we go there to ask God's forgiveness for our sins. The *hajj* belongs to the Prophet Ibrahim as does the *eid*. There are two sunnas, Ibrahim's and Mohammad's. It moves from Adam to Ibrahim. The Prophet did the same [when he performed the first *hajj*].

Although the transformation effected in pilgrims is fundamentally a spiritual one, nevertheless pilgrims return from *hajj* bearing with them sacred tokens – bottles of water from the holy spring, the *zamzam*, as well as dates, rosaries and shawls. They sprinkle this water on people back home, spreading the blessings they received (for similar metonymic transfer in Turkey see Delaney 1990: 520).

The making of *qurbáni* sacrifice during the *hajj* is thus a moment in a sequence of structural transformations which effects the movement of pilgrims on *hajj* towards blessed innocence, a state embodied in the sacred water and dates they carry home with them. Sacrifice is a key moment of transition in this process. In saints' lodges and shrines in South Asia, this moment is expanded and magnified to become the central trope of the lodge, binding together the moral ideas of mystical Sufism with the organisational agendas of the lodges as centres of far-flung regional cults.

Sacrifice in Islam as performed during the *hajj* is a moment of ordeal and release, in which a person's faith in God is tested. One of the key features of the *eid* sacrifice on the *hajj* is that both the sacrificial slaughter and the prayers accompanying it are multiplied a thousand times. In explaining the *hajj*, Sharif Ahmad, a distinguished British *'alim*, (religious scholar or official) told his congregation:

> When one person asks blessings alone from his God, he shall get the blessing. But if many people ask for blessing all together, they will get manifold blessings. The bigger the congregation is when they ask for

blessings, the more blessings Allah will give them, and in the whole world there is no gathering of human beings asking for Allah's blessings as large at that of the *hajj*. And this gathering only takes place on the Mount of Rehemat and in Arafat, nowhere else. And on the day of *hajj* millions and millions of people, on the same day and with the same intention, call out to their God. So the blessings of God come running towards them. This state, this atmosphere, and this situation cannot be found on any other day, any other time or any other situation.

The time of *hajj* is the time of blessing. On that day if a person asks for blessing with a true heart, he will get a river of blessings and will be purified. Such a person will feel so pure, as though he was just born from his mother's belly.

What is stressed here is mediation with God not by a single person but by the community of believers, united in their intentionality and all focusing on Allah. While for Sufis the mediation of the Prophet and of saints on the Day of Judgement is a cornerstone of their belief, this mediation is itself mediated by the ability of these saints to mobilise the multitude in a shared ordeal. Like the sacrifice, the day in the valley of Arafat, exposed to the heat of the sun, is regarded as a test of faith.

To develop this point in relation to sacrifice at saints' lodges in India and Pakistan, let me begin by describing the annual sacrifice as a cultural performance held in Ghamkol Sharif, the lodge of Zindapir, in a little valley outside the town of Kohat in north western Pakistan.

Perpetual sacrifice

The annual sacrifice on the *'urs* (commemoration of the saint's death) at Ghamkol Sharif is a major event. In 1990 ninety-five goats, thirteen sheep, and seventeen cattle and buffalo were slaughtered over a three-day period, the equivalent of over 3,000 kg of meat, distributed to some 20,000 or more pilgrims and supplicants. In preparation for this annual feast local high-class *Sayyid* women of wealthy families who claim descent from the Prophet, along with a large number of women from other respected families throughout Pakistan, clean and scrape thousands of clay dishes, hundreds of flat bread baskets, about twenty or thirty giant clay pots and an equivalent number of iron chappati stoves (*loh*). The latter accumulate a layer of rust over the year and need to be scraped and polished in readiness for the thousands of chappatis that are to be baked on them during the major three-day festival. Once cleaned, they have to be reinstalled in the earth and the women – again I must stress their wealthy, high-caste origins – use heavy iron picks to dig up the dry earth in order to install the ovens. Then the women smear the surface around the ovens with mud. The labour of the women is all voluntary, an act of *khidmat*, of public service; or, as the living saint of Ghamkol Sharif, Zindapir, stressed to me repeatedly, it is all done out of *muhabbat*, the love of God. The women explain that they work for *sawab*, merit, and for God's forgiveness, *Allah mu'af kare*.

While the women wash, scrape and polish, the men invest their voluntary labour in piling up vast quantities of wood in preparation for the enormous quantities of food to be cooked.

The occasion of the sacrificial feast is the *'urs*, the commemoration of the death/rebirth of Zindapir's Sufi master, Baba Qasim. Every year on the *'urs*, the valley of the lodge fills with disciples coming in convoys from all over Pakistan. They bear with them tributary gifts for the saint known as *nazrana* and offerings for the *langar*, the sacred food provided freely at the lodge for all supplicants, disciples and pilgrims who visit it. The food is pure, I was told, because it is cooked by men of pure heart who chant *zikr* (the incantation of God's name) as they cook.

The *'urs* is the high point of a continuous flow of food provided at the lodge by the saint all year round. This food may be conceived of as a perpetual sacrifice, one that provides an apparently endless supply of sacrificial meat every day throughout the year.

A key feature here is, first, the need to conceptualise the difference between Islamic ritual slaughter (*halal*) and ritual sacrifice, since nominally in Islam every animal slaughtered is a sacrifice (see contributions in Brisbarre and Gokalp 1993). Ritual sacrifices are, however, set apart from routine Islamic slaughter by additional customs related to particular festive occasions – the *eid*, *'aqiqa* (on the birth of a son) or *sadaqa* (sacrifices of exorcism or expiation) (see Werbner 1990). The second question is: how can one speak of *perpetual* sacrifice, quotidian sacrifice, sacrifice as a routine of daily life?

Plate 5.1 Cooking pots and wood piled high in anticipation of the *'urs* at Ghamkol Sharif

The key difference between routine ritual slaughter (*halal*) and ritual sacrifice, I suggest, is related to an act of conversion. The conversion is from the cash economy to the moral economy, the good faith economy, the gift economy. Unlike ordinary *halal* slaughter, a ritual sacrifice is the slaughter of an animal freely given, removed from the cash nexus of commercial buying and selling. This means that a purchased animal must be transformed through rites of sacralisation before it can be sacrificed or defined as an offering. Among Pakistanis this sacralisation is usually achieved through a communal reading of the whole Qur'an in a cooperative gathering, or through a special specified prayer of dedication – such as the *eid* morning prayer – which takes place before the slaughter of the animal, or the cooking and eating of an offering of vegetarian food known as *tabarruk*.

It is in the light of this that the slaughter of animals at the lodges of Sufi saints in Pakistan can be regarded as perpetual sacrifice. All the animals slaughtered for the *langar* are freely given by pilgrims, disciples and supplicants – none is purchased. Moreover, the sacrifice takes place in a space which has been sacralised by continuous prayer. Zindapir, the saint of Ghamkol Sharif, is said never to sleep but to spend all his time meditating and praying. The lodge itself is a place of *zikr*

Plate 5.2 A pilgrim leads his sacrificial goat for the *langar*

– the remembrance of God, the incantation of God's name. The sound of *zikr* – *Allah hu* or *La'illa il allah hu*, both individually and communally sung – echoes continuously through the valley. The men who slaughter and cook the animals for the *langar* do so as a meritorious, freely given act, an act of selfless service (*khidmat*). All the labour in the lodge is freely given in the name of God. Hence the lodge is a space set apart from the commodity economy, and capitalist logic does not hold there. During the *'urs* the convoys of trucks and buses coming from the different villages, towns, factories, army barracks or workplaces throughout Pakistan and beyond it, including from Britain, where Zindapir's order extends, bear with them not only animals but sacks of flour, bags of rice, large containers of clarified butter (*ghee*) and money donated for the purchase of food for the *langar*. These staples and animals, like the cash and the voluntary labour, are freely given. Perpetual sacrifice and other forms of offering are in this respect identical.

To understand this further we need also to appreciate that Islamic sacrifice in South Asia, as I have argued elsewhere (Werbner 1990: chs 5, 8), is framed by a semiotic of inequality characterising what I call hierarchical gift economies (see Figure 5.1).

The hierarchical nature of South Asian Islamic gift-giving is clearly expressed in the ideas and practices surrounding sacrificial giving. Gifts to God, including animal sacrifices and offerings of food and money, are always unilateral – given without expectation of return. Yet the direction of this gifting is highly significant. Gifts to God are directed either 'downwards', to the poor, in the form of *sadaqa* (alms), or 'upwards', as religious tribute to saints and holy men, whether alive or dead. Alternatively, offerings are made to communal causes such as the building of a mosque or the *langar*.

Saints, regarded as descendants of the Prophet or his close companions, are

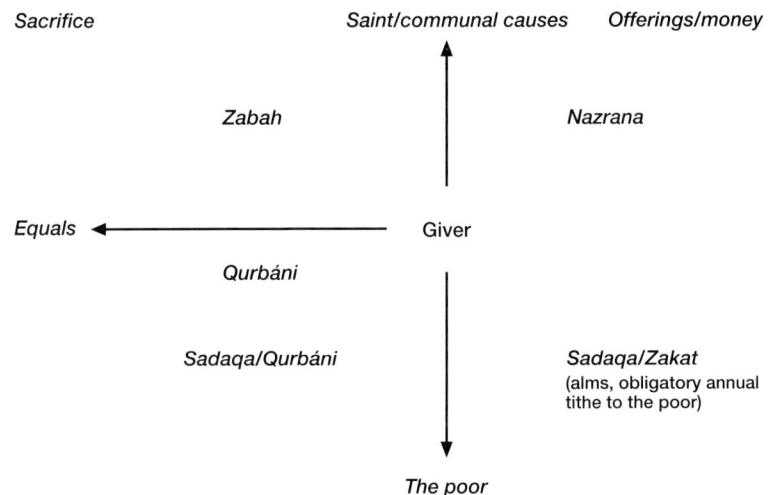

Figure 5.1 The structure of sacrificial giving

almost invariably members of the highest *Sayyid* or *Siddiqi* Muslim castes. Members of these castes, I was told, will not accept *sadaqa* (gifts to the poor), but only *nazrana*, a religious tributary gift of money, valuable objects or food given as a mark of respect or in gratitude for a blessing bestowed. The remains of communal meals held after religious gatherings (usually fruit or cooked food) are distributed as *tabarruk* (blessing, thanksgiving) among the people to be taken home; the food is sacrificial and dedicated and hence it cannot be thrown away. Again, I was told that *Sayyids* are not offered and do not usually accept *tabarruk*.

In accord with this distinction between gifts to God via the poor and gifts to God via a superior religious intercessor (a saint), Pakistani Muslims also distinguish between different forms of animal sacrifice: *sadaqa* is an expiatory gift at the time of extreme danger of a life-threatening kind, in which the victim is given to the poor in its entirety; in *qurbáni*, the *eid* sacrifice, a portion is given to the poor and the rest shared among kin and friends conceived of as equals; and in *zabah*, an animal is given as a tribute at a saint's lodge and is usually shared out as *langar* (see Figures 5.1 and 5.2).

The hierarchical nature of religious giving was made evident to me in Pakistan by Zindapir, the living saint of Ghamkol Sharif. Zindapir described himself as a *faqir* (an ascetic), and he explained: 'A *faqir* is the friend of Allah. Even if he is offered one lakh [100,000] rupees or nothing to eat for Allah's sake, he would choose to go hungry.' The *faqir*, he said, denies himself while giving to others: 'This is the way of a *faqir*. He fasts all day while making sure that everyone else is given food.' Remarkably, the saint gives not just at his own lodge. Hence Zindapir explained: 'I have arrangements to host people wherever I go, all over Pakistan and even all over the world. Wherever I go, whether here [at the lodge] or in Mecca, Allah provides the *langar* and hospitality for my guests.' Here Zindapir is referring to his regional cult, the network of satellite lodges distributed through-

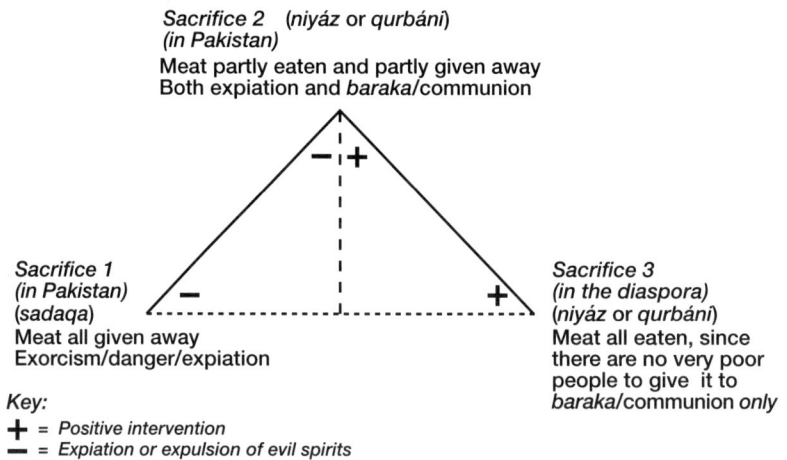

Figure 5.2 Sacrifice and offering in the context of migration

out Pakistan and Britain which provide *langar* for visitors. On the annual *hajj*, Zindapir distributes *langar* in Mecca. This *langar* is organised and funded by his vicegerent in Britain – Sufi Abdullah, a saint in his own right, based in Birmingham, itself the centre of a regional cult with satellite centres in nine British cities. The money for the *hajj langar* is donated by British Pakistanis, while the pots and utensils are kept by disciples of Zindapir living in Mecca who are labour migrants working in Saudi Arabia.

Explaining his remarkable generosity, Zindapir told me: 'I have to be generous because this [the lodge, or Mecca] is not my house. It is the house of Allah. I too am a guest here. It is easy to be generous in someone else's house. If it were my own house, it might be hard for me to part even with a glass of water.' We see in this statement the close identification of the saint with Allah, his proximity to God. But it is also a commentary on the identification between the saint and the community. Commenting on the difference between himself, as a *faqir* and friend of Allah, and the *'ulama*, the learned doctors who are paid officials, he said: 'Allah will undoubtedly take the *'ulama* to Paradise on the Day of Judgement. But Allah gives paradise to his *faqirs* on earth. I can give all the blessings of Allah.'

Zindapir repeatedly reminded me of the enormous crowds his *langar* had just fed during the *'urs* festival and the vast number of gifts of money and cloth he had bestowed on his followers and the needy. The *'urs* is said, somewhat hyperbolically, to draw 300,000 pilgrims to the lodge, all of whom are fed by the saint. By contrast, *'ulama* are mere employees. Zindapir told me: 'Only yesterday I paid a *maulvi* [Islamic scholar] 400 rupees [about £15] for giving a sermon at the mosque'.

The saint, friend of Allah, most elevated and closest to him, asks for nothing except from Allah. He is the infinite giver through whom flows the bounty of Allah to his followers below him. If he takes, it is only as tribute, a mark of respect and gratitude made towards him by his followers. By contrast the *'ulama*, although undoubtedly pious men, are mere receivers, dependent on human generosity, employees of low status and honour.

Mediation with God is thus achieved either by giving to the poor or, indirectly, via a tribute to a saint who, in turn, is expected to use the tribute, if it is a sacrificial animal, for the *langar*; or by giving directly to the *langar*, for the sake of the people (*makhluqat*, the community). In Pakistan, and throughout South Asia, most major Muslim shrines and lodges have *langar* arrangements at festivals and often daily. In Britain, the *langar* is provided for the celebration of the *'urs*, of *eid milad-un nabi* (the commemoration of the Prophet's birth/death), and during monthly rituals at a celebration commemorating the birth/death of Abdul Qadr Gilani, regarded as the founder of all the Sufi orders in India. These monthly rituals are known as *gyarvin sharif*, the eleventh of the month, and are held in most of Zindapir's satellite lodges and mosques throughout his regional cult. In addition, during the month of Ramadan, food and offering are distributed daily at the mosque branches of Zindapir's Sufi order in Manchester and throughout Britain. In all these instances the food is donated and its cooking is voluntary. The slaughter of the animal in Britain is, however, entrusted to the Pakistani butcher, who slaughters it at the abattoir. There appears to be very little sentimental value attached to the act of personal slaughter, and similarly, people do not appear to attach much value to the appearance of the live animal. The choice of the animal, like the slaughter itself, is entrusted to the butcher.

At Ghamkol Sharif, however, animals are donated on the hoof and one of the disciples slaughters them, assisted by several companions. The same disciple acts as chief slaughterer for the lodge on all major festivals. The *langar* at Ghamkol Sharif is open twenty-four hours a day all year to all supplicants and pilgrims, from the very poor to the most elevated and powerful in the land. Zindapir is a well-known saint, and he is regularly visited by top civil servants, army brigadeers and generals, and even politicians. All partake of the *langar*. To partake of the *langar* is to partake of the blessings of the Shaikh, the divine blessing, *faiz*, which endows him with *barkat*, and indeed, the *langar* objectifies this perpetual source of saintly divine spiritual power.

The hierarchical nature of South Asian giving does, however, imbue even the *langar* with some ambiguity. At Zindapir's lodge there are, in effect, two *langars*. One is an open, general *langar*, and the other is run by his son's wife. Many of the most respected guests are fed from this more exclusive *langar*, although chappati bread usually comes from the central *langar*. The *Sayyid* women with whom I spent the *'urs* had brought their own food with them for the festival, and ate almost nothing from the central *langar*, although they denied that this avoidance had any significance, beyond a matter of taste preferences.

The *langar*, conceived of as perpetual sacrifice, is the key organising feature of Sufi lodges in South Asia. Such lodges are centres for the collection and redistribution of food on a vast scale. Virtually all the activity of the lodge is geared to

Plate 5.3 Distributing the *langar* to the pilgrims

this continuous provision of ritually sacred food. Ghamkol Sharif has its herds of cattle, goats and other livestock, its orange groves and fruit orchards, its vegetable gardens, as well as storage rooms for grain, rice and clarified butter, brought by supplicants or purchased with their donations. Gifts of camels and horses, and of strange and beautiful wild birds and animals, as well as of goats, sheep and buffalo are not unusual. Many are dedicated to the *langar* and cannot be used for any other purpose.

The saint himself is a vegetarian who eats no meat and regards himself as the protector of all living creatures. Every morning he feeds the ants with the remains of his sweet morning tea. Killing ants and any other creatures, however minute, is prohibited within the lodge area. This is also true of his conduct during the *hajj*, I was told. A special water trough has been constructed by the saint's son for the wild animals that descend from the hills at night to drink from, while the legends about the Zindapir recount his conquest of the wild. He can cure poisonous snake bites, honey bees are said not to sting, and wild animals do not invade the lodge or attack its inhabitants. The saint is conceived of as the source of natural fertility, and his command over nature is a metaphor for his command over his passionate soul, his *nafs*. He is a source of both infinite nurture and infinite love.

Yet his abstention from meat underlines once again the hierarchical logic informing sacrifice. As a perpetual giver he cannot take. The unilateral nature of gifting would be compromised if he took of what was given him. God is the ultimate source of both food and life, which flow from him downwards into the world of ephemeral creations.

Sacrifice is a tribute to God just as *nazrana* is a tribute to the saint. The offerings or tributes are meritorious acts of respect, but neither God nor the saint needs the gifts offered them. Need implies a lack and hence imperfection. The saint is an exemplar of the perfect man, *insan kamil*. Just as God needs no sustenance from humans, so too the saint needs sustenance from God alone. The saint gives generously and accepts tribute, which he himself does not consume but redirects to the *langar* – and hence ultimately to the whole community. He fasts all day and is a vegetarian while being the source of meat.

Why do people give to the *langar*? They do so in fulfilment of a vow (*niyat*) or to seek merit (*sawab*), but also as an act of identification with an unbounded Muslim community, the *umma*. By contrast, the giving of *nazrana*, even if the expectation is that the tribute will ultimately be redirected to the *langar*, is much more simply an expression of love and respect for the saint by his disciples, or of gratitude, with the added assumption that God loves those who love God's friends, his *awliya*. Although giving *nazrana* may be construed as meritorious and efficacious, it is not an act of sacrifice, unless we recognise the identification of the saint, as the exemplary person, within the community. Sacrifice is necessarily mediated either by the poor or by the community. It is an act of expiation, and – in the case of *sadaqa* sacrifice – of exorcism of afflicting spirits (see Figure 5.2). The poor are not conceived of as scapegoats: since they need the meat for their sustenance and survival, it is assumed it will do them no harm.

The encounter between the good faith and bad faith political economies

To understand fully, however, why people give the *langar*, or why they devote their time and labour to voluntary work at the lodge, we need to recognise the contrast that they and the *pir* draw between the greed and corruption of the 'world' (*dunya*) and the purity of the lodge as a place of true religion (*din*). The postcolonial reality of contemporary Pakistan is seen by pilgrims as one of mendacious politicians, of greed, selfishness and violence. Even the politicians themselves acknowledge this reality: the celebrations of fifty years of Pakistani independence, which took place in August 1997, were an occasion for political leaders to beat their breasts in public about the endemic corruption and social divisions afflicting the nation. To lead the good life of a Muslim in this world is, people say, virtually impossible. Only *pir*s, *awliya* (friends of God), can therefore guarantee God's forgiveness for their followers on the Day of Judgement.

Hajji Bashir, Zindapir's vicegerent in Manchester and my companion and guide during my 1989 visit to Ghamkol Sharif, told me:

> People believe that on the Day of Judgement they will appear before God as a group and the *pir*s will speak for them and ask God to forgive them, and they will then be forgiven and go to heaven. . . . They know that if they stood alone before God they would definitely not go to heaven.

'Why not?' I asked. 'You are a good man, why should you fear God's judgement?' 'Because this is not an Islamic country and it is very hard to be a good Muslim here.'

Zindapir repeatedly explained that he refused to get involved in elections because, he said, 'God is not elected, and to become a Sufi you don't need to be elected' (that is, a saint is chosen not by the people but by God). He continued:

> Politicians come to me and ask me for my support but I always refuse. Once, a local politician who had cheated in the elections came to me. He wanted to put two of his political opponents in jail. But I said to him: 'Even though you got elected by cheating, now you must do what is good for the people, and you should not put those people who fought against you in jail.' Politicians come to me for *du'a* [prayer, supplication] and I pray for them, but still they have the thoughts of politicians – by coming to me they are making a public demonstration that they respect me, in order to get the people's support.

'Why don't you like them?' I asked. He replied, 'Because they tells lies [*jhut*].'

The corruption of politicians and large zymindars (landowners) is associated also with an unbridled hubris: they believe that their wealth can buy anything, even God's approval. Zindapir is fond of telling stories of politicians who have wanted to supply the *langar* with vast quantities of food or money, and whom he has refused:

> A very great landowner came to see me from Sahiwal district. He offered to provide all the food for the *langar* for three days if I gave him permission to heal by *dam* [healing breath]. I said to him: 'If I let you provide the *langar* for three days I will make you a partner with God which would be *shirk* [polytheism, blasphemy].' Indeed, I refused even to make him my *murid* [disciple].

In another version of this tale, it was the uncle of the Minister of Finance, Mian Muhammad Yasin Khan Watto, who made the offer after Zindapir cured him of an incurable disease. *Pir* Sahab cast *dam* (blew a prayer) on him and said: 'Let him eat from the *langar*'s food and he will be cured.' Once cured, the minister's uncle offered to supply the *langar* for three days but was refused. Zindapir told him: 'You will provide for the *langar* for three days but what will happen after that? I cannot make you a partner (*sharik*) with God.'

The paradigmatic tale which illuminates the place of the lodge as the sole source of God's boundless nurture is contained in the founding myth of Ghamkol Sharif. On their first journey to establish the lodge, Zindapir recalled, he saw one of his companions carrying a sack of flour. He told the man: 'What will you eat when the flour is finished? Throw it away and trust in Allah.' This story, like others, stresses the finitude of men's resources, whatever their wealth or power, set against the infinity of God's capacity to feed the world. Wherever he goes, Zindapir regards himself as dwelling in the house of God. On one occasion he was invited by an important Saudi politician to stay at his home in Jedda, but he replied: 'When I visit the house of God, I am the guest only of Allah.'

On my visit in 1991 I was told confidentially that one of the leading political figures in Pakistan had visited the lodge and had wanted to write Zindapir a cheque for a very large sum of money. The saint refused the donation and instead offered the politician and his entourage food from the *langar* to eat. If it even crosses the mind of a saint to influence politicians, he told me, then he is no longer a *faqir*, a man of God.

The evidence for the superiority of saints over politicians is proven, Zindapir repeatedly asserted, by the honour given to saints' shrines after their death:

> The tombs of kings do not get *izzat* [honour]; only those of *awliya*. The men whom God gives respect to in their lifetimes, in their death their respect grows and grows. Like Data Ganj Baksh in Lahore [the shrine of the eleventh-century Sufi saint Hujweri]. If you go to the Emperor's tomb [Shah Jahangir's] you will find no people there. But at Data Ganj Baksh there are thousands of people all the time.

In similar vein he recalled: 'When the Viceroy of India visited the shrine of Khwaja Ajmeri [one of the great Muslim saints of India] he saw all the people coming there – Hindus, Muslims, Sikhs. After his visit he said: "India is ruled by two governments – the British government and the government of Khwaja [lord, gentleman] Ajmeri, and the second one is the greater power because it rules people's hearts.'

Zindapir stresses that he asks no one his name, *badshah* (king) or *garib* (poor man). All are equal. The Chief Minister of Azad Kashmir visited him several times, but Zindapir told me, he never asked his name. When this was commented upon Zindapir responded: 'I have no need to know anyone's name. I know only the name of Allah' (that is, Zindapir needs no favours from those who come to see him; he is a giver, never a taker).

The polar contrast between the world of everyday greed and corruption and the infinite generosity of the lodge are captured by Zindapir in a series of aphorisms: '*Dunya ki taraf pith kare, ton khuda ki taraf munh hote hey*' ('if you turn your back to the world you will face God') and 'The world and religion [*dunya te din*] are like two sisters. If you marry one, you cannot marry the other.'

In his encounters with politicians, the *shaikh* presents himself as tough and definite. Politicians who aspire to acquire some of his powers must confront the fact that they cannot compete with the divine spiritual power of God's chosen saints. Again and again, it is the *shaikh*'s ability to provide nurture on a daily and annual basis to all who come, from an unending source, which the morality tales stress. It is this which makes it impossible for politicians to compete with him, and which proves that his following is much vaster than that of any politician. This world of generosity and giving as constructed by the saint is the one pilgrims enter into when they arrive at the lodge, bearing their gifts for the saint and the *langar*, in what may be conceived of as an imaginative as much as a real journey.

Yet just as he denies the importance of the visits and honours granted him by state officials and politicians, so too, paradoxically, do the visits prove that Zindapir is indeed a great and spiritually powerful friend (*wali*) of Allah. And despite the constructed ideological opposition between the lodge and the world, the growth and success of the lodge have profited from official goodwill. Land, telephone lines, water, roads and transport have all been provided free through official channels, and Zindapir takes great care, in reality, not to offend politicians. Moreover, there is a symbolic economy of gifting which pervades pilgrims' and supplicants' relations with the saint.

In exchange for the gifts of money, perfume, flour, animals, rice and clarified butter given to the *pir* as *nazrana*, or donated directly to the *langar*, the saint gives his close disciples white chiffon headscarves, embroidered praying caps and perfumes. These he draws, with the almost magical gesture of a conjurer, out of the treasure house of objects he accumulates in his room, buried in the silk and brocade cushions on which he reclines. He distributes salt and amulets to the supplicants who visit him, along with *du'a* and *dam*. He also donates money generously to the poor and needy who come to him with requests for help. I myself was showered with gifts: several clothing outfits, jewellery, perfume and a handbag from the *shaikh*'s son's family; four large bottles of honey collected from the lodge's beehives; a lovely white, finely woven cotton headscarf of a type usually reserved for disciples; a beautiful length of silk cloth; and a box of sweets (*mithai*), all to take home with me to England, gifts from the *shaikh*. My attempts to reciprocate were of little avail. The gifts embodied the saint's generosity but, even beyond that, they proved his supreme elevation above the anthropologist and, indeed, any educated, non-Muslim Westerner.

Experiencing the good faith economy

We see the limitations of the suggestion put foward by Eade and Sallnow (1991) according to which much of the activity at saints' lodges is a matter of 'sacred commerce'. Such a conception denies, moreover, the experiential dimensions of voluntary labour and sacrifice, particularly in the case of close disciples of the saint. Most of the women who work as volunteers in preparation for the *langar* of the *'urs* say they are seeking merit, but I would argue that the reality of the transformation they experience is both far more immediate and far more complex.

For three weeks before the *'urs* both men and women begin arriving at the lodge to contribute their voluntary labour to the preparations for the festival. Much of the building of the lodge takes place during this period, including the extension of water pipes, sewerage and electricity. New hostels are constructed for pilgrims. The women arrive daily, increasing in numbers as the festival approaches. They come from throughout the Frontier and even from Lahore. But a core of women come from neighbouring Jungel Khel, the birthplace of Zindapir himself. Most of the women are, as I mentioned, from the high-ranking *Sayyid* family, which is the largest, wealthiest and most important in Jungel Khel, now a small town of 20,000 inhabitants. Members of this large family are scattered throughout the world, occupying professional positions as doctors, engineers or pilots. They hold, and held in the past, many of the top administrative positions in the town. They own large houses and the women who run these have servants to assist them. Yet these very women are willing to take on the most menial, dirty, unpleasant tasks, hard, tiring, physical labour, and live in crowded conditions, sleeping on mats on the floor if they come from some distance, in preparation for the sacrificial feast of the *'urs*. During the *'urs* they also help supervise the visits of women supplicants to the saint.

Paralleling the seasonal pilgrimage of organised groups to the lodge on major festivals is a constant daily flow of supplicants seeking healing for their ailments or divine blessings in their jobs, careers and marital fortunes. The healing powers of the saint are grounded in a belief in his ability to see below the surface, to the occult and social causes of illnesses, the thoughts, feelings and accidental transgressions which have brought about pain, chronic illness, infertility, depression, business failures and so forth. As an agent of God, the saint is able to act on these hidden forces and change the course of natural illnesses and social fortunes.

The saint is visited by both male and female supplicants. They sit at some distance from him. Both men and women expose their faces, the women drawing their veils above their heads. The exposure underlines the belief that the saint transcends sexuality. His persona combines male and female qualities – the gentleness, love and tenderness of a woman with the power, authority and honour of a man (see also Kurin 1984).[1] He communicates very briefly with the supplicants, addressing them in short, distant tones. Once they have explained their problem to him, he usually instructs them to perform their daily prayers, sometimes throwing a rolled-up, inscribed paper amulet in their general direction. At other times, he instructs them to collect amulets 'outside'. Once he has heard a whole round of supplicants (he takes in about ten at a time) he raises his hands in prayer (*du'a*). Even in these brief interchanges, however, the symbolic transference appears to be very powerful. One can only speculate that for the supplicants his immense healing power derives precisely from his gendered ambiguity: he combines maternal and paternal qualities: he is a maternal father or a paternal mother, protective yet authoritative.[2]

His relationship to the women preparing for the *'urs* is radically different. Every day during the weeks of preparation for the *'urs*, the saint visits the women at their work. They greet him *'asalam u pir'* ('greetings, saint'). There is no bowing or scraping. He does not allow it. They smile at him, an elderly man limping along slowly since his knees are painful and have been causing him some trouble. It is clear that the women are very fond of the saint.

After work every day the women workers come into the saint's inner sanctum to receive his blessings. During these meetings he prays a *du'a*, (supplication) for them. The meetings are marked by their atmosphere of intimacy. To most women supplicants the saint is a distant, charismatic figure, fearful and awe-inspiring. His face as he distributes amulets, salts and prayers is expressionless, his tone matter-of-fact, verging on abruptness. The vast majority of his male disciples treat him with awe and respect. The saint is a remote figure, revered, feared and respected. His commands are instantly obeyed. Grown men tremble at his anger and sink into despair. He is treated as a king or prince. On their visits to his room women supplicants sit behind a low wooden barrier to prevent them from reaching too close to him.

This remoteness contrasts with his relationship with his close disciples, those who work on the preparations for the *'urs*. The women disciples who assist in the preparations for the sacrificial meal of the *'urs* treat him with the freedom of companions. The *shaikh* (saint, spiritual mentor) clearly enjoys the company of these women, and they entertain him with anecdotes and tales of amusing incidents and gossip, including the ridiculous behaviour of the anthropologist, which he finds particularly amusing. They are an invaluable source of information to him about what goes on beyond the confines of the room in which he meditates. They are also privy to a good deal of information about his family and private life to which others have no access. They say they fear him, but in practice, what they mainly express is their fondness for him. During my visit to the lodge in

LANGAR: PERPETUAL SACRIFICE

1991 Zindapir's son's wife was undergoing an operation on her throat in England. On the day of the operation the women visited the saint. Earlier he had been to pray in the northern guest house for the success of the operation. The women disciples kept trying to comfort him by discussing the details of his son's wife's condition. But he kept sighing and lapsing into long silences, then renewing the conversation. They too would lapse into sympathetic silence. This went on for about forty minutes. As time passed with no news of the operation from England, the whole lodge entered into a state of worried expectation. Eventually, at 9.30 p.m., the telephone message arrived, informing the saint that the operation had been a success.

I tell this story to underline the clear connection between sacrifice and moral amity. If sacrifice in Islam hinges on the existence of inequalities, of a category willing to define themselves as 'poor', it nevertheless also encompasses notions of moral responsibility within a moral community. The *langar* objectifies the moral community embodied by the saint himself as a figure of infinite generosity. This underlines the fact that in Islam voluntary labour, sacrifice, donations, offering and charity merge. All these acts are vehicles mediating the relationship between person and God. In all, moral space is extended, objectified and personified, while the identification between person and community is revitalised.

It is remarkable that in many ways the *langar* at Sufi *dar ul ulooms* (places of learning) in Britain differs rather little in organisation and ideology from the *langar* in Pakistan, except for the fact that, as yet, it is not a perpetual sacrifice. The same discourses and practices characterise both *langars*. The resemblance underlines the transnational nature of Zindapir's order. British branches of the saint's regional cult, like the branches of the cult in Pakistan, provide *langar* for the same major Islamic and Sufi holidays and festivals, just as the branches in both countries send tribute to the *shaikh* himself. The ultimate objectification of this diasporic transnationalism is through the *langar* provided annually by the order on the *hajj*. Members of the cult from Pakistan in the east and from Britain in the west, along with disciples working as labour migrants in the Middle East and Gulf states, meet in Mecca annually for the *hajj*. From the east comes Zindapir, the source of powerful blessing; from the west Sufi Abdullah, his most trusted and highly ranked *khalifa* (vicegerent). It is, however, Sufi Abdullah who provides the sacrificial offering, the *langar* (as against the *eid* sacrifice) which objectifies the saint's *baraka* and his infinite generosity. This ritual international division of labour produces a perpetual sacrifice at the global centre of Islam. What is evident is that the spread of Zindapir's cult has been associated with contemporary global movements of migrant labour from Pakistan to the West.

The global regional cult which has emerged as a result of this international migration process mediates between the universalism of Islam and the particularism of migrants' networks of associations (see Werbner 1989). The focus on a central lodge and its charismatic saint, and on periodic mobilisations – local, national and global – brings together a widespread network of disciples from the various branches of the cult for the purpose of sharing in a sacrificial feast.

On the surface, however, the saint's relation to the majority of supplicants is nevertheless based on a calculus of exchange. If we deploy familiar religious terms such as penance and salvation, we may easily mistake the work of the women and men for what they explicitly say it is – a calculating act of service before God for the purpose of accumulating merit. So too offerings and sacrifices, whether directly to the saint or to the *langar*, can be understood as they are apparently intended: as acts of reciprocity in which a favour is sought from the saint or from God in return for an offering. The saint's gifts to pilgrims – white cotton scarves and white embroidered hats for his disciples, gowns for his khalifa, amulets and salts for supplicants – may all be seen as items in a simple relationship of reciprocal exchange. If, however, as I believe, these ideological statements tell only a very partial truth, then the need is to consider what the sacred exchange effected in the pilgrimage to the *'urs* is. At first glance, there is no elaborate sacred text or metonymic acts in the *'urs* which may be said to parallel and comment upon those of the *hajj*.

Yet the *'urs* too has its pretexts. Hence, a key feature of Ghamkol Sharif is its sacred peripherality (Turner 1974). The lodge was built outside any established settlement, very gradually, over many years, in what was previously an uncultivated valley. The men and women who return annually to work for the *'urs* have participated in this gradual transformation of the lodge. Each year they retrace the footsteps both of the saint and of themselves in prior years as they move beyond the boundaries of their settled communities. Metaphorically, they move back in time by journeying once again to the lodge in order to be renewed. As they work they often recall the early days of the lodge. The women's gossip during the long working hours is in itself a work of making history, reliving the myth of the lodge's establishment.

The same is true for all the pilgrims who visit the lodge annually. The journey to the lodge is a movement back in time in the sense that it repeats an earlier journey. In his final supplication for the sake of the community, the saint recalls his own first arduous journey to the lodge. Indeed, he repeats the story of this legendary journey almost verbatim every year. The assembled crowd wait for this final *du'a*, the request for God's blessing, the peak moment of this three-day ritual festival. Yet as in the *hajj*, the supplication is more than the voice of a single individual: it is the sum of all the silent prayers of the multitude present, even if it is embodied in the trembling tones of the saint. So too the sacrificial feast is perceived to be more than the multiplication of individual acts of sacrifice. It is an achievement of a community that has stepped outside the world. As in the *hajj*, pilgrimage to Ghamkol Sharif is a fleeting act of world renunciation in which the pilgrims identify with their saint. In a sermon delivered in Rochdale on the day of the *hajj*, Ahmad Sharif, a well-known *maulvi*, told his congregation: 'While the real test of faith is faith *in* the world then . . . if someone wants to renounce this world, it is possible for him to do so on *hajj*; a pilgrim, as long as he keeps his *ihram* on [the two sheets the *hajji* wears], is a *faqir* of God.' The food of the *langar* eaten in this extramundane world differs in every respect from the sacrificial *halal* meat normally consumed.

This may be taken to imply that the annual pilgrimage to Ghamkol Sharif is a text (in the Ricoeurian sense) enacting Eliade's myth of eternal return to a point of original creation (Ricoeur 1981: 197–221; Eliade 1954). It may also be taken to be a reiteration of Turner's (1974) view that pilgrims both to the *hajj* and to the *'urs* experience a sense of communitas in which the boundaries between individual and community are obliterated. The *'urs* is a cultural performance which can be analysed from different perspectives (on this see Weingrod 1990). Beyond calculus or communitas, I want to stress a further point: pilgrimage to the *'urs*, and especially the voluntary labour vested in preparation for it, is a text which is both personal and performative: each pilgrim re-enacts his or her own text, her or his annual visit and contribution to the growth of the lodge. Each personal text reflects on all the prior personal texts, as a series of reflexive memorials of positive action. In addition, each personal text also allegorises the shared pretext of the saint's first journey to the lodge, itself an allegory of the texts of the Prophet's migration and return to Mecca, for which Ibrahim's test of faith by sacrifice, and Hajara's ordeal in the desert, searching for water for her infant son, are the ultimate pretexts. Hence also, for example, the text of the *'urs* in Britain echoes that at Ghamkol Sharif while being uniquely British. These acts of identification imbue the sacred exchange at a saint's lodge with moral meaning in the world. The gifts, amulets and blessings, charged with saintly charisma, which are carried back from the pilgrimage have to be understood as tokens of moral renewal, energising this mundane world of the here and now in which pilgrims live their daily lives.

Acknowledgements

This chapter is based on research in Pakistan at the lodge of Zindapir during several weeks in 1989 and 1991, and on research in Manchester among returning pilgrims from *hajj* during 1988–1989. The research was supported by the ESRC, UK, and the Leverhulme Trust, and I am grateful to these foundations for their assistance. The sayings quoted here are from a sermon delivered by Sharif Ahmad at the Blue Mosque in Rochdale on the day of the *hajj* in 1989. The sermon was in Urdu and was translated by his daughter and son, Nyla and Arshad Ahmed. I would like to thank both Arshad and Nyla for their help. I would also like to thank Hajji Bashir Ahmed, who clarified many of the points about sacrifice at a saint's lodge discussed here. An early version of this chapter was given at Nanterre University in Paris in 1991 to a seminar series on Muslim sacrifice organised by Anne-Marie Brisbarre and Altan Gokalp, of the Laboratoire d'Ethnologie et de Sociologie Comparative. I would like to thank the participants at the seminar for their comments.

Notes

1 The belief that this professional distance is abused is widespread, fuelled by tales of the excessive sexual appetite of saints (see Lindholm 1990: 33) and periodic scandals. The power of the cultural ideal of saints as world renouncers is evidenced, however, by the fact the women continue to unveil before the saint. In the case of Zindapir, his reputation was quite immaculate.
2 That healing is achieved through transference is suggested by Kakar (1982:91) and Ewing (1984). Ewing (1993) also suggests a similar view on the saint's qualities.

References

Brisbarre, Anne-Marie and Altan Gokalp (eds) (1993) *Islamic Sacrifice: The Spaces and Occasions of Ritual*, Paris: CNRS.
Delaney, Carol (1990) 'The *Hajj*: Sacred and Secular', *American Ethnologist* 17, 3: 513–530.
Eade, John and Michael J. Sallnow (1991) 'Introduction', in John Eade and Michael J. Sallnow (eds) *Contesting the Sacred: The Anthropology of Christian Pilgrimage*, London: Routlege, pp. 1–29.
Eickelman, Dale (1976) *Moroccan Islam: Tradition and Society in a Pilgrimage Centre*, Austin: University of Texas Press.
Eliade, M. (1954) [1948] *The Myth of Eternal Return*, New York: Bollingen.
Ewing, Katherine (1984) 'The Sufi as Saint, Curer and Exorcist in Northern Pakistan', *Contributions to Asian Studies* XVIII: 106–114.
Ewing, Katherine (1993) 'The Modern Businessman and the Pakistani Saint: The Interpretation of Worlds', in Grace M. Smith and Carl Ernst (eds) *Manifestations of Sainthood in Islam*, Istanbul: Editions Isis, pp. 69–84.
de Heusch, Luc (1985) *Sacrifice in Africa: A Structuralist Approach*. Bloomington: Indiana University Press.
Hubert, Henri and Marcel Mauss (1964) [1898] *Sacrifice*, London: Cohen and West.
Kakar, Sudhir (1982) *Shamans, Mystics and Doctors*, Chicago: University of Chicago Press.
Kurin, Richard (1984) 'Morality, Personhood, and the Exemplary Life: Popular Conceptions of Muslims in Paradise', in Barbara Daly Metcalf (ed.) *Moral Conduct and Authority* Berkeley: University of California Press, pp. 196–220.
Lindholm, Charles (1990) 'Validating Domination among Egalitarian Individuals: Swat, Northern Pakistan and the USA', in Pnina Werbner (ed.) *Person, Myth and Society in South Asian Islam*, special issue of *Social Analysis* 28, University of Adelaide, pp. 26–37.
Meyerhoff, Barbara (1974) *Peyote Hunt: The Sacred Journey of the Huichol Indians*, Ithaca NY: Cornell University Press.
Parry, Jonathan P. (1994) *Death in Banaras*. Cambridge: Cambridge University Press.
Ricoeur, Paul (1981) *Hermeneutics and the Social Sciences*, trans. John B. Thompson. Cambridge: Cambridge University Press.
Turner, Victor (1974) 'Pilgrimages as Social Processes', in Victor Turner *Dramas, Fields, and Metaphors: Symbolic Action in Human Society*, Ithaca NY: Cornell: Cornell University Press.
Weingrod, Alex (1990) *The Saint of Beersheba*, Albany NY: State University of New York Press.
Werbner, Pnina (1990) *The Migration Process: Capital, Gifts and Offerings among British Pakistanis*, Oxford: Berg.
Werbner, Richard (1989) *Ritual Passage, Sacred Journey: The Process and Organization of Religious Movement*, Washington DC: Smithsonian Institution Press.

6

HIERARCHY AND EMOTION

Love, joy and sorrow in a cult of black saints in Gujarat, India

Helene Basu

Introduction: the hierarchy of saints' cults

Sufism is often presented as a realm of Islamic emotional discourse opposed to the cold and 'technical' constructions put forward by theologians and judicial scholars (Schimmel 1975; Rahman 1979). The core of Sufi mysticism consists of divine love conceptualised as inner experiences of growth and realisation in the relationship between individual worshippers and a Saint (cf. Pinto 1989). Such concepts, historically developed by Sufi literati, also shape contemporary cults of saints. Emotional experiences, especially love (*'ishq, muhabbat*), are crucial to Sufi practices (cf. Nanda and Talib 1989; Pinto 1989). It would be misleading, however, to assume that the meanings of these terms always accord with those established by the textual tradition. Nor do they refer exclusively to inner experiences of the self characteristic of Western individualism. Rather, they are constituted situationally in social discourses by eliciting and evaluating social relationships (cf. Abu-Lughod and Lutz 1990; Abu-Lughod 1986; Lutz 1986, 1988). In some cults, as in the one I deal with below, emotional constructs are used to enact hierarchical relationships *against* dominant social and moral evaluations. It is this connection between constructions of emotions and the creation of a counter-hegemonic world view, one that seeks to give asymmetrical ritual exchanges a different meaning, which is the subject of the present chapter.

In Gujarat, Muslim conceptions of social hierarchy are often merged with ideas about the embodied charisma of saints (cf. Gaborieau 1986). Shrine cults revolve around exchanges of ritual services and gifts between unequals, and the rank of different regional cults, co-existing within a single area, may be inferred from the direction of the gifts between cults. The most important cult centres are managed by *Sayyid pir*s who deny taking gifts altogether, but assert their supreme status by displaying generosity and giving. God is perceived as the ultimate source of wealth and *Sayyid pir*s act as mediators through whom the grace of Allah flows downwards (cf. Werbner 1990b and this volume). The poor, on the other hand, appear as paradigmatic recipients of the grace of superiors. In the moral vision animating ritual worship at saints' cults, the poor are elevated as the subjects of specific saintly love because of the purity of their faith. According to Pinto (1989: 124), divine love is a mystery that should be received in the same way a poor person reciprocates, with 'gratefulness, faith and a pure heart'.

Besides those shrine cults that are dominated by high-status *Sayyid*s, credited with inherited charisma originating in the family of the Prophet, there are cults venerating non-*Sayyid* saints who derive their charisma from other sources. The cult I am concerned with here is managed by *faqirs* of black African saints said to be descended from Bilal, an Ethiopian who was the companion of the Prophet Muhammad. In Islamic history, Bilal is famous for his loyalty to the Prophet and recognised as the first to call the faithful to prayer at the mosque. In Gujarat, the cult of black saints, an assembly referred to as *kulpir* (clan saints), is a cult of the poor, managed by a small African diaspora who identify themselves as *Sidi faqirs*. For them, the idea of the 'pure love' that saints in general are said to harbour for the poor is of great importance in constructing a self-image that reconciles ideas of moral and ritual superiority with the acceptance of alms.

When the *Sidi* in Gujarat talk about the cult of Bava Gor, emotional concepts such as love (*muhabbat*), joy (*maja*) and sorrow (*dukh*) are often evoked in association with social relations between supplicants and *Sidi* saints, and between *Sidi* and *Sayyid* saints, both of which are governed by hierarchical exchanges of gifts and services.

Dumont defines the notion of hierarchy in terms of a logic of encompassment by higher of lower levels and their situational reversal of qualities such as purity and pollution (1980, 1986). A similar hierarchical logic is operative in the realm of Muslim shrines, in which the pure saint encompasses the impure temporal order. Against this logic, the *Sidi* operate through a complementary and encompasssing logic of heating and cooling. Hot and cold qualities are understood as embodiments of ethically grounded emotions (cf. Kurin 1982, 1983a, 1983b), and their use by the *Sidi* inverts the hierarchy of purity and pollution by posing an alternative moral order which is also connected to fertility and social reproduction. This is of critical importance when looking at the regional cult hierarchy in Gujarat from the point of view of those who represent the lower pole, in this case the *Sidi*. It highlights the fact that shrine hierarchies are not merely imposed givens but are constantly created and recreated through asymmetrical social interactions. Cosmologically, the hierarchies are articulated by the *Sidi* through the complex of relations said to exist between saints, demons and humans.

In Gujarat, Muslims represent a heterogeneous social ensemble comprising about 10 per cent of the population. Organised in different castes and sects (Sunni and Shi'a), the higher categories correspond principally to the pattern prevalent in north India (where they are called *ashraf*, the 'noble ones'), whereas the middle and lower rungs display regional particularity. As elsewhere, the *Sayyid* are accorded the highest prestige due to their claim of descent from the family of the Holy Prophet through his daughter Fatimah. On the basis of notions of genealogical closeness to the Prophet, the *Sayyid* claim an inherited charisma, in the form of *baraka* (blessings, spiritual power) and *karāmāt* (capacity to perform miracles), that is manifested and routinised in shrines managed by their families. Inheritable charisma ('blood') distinguishes *Sayyid* from all other Muslim castes (Misra 1985). A large section of Muslims in Gujarat belong to one of the many regional trading castes such as *Bohra* (or *Vohra*), *Memmon*, *Khoja* and *Khatri*, settled mostly in town.

The *Sidi* constitute one of several other Muslim servant castes who are also predominantly urban based. They, however, differ from other servant castes due to their African origin. They are descendents of slaves from the shores of East Africa who were sold in western India until the late nineteenth century, often by Muslim traders (cf. Basu 1995). The *Sidi* in Gujarat number around 6,000–7,000, and some live in town working as domestics. Yet, while acknowledging the ritual superiority of the *Sayyid*, the *Sidi* claim a similar though lower-order charisma transmitted by birth from their African saintly ancestors. Most *Sidi* are convinced that a special *bakshish* (gift) has been bestowed upon them by their apical ancestor, Bilal.

Despite systematic attacks by Muslim reformers, ritual worship at saints' shrines remains for many Muslims an expression of true faith. In Gujarat, the hierarchical network connecting shrines is controlled by men. Status differences between shrines and their spiritual representatives are emphasised by a terminology distinguishing *Sayyid* from non-*Sayyid* saints. The *Sidi* address only *Sayyid* saints with the title *pir*, whereas the terms *murshid* or *faqir* denote a holy person from their own *jama'at* (caste) or any other non-*Sayyid* social category (for a variation, see Mayer 1967).

The *Sidi* maintain many small shrines all over Gujarat. In each of their settlements there is at least one shrine housing ancestor saints, but the highest place is accorded the shrine of Bava Gor in South Gujarat (another large shrine, Nagarchi *Pir*, is situated at Saurashtra). The three saints enshrined at Bava Gor – the elder brother, Bava Gor, his sister, Mai Mishra, and his younger brother, Bava Habash – are regarded as the founding ancestors of the *Sidi jama'at*. Bava Gor is the largest shrine maintained by the *Sidi* and the only one that provides a basic livelihood to a few families. Those *Sidi* who perform ritual services on behalf of the ancestor saints are distinguished as *faqirs* – a term which in this context includes women as well, unlike the Malang described by Ewing (1984b). The role of a *faqir* is explained in two ways: as a spontaneous charismatic calling based on a *hukm* (order) received from one of the ancestor saints, or as privileged access to shrine service inherited from a kinsman or kinswoman.

Whereas in the past the shrine seems to have been mainly a centre for *Sidi faqirs*, their families and peasants from the area, during the last thirty years the cult following has expanded considerably. In addition to 'Tribals' (Bhil) and Hindus from surrounding towns and villages, the *dargah* (court or shrine) of Bava Gor is visited by an ever increasing number of Muslims. In the large industrial centres such as Surat, Bharuch, Baroda or Ahmadabad the *dargah* has, since the mid-1980s, been discovered as a major destination of weekly pilgrimages. Followers originate from an urban, lower middle-class milieu, many from the Sunni *Bohra* caste. The clientele includes shopkeepers, small traders, manufacturers, artisans and workers from the industrial cities of mainland Gujarat, all of whom visit the shrine on a regular basis. This trend is also noticeable in the shift in the day of the week attracting the most visitors. Whereas formerly it was Thursdays, the day reserved for the memory of the dead, which drew the largest crowds (*c.*150–200), nowadays Sundays tend to be even busier. Such expansion and shifts in the cult clientele are accompanied, moreover, by changes in its organisational structure.

Legally, the shrine falls under the laws of the religious endowment act, which places it under state control vested in the charity commissioner. Formally managed by a trust consisting of three male members – two *Bohras*, one *Sidi* – control over the shrine and access to its ritual positions have long since been contested amongst different *Sidi* factions. Conflicts over traditional rights at the shrine originated in the seventies, when the charity commissioner's officers charged the customarily installed *mujavir*s (officiating *faqirs*) with misuse of religious donations and subsequently dismissed them from their offices. Many *Sidi* emphasise that until this time the shrine was managed on behalf of the *jama'at* as a whole. Shrine services were carried out by three *faqir* families taking weekly turns. In addition, *Sidi faqirs* fulfilled several distinct roles related to the performance of specific shrine rituals. Authority over shrine rituals was held by the elders, several of whom happened to be women. At the occasions of large shrine festivals, gifts of money and natural products given to the saints were redistributed among the other members of the *Sidi jama'at*. Whereas the traditional system focused upon the collectivity as a whole, the intervention by state agencies into the formal organisation of the cult resulted in the centralisation of authority in the family of the *Sidi* trustee and an increasing dependence or marginalisation of other *Sidi*.

Gender and the cosmic order

The *Sidi* cult differs importantly from other saint cults practised in the area in the emphasis it places upon complementary male and female ritual domains. Although most *dargah*s of Muslim saints contain tombs of female relatives within their precincts, these are usually not treated as the object of special ritual attention. Such tombs are declared sacred and accorded respect by virtue of the dead saint's relation to deceased kinswomen buried there. By contrast, the sister of Bava Gor, Mai Mishra, occupies a central, designated symbolic space associated with values of femininity. To worship Mai Mishra requires the performance of rituals by women. Moreover, complementing the exclusion of women from the inner sanctum of a *Sayyid* shrine (cf. Pfleiderer 1981: 226), no men may enter or touch the interior of the shrine of the female saint. Close contact with Mai Mishra is restricted to women, who also keep the tomb and receive the offerings of visiting devotees.

In this and other ways *Sidi* women are actively involved in the routine of the shrine. Those who organise rituals and other services mostly belong to the households of men employed by the trust as *mujavir*. The shrine of the female saint Mai Mishra is looked after by the female members (wife, daughters and daughters-in-law) of the household of the *Sidi* trustee. On Thursdays and Sundays, when pilgrims visit the shrine in greater numbers, other *Sidi* women sit at one of the many tombs scattered over the landscape – which do not fall under the direct management of the trust – ready to receive alms (*jakat*).

The ideology of the cult of Bava Gor is embedded in a cosmology that places God (Allah) over and above a hierarchy of saints, humans and (Satanic) demons. The cosmic order is structured by Sufi principles of closeness and distance to God that define high (*uncha*) and low (*niche*) status. Saints are closer to God and higher than human beings, to whom they mediate his grace. Among themselves, saints are divided according to the same principles. Situated beneath the level of humans, the lowest category of beings, comprising demons and evil spirits, is not only distant from but opposed to God.

The distinctions between saints, humans and demons may be conceptualised in terms of the relation between 'type' and 'token' suggested by Valerio Valeri (1985: 54), according to which the deity is 'a paragon for empirical actions and subjects . . . and endows their actions with significance'. Applying this in our context, saints and demons represent opposed types of positively and negatively evaluated exemplary moral person. At the same time, both work upon each other through human embodiment and mediation, since human actions and conditions may instantiate either saintly or demonic attributes. In *Sidi* discourse, qualities of hot and cold are critical characterisations of saints and demons. But when attempting to ascertain their respective values, what becomes evident is the fundamental ambivalence inherent in these qualities: they refer metonymically to both physical and mental processes, to fertility, death, gender, power, ecstasy, possession, emotion, purity and impurity. They are thus manifestations of a scale of evaluation that depends on relationships and transformation.

The hierarchy produced by the categories of heat and coolness is in continuous oscillation, displaying reversals and combinatorial juxtapositions. The *Sidi* hierarchy appears itself as a reversal: the assembly of *Sidi* saints is divided by gender according to a male–female duality as represented by the brothers (Bava Gor and Bava Habash) and the sister (Mai Mishra). At the same time, they refer to ancillary forms of dual hierarchies of male and female saints. Bava Gor encompasses a group of subordinate, locally enshrined brother-saints, Mai Mishra a group of seven sisters. But whereas the category of male saints is internally divided according to senior and junior status, the category of female saints remains undifferentiated. Mai Mishra represents female to male as a sister–brother relationship, as well as female relationships between sisters unaffected by seniority.

The spatial pattern of the tombs provides another clue to the relationship between brothers and sister. The tombs of the three saints are situated on top of a series of hills rising abruptly from the plains below. That of the elder brother,

Bava Gor, is sheltered by the largest shrine, indicating by its architecture its position at the apex of the shrine hierarchy. Attached to it is a small mosque. At the left, somewhat behind the sanctuary of Bava Gor but on the same hill, lies the shrine of the sister, smaller in size and placed at the back. The female saint's subordinate position in relation to the male saints is implied by the spatial order. Further away, on a second hill, rests the tomb of the younger brother, Bava Habash. It is slightly bigger than Mai Mishra's, but smaller than the shrine of Bava Gor. This spatial constellation maps the asymmetry between brothers, defined by order of seniority, and the closeness between brothers and sisters.

The male–female bisection of the saintly order is matched by a similar division between demons or spirits (*bhut*) and saints. While the latter reside in higher spheres ('up' on a hill), demons inhabit the lower realms, an underworld beneath the earth. The category of *bhut* includes the restless spirits of men or women who died an unnatural death or the sexually lustful and amoral male and female *jinn* (spirits). All of them are classified as hot. The *bhut* prefer impure, filthy surroundings such as cremation places, graveyards and public latrines. Jealous of the power of the saints, spirits make use of human bodies to destroy the moral order and to satisfy their own greedy desires. According to a psychoanalytic interpretation put forward by Sudhir Kakar, spirits 'are the reification of certain unconscious fantasies of men and women which provoke strong anxiety in the Indian cultural setting' (1982: 29). However, as Kapferer (1983) has convincingly shown, demonic illness cannot be reduced to the individual that is the focus of Western therapeutical models. It involves not only the social context of a patient but also, more generally, the society as a whole. Seen at this level, demons and malign spirits are reifications of social disorder. When low and impure spirits take control over human beings, the hierarchical social order is threatened.

Healing cosmic disorder

Within the context of the cult of Bava Gor, the healing of possession is seen more as a means of countering a cosmic threat to the hierarchical order than as a cure centred upon the individual patient. Attacking their victims from below, through the genitals and excretory organs, male spirits may demand sexual intercourse with female victims of possession, whereas female spirits crave for the blood (semen) of men.

Both saints and demons are distinguished by their thermodynamic qualities of heat and coolness. According to dominant taxonomies, being cool carries superior value. In relation to humans, saints (*pir*s) are said to be cold because they have overcome the hot *nafs* (desiring soul), that is, the instinctual, 'animal' nature of humans (Kurin 1984). Whereas *nafs* are classified as hot and low – like demons that leave humans with unfulfilled desires and strivings – the blessings (*baraka*) transmitted by saints have positive, cooling effects upon humans troubled by the heat of the *nafs* (cf. Kurin 1983b).

Yet when confronted with the *Sidi* hierarchy, the ambiguous qualities of heat and cold become evident. For one thing, hot and cold reflect gender distinctions: Bava Gor, the senior saint, is reputed to be cool minded (*thanda magaj*); Bava Habash, the young saint, is hot minded (*garam magaj*); while the female saint is 'hot–cold' (*garam–thanda*). In terms of seniority, then, heat is encompassed by the superior quality of coolness, while male encompasses female. Yet the female encompassing of heat, mediating between male coolness and hot youth, is grasped as generative, embodying fertility and reproduction. The connection between gender distinctions and thermodynamic qualities is thus most evident in relation to sexual reproduction.

According to fundamental assumptions of femininity in South Asia, shared by both Hindus and Muslims, menstruation, pregnancy and parturition are hot (and impure) bodily states. Since heat is a necessary precondition of female fertility, it must be successively transformed into a cold state of nurturing motherhood in order to control its dangerous potential. As is well known, the control of feminine (and male) heat is a major theme of life-cycle rituals, especially marriage (cf. Werbner 1986). Mai Mishra, the 'hot–cold' female saint, therefore embodies a basic cultural paradigm of femininity.

Male virility (semen), on the other hand, is equally perceived as hot and potentially dangerous, though for different reasons. Male heat may turn dangerous if controlled too much, especially through the asceticism of renouncers, as a powerful cultural stereotype personified by the Hindu god Shiva exemplifies (cf. O'Flaherty 1973). As is hinted in the myth I shall examine below, Bava Gor shares with the renouncer a rejection of sexuality. His cold attributes seem to be derived not only from sexual control but from a complete victory over sexual desire (in accordance with ideas regarding the *nafs*). Such a transformation is, moreover, hinted at by a fire kept continuously burning near his tomb, at a site where Bava Gor is reputed to have meditated for twelve years. Bava Gor is cold because he burned his own desire as the fire consumes wood and turns it into cold ash. Bava Habash, by contrast, represents the male virility necessary for human reproduction. This aspect is particularly elaborated in the ritual context to which I shall return soon.

Overcoming evil: the myth of the powerful demoness

While the categories of hot and cold construe asymmetrical relationships between saints, they are differently evaluated in relation to the demonic, marked by a reversal of levels. The relationship between saints and demons is established in a myth that is often told by the *Sidi*. In this narrative, Bava Gor is represented as a fighting holy man who came to Gujarat in obedience to the commands of the Prophet to spread Islam in this part of the world. The saint met his opponent in the form of Makhan Devi (*sic*), a powerful, evil demoness typifying hot, uncontrolled and dangerous spirits. Characterised by a series of inversions of female heat, Makhan Devi is associated with blood and unrestrained sexuality. Her rule, the narrative continues, was based on the workings of evil spirits, who brought sorrow and destruction to the population. Instead of harvesting fertile crops, people were famished and died of starvation; in place of truth, Makhan Devi used trickery and illusion to uphold her power. Most dramatically, Makhan Devi did not give birth but 'consumed' embryos and small children out of a perverse desire for blood. The rule of Makhan Devi meant chaos, destruction and death. This was the situation when Bava Gor arrived. However, the saint refused to enter into battle, because, as narrators emphatically stress, the demoness was a woman and a man cannot fight a woman. Given the implication of physical contact in battle, Bava Gor appears to have rejected a situation of sexual seduction. When his hot-headed younger brother came on the stage and threatened to kill the demoness in great rage, he was restrained by the saint and sent to another hill. Finally, the female saint arrived on the scene. Enraged like her brother Bava Habash, Mai Mishra overwhelmed the demoness by pushing her into the interior of the earth.

This narrative reveals a striking reversal of hierarchy in the relation between male and female saints, according superior value to female actions. Whereas the spatial order of the shrine manifests the superiority of male over female, the myth establishes an inversion of female and male positions. This is achieved by the transformative logic of hierarchy that creates a continuous process of balancing ambiguous hot and cold forces. Its logic requires that heat should be cooled and cold be heated. The cold saint is simultaneously superior to heat and juxtaposed to (positive) fire, while the hot saint encompasses (negative) coolness through his impotent followers. In successive stages of the ritual process, one of the poles gains prominence over the other and vice versa. The battle between the demoness and the female saint represents, symbolically, the transformation of female ambivalence. Negatively evaluated, uncontrolled female heat is projected upon the demoness, who embodies the terrifying aspects of femininity. The female saint, by contrast, represents in this constellation the positive or cold aspect of femininity; that is, controlled, dangerous heat is transformed into potentially nurturing motherhood. Thus, the male–female hierarchy is reversed when cold or superior femininity is marked. Its relationship to the male domain is, moreover, indicated by the battle scene. While the battlefield is normally the domain of men, in contrast with the domestic as the female realm, at a cosmic level, male actions of power and war are attributed to women. This temporary female superiority is expressed by evoking a male idiom.

However, although Makhan Devi's power has been subdued it cannot be completely extinguished. From below, spirits continue to harass people, who seek the power of the *Sidi* saints in order to get rid of them. Thus the struggle of Mai Mishra against evil forces is continuously recreated through ritual exorcism. In the relationships between saints, humans and demons the complementary categories of hot and cold serve to distinguish several parallel hierarchies. One is the hierarchy established between saints, humans and demons; the second is a discourse of gendered substances and conditions; the third is that of emotions and emotionality.

Emotional states

In *Sidi* ideology, the hot and cold qualities of saints are related to special emotional dispositions. These are crucial for defining them as archetypal representations of morally grounded human action. Emotions are thus localised in a configuration that resembles English notions of temperament, and is called *magaj* by the *Sidi*. *Magaj* is a key term used to refer to experiences of the self embedded in a mind–body–emotion ensemble. Thus the cold saint Bava Gor represents an exemplary *thanda magaj* (cold temperament) that includes patience, personal restraint, leniency, empathy ('understanding'), *muhabbat* and generel benevolence. Such a cold saint or person inspires trust, love, loyalty, and a sense of protection and shelter in others. In contrast, Bava Habash represents the distinct emotional pattern of an exemplary *garam magaj* (hot temperament). Bava Habash is also referred to as the saint with an 'angry mind' (*gusso magaj*). This includes wilfullness, anger, rage and passion. The hot saint is perceived as both powerful and fierce. He may inspire raging passion or deadly fears in his followers. Easily angered by minor offences, Bava Habash is said to pursue his enemies in his anger and bring misfortune on their homes and families. Moreover, the hot saint is said to react especially fiercely against those who take a favour but neglect to fulfil their promises. On the other hand, people stress that once the hot saint has accepted a devotee, his love and support knows no limits.

Compared to the male saints, the female saint is less elaborately identified with a specific emotional pattern. More importantly, she represents ideals of Muslim womanhood. Chaste ('in *parda*') and in control of the dangerous aspects of femininity, Mai Mishra manifests cold motherly love and nurturing aspects. The demoness, by contrast, represents a negatively evaluated hot emotional pattern consisting of selfishness, jealousy, hatred, greed and dishonesty.

Saints and demons, thus defined by hot and cold qualities that are associated with specific emotional patterns, represent types of morally approved or disapproved actions. Interaction between saints and demons is embodied in human struggles. *Sidi faqirs* become tokens of the saints, whereas those of demons and spirits are embodied in the possessed supplicants who seek a cure at the shrine of Bava Gor. The interactive process involving shrine followers, *faqirs* and saints is again conceptualised in an emotional idiom constituted by the categories of *dukh* (sorrow, suffering, pain) and *maja* (joy, fun). The ritual routine of the shrine is designed to transform *dukh* into *maja*. The category of sorrow encompasses hunger, unemployment, illnesses, marital problems (divorce), imprisonment of family members, and material and physical injuries inflicted by communal riots. In addition to such experiences of suffering characteristic of the life of the poor, the evil doings of the demoness stop human fertility, creating female barrenness and male impotence, and affect people's mental wellbeing through possession. People coming to the shrine seek a change in their own personal conditions experienced as suffering. Whereas *dukh* is located close to the demonic, *maja* is associated with the relationship to the saints. Ritually enacted by their tokens, the *Sidi faqirs*, *maja* is principally mediated through music and dance (*goma/dammal*).

In *Sidi* discourse, the musical repertoire of *goma* (possibly derived from Swahili *ngoma*, dance, and also known as *dammal* in Hindi, from *dam*, healing breath) is specific to the *Sidi* caste. *Goma* refers to rhythms and movements not practised otherwise by Gujaratis. Vaguely associated with their African origins, the performance of percussion and dance is restricted to *Sidi* as agents of joy. These ideas are, moreover, embedded in a cluster of concepts arising from the transformative qualities of hot and cold; an emotional idiom that articulates the self-perception of the *Sidi* as a caste descended from saintly ancestors.

To begin with, the collective image of the *Sidi* caste is modelled upon Bava Habash, the hot saint. The *Sidi* are hot. Their 'hotness' manifests itself on several levels, starting with food. A *Sidi*, it is maintained, needs two types of food: hot (meat and chillies) and 'sweet' food. Second, the *Sidi* get easily angered by insolence (*abhiman*) and hypocrisy. Such behaviour is attributed to the faculty of *'aql* (reason) that governs desire for social prestige, material wealth and worldly power. According to the *Sidi*, such strivings are built upon deceit, cheating and cunning. *'Aql* is devalued by *Sidi* ideals, which emphasise their identity as 'people without reason' (*'aql vagar loko*). Thus the *Sidi* often refer to the members of their caste as 'mad people' (*ganda loko*). Whereas madness is normally seen as a negative state closely connected with spirit possession, this value inversion is related to privileging the faculty of emotion located in the heart (*dil*) over *'aql*.

By defining themselves as mad the *Sidi* also claim a superior status as *dilvale* or 'people of the heart'. Thus, another name by which the *Sidi* call themselves is 'Badshah *loko*' or kingly people. They see themselves as superior in terms of emotional experiences especially, expressed through royal metaphors. *Sidi* are 'kings of the heart'. Abundant emotional experiences of joy are summarised in the concept of *mast*, which refers to ecstasy, spiritual intoxication, fun, joy, pleasure and trance induced by the saints (for another context for *mast*, see Lynch 1990). The concept of *mast* is also related to ideas of the *majzub* (intoxicated or mad with divine love), as Frembgen and Ewing show in this volume. Consonant with *maja*, *mast* appears as another key concept of the *Sidi* cult.

As I mentioned before, the *Sidi jamat* is divided into ritual specialists and lay persons. Among the *faqirs* those who are called *mastan*s stand out as tokens of particular saints. Whereas *mast* as an emotional state may be experienced temporarily by any *Sidi*, *mastan*s are permanently absorbed in this blissful state. They are believed to have been selected by one of the saints to act as mediums, which intoxicates them with *muhabbat*. Therefore *mastan*s experience reality in other ways than ordinary people. Their behaviour might seem bizarre when considered from the perspective of norms that ordinarily govern social interactions. At times, a *mastan* talks in a seemingly silly manner, uses abusive language, mocks expressions of respectability and refuses to use gestures of respect towards superiors. Such actions are seen not as offensive but as confirmations of his or her closeness to the saints. Through his unexpected utterances and gestures he or she exposes the hypocrisy and falseness of the world, contrasting it with the truth of the saints.

An outstanding place amongst *mastan*s is accorded the *gaddivaras*, the ritual head of the cult and representative of the senior saint Bava Gor. As the *gaddivaras* also emblematically respresents the *Sidi* caste, the relationship between saint and *gaddivaras* introduces a hierarchical distinction between saints and humans that is consituted through the relative encompassment of cold and hot: the superior, cold saint is represented by an inferior, hot man. The hotness of the *gaddivaras*, however, is induced by the saint, whose 'throne' (*gaddi*, pillow) is extremely hot and affects successors instantly. Thus the ambiguity of the position of the *gaddivaras*, who mediates in two directions – upwards and downwards – is matched by the shifting value of heat as a negative or positive quality. While being hot marks him as inferior in relation to the superior, cold saint, his powerful heat distinguishes him as superior in relation to ordinary devotees, because of the supreme intensity of his devotional emotionality.

The transformative power of heat and coolness, and the emotional qualities they substantialise symbolically, are embodied in the powers of healing, exorcism and divine judgement that *Sidi faqirs* possess.

The transformative power of saintly rituals

Devotees come to the shrine to 'work' (*kam*) with the saints, who are seen as powerful agents capable of controlling both worldly and other-worldly conditions. Using the general word for work, people indicate that they need the services of *Sidi faqirs* to mediate their request for saintly intervention or protection against personal misfortune. Such services (*seva*) are carried out not by the *gaddivaras* or by *mastan*s but by the shrine servants called *mujavir*. Whereas the ritual transactions I am considering here are aimed at a concrete change in the personal condition of supplicants, the *gaddivaras* and *mastan*s assume prominent roles, as we shall see, in another type of ritual, the *'urs* (commemoration of a saint's death), performed on behalf of the black saints.

Most cases brought to the shrines are concerned with one of three distinct spheres of power vested in them: divination through ordeal, human fertility and exorcism. Each of these requires a different type of ritual, specifically related to one of the saints. Thus, truth ordeals are performed in the name of the senior saint, Bava Gor, who represents the highest authority and absolute truth; the female saint Mai Mishra is addressed in female fertility rituals; while exorcised spirits are banished to the trunk of a tree overlooking her shrine. The hot saint, Bava Habash, is invoked to restore virility or male fertility. The supplications and rituals thus reinforce the saintly images constructed in the myth and their reality as symbolic types. Accordingly, some rituals must be performed exclusively by male or female *faqirs*, others by men and women together. I shall begin with the ordeal.

Bava Gor: divination through ordeal

The coolness of Bava Gor is associated with the power of truth, knowledge and divinely inspired judgement. Hence, divination ordeals transform his shrine into a court of law. Called *bedi*, the term literally denotes the iron rings put around the ankles of a criminal suspect. Most common ordeals relate to accusations of witchcraft, adultery or theft. Whereas only male *faqirs* may perform the *bedi* divination ritual, accused subjects are frequently women, especially when the accusation concerns witchcraft or adultery.

Within the cultural context of the cult, witchcraft is related to ideas of inverted motherhood, personified by the demoness Makhan Devi. Women accused of being witches (*dakan*) are taken to the shrine to disclose their 'true nature'. Most come from the Tribal (Bhil) population of the area. Whereas neither *Sidi* nor other Muslims level such accusations, few among them seriously doubt the reality of witches, who are said to crave for the blood of embryos and newborn babies. That they are found mainly amongst the *jungli* (uncivilised) Bhil seems only natural.

More common, however, are accusations of adultery or theft. To find out whether a suspicion is justified, the accusing party takes the suspect to the shrine. Refusal to undergo this ordeal is almost impossible, being tantamount to an admission of guilt. At the time of my fieldwork, every week between ten and thirty *bedi* cases were brought before the saint. The majority came from towns and big industrial centres. Among the accusers were *kharkhana* (factory) and shop owners who suspected their employees of stealing money from their businesses, middle-class women suspicious of their maidservants, and several husbands, accompanied by their mothers, who suspected their wives of sexual infidelity.

The procedure of the ordeal is a serious affair. The saint is believed to see through the person, right into his heart. The necessary acts are usually carried out by the *Sidi* trustee himself. At first, the suspect is given a purificatory bath behind the shrine by another *Sidi mujavir*. Only a person rendered *pak* (pure) is allowed to receive the judgement of Bava Gor. Performed in public under the eyes of many uninvolved spectators, this phase of the ordeal is itself a humiliating affair. Clad only in a wet loincloth in the case of a man, or in a wet sari in case of a woman, the accused must stand at a place outside the shrine where *bedi* (iron rings) are put around his or her ankles by the *mujavir* performing the ordeal. He purifies the person and the area with burning *loban* (incense) and utters an oath promising to accept the judgement of Bava Gor, which the accused must repeat. While a large drum is beaten inside the shrine, the *mujavir* takes the lead and runs towards the tomb of the saint at great speed, followed by the accused. If the iron rings spring open during the run, the innocence of the suspect is established. But if the rings do not open, he or she is plainly proved guilty. The iron rings are seen as signs through which the saint directly communicates the truth to the people. If they do not open, there is no way to deny the accusation. The punishment of a culprit, however, is beyond the jurisdiction of the shrine. It is left to the accusers to mete out appropriate retribution.

In the context of the ordeal, the leading saint's supernatural powers are constructed in relation to worldly hierarchies and economic powers: Bava Gor supports the more powerful against the less powerful; the dominant – patrons, employers – against the dominated – labourers, clients, and women. Seen in this context, the *dargah* is a place where class-based social control is publicly exercised. It is an attempt to check transgressions against the morally sanctioned cultural order that are seen to arise from selfishness and greed (theft) or from a lack of control over negative femininity (witchcraft, adultery).

Mai Mishra: rituals of motherhood

Mai Mishra, it will be recalled, is the 'hot–cold' saint able to transform infertile heat into cooling nurture. Hence, the second domain of saintly power is the restoration of fertility and the rituals confirming a vow (*mannat*), made either by a woman or by a man, in order to secure the birth of a child. In the cultural context of South Asia female barrenness is dreaded by married women as the cause of great *dukh*. Men, on the other hand, often suffer from fear of or actual impotence (cf. Kakar 1989: 31). Procreation and sexuality seem to be under a perpetual threat of malfunction, caused by a physical imbalance of hot and cold forces. A barren woman is said to be too hot, because the heat necessary for procreation is not transformed into cool motherhood after having given birth.

The desire for offspring and the belief that fulfilment is dependent upon the beneficial powers of saints are visibly manifested by numerous small, wooden, brightly painted cradles that are decoratively placed upon the frames protecting the tombs of the three saints. In more severe cases of childlessness, suspected of being caused by female infertility, a ritual called *Mai Mishra ni khichadi*, performed by *Sidi* women, is sponsored by the barren woman herself or by a close relative (usually her mother). This ritual requires that seven *Sidi* women, who represent the seven sisters of the female saint, consume a dish made from rice and lentils mixed with sugar and ghee. Seven is, of course, an auspicious number, and it is used by Hindus as well to refer to seven goddesses. Here, sweetness is associated with special food prepared for the female saint. One of the women, usually a wife of one of the *mujavir*, is responsible for the organisation of the ritual, including the purchase of the necessary food items. She receives a lump sum from the sponsor which covers the food expenses and a small money gift for each of the participating *Sidi* women.

After the dish has been cooked by the seven 'sisters' themselves, they gather in a room adjacent to the shrine of Bava Gor. The first stage of the ritual requires that the women eat 'in *parda*', that is, hidden from the gaze of men and strangers not involved in its performance. As is the custom in this Muslim social milieu, the women share the food from one common dish. Their leftovers are afterwards distributed as *niaz* (blessed food), first to the afflicted woman herself, then to other women devotees. Mai Mishra's *khichadi* is not shared with men.

The second part of this ritual consists of *goma*, the dance which is performed in different ritual contexts. The *Sidi* women gather next to the shrine of the female saint and sing songs (*jikkar*) dedicated to Mai Mishra and her saintly sisters. This performance is intended to give them *maja* and to invite them to show their benevolence. For a short time, one or two of the women actually begin to move and dance, swinging their hips while spectators wave rupee notes over the heads of the musicians as a sign of auspiciousness. Throughout the ritual the afflicted woman presides over the whole event.

Bava Habash: restoring virility

A man who doubts his virility will sponsor a ritual, performed by *Sidi* men, that addresses the hot saint Bava Habash and is therefore called *Bava Habash ni dudh*. Impotence is regarded as arising from a lack of the bodily heat considered necessary to transform blood into semen. The ritual of *Bava Habash ni dudh* is structured very similarly to the one performed for Mai Mishra, but involves exclusively male actors. A man concerned about his virility will select one of the *Sidi mujavir* to organise the rite, which requires that at least seven *Sidi* men (it might be more) gather in front of Bava Habash's shrine and consume a hot liquid mixture made from milk, ginger and spices. Again, the leftover is given as *niaz*, first to the sponsor and then to other men present. Afterwards, a short drumming and dancing session is performed by *Sidi* men.

The main media employed in both these gendered rituals is food given to the *Sidi* as the recipients of a conditional sacrifice. The rituals mimetically enact what they want to achieve: female fertility and male virility. The blockage within the female body – hot procreative powers that are not cooled through motherhood – is metonymically overcome through the consumption of solid, sweet and cool food. The male body, by contrast, is metonymically worked upon through milk. Milk, a cool substance, is turned hot through the addition of hot spices. The weak male body is re-empowered through the consumption of a hot liquid carrying the heat of the powerful saint. Both substances, the solid and the liquid, are consecrated through their conversion into a sacrifice mediated by *Sidi* men and women as representatives of their respective saints. Such thermodynamic 'tempering' and 'framing' of heat in coolness for the sake of fertility are widely found throughout South Asia (see Beck 1969; Werbner 1986, 1990a; Fuller and Logan 1985; O'Flaherty 1980) and even beyond it (R. Werbner 1989). They embody, synergetically, emotional, physiological and social transformations in the condition of the afflicted, simultaneously setting limits to heat, casting out anger or pollution, and bringing a personal support circle concerned about the person's suffering.

Bava Gor: rites of exorcism

Bava Gor, the cool saint, is also the saint with the power to overcome and exorcise hot demons. At the time of fieldwork, between thirty and fifty people suffering from symptoms of spirit possession came to the shrine on Thursdays. They are called *hajrivale*, that is, people experiencing a trance. *Hajri* literally means 'presence' and refers here to the presence of a possessing spirit that manifests itself and speaks when the patient is entranced. The majority being women, *hajrivale* settle close to the tomb of Bava Gor, where the drama of possession trance unfolds. At the shrine of Bava Gor, *hajrivale* are completely left to themselves until the behaviour of the patients indicates that the *bhut* is ready to leave their body.

Dyadic relationships between *Sidi* healers and patients suffering from demonic illness, comparable to those reported from other Muslim contexts (Ewing 1984a; Kakar 1982: 15ff; Pfleiderer 1981), are operative only at the local levels of the cult. *Faqirs* performing healing functions are usually based at a small *Sidi* shrine in an urban neighbourhood. They provide the first remedies for people in distress and, most importantly, decide whether a person showing symptoms not yet clearly identified is possessed by a *bhut* or suffering from some other affliction. When such a healer diagnoses a demonic illness he usually prescribes at least five visits to the shrine of Bava Gor. The place is considered more important than the individual healer since the sacred area represented by the tombs is imbued with those saintly powers (*karāmāt*) that ultimately provide the most effective means of exorcising spirits. Seen from this angle, the shrine appears as a healing space.

At the same time, the shrine is a battlefield where the saints fight directly with the spirits. Proximity to a tomb provokes the spirit to reveal itself, which it often does by shows of resistance. Some *hajrivali* scream their protest as their relatives drag them close to the tomb, and refuse to drink the water of Bava Gor or eat the ash from his fire – both of which carry powerful healing substances. Some of them spit at the tomb, heap insults upon the saints or boast that they will never succumb. If the initial resistance is broken, patients often remain in a trance induced by hyperventilation for hours. The saint may chase the spirit by making the patient move between the different tombs of the three saints. While the *bhut* speaks through the mouth of the patient, relatives try to find out its identity and demands (for an elaborate account of this, see Pfleiderer 1981). In successful cases, a *bhut* finally accepts the superior power of the saints and agrees to leave the body of his victim. Only then is a *Sidi mujavir* called. In accordance with the pattern established in the myths, departing spirits are banished to a large tree overshadowing the *dargah* of Mai Mishra, the female saint. Strands of the patient's hair are nailed to its trunk by a *mujavir* while he again confirms the final identity of the *bhut*.

Sorrow and suffering: saintly rituals and worldly hierarchies

The rituals described so far are classified as *seva*, service performed for the sake of supplicants. Through such rituals, I propose, worldly and cosmic hierarchies of superior *Sidi* and inferior cult followers are constructed. The lowest position at the shrine is accorded to Hindu and Tribal women afflicted by spirit possession. Embodying evil spirits, they are identified with this category of beings. In accordance with the hot identities of the *gadivaras* and *Sidi* caste, most rituals, as we have seen – although, significantly, not all – emphasise thermal transformations. The superior qualities of coolness are most clearly revealed in the truth ordeals which affirm the spiritual authority of Bava Gor, the cool saint. In this ritual, people who normally wield greater worldly power and influence than the *Sidi* (for example, small-scale manufacturers) accept the *Sidi*'s superior authority when submitting to the revelatory powers of the saint. The ritual addressing Mai Mishra, the female saint, frames heat in positive coolness, that is, motherhood. The reverse is true for the ritual involving Bava Habash, the hot saint: here negative cold is transformed into positive 'heat'. Again, exorcism involves cooling a dangerously hot state. Thus, *seva* rituals display a series of movements between cooling and heating and the implicit positive and negative emotional conditions underpinning these qualities.

In contrast to *seva* rituals which emphasise hierarchy and its transformations, at the large annual shrine rituals ('*urs*) hierarchy is temporarily collapsed. The context, however, is provided not by the relationship between cult followers and the *Sidi* but by that between saints and humans. The radical break of context is signified by a different style of *goma* stressing experiences of trance. It is here that the concept of *mast* is most prominently invoked.

Joy and fun: embodying community

'*Urs* celebrations stress the relationship between the saints as ancestors and their *Sidi* descendants. They involve the *Sidi* collectivity whose members travel from all over Gujarat to the shrine of Bava Gor – far in the south by local standards – in order to celebrate the death anniversary of their *kulpir* (clan saints). This also means that large groups of *Sidi* dance together, which is seen by many as a major attraction promising a lot of *maja*. Such dancing sessions differ considerably in scope from those performed in the context of *seva* rituals. Most importantly, they involve a positively evaluated trance (*hal*) that is opposed to the trance of spirit possession (*hajri*). During trance dances many *Sidi* experience temporarily a state of ecstatic love for the saints, which is the permanent condition of *mastans*.

In '*urs* rituals, the *Sidi* seem to express literally the metaphorical Sufi idea that for a saint, death means spiritual marriage to God. The last day of the '*urs* is not only referred to as the *sagai* (engagement) of Mai Mishra, but throughout the festive period *maja* is produced. This joy is related to an inversion of the mystical notion of 'union with the divine'. Instead of merging with God, *Sidi* saints unite with their living descendants. They step down to earth for a few moments. Such moments are extremely hot. However, while the hierarchy of saints and humans is collapsed in trance, the gender hierarchy is maintained and emphasised. Consequently, men are possessed exclusively by male saints, women by Mai Mishra or another female saint. A woman seized by the female saint is easily recognisable by the veil put over her face. Men in trance tie a green cloth around the lower parts of their bodies. *Sidi* trance implies a complete abandonment of control over physical movements, with the entranced possessed by a saint who speaks through his or her body. While in trance, men and women are looked after by other *Sidi* not presently possessed. They see to it that the clothes of the dancers are modestly arranged, they give them water to drink when exhausted, and they keep a lemon over the head of a person entranced too violently. A cool lemon is said to balance an overdose of saintly heat.

Thus, different styles of *goma* correspond to different types of relationship implicit in the performances. In its 'small version', carried out by a few *Sidi* singing songs in praise of the saints in the context of a conditional sacrifice, the relationship between *Sidi faqirs* and cult followers is distinguished. When *goma* involves large numbers of *Sidi* and practices of trance, the relationship between *Sidi* and ancestor-saints is saliently marked. A third type of dance is performed in the context of the wider shrine regional network hierarchy to which I shall turn below. In advance it can be stated that each type of *goma* involves an inversion of hierarchy at a different level. By way of a conclusion, I would like to examine the discourses of the cult of Bava Gor in the context of the regional shrine hierarchy.

Saintly regional hierarchies

So far we have seen that the shrine of Bava Gor constitutes hierarchical space in which *Sidi faqirs* are constructed as superior to cult followers. At the same time, it is encompassed by a wider hierarchical system of regional shrines. Within this context, the shrine of Bava Gor and *Sidi faqirs* are accorded a lower place *vis-à-vis* high-ranking *Sayyid* shrines and *pir*s. That shrines, *faqirs* and *pir*s do not constitute separate and atomistic local universes but are systematically related to each other becomes manifest in several ways.

Shrines of reputedly high status are usually not confined to narrow functions but are instead taken to transmit general and powerful *baraka* to human beings as a necessary life-giving force (Kurin 1983d; Currie 1989). The power of small saints and lower-order shrines is conceived as more limited and specific, as in the case of the *dargah* of Bava Gor, the reputation of which derives from its specific healing and divinatory powers. Such shrines do not exist in isolation but are connected by spiritual master–disciple bonds (*pir–khalifa*, *pir–murid*). Higher and lower saints are linked through a spiritual genealogy (*silsila*) and, most importantly, by the master–disciple relations of *pir* (spiritual guide, teacher) and *murid* (spiritual disciple). An intermediate position between *pir* and *murid* is accorded to *khalifa*s, that is, delegates or vicegerents of the *pir*, often carrying the message of his spiritual authority to geographically or socially distant places and contexts.

In the present case, *Sidi faqirs* are linked to a hierarchically structured universe of saints through the *pir*–khalifa bond which existed between Bava Gor and Sayyid Ahmad Kabir Rifa'i, the founder of a Middle Eastern Sufi order which has branches in Gujarat (cf. Trimingham 1971; van der Veer 1992). As is told in more elaborate versions of the myth, on his journey to India Bava Gor passed through Baghdad, where he met Sayyid Ahmad Kabir Rifa'i and became his *murid*. It was Rifa'i who changed his name from Sidi Mubarak Nobi to Bava Gor. The *pir* made him a *khalifa* for the area where he ultimately settled. The symbolic logic of the myth constitutes a pardigmatic template of the asymmetrical relationship between Rifa'i *Sayyid pirs* and *Sidi faqir* (Basu 1996). This relationship is revealed particularly at *'urs* celebrations at Rifa'i shrines when *Sidi* men and women perform ritual services for the *pir*. Thus the *Sidi*, although low and marginal, are not beyond the fold of a regional Muslim hierarchical system represented by shrines.

Most importantly, the hierarchy of shrines is continuously recreated through asymmetrical exchanges of gifts to God. Analysing different categories of gifts through which hierarchical relationships are established between donor and recipient, Pnina Werbner writes: 'Gifts to God, including animal sacrifices and offerings of food and money, while always unilateral, are directed either "downwards", to the poor, in the form of *sadaqa*, or "upwards" as religious tribute to saints and holy men, whether alive or dead' (Werbner 1990b: 271; see also Chapter 5 in this volume). In accordance with values of generosity associated with high status, the *pir* is the ultimate giver, who accepts gifts only from God (Werbner 1990b: 272). The goods and donations he receives from his followers are classified as *nazrana*, that is, tributary gifts such as those given by a client to a patron. *Nazrana*, formally the possession of the saint, are usually redistributed at the shrine and used for the benefit of all, as are other offerings to the *langar*, blessed food handed out to all pilgrims and supplicants at the shrine (see Werbner, this volume). The distribution of *langar* to devotees is a common practice at higher-status shrines, and especially so during the festive days of the *'urs* celebration (cf. Currie 1989; van der Veer 1992).

At the shrine of Bava Gor, by contrast, *Sidi faqirs* receive gifts to God in a downwards direction. They embody the category of the poor whose gifting increases the religious merits of the donor. In addition to *jakat* (alms), the *Sidi* accept *sadaqa* and *qurbáni* (animal sacrifices). At the Islamic festival of *eid* celebrated at the end of Ramadan, the month of fasting, for example, other Muslims visit *Sidi* hamlets and distribute parts of a sacrificial ram. Moreover, no *langar* is provided at the shrine of Bava Gor. Instead, *niaz* is given by individual cult followers in fulfilment of a vow. The term *niaz* refers generally to food consecrated by sacrifice. Although such a meal is shared by all those who happen to be at the shrine at the moment of its distribution, it is explicitly prepared for and directed to the *Sidi* as recipients.

As is well known, however, gifts are not neutral objects but imbued with the 'spirit of the donor' (Mauss 1966). According to Parry (1980) gifts (*dan*) given to the brahmin funeral priests at Benaras are negatively charged with the sins of devotees. These sins, transmitted to the priests, render them inauspicious and impure. Gifts given to *Sidi faqirs* are similarly charged with ambivalence. In this context, instead of sins, they are perceived to be loaded with negatively evaluated emotions of hot *dukh*. But unlike Hindu funeral priests in Benaras, the *Sidi* do not absorb *dukh* but transform it into positive emotions of *maja*. This, again, is achieved through a situational inversion of hierarchy.

The ambiguity of gifts given in a 'downwards' direction corresponds to the ambivalence contained in the image of a poor *faqir*. Although routinely invoked by high-status *pirs* for themselves, mendicant *faqirs* are in practice often despised and feared for their powers to bless *and* curse (cf. Ewing 1984b). Opposed to the superior *pir*, the category of inferior *faqir* is at the same time encompassed by the former. For the present context, this encompassing relationship can be detected in the use of the concept of *mastan* by the Rifa'i. As noted by van der Veer, in each generation one member of the family which inherits the *sajjada nishin* (the spiritual succession of Sayyid Ahmad Kabir Rifa'i) becomes a *mastan*: 'Stories abound about these men who combine strong spiritual powers with anti-social, unpredictable behaviour ... A *mastan* is clearly beyond the Law but ... he can never be head of the family, *sajjada nishin*' (van der Veer 1992: 560). Hence we are confronted with the same type of hierarchical relationship within the category of superior *pirs* that also marks the asymmetrical alliance between *Sayyid* (Rifa'i) *pirs* and *Sidi faqirs*.

Conclusion: the emotional reversal of the status hierarchy

Sidi constructions of hierarchy are built upon a productive ambivalence, implying a constant shift between positive and negative evaluations of hot and cold. While coolness and the complex of ethical imperatives and emotional temperaments associated with these qualities marks the unequivocal superiority embodied by the *Sayyid*, the subordinate and encompassed quality of the 'hot' is ambiguously defined – powerfully good or dangerously bad. The positively hot *mastan* overcomes negatively hot spirits. By adopting a discourse of emotions, the *Sidi* create an alternative taxonomy of values that undermines the fixed, frozen truths of the status hierarchy, based on the absolute opposition between purity and pollution. Thus the *dukh* of cult followers is confronted with the *maja* associated with saints and their tokens. The ambivalence connected to receiving gifts and alms is rejected by the evocation of *maja*, which inverses its negative value and symbolically devalues the donors. This is most prominently displayed in yet another style of *goma* performed at the shrines of high-status saints.

When *Sidi faqirs* follow the call of a *Sayyid pir* of another shrine, *goma* does not include *hal* but is concerned with the comic. This type of *goma* is performed in a courtyard of *Sayyid* shrines by relatively large groups of male *Sidi* dancers. Watched by an audience of shrine devotees and pilgrims, some of the *Sidi* performers jump into an interior circle formed by those who beat the drums. Individual dancers display a wild show of contorted bodies and funny gesturings while the audience interacts with the performers by throwing money (coins and notes) into the circle. A large part of the fun derives from the ways in which this money is picked up – dancers might enact a mock fight, wipe the money on their buttocks and present this rear view to the spectators, or pretend to devour it greedily. In addition, through obscene gesturing and acrobatic stunts, gestures marking respectability, seriousness and high status are mocked and imitated. The whole carnevalesque performance seems designed to bring down the high to a low bodily realm (cf. Bakhtin 1968; Basu 1996). Through movements and facial grimacing, the hierarchy inscribed upon social bodies is pulled down and its seriousness is laughed at. Most especially, the act of giving that usually bestows superiority upon the giver and inferiority upon the recipient is exposed as ridiculous. Hence, in contrast to the brahmins of Benares who act as vessels of inauspiciousness (cf. Parry 1989), the *Sidi* purify the alms they receive of their negative associations, ridding them of their evil stigmata and simultaneously rejecting their role as scapegoats for the sins of others. Laden with emotions, the gifts they receive are transformed by inverting their *dukh* into *maja*.

Thus, although the *Sidi* cult recognises, and is partly resonant with, the hegemonic Muslim status hierarchy which places *Sayyid*s at its apex, a counter-discourse simultaneously subverts the basic premises of this hierarchy. The threads of ambivalence outlined above weave an alternative order of values by juxtaposing the taxonomic qualities of hot and cold to cosmogonic emotional and ethical values that contradict and undermine a fixed and rigid, purity-based caste order. Instead, another discourse emerges that redefines people normally judged as extremely low (black, begging, servile) as morally and cosmically superior. The inbuilt ambivalence of the *Sidi* discourse thus undermines the universal claims to authority of those in control of power and status.

Acknowledgements

I would like to thank Pnina Werbner for her sustained interest in this chapter, her careful readings and a host of valuable critiques and suggestions.

References

Abu-Lughod, Lila (1986) *Veiled Sentiments: Honour and Poetry in a Bedouin Society*, Berkeley: University of California Press.

Abu-Lughod, Lila and Catherine A. Lutz (1990) 'Introduction: Emotion, Discourse and the Politics of Everyday Life', in Catherine A. Lutz and Lila Abu-Lughod *Language and the Politics of Emotion*, Cambridge: Cambridge University Press, pp. 1–23.

Ahmad, Aziz (1969) *An Intellectual History of Islam in India*, Edinburgh: Edinburgh University Press.

Bakhtin, Mikhail (1968) *Rabelais and his World*, transl. H. Iswolsky, Cambridge MA: MIT Press.

Basu, Helene (1995) *Habshi-Sklaven, Sidi Fakire: Muslimische Heiligenverehrung im westlichen Indien*, Berlin: Das Arabische Buch.

Basu, Helene (1996) 'Muslimische Lachkultur in Gujarat/Indien', in Georg Elwert, Jürgen Jensen and Ivan R. Kortt (eds) *Kulturen und Innovationen: Festschrift für Wolfgang Rudolph*, Berlin: Duncker and Humblot.

Beck, Brenda (1969) 'Colour and Heat in South Asian Ritual', *Man* n.s. 4: 553–572.

Currie, P.M. (1989) *The Shrine and Cult of Mu'in al-din Chishti of Ajmer*, Delhi: Oxford University Press.

Dumont, Louis (1980) [1966] *Homo Hierarchicus: The Caste System and its Implication*, Chicago: University of Chicago Press.

Dumont, Louis (1986) *Essays on Individualism: Modern Ideology in Anthropological Perspective*, Chicago and London: The University of Chicago Press.

Ewing, Katherine (1984a) 'The Sufi as Saint, Curer and Exorcist in Modern Pakistan', *Contributions to Asian Studies*, XVIII: 106–114.

Ewing, Katherine (1984b) 'Malangs of the Punjab: Intoxication or *Adab* as the Path to God?', in Barbara Daly Metcalf (ed.) *Moral Conduct and Authority: The Place of Adab in South Asian Islam*, Berkeley: University of California University Press, pp. 357–371.

Fuller, C.J. and Penny Logan (1985) 'The Navratri Festival in Madurai', *Bulletin of the School of Oriental and African Studies, University of London*, XLVIII, I: 79–105.

Gaborieau, Marc (1986) 'Les ordres mystiques dancs le sous-coninent indien', in A. Popovic and G. Vensten (eds) *Les ordres mystiques dans l'Islam*, Paris: Editions de L'Ecole des Hautes Etudes en Sciences Sociales, pp. 105–134.

Kakar, Sudhir (1982) *Mystics, Shamans and Doctors: A Psychological Inquiry into India and its Healing Traditions*, Delhi: Oxford University Press.

Kakar, Sudhir (1989) *Intimate Relations: Exploring Indian Sexuality*, New Delhi: Viking.

Kapferer, Bruce (1983) *A Celebration of Demons: Exorcism and the Aesthetics of Healing in Sri Lanka*, Bloomington: Indiana University Press.

Kurin, Richard (1982) '"Hot" and "Cold": Towards an Indigenous Model of Group Identity and Strategy in Pakistani society', in S. Pastner and L. Flam (eds) *Anthropology in Pakistan: Recent Sociocultural and Archaeological Perspectives*, South Asia Program Occcasional Papers and Theses, 8, Ithaca NY: Cornell University Press pp. 89–102.

Kurin, Richard (1983a) 'Modernization and Traditionalism: "Hot" and "Cold" Agriculture in Punjab, Pakistan', *South Asian Anthropologist* 4, 2: 65–75.

Kurin, Richard (1983b) 'Indigenous Agronomics and Agricultural Development in the Indus Basin', *Human Organization* 42, 4: 283–294.

Kurin, Richard (1983c) 'The Structure of Blessedness at a Muslim Shrine in Pakistan', *Middle Eastern Studies* 19, 3: 312–325.

Kurin, Richard (1984) 'Morality, Personhood and the Exemplary Life: Popular Conceptions of Muslims in Paradise', in Barbara Daly Metcalf (ed.) *Moral Conduct and Authority: The Place of Adab in South Asian Islam*, Berkeley: University of California Press, pp. 196–220.

Lutz, Catherine A. (1986 [1982] 'The Domain of Emotion Words in Ifaluk', in Romano Harré (ed.) *The Social Construction of Emotion*, Oxford: Blackwell, pp. 267–288.

Lutz, Catherine A. (1988) *Unnatural Emotions: Everyday Sentiments in a Micronesian Atoll and their Challenge to Western Theory*, Chicago: University of Chicago Press.

Lutz, Catherine A. and Lila Abu-Lughod (eds) (1990) *Language and the Politics of Emotion*, Cambridge: Cambridge University Press.

Lynch, Owen M. (1990) 'The Mastram: Emotion and Person among Mathura's Chaubes', in Owen M. Lynch (ed.) *Divine Passions: The Social Construction of Emotion in India*, Berkeley: University of California Press, pp. 91–115.

Mauss, Marcel (1966) *The Gift*, London: Cohen and West.

Mayer, A.C. (1967) 'Pir and Murshid: An Aspect of Religious Leadership in West Pakistan', *Middle Eastern Studies* 3, 2: 160–169

Metcalf, Barbara Daly (1986) 'Introduction', in Barbara Daly Metcalf (ed.) *Moral Conduct and Authority: The Place of Adab in South Asian Islam*, Berkeley: University of California Press, pp.1–20.

Misra, S.C. (1985) [1961] *Muslim Communities in Gujarat*, New Delhi: Munshiram Monoharlal.

Nanda, Bikman, N. and Mohammad Talib (1989) 'Soul of the Soulless: An Analysis of Pir–Murid Relationships in Sufi Discourse', in Christian W. Troll (ed.) *Muslim Shrines in India: Their Character, History and Significance*, Delhi: Oxford University Press, pp. 125–144.

O'Flaherty, Wendy Doniger (1973) *Siva the Erotic Ascetic*, Oxford: Oxford University Press.

O'Flaherty, Wendy Doniger (1980) *Women, Androgynes and Other Mythical Beasts*, Chicago: University of Chicago Press.

Obeyesekere, Grananath (1990) *The Work of Culture: Symbolic Transformation in Psychoanalysis and Anthropology*, Chicago: University of Chicago Press.

Parry, Jonathan (1980) 'Ghosts, Greed and Sin: The Occupational Identity of the Benares Funeral Priests', *Man* n.s. 15, 1: 88–111.

Parry, Jonathan (1989) 'On the Moral Perils of Exchange', in Jonathan Parry and Maurice Bloch (eds) *Money and the Morality of Exchange*, Cambridge: Cambridge University Press, pp. 64–93.

Pfleiderer, Beatrix (1981) 'Mira Datar Dargah: The Psychiatry of a Muslim Shrine', in Imtiaz Ahmad (ed.) *Ritual and Religion among Muslims in India*, New Delhi: Manohar, pp. 195–234.

Pinto, Desiderio (1989) 'The Mystery of the Nizamuddin Dargah: The Accounts of Pilgrims', in Christian W. Troll (ed.) *Muslim Shrines in India: Their Character, History and Significance*, Delhi: Oxford University Press, pp. 112–124.

Rahman, Fazlur (1979) *Islam*, 2nd edn, Chicago: University of Chicago Press.

Schimmel, Annemarie (1975) *Mystical Dimensions of Islam*, Chapel Hill: University of North Carolina Press.

Trimingham, J. Spencer (1971) *The Sufi Orders of Islam*, Oxford: Oxford University Press.

Valeri, Valerio (1985) *Kingship and Sacrifice: Ritual and Society in Ancient Hawaii*, Chicago: University of Chicago Press.

van der Veer, Peter (1992) 'Playing or Praying: A Sufi Saint's Day in Surat', *Journal of Asian Studies* 51, 3: 545–564.

Werbner, Pnina (1986) 'The Virgin and the Clown: Ritual Elaboration in Pakistani Migrants' Weddings', *Man* n.s. 21: 227–250.

Werbner, Pnina (1990a) *The Migration Process: Capital, Gifts and Offerings among British Pakistanis*, Oxford: Berg.

Werbner, Pnina (1990b) 'Economic Rationality and Hierarchical Gift Economies: Value and Ranking among British Pakistanis', *Man* n.s. 25: 266–285.
Werbner, Richard (1989) *Ritual Passage, Sacred Journey: The Process and Organisation of Religious Movement*, Washington DC: Smithsonian Institution Press.

7

THE *MAJZUB* MAMA JI SARKAR

'A friend of God moves from one house to another'

Jürgen Wasim Frembgen

Introduction

For the *wali* (friend of God) physical death marks the entry into the 'real' life embodied in the mystical union (*maqam al-wisal*) with Allah, a moment of unification which is ritually celebrated as a 'holy marriage', an *'urs*, with God. In the words of the well-known *hadith* (saying of the Prophet) cited above, the movement is from the mundane 'house' of life-in-the-world to eternal life in the 'house' of God.

The present chapter seeks to illuminate this transition not merely in its classical, mystical sense, but as it throws light on a cult in transition. The movement I disclose is from a cult centred on devotion to a living *majzub* residing in a *darbar* (court, Sufi lodge) to the establishment, after his death, of a *dargah/mazar* (shrine complex) and the reconstruction of the cult around this new focal place of devotion. The central aim of this chapter is thus not only to illuminate the personality of a particular *majzub* (religious ecstatic) or to locate ecstatics like him in the Muslim South Asian religious universe; the broader aim is to understand the 'holy houses' of such *majzub*s, alive or dead, as lived-in, concrete, everyday realities.

The first shrine analysed here is situated in the old city of Rawalpindi in Punjab, Pakistan; the second, which was established after the saint's death in 1991, is located in the nearby village of Nurpur Shahan, on the outskirts of Pakistan's capital city, Islamabad.[1]

To portray a living *majzub* and his cult is to deal with embodied, concrete religion as a living force. From this perspective, the focal point of analysis is necessarily the personal piety of believers, their experiences, emotions, intentions, and hopes of salvation. Such reflexivity, to quote Wilfred Cantwell Smith, makes 'the study of religions . . . the study of persons' (1959: 35). By interrogating the subjective realities of followers we may gain new insight into what is normally referred to, somewhat dismissively, as 'folk' Islam.

Plate 7.1 The *majzub* Mama Ji Sarkar (watercolour painting by Sayyid Ishrat, 1988)
Photo by M. Weidner-El Salamouny. Courtesy, State Museum of Anthropology Munich

The biography of a living saint

The Muslim saint Hazrat Gul Warith Khan – some say his real name was Gulshan Warith Khan – is better known in Rawalpindi by the affectionate title 'Mama Ji Sarkar'; *mama* being the Punjabi term for mother's brother. His devotees also explain the meaning of *ma-ma* as 'double-love'. In addition the *pir* (saint, divine) is variously addressed as 'Pia', 'Bhai Ji', 'Badshah Ji', and 'Qalandar Badshah'. The last title of honour refers to his association with the 'free', heterodox Qalandariyya brotherhood. Mama Ji is said to be a *majzub-Qalandar-bacha*, who also belongs to the Qadiriyya *silsila* (spiritual genealogy), like his *murshid* (spiritual guide), Barri Imam (1617–1705/1706). Hence the complete title of honour used on printings and paintings of the saint is *Hazrat Gul Warith Khan (Pia) al-ma'ruf Mama Ji Sarkar Majzub Qalandar*.

The *mujawir*s (attendants), who are able to depict only the bare contours of the saint's life, report that Mama Ji was born in Peshawar (Dabgari-bazaar) about 1910–1920, and lived there together with his father, Aziz Khan, his mother, Gul Makay, and a sister called Sanbari. They are uncertain if his father was an Awan or a Pakhtun of the Shinwari or Khattak tribe. Some say that he worked as a trader and belonged to a Mian family. As the pious tradition goes, the pregnant mother of the saint-to-be went to the shrine of the *panj pir* (the five *pir*s) and prayed there for the birth of a son. One of the *gaddi-nishin*s (heirs of a saint's throne) gave her a little sugar and advised her to name her future son Gul. Nothing handed down from the saint's early childhood provides any clues to a psychological interpretation of his further development. When I met him he was no longer able to respond to such questions. In Peshawar I heard that as a youth, he preferred to stay at the *mazar* of the Qadiri saint, Sayyid Shah Qabul Auliya (late eighteenth century), close to Dabgari-bazaar. Until the end of the 1970s, he used to travel together with his followers from Rawalpindi to Peshawar in order to attend the *'urs* of that saint. Rahim Gul Motilala, the oldest and most respected *mujawir* of Mama Ji's shrine, links him to a legend about Barri Imam: he sees the *majzub* as a descendant of the saint Chan Agha Badshah (seventeenth century) from Peshawar who once insulted Barri Imam, not recognising his saintliness. The moment he realised his mistake, Chan Agha's regret was such that he made a vow to journey every year by foot to the saint's *dargah*.

Around the age of 14–16, Mama Ji accompanied this traditional procession of devotees from Peshawar to Nurpur, organised by the descendants of the repentant Chan Agha and the later, better-known *pir* Agha Sayyid Mir Jani Shah (d. 1883) (see Einzmann 1988: 56–58). The unique sense of communal solidarity and love evoked both by the week-long procession and by the subsequent five days of *'urs*-celebrations apparently had a strong impact on the young *majzub*. According to his *mujawir*s, he remained near Barri Imam's shrine for about ten or twelve years. Living for longer periods in the wilderness surrounding the village, he avoided women and any polluting sexuality. Next, Mama Ji began shuttling between Nurpur and Rawalpindi, where he finally settled in the 1960s in the Bunni Mohalla, Warith Khan quarter, which gave the saint his *misba* name. It is said that he used to move around the area between Murree Road, Jama' Masjid Road, and Raja Bazaar. In 1978/1979 his followers rented one of the rooms behind the Jama' Masjid on his behalf, situated in a very narrow lane which falls steeply away to a dirty channel (*ganda nala*), a place now called Mama Ji Sarkar Mohalla.

The saint remained unmarried just like Barri Imam, the saint whom he adopted as his spiritual guide. By practising celibacy he tamed and eliminated his *nafs* (soul, lower self), revealing the ideal moral behaviour of a mystic. Mama Ji used to wear a long Sufi garment (*chola*), preferably green in colour, and a necklace. He spent most of his days resting on his lower legs with his soles turned towards the back. In addition to this difficult position, a characteristic mystic posture, he also liked to sit cross-legged, with raised-up knees, while at the same time vehemently shaking his right foot. It is said that he loved *qawwali* and especially *rubab* music from the North-West Frontier Province; further, he liked to see *dhamal* dancing but he never participated in the dancing himself. He practised the *zikr-e ruh* (silent commemoration of God), taking the *basmala* (invocation of God) as his formula. The state of being taciturn or silent, sometimes for long periods, is interpreted by his disciples either as being in the state of reciting this *zikr* or as remaining in *maqam al-qurb* - an expression for the highest form of rapture and proximity to God.[2] The *majzub*'s silence, which is also an important exercise of Christian and Buddhist monks as well as of Hindu ascetics, is realised as an element of the divine and as an experience of God that can not be expressed in words.

I was told of the saint's *karāmāt* (spiritual powers, miracles) and mannerisms by his *mujawir*s and *murid*s (disciples). These narratives, despite their anecdotal character, not only prove but constitute the authenticity of the devotees' faith. In the beginning, I was told, when Mama Ji moved from Nurpur to 'Pindi, he used to run up and down the streets in a state of divine ecstasy *(jazba-e jalal)* shouting 'I am the Qalandar of God', or 'Ah, Gul Makay.' Once the enraptured one seized a man by the throat, lifted him up easily, and threw him from one side of the road to the other. The man remained completely unhurt. This deed was interpreted as a *karāmāt* rather like another event which occurred at Bunni Chowk in the 1960s, during Ayub Khan's rule: the *sahib-e kashf* (lit. 'the revealed Lord') was at that time considered only a beggar and hashish addict by the local authorities. So the police picked him up on the road and put him in a van, together with some other destitutes. But when the driver tried to move off, his motor refused to start. All the efforts to get it going were in vain. Next, two of the van's tyres burst without any visible reason. It was then that the police finally realised that they had arrested a holy man. They apologised to Mama Ji and begged his forgiveness. As soon as the saint descended from the vehicle, the motor started.

'Modern' hagiographic tales, particularly of this type, are prevalent throughout South Asia. A taxi-driver from 'Pindi told me of a similar incident: his car was stuck on the road and the saint, arriving on the scene, told him gently: 'Try it again now!' With these words the motor started up. In another case, a young man fell down in the *ganda nala* near Mama Ji's *darbar* and badly injured one of his feet with cuts from broken glass. Staying for some time with the holy man, he soon got cured; today, he is Mama Ji's youngest *mujawir*. Another *murid*, Liaqat 'Ali Bhatti, was dismissed from his job in 1987 and in desperation planned to migrate to Iraq. There were just twenty-five minutes left before he was due to sail out of Karachi port when, standing lost in thought at the quay, he gazed into the water and perceived the face of his *murshid*. Being under the influence of hashish, he was uncertain whether his vision was real, so he asked a security man standing nearby if he would be willing to look into the water as well. The security guard obliged and confirmed that a long-haired, bearded saint's face was reflected in the water. Knowing that all his endeavours would succeed now, the disciple went straight back to Rawalpindi. Within a few days he was reinstated in his former job.

In the final twelve years of his life, Mama Ji mostly remained in his *baithak* (sitting place) behind the Jama' Masjid, visited by a steady flow of *murid*s and other pious people. It is said that when a person entered his room the saint directly knew about the problems and difficulties facing the visitor. When high officials and dignitaries came to pay their respects to him, Mama Ji addressed them with their proper names without ever having met them before. Generally, he gave comfort and advice to supplicants seeking help, prayed for them, and kept a *langar* (centre for communal distribution of food) to feed the poor. Sometimes he described to his devotees in great detail what they had done the day before, in his absence, or foretold future events (like the coming of rain, the imminent arrival of particular persons, and so forth). Knowing their inner thoughts, he used to rebuke his *murids*, saying: 'You there in the front, you are a *lafanga* [good-for-nothing]!' or 'You are fond of drinking and smoking, give it up!'.

He spoke either in Pashto, Hindko, Potohari or Urdu, or in his own language, incomprehensible to those present, with the exception of the person he was addressing. The use of a sacred language, here in the form of charismatic words, is related to the phenomenon of speaking in tongues. There is as yet no indication that Mama Ji's utterances have anything to do with the ecstatic pronouncements and theopathic locutions (*shathiyat*) of famous Sufis like Mansur al-Hallaj (d. 922) or Bayezid Bistami (d. 874); as an incomprehensible idiom they seem even more indecipherable.

A peculiarity of Mama Ji was the power of his eyes, a fact which I can confirm myself. People said: 'His eyes are so powerful that one cannot return his look', or 'He can see behind the faces of people.' This is a characteristic trait of *majzub*s, called *nazarbazi* – literally 'playing with looks', but in fact influencing, teaching, and healing persons (Frembgen, in press). *Nazarbazi* is especially known as a practice on the mystical path of the Iranian Khaksar dervishes, a brotherhood in which the *shaikh* (saint, divine) trains the novice in this way (Gramlich 1965: 76). In his *Saints of Sindh* Moin Bari concludes: 'A saint can be judged from his eyes. His looks are extraordinary as compared to others. Reddish, piercing and enlightening. Their eyes are the real source of inspiration' (1994: 75).

The category of *majzub*

Belonging either to an orthodox or a heterodox brotherhood, the *majzub* embodies a very special, but many-faceted type of ecstatic who is 'at the wilder end of the Sufi spectrum', as Simon Digby aptly puts it.[3] Hagiographic sources show that he can be a thorough ascetic at one time and a complete pleasure-lover at other times, indulging in gluttony and seeking the company of dancing girls and prostitutes. The swing of the pendulum between these extremes becomes clear in the cases where the saint proves his resistance to feminine charms. As a 'wise fool' (*'uqala' al-majanin*), he is considered exempted from following the religious law by God himself; he has the free rein of the religiously confused. A feature usually tolerated by the common people but vehemently condemned by the religious orthodoxy is the practice of some *majzub*s of roaming about naked, a custom often expressed in the epithet *nanga*. The 'dress of nakedness', for example, worn by the famous poet and *majzub* Sa'id Sarmad (d. 1661), can be understood as a humiliation before Allah and a trusting devotion to him; ecstatics like Sarmad need nothing more than the proximity to God. Many of these strange mystics – like Buhlul al-Majnun (ninth century), the Algerian Shudhi al-Halwi (twelfth century), or the Moroccan Haddawa-saint *Sidi* 'Abdur Rahman al-Majzub (d. 1674/1675) – lived in the way of the ancient cynics, provoking the people, admonishing them, and mixing freely with social outcasts. The charismatic quality of the 'holy fool' is known in oriental Christianity (for example, Symeon Salos of Emesa in the sixth century, or Saint Andreas, d. 947), as well as in Islam. Among Bengali Vaishnava mystics we encounter a kind of 'religious madness' called *divyonmada*, expressed in an ecstatic state where the saint self-abandons in God.[4]

A core aspect of being a *majzub*, frequently mentioned by Pakistani informants, is the attachment to the solitude of the wilderness. The rejection of the 'life in this world' is generally typical of Islamic mystics, and particularly so of the *majzub*. By contrast, the *gaddi-nishin*s are widely seen as rooted in 'this life'. In keeping with such ideal ascetic behaviour, Mama Ji wandered around in the forests and hills of the Margalla mountains near Nurpur before settling in Rawalpindi. Like other dervishes and *majzub*s he relied for his survival on the alms distributed by villagers and city-dwellers.

At the end of the 1940s, a dervish of this type used to live in and around the town of Tank (North-West Frontier Province). The following story about this ecstatic was told to me by an eye-witness, *Sayyid* 'Alam Shah Bukhari,[5] who worked in 1948 as a dispenser in the civil hospital of Tank. The dervish in question, whose words nobody could understand, was considered a true *majzub* by the local people as he was extremely modest, never asking for anything; shopkeepers in the bazaar gave him food of their own free will. He was especially happy if somebody offered him a puff of their water-pipe. One day he died and his corpse was brought to the civil hospital for a post mortem. The moment the sweeper, following the orders of the medical doctor and the dispenser, put the knife to the body, the new operating table broke down – a fact widely interpreted as proof of the magical power of the *majzub*. It further shows that the perfect body of a Muslim saint should never be violated.

Advocates of Western orthodox biomedicine might suggest as a diagnosis that many *majzub*s are actually schizophrenics, hysterics, epileptics or autistics. Beyond the questionable transfer of Western medical concepts and terms to another culture, what such a diagnosis misses are the emic perspectives on charismatic 'possession'. In the Islamic world, a *majzub* means a person being in a permanent state of ecstasy and divine emotion, in most cases enraptured since birth, but sometimes in response to dramatic visions or far-reaching experiences of the soul. The Arabic term *majzub* is derived from the verb *yazaba – jazaba* in the vernacular – meaning 'to be attracted to' or 'drawn to'. A *majzub* is therefore 'drawn' to God.

When he follows the divine call, his heart is fully captured and enveloped by the Almighty. Mental disorders prove that his soul is overflowing with God's light and that he is absorbed by him. To draw a comparison with antiquity, epilepsy was called the 'holy disease', hence *epileptos* means in Greek 'enraptured' (Benz 1972: 127). In the language of Christian religious experience, being moved by divine emotions points to the seizing hand of God.

In this sense Mama Ji Sarkar is respected by his devotees as having been a true *majzub*. Being in God's hands since birth, he shared some of the attributes described as common for these ecstatics, like, for example, the ability to foretell the future and to perform miracles, to speak clearly and lucidly at times, while being at other times incoherent and incomprehensible, and a love of hashish.

Finally, the *murid*s explain the fact that Mama Ji scarcely had excretions in his last years and that they did not smell at all – so they say – as a further proof of saintliness, because the physical body of a saint is intrinsically pure and free of decay. In fact, all those present during his excreting have to get up and stand in silence as a mark of respect. This aspect evokes the Iranian folk-belief that in paradise, Hazrat Adam 'got paradisic fruits to eat, these became sweat and evaporated without defecation' (Loeffler 1988: 44).

Whereas certain heretical *majzub*s, especially of the Qalandar order, go naked, dance, provoke the people, or reject disciples in a rude manner, other mystics like Mama Ji tend to be more inconspicuous, being gentle and calm (Frembgen 1993: 96). The 'Pindi saint is venerated by his *murid*s as a man with a pure soul, with high moral qualities, and without any badness, who is very close to God and brings peace and inner harmony (*sokun*) to his devotees. Being a real *majzub* gifted with a miraculous charisma makes him superior to any *sajjada-nishin* or *gaddi-nishin*, descendants of former respected saints, who are nothing more than 'heirs of prayer carpets'; he is therefore considered as having far more personal *baraka* (blessings) than those embodying a mystical hierarchical order. His followers state that Mama Ji was neither a poet nor a philosopher, but a man of simple manners with a powerful aura, whose heart was not attached to worldly things. As he renounced the world, his intercession with God through prayers and invocations is considered very efficacious. Mama Ji knew the hearts of people and preached the love of God, the Prophet, and the Saints (*'ishq-e haqiqi*) and the love of man (*'ishq-e majazi*).[6] He himself is full of love, especially for the poor, which proves him to be a recipient of divine grace. And this love is transmitted to his devotees, who find it in their own selves.

The saint's *darbar* in Rawalpindi: his first house

The living-room with anteroom at the *ganda nala* in which the saint lived is part of the *waqf* (religious endowment) property of the adjacent Jama' Masjid. Mama Ji's followers collect the monthly rent for this property among themselves. The house served as a *darbar* and *baithak* for the *pir* and his devotees during the saint's

THE *MAJZUB* MAMA JI SARKAR

lifetime; after his physical death it is now called an *astan*. Opposite the anteroom, just across the narrow lane, there is the half-open *langar*, built with wooden planks over the dirty *nala*.

Seen from the entrance, the left side of the anteroom is used for shoes while on the right is a very narrow and low partitioned area, lockable with a metal door. This tiny room is decorated with a fresco, painted by Sayyid Ishrat, the local artist whom I discuss below, which depicts a Punjabi landscape. It was the saint's *chillagah* (place of seclusion) and is now used as a place either for sleeping or for smoking hashish. Sometimes pigeons, traditionally associated with saint's abodes in South and West Asia, are kept above this room.

Within the square living-room, the saint's bed stands in the right-hand corner by the end wall, with a space reserved for women between the foot of the bed and the door. The place of the *mutawalli/mujawir* on duty is between the bedhead and the fireplace, situated along the middle of the end wall. The rest of the floor serves as a sitting space for the male visitors who come and go freely. Privileged seats for high-ranking persons are near the end wall, close to the *mutawalli*. Others

Plate 7.2 The living saint Mama Ji Sarkar in his *darbar* in Rawalpindi, to the left his attendant 'Abdul Rashid
Photo by J.W. Frembgen

occupy the middle of the left side under a low roof supported by two pillars. The lowest-ranking seats are, of course, near the door.

The living-room is richly decorated with devotional objects donated by pious *murids*; these range from colourful kitsch knick-knacks to a *kashkol* (begging bowl), *shanka* (conch), four photographs of the *pir* adorned with flower garlands, and various pictures. There are, for example, popular prints of the saints 'Abdul Qadir Jilani (Bagdad), Pir Mehr 'Ali Shah (Golra/Islamabad), and Baba Lal Shah (Sorasi/Murree). A big portrait of Mama Ji, the fresco on the left wall which depicts a Punjabi landscape with a huge lion, and a shrine in the background resembling that of Barri Imam were painted by Sayyid Ishrat, an old *murid* of the saint.

Up to 1989, Ishrat rented a part of a shop adjacent to the *astan* where he sold hand-painted portraits of the saint (see the illustration in Frembgen 1993: 110), as well as individual portraits based upon passport photographs. The self-taught painter, who is about 70 years old, originally comes from Saharanpur (Uttar Pradesh/India) and migrated to Pakistan in 1947. Since childhood, he told me, he loved to paint, perhaps stimulated by his mother, who was an experienced embroiderer. Ishrat's portraits of Mama Ji are placed by devotees in their homes and sometimes also in shops. Serving, above all, as devotional pictures, they also have a popularising, if not advertising, effect when put in the right place. So the bus driver Izhar from 'Pindi, for example, displays a framed photograph of his *pir*, Mama Ji, with a plastic board giving his name, honorary titles and address in the front window of his vehicle.

Through Sayyid Ishrat's paintings the appearance of the *darbar* has a charming touch of religious folk-art. Yet influenced by 'modern' aesthetics and current nostalgic 'fashions', the *mujawir*s decided to order a change of the living-room into a *shish mahal* (lit. 'palace of mirrors'). Mirror mosaic became popular in the time of the emperor Shah Jahan (1628–1658) and was used to give Mughal splendour to the court. So in February/March 1990, the local *ustad* (master), Shabir Ahmad, and his *shagird* (apprentice), Mohammad Amin, carried out extensive mosaic work, using motifs like the Kaaba, the tomb of the Holy Prophet in Medina, the shrine of Barri Imam, calligraphies with different blessing formulas, and the depiction of flower gardens in the Mughal style.

The entrance to the *langar* is marked by a glass case on a base built with mortar. It is used as a *cheragh-khana* (oil-lamp house) and contains five oil lamps symbolising the Holy Family, which burn in honour of Mama Ji's *murshid*, Barri Imam. Devotees take the oil as a remedy against any physical pain. In the *langar* the *mujawir*s, *cheragh-wala*s (attendants looking after the oil lamps) and *kismatgar*s (servants) offer food and tea as well as the *huqqa* (water-pipe) to the visitors; hashish is also consumed extensively. Sometimes, a few chicken or quails are kept in a hutch, cats play around, and before a *mela* (fair) one or two goats are fattened in advance of being butchered. Among Sayyid Ishrat's paintings are two big portraits of Mama Ji, one of Pir Chan Agha Badshah of Peshawar, and, as mentioned, a large fresco showing a Punjabi landscape with lions. Other religious posters

Plate 7.3 The painter and devotee Sayyid Ishrat
Photo by J.W. Frembgen

include portraits of Lal Shahbaz Qalandar (Sehwan) and Sain Kanwan Wali (Gujrat). In a corner there is a model (*dali*) of Barri Imam's shrine, which is taken to Nurpur on the occasion of the *'urs*.

> *Mama Ji Sarkar sarmast,*
> *do sauda dast-ba-dast!*
>
> Hand in hand [with the]
> intoxicated Mama Ji Sarkar,
> give in plenty!

The veneration of Mama Ji Sarkar

From morning until evening on an average day ten to fifteen persons – mostly men but usually also a few women – were constantly present in the *darbar*. The total number of visitors per day was around fifty to a hundred. They were mostly members of the urban unprivileged classes, including labourers, craftworkers, small employees, drug addicts, unemployed and the poor generally. Acts of patronage mainly came from a few persons belonging to the middle classes. As Mama Ji was not a *Sayyid* (one claiming blood descent from the Prophet), and consequently not a member of the religious elite, non-adherents see him in a lower position within the hierarchy of saints, a perception which coincides with the social standing of his followers.

Some *murid*s just touched their heart with the right hand while greeting the saint; others bent down at the foot of the bed to touch or kiss it, afterwards stroking their faces or hearts with their hands. Having thereby transferred something of the *majzub*'s divine power to themselves, they sat down on the floor quietly or chatted with a neighbour in a low voice. Some lit joss sticks. If the *mujawir* on duty gave his permission, people could come forward to make a request to Mama Ji for a prayer or to ask advice. As *nazr* (offerings) they donated money and brought food to him, especially eggs, because he liked eggs very much. The *mujawir*s interpreted this preference for *bahut garm asar* ('very hot' food as classified in the local folk medicine, derived from the classical Galenic version) as a sign of Mama Ji's 'hot state' of intoxication with God. They looked after him in a loving way and did everything for him, pushing strands of hair back from his forehead, fanning him, wiping his nose, putting a blanket around his shoulders, massaging him, feeding him, removing his faeces, etc. It should be remembered that the old man was confined to his bed for the last six years of his life.

Many *murid*s told me that in the presence of Mama Ji they experienced a direct transmission of the saint's blessings and his spiritual power. They described it as comparable to the flow of energy received in a normal *mazar*, but much stronger and of a superior quality. Being close to a living saint is thus something like a *darshan* – obtaining audience – in the Hindu context. The devotees felt free of their daily worries, unburdened by social pressure, and protected from evil and bad luck. They compared their mood to being happy and relaxed near a fountain with fresh healing water. This was visible in the shine reflected on their faces while they attended the saint's *darbar*.

Generally the atmosphere in Mama Ji's *darbar/astan* was informal, as it is in so many other 'small shrines'. The living saint seemed to stimulate communication among his followers, which went on in a casual, elated way, less ritualised than in the realm of an institutionalised tomb-cult. In Mama Ji's presence they conversed in whispers about personal spiritual experiences, dreams, favours bestowed upon them by the *majzub*, and his qualities, which ranked him superior to other saints. Here the narrative context was moulded by the devotees' confidence in the mystical power of their saint and a general positive tone. The emotional style of these conversations was therefore notably different to that, for example, at ritual meetings of women in the neighbouring North-West Frontier Province, Afghanistan, and Iran with their emphasis on *gham pasandi* ('loving grief') or *dard-e del* ('telling one's heart's sorrow') in a lamenting way (Fischer 1988: 38).

It should be added that each Thursday evening, and often on other weekdays as well, a *mehfil* (assembly) with *qawwali* was held in front of a congregation of twenty, thirty or even fifty people. If musicians were not present then cassettes by the Sabri Brothers were played. Frequently, also, drummers came to perform *naubat* (ritual drumming) at the saint's *baithak*. According to my observations, in both sanctuaries, in 'Pindi and Nurpur, expressions of high ecstasy and excitement by the saint's adherents were disapproved of and seldom seemed to occur. The group of *mujawir*s successfully promoted a serious framework of rituals in order to bring them into line with other orthodox Qadiri and Chishti tomb-cults.

Mama Ji's *dargah* in Nurpur: his second house

The *majzub* passed away on the 27th of the Muslim month of Ramadan AH1411 (12 April AD 1991), at 3.08 p.m.; shortly before he died, he is said to have uttered the *basmala* (invocation of God) and the *kalima* (the Muslim creed). In the morning, the saint was taken in a long procession from Rawalpindi to Nurpur and buried there at the Nuri Bagh, close to the shrine of Baba Juman Shah Bukhari, on the south-eastern outskirts of the village.

In the same month, the *mujawir*s and prominent *murid*s collected enough money to start building the frame of a shrine, which was structurally already complete by July 1991.[7] A period of stagnation followed in the construction of the *mazar* because of a deep disagreement and rift with Mahbub Ilahi, a 42-year-old man from Fatehjang, living in 'Pindi, who had been considered as the *fuqra-khadim* (leader of the followers) of the saint. He embezzled money donated for the shrine and was compelled eventually to leave 'Pindi. In Ramadan 1992, the followers of Mama Ji formed an *anjuman* ('society'), called *muridan muntazim kamiti Mama Ji Sarkar* (Committee of the Associated Followers of Mama Ji Sarkar) or sometimes also *intizamia bara-ye ta'mir darbar Mama Ji Sarkar* (Organisation for Building the Shrine of Mami Ji Sarkar), for the maintenance and organisation of the Nurpur-*mazar* and of the *astan* in 'Pindi, now the *akhir maqam* (last place) of the saint, where a framed painting of the *majzub* is placed on his bed. The latter symbolises the saint's 'empty throne'. The presidents of the *anjuman* were first Babu Mohammad Iqbal and then, since 1994, Shaikh Khalid Mahmud. As its degree of institutionalisation is still limited, arrangements are not yet bureaucratised.

The *anjuman* organised the first '*urs* on 1 April 1992: with a kitchen *langar* consisting only of two huts and one tent, it was still a modest event, with about 100–130 visitors coming in the evening. After the '*isha*' prayer, the guests were served with rice, meat, and tea, under a *shamiana* tent; a generator provided light for the *langar*. The tomb under construction was illuminated with neon garlands. Later on, a *mirasi* drummer and a young professional *dhamal* dancer were invited to perform. The visitors at that event were exclusively male and the majority belonged to the urban lower classes.

Mama Ji's '*urs* can be interpreted as a liminal situation for the pilgrims, who developed among themselves a communitas-type relationship characterised by a sense of equality, fraternity and solidarity. But Victor Turner's notion that 'the

Plate 7.4 The veneration of the dead saint in the *astan* in Rawalpindi; the *majzub* is depicted in a painting by Sayyid Ishrat
Photo by J.W. Frembgen

"other" becomes a "brother"' (Turner 1973: 207) holds even more true for the *majzub*'s sanctuary in 'Pindi, where the devotees living in the neighbourhood habitually just went around the corner to experience communitas in the presence of their saint. Such 'normative' communitas was part of their ordinary lives and, as such, it did not need to be embedded in the liminal situation of a temporary pilgrimage setting, outside the familiar, in Turner's terms.[8]

In the folk veneration of saints it is usually women who are more involved than men. Interestingly, in the case of Mama Ji, women are conspicuously absent in Nurpur, partly since, during this provisional stage of transition, no suitable arrangements have yet been made for their stay and proper social contacts. But it should be remembered that Mama Ji's *astan* in 'Pindi is already very confined and, in my observation, women do not find it easy to go there. In his lifetime he sometimes sent them away from his bed – even if they were not menstruating, as stated by informants – and only allowed access to men. A higher participation of women in the cult would most probably have lent it another character, with a different intensity of devotional sentiments displayed at the shrine.

During my subsequent visits, in 1992 and 1993, the devotees were increasingly discontented with the initial hasty planning of the new shrine and decided they wanted a more generous layout. So both in Nurpur and in 'Pindi, two large paintings by Sayyid Ishrat of the future shrine building are displayed, showing a prestigious, cube-shaped, domed structure with a veranda surrounding it. In September 1992, a forged iron door was erected at the entrance to the shrine, to protect it from goats. Heavy monsoon rains in summer 1994 threatened to wash away the tomb. In response, a solidly cemented basement, accessible by four stairs, was built and the tomb itself was brought down. By April 1994, the *langar* had already mushroomed, with several makeshift huts, small gardens, and fences for the *langar*'s property – now consisting of five goats and one sheep! It is still a casual, unstructured hang-out which, in its informality and availability of hashish, attracts free spirits and easy-goers, as well as seekers of mystical blessings.

During Barri Imam's *'urs* in 1994, in the first week of May, the *anjuman* was able to attract crowds of visitors to Mama Ji's shrine and to his former *baithak*, a holy place with a *cheragh-khana* in honour of the *majzub*, maintained by Sain 'Abdul Majid near the roadside. The latter was one of the closest *murid*s of the saint, who lives out the mystic ideals in an apparently authentic way. Even if not a *majzub* himself, 'Abdul Majid is inwardly and outwardly following in the footsteps of his *pir*. During Barri Imam's *'urs*, both places of devotion were richly decorated and the event was successfully used to publicise the name and sacred power of Mama Ji Sarkar. His own *'urs*, the fourth one, attracted hundreds of pilgrims – if not thousands as proclaimed by his followers.

The aesthetics of embodiment

Having now presented the ethnographic particulars, what insight can we get into the meaning of this cult, and which theoretical issues does it raise?

Fundamental is the problem of charisma: in one of his key theories, Max Weber argues that with the death of the charismatic, his mystical power either is converted into a 'charisma of office' and thereby routinised, or becomes 'tradition' in the form of a hereditary charisma.[9] In the case of Mama Ji his charisma is seen as a positive force, a benign mystical energy which is derived from his intimate contact with God. As it is in the nature of a *majzub* not to have an heir, the saint's pristine source of authority has obviously been lost. Consequently one would expect a decline in the 'personalised' character of his charisma and a growing institutionalisation in managing the affairs of both 'houses'. Yet the *majzub*'s disciples did not become real officials, and the rational organisation remains modest and unstructured.

In the present transitional phase from an emotionally intense, 'personalised' charisma to routinisation in the Weberian sense, interviews with followers already furnished the evidence of a contrast in the expressive forms of emotional devotion. The fountain of the devotees' love to Mama Ji goes on flowing, seeking immortality, but yet the saint's transition to the 'real life' with God means a break

Plate 7.5 The devotee Sain 'Abdul Majid, residing in the village of Nurpur Shahan
Photo by J.W. Frembgen

in his followers' ordinary lives, a kind of set-back into normalcy. Devotees confessed to me that they felt stronger in his presence in facing the hardships of daily life. Many of them often think: 'When Mama Ji was alive, all things went better!'. In the sacred intimacy of Mama Ji's *baithak* their *ta'alluq* (relation) was of another quality, namely, the personal encounter with a saint living among them. He was accessible and they could transfer his holiness through direct physical contact. He was an integral part of their everyday emotional experience; many devotees virtually shared his life. They were proud to have a living *majzub* among them, something which seems to be extraordinary, at least among the shrines of Rawalpindi. His followers miss the peculiar atmosphere in his shrine, the saint's comforting presence, his sensibility, and the balanced nature he induced in them. Mama Ji Sarkar has now withdrawn behind a *parda* (veil).

In theory, there seems little to choose between the political imaginaries of mystical power portrayed here, namely the 'pure', albeit short-lived and unstable, 'living' charisma of the saint in his first house and the manifestation of his *baraka* in the second house's tomb: in both, the saint embodies the vitalising force of his disciples' lives and remains himself, as the subject/object of devotion, relatively passive. In both, his presence inspires organisational activities and a sense of communitas between devotees. In accordance with the ideas of Emile Durkheim (1915), we observe that the saint's disciples form a close community sharing enthusiasm and common memories focused on their *murshid*. Yet this conceptualisation of charisma as 'imagined' and 'constructed' must contend with an ontological difference: the live saint was experienced not only as powerfully sacred but also as human, as vulnerable, as requiring care and loving attention. Mama Ji was 'mother' in two senses (hence the name *ma-ma*) – as protector and giver but also as an object of protection. So the *mujawir*s were concerned with his health and with the vigour of his body: they fed him, applied, and massaged him. But as his body was intrinsically pure, without emitting any odour, it did not need more care (washing, etc.), in the same way as with the famous *majzub* Baba Dhannaka (living near Manschra in the Hazara District) who has not moved from his sitting position for the past twenty-nine years. These examples show that among saints bodily qualities correspond to mystical qualities of the mind and soul.

Even though in the philosophy of Islamic mysticism we find the concept of the saint's power being considerably enhanced after his death, which means that the soul passes the door to the 'real life' with God whereas the physical body decomposes, my observations of living Sufism show that the presence of the *majzub* amidst his followers is of crucial importance to them. Consequently, disciples attach value to the living, physical body of their saint, whereas in the ideology of mysticism the body is seen as an obstacle and considered to be just a container for the soul, whose bonds have to be loosened in order for the soul to be purified. The body has been a project for mystics not only in Islam but also in other world religions (Shilling 1993; Feher 1989). Mystics control their body; they keep an extreme discipline and a strict dietary scheme, and deny sexual desire (Frembgen 1993: 166–170, 190–196).

In practical 'folk' Islam we find another concern with the ascetic body: because Mama Ji's body bore the imprint of saintliness, it was not perceived as equal to other humans'. Devotees were conscious about his body as an entity. They thought of his bones, flesh, bodily fluids and 'residues' (hair) as consisting of *baraka*, or having sacred qualities (hence the importance of relics; besides the theft of the saint's body, even the killing of the saint so as to get his body is known in the history of Sufism). Through touching the saint's body and paying loving attention to it, they transmitted this mystical power to themselves. If, as René Devisch points out, 'the human body is the central device or principal key that opens up and stimulates the whole system of healing' (1993: 264), then similarly Mama Ji's body appeared to be the source of curative powers.[10] Its healing capacity was an underlying factor in the love and devotion paid to the saint. Even though he remained a passive healer, through his body energy flowed to his disciples, conveying wellbeing and consolation to them. So Mama Ji's cult demonstrates how love and devotion are operative through the saint's body. In the veneration of the *majzub* his body became a 'lived experience' (Turner 1992; see also Shilling 1993: 101) for his devotees. They experienced the saint through a *darshan*-like contemplation as well as through his body as a medium of interaction; in this way they perceived Mama Ji as a psychosomatic unity, as soul and body together. Their orientation to him had therefore a high degree of concreteness differing in quality from the cult of a dead saint whose body is enshrined in a tomb.

'Knowing' and experiencing a saint as a living presence, feeling his personal magnetism, direct and intimate, touching his body, having actual eye contact with him, asking and getting response from him, and so forth, were all things that created a quality of emotion and rapture among the devotees otherwise unknown in Muslim tomb-cults. Charisma and love are intertwined like the warp and weft of a woven fabric. In our case this link seems to be strong enough to personalise the saint even after death. The personalised charismatic relation between the *majzub* and his disciples is kept alive in the shrine in 'Pindi. It is manifested in an 'original charismatic community', to use Weber's words (Weber 1947: 297), which has formed a strong 'We-relation'[11] among its members. This emotionally bound community, the first generation of disciples who encountered their saint face-to-face, tries to retain his personal charisma.

The peculiar, essentially irrational charisma of a religious virtuoso stands as anti-structure to the rational (anti-mystical), rule-oriented, official Islam represented by the 'religion of the mosque'. In the case of Mama Ji's shrine in 'Pindi, which is adjacent to the Jama' Masjid, this opposition is aptly reflected in the geographical setting. It becomes clearly recognisable and audible in the saint's silence as well as in his charismatic utterances, which are mystical revelations *per viam negationis* (on the road of negation) and stand in sharp contrast to the stereotyped prayers recited at the mosque, immediately behind it.

The first house in 'Pindi remains the real 'internal centre' for the devotees, where they experience communitas among themselves. Here, the aesthetic features of the setting are part of the peculiar devotion displayed at the shrine. Visual and auditory elements create a mystical 'climate'. Pictorial representations of Mama Ji and other, related saints have the role of mediating symbolic forms which touch the inner experience of the pious. In the intimacy of the shrine and *langar* they help to produce a stimulating atmosphere where the saint, whose lifestory is told, becomes familiar and close. Surrounded by Mama Ji's portraits, his *murid*s extol the virtues of their *murshid*, tell their dreams in which he appears as a saviour, and make his saintly qualities a topic of everyday discourse. As Bruce Kapferer puts it: 'The aesthetic object frames individual experience, sets it in motion, and establishes the context of its experiencing' (1983: 191). In addition to the aesthetic mode of paintings which covers a peculiar domain in the 'Pindi shrine, devotees are further sensitised by the flow of *qawwali*-music. This is a style of mystical music associated with divine love in its most intense form. 'It demands the living of the reality it creates', to quote Kapferer again (ibid.: 187). Religious folk-art here serves as a formula of experience and emotion, creating a context in which devotees feel again the presence of their saint.

As 'charisma has an implicit structural form as a process that takes place over time and under certain conditions' (Lindholm 1990: 7), the further development of Mama Ji's (male?) cult remains an interesting topic. The saint's *baraka* works in both houses and foci of veneration. Yet devotees are especially aware of his 'living', personalised charisma in the setting of the shrine in 'Pindi. They celebrate a form of Islam which offers a lot to the emotional needs of its adherents.

Acknowledgements

I am especially grateful to Pnina Werbner for reading different versions of the present chapter and providing very useful and inspiring comments. Hugh van Skyhawk's help in reading an earlier draft is also warmly appreciated.

Notes

1 During a seven-year period from March 1988 to September 1995 (in the course of twelve trips to Pakistan) I visited these two shrines frequently. Following the death of the *majzub* in 1991, the visits were also to the Nurpur *mazar*. What first started as a way of passing the time between arriving in Islamabad and embarking upon fieldwork in Northern Pakistan (Nager, Harban) matured over the period into a serious topic of research and has finally become a kind of possession (meaning that the saint and his cult possess me; compare Lewis 1986: 7). I am grateful to the *mujawir*s Rahim Gul Motilala, Nauroz, 'Abdul Majid, Tariq, and 'Abdul Rashid as well as to the *murids* Sayyid Ishrat, Sain 'Abdul Majid, Mohammad Rafique Qureshi, Liaqat 'Ali Bhatti (who first introduced me to the saint), Babu Mohammad Iqbal, and to my Sufi friend 'Abdul Qayyum from Gilgit for their help, cooperation and friendliness.
2 Compare Benz (1972: 132): 'Das Verstummen wird in einer religiösen Umwelt, die mit dem Phänomen der Ergriffenheit vertraut ist, geradezu als Zeichen der Begegnung mit der himmlischen Welt verstanden.'
3 See Digby (1986: 67). For the following, see Frembgen (1993: 95–115) with further bibliographical data.
4 McDaniel (1989). Similarly, wandering ecstatics among the Nigerian Tiv, who live like the *majzub* of the Qalandar order, are called people with the 'small madness' (Bowen 1964: 262).
5 'Alam Shah Bukhari was born in Kulachi (near Dera Ismail Khan) and lives now as a retired ward-master in the village of Aliabad (Hunza/Karakorum).
6 In addition to these emic explanations of the category of *majzub*, I would like to add an etic perspective, based on a strange neurological condition spread worldwide, but still little known outside medical science. It is a bio-psycho-social functional disorder investigated by the French neurologist Gilles de la Tourette at the end of the last century, and called after him Tourette's syndrome (Shapiro *et al*. 1988). This nervous condition, which mostly strikes young boys between the ages of 2 and 15, manifests itself in restlessness, impulsiveness, convulsions, hopping around, and the urge to touch things. Further features of this syndrome are: expressing oneself in a confused way, including curious neologisms; echolalia; strange gestures; sudden curses; and even blasphemous remarks and obscenities (coprolalia). These characteristic traits, which mark a grey area between 'normal' and 'disturbed', could, in my opinion, be a clue to an understanding of some *majzub*s. Not being a physician, I can obviously only suggest

the possibility of studying *majzub*s from this neurological perspective. It seems to me as an ethnographer that a lot of *majzub*s – including Mama Ji Sarkar – seem to answer to several traits of Tourette's syndrome.
7 The plot belongs to the villager Sain Ikram.
8 For a critical review of Turner's concept, see Bilu (1988: 302–330).
9 Weber (1947: 297, compare 54); Weber (1972: 143–145); compare Turner (1974: Ch. 2); Lindholm (1990: 23–27).
10 Compare Devisch (1993: 246, 257–258).
11 Schütz (1964: 24–33).

References

Bari, Moin (1994) *Saints of Sindh*, Lahore: Jang.
Benz, Ernst (1972) 'Ergriffenheit und Besessenheit als Grundformen Religiöser Erfahrung', in J. Zutt (ed.) *Ergriffenheit und Besessenheit: Ein interdisziplinäres Gespräch über transkulturell-anthropologische und -psychiatrische Fragen*, Bern and Munich: Francke, pp. 125–148.
Bilu, Yoram (1988) 'The Inner Limits of Communitas: A Covert Dimension of Pilgrimage Experience', *Ethos* 16, 3: 302–325.
Bowen, Elenore Smith [Laura Bohannan] (1964) *Return to Laughter: An Anthropological Novel*, New York: Doubleday.
Devisch, René (1993) *Weaving the Threads of Life: The Khita Gyn-Eco-Logical Healing Cult among the Yaka*, Chicago: Chicago University Press.
Digby, Simon (1986) 'The Sufi Shaikh as a Source of Authority in Mediaeval India', in M. Gaborieau (ed.) *Islam et Société en Asie du Sud*, Paris: Collection Purushartha, pp. 57–77.
Durkheim, Emile (1915) *The Elementary Forms of Religious Life*. London: George Allen and Unwin.
Einzmann, Harald (1988) 'Ziarat und Pir-e-Muridi: Golra Sharif, Nurpur Shahan und Pir Baba', *Drei muslimische Wallfahrtsstätten in Nordpakistan*, Stuttgart: Franz Steiner Verlag.
Feher, Michel (ed.) (1989) *Fragments for a History of the Human Body*, Vols 1–3, New York: Zone.
Fischer, Michael M.J. (1988) 'Aestheticized Emotions and Critical Hermeneutics', *Culture, Medicine and Psychiatry* 12: 31–42.
Frembgen, Jürgen W. (1993) *Derwische: Gelebter Sufismus. Wandernde Mystiker und Asketen im islamischen Orient*, Cologne: DuMont Verlag.
Frembgen, Jürgen W. (forthcoming 1999) 'Saints in Modern Devotional Poster-Portraits: Meanings and Uses of Popular Religious Folk-Art in Pakistan', *RES: Anthropology and Aesthetics*.
Gramlich, Richard (1965) *Die schiitischen Derwischorden Persiens*. Teil 1: Die Affiliationen, Wiesbaden: Franz Steiner Verlag.
Kapferer, Bruce (1983) *A Celebration of Demons: Exorcism and the Aesthetics of Healing in Sri Lanka*, Bloomington: University of Indiana Press.
Lewis, I.M. (1986) *Religion in Context: Cults and Charisma*, Cambridge: Cambridge University Press.
Lindholm, Charles (1990) *Charisma*, Oxford: Blackwell.
Loeffler, Reinhold (1988) *Islam in Practice: Religious Beliefs in a Persian Village*, Albany NY: State University of New York Press.
McDaniel, June (1989) *The Madness of the Saints: Ecstatic Religion in Bengal*, Chicago: University of Chicago Press.

Schütz, Alfred (1964) *Collected Papers II: Studies in Social Theory*, ed. and intro. Arvid Brodersen, The Hague: Mouton.

Shapiro, Arthur K., Elaine S. Shapiro, J. Gerald Young and Todd E. Feinberg (1988) *Gilles de la Tourette Syndrome*, 2nd edn, New York: Raven Press.

Shilling, Chris (1993) *The Body and Social Theory*, London: Sage.

Smith, Wilfred Cantwell (1959) 'Comparative Religion: Whither – and Why?', in M. Eliade and J.M. Kitagawa (eds) *The History of Religions*, Chicago: University of Chicago Press.

Turner, Bryan S. (1974) *Weber and Islam: A Critical Study*, London: Routledge and Kegan Paul.

Turner, Bryan S. (1992) *Regulating Bodies: Essays in Medical Sociology*, London: Routledge.

Turner, Victor (1973) 'The Center Out There: Pilgrim's Goal', *History of Religions* 12, 3: 191–230.

Weber, Max (1947) *From Max Weber: Essays in Sociology*, trans., eds and intro. H.H. Gerth and C. Wright Mills, London: Routledge and Kegan Paul.

Weber, Max (1972) *Wirtschaft und Gesellschaft*, 5th edn, Tübingen: J.C.B. Mohr.

8

A *MAJZUB* AND HIS MOTHER

The place of sainthood in a family's emotional memory

Katherine P. Ewing

Introduction

It has been noted that in popular Muslim belief madness and feeblemindedness are regarded not as disease, but as a sign that the affected person lives in a state closer to God than do most of us. In my own fieldwork in the vicinity of Lahore, Pakistan, I heard many stories of men and women acknowledged to be mad (*pagal*) who did such things as wandering the streets half-naked or spouting nonsense. Many people will go up to such unfortunates and touch them to receive God's blessing through them. Among those who could be labelled *pagal*, there were some – called *majzub* – who were treated with all the reverence and deference bestowed upon saints. In the Urdu language, the *majzub* is "one whom God draws to Himself" (Platts 1983: 1002). The *majzub* is one whose speech and actions appear to lack sense because his or her mind has been "burned" by the closeness to God.[1]

Once on a visit to a shrine, I was introduced to a Sufi living there. He was described to me as a great saint, and as far as I could see, he was treated with great deference. As I stood before the man, he pressed his thumb against my forehead and uttered buzzing noises. I was startled. My escorts, who were disciples of another Sufi who lived at the same shrine, explained that the saint had gotten so close to God that the encounter had "burned" his mind: he had become *majzub* – so close to God that he could not communicate normally with other people. This particular *majzub* was introduced to me in a formal, public setting: I was a scholar visiting the shrine on a crowded religious holiday and met him on a tour of the shrine, under the gaze of many disciples and onlookers. This public experience certainly seemed to support the general statement that madness and mental deficiency are not regarded as disease but as blessing among those who have been labeled "traditional" Pakistani Muslims. Stories I heard about other *majzub*s reinforced this impression.

But a general statement such as this is, of course, wrong. It highlights (or, rather, creates) a gulf that separates a modern Western discourse that constitutes "mental illness" as an observable, clinical, medical entity (see Foucault 1973) from a Muslim discourse that apparently does not. It obscures the nuances and contextual specificity with which Pakistani Muslims assess and react to those they label *pagal*. I did not feel a conceptual gulf when I participated in these people's lives and observed their behavior toward those whom they acknowledge to be *pagal* or *majzub*, even when I was introduced to the *majzub* who buzzed at me. Sure, I was startled when the man put his thumb on my forehead, but my nonverbal reaction seemed to be perfectly understandable to my companions, and their explanation seemed to answer my unasked questions about what was going on. I did not feel the gulf because it is actually much narrower than an interpretive stance embedded in general statements of cultural difference would have us believe. At that time I had no inkling of what it might mean at an experiential level to be a *majzub*, but neither did many of those around me. The difference between us was that they held it open as a real possibility that could, with sufficient insight, be understood. At this point I must ask, then, what does it mean to be "burned by God," beyond the stance of taking it as some strange idea engendered by another cultural system? How do people living in close contact with a *majzub* find meaning in the strange practices of the *majzub*? And how could such an idea be meaningful for me as a human being, as a reflection of a possible reality?

Statements of cultural difference articulated in terms of "modernity" and "tradition" are particularly powerful because they are distinctions organized in terms of a dominant discourse that posits progress and locates signs of this progression in Western practices (see, for example, Said 1979; Mudimbe 1988). The rhetorical power of this discourse has been challenged by anthropologists' articulations of the principle of cultural relativism and by recent questionings of a "grand narrative" of history that locates the West as the pinnacle of development. A tenet of cultural relativism is that the culturally other constitutes and occupies a reality grounded in principles incommensurable with those that organize Western experience. But the cultural relativist's stance also draws an artificial boundary between "us" and "them" that is insupportable when the day-to-day management of relationships involving those considered *pagal* or *majzub* is examined.[2] Anthropology has frequently been guilty of exoticizing the other, a sin that many in the discipline have been acutely self-conscious about in recent years.

One way of escaping an interpretive stance that constitutes an exoticized other is by shifting to a lens that focuses on the complexities of this day-to-day experience. The religious framework in terms of which the experiences of an unusual individual such as the *majzub* are explained does not operate as a totalizing interpretive grid that simply constitutes reality. This becomes visible when we examine how followers and associates of such a person articulate their own identities *vis-à-vis* their ties to the saint in a variety of discursive contexts. Though the *majzub* is explicitly associated with sainthood, the same individual may in another setting be called *pagal* (mad) and be rendered powerless.[3] In a context where his sainthood is recognized, is this recognition open only to "traditional" Pakistanis – the culturally "other"? Or is it open to "us" as well, to me as an anthropologist, as a thoughtful human being? Is there space for the truth of the experience of the *majzub* in our models?

In this chapter, I focus on the stories of the mother of a *majzub*. This mother's stories about two saints – her own son and her brother-in-law – express an ambivalence that reflects not so much a tension or discontinuity between tradition and modernity as her own conflictual positionings *vis-à-vis* discourses about family dynamics, assessments of disease, and attributions of sainthood. Modernity and tradition do not stand dichotomized as alternative explanatory models. Rather, explanations are closely tied up with identities, which are situationally specific and shift from one discursive context to another. In one positioning, Rabi'a is a member of a family that assesses and characterizes its members in terms of socially normative expectations about proper behavior, and she is affected by the tensions that emerge from a specific family dynamic. In another, Rabi'a is talking about people who are saints and who, therefore, stand outside of an everyday discourse of family and respectability; their identities have been bestowed by God. Because of her shifts in positioning, the significances of everyday events (and the memories of them) are unstable and polyvocal.

My approach is different from one to be found in studies of ethnopsychiatry and medical anthropology, in which the anthropologist identifies a range of "choices" available to actors, who as rational actors arrange the choices in some kind of hierarchy, these choices usually being based on competing indigenous and Western medical models of distress and cure. Another similar approach links the process of treatment choice to the issue of "diagnosis," so that the villager with a loved one who has been characterized as "crazy" or "not right" sees a range of possible causes for this problem and seeks a diagnosis and then an appropriate cure based on that diagnosis.

These models of rational choice do not do justice to the experience of individuals. On the one hand, such approaches make the observed, the other, appear "like us" – or like what we imagine ourselves to be – in ways that he or she actually is not: the informant is said to differ from us only in using a religiously grounded explanatory model rather than a scientifically grounded one as the basis for rational decisions. Thus, the cultural statement that Pakistanis view madness and feeblemindedness as a condition caused by God's favor is plugged into a Western, medical, empirically grounded interpretive frame. The approach is reminiscent of that of Frazer's and Tylor's theories of primitive religious practices and of Malinowski's (1948) description of magic as stepping in where science has not yet been sufficiently developed: it assumes that the natives are really rational if we only understand the misconceptions they have been forced to labor under.

On the other hand, such an interpretive procedure also makes the other more alien than, I argue, he or she actually is. It posits that we Westerners have access to "reality" and that those mired in "tradition" do not, that the idea of having one's mind burned by God is not a meaningful or real possibility for us.

I propose looking at the person who behaves oddly as a nexus of conflicting interpretive processes that serve as a vehicle for articulating self-experience and identity. The reverence shown such a person is one of many interpretive efforts made by people to account for the subjective experience and "otherness" of that person. This process of interpretation is especially complex for family members, for whom the act of caring for and experiencing a loved one is intimately linked with one's own self-images, conflicts, and complex, inconsistent social embeddedness. These interpretive efforts are not so different from the ones I (and probably most of my readers) might make under similar circumstances. Tracing out the conflictual process of interpretation itself highlights neither a cultural gulf between tradition and modernity nor a hermeneutic gap between cultures, but rather an array of responses that manifest our common humanity.

Rabi'a

When I met her, Rabi'a was an elderly woman who lived in Lahore, one of Pakistan's major cities, with her husband and her two youngest grown children. Her husband was a government servant, and so she and her family live in government quarters, a sterile-looking development of uniform brick houses on the outskirts of the city. Though Rabi'a was herself illiterate, her children had attended college. Despite twenty-five years of city living, Rabi'a continued to keep goats in the small courtyard of her home, much to her daughter's annoyance and embarrassment. She claimed that she had never used "Western" medicine.

Rabi'a could be described, undoubtedly with some distortion, as the mother of a revered "saint" (sa'in)[4] who was regarded as *majzub*. This son, whose name was Ashiq, was only 23 when he died. His ancestors had been saints. Their shrine dominates the small village north of Lahore where most of their relatives continue to live, and Ashiq had been designated the future successor of his paternal uncle, who is the current caretaker (*gaddi nishin*) of the family shrine.

I met Rabi'a through a young man, Anwar, a close school friend of Rabi'a's youngest son Tariq, who had recently graduated from college and had taken a job with the government. Anwar and I met with Rabi'a four times over the course of as many weeks and encouraged her to speak about her life, thoughts, and feelings. At each meeting, she spoke of her dead son Ashiq. We also had conversations with Tariq and with Talat, her youngest daughter, who together subsequently took us to the village to participate in and observe the annual *'urs* celebration at the shrine.

The death at age 23 of her son Ashiq twelve years before I met her was one of Rabi'a's great sorrows. In death, Ashiq affirmed Rabi'a's identity as mother of a saint, but during his lifetime Ashiq had been a constant source of worry for her because of his poor health and because of peculiarities in his speech and actions.

Plate 8.1 Rabi'a, mother of a *majzub*

Though his social positioning as a descendant of saints had made it possible for Ashiq to assume the identity of "saint," this positioning alone would not have been sufficient to account for the reverence with which he seemed to be viewed. Ironically, it was precisely the qualities that had given Rabi'a so much worry and concern that led to his acquisition of this identity. And this designation as "saint," though it affected Rabi'a's own identity, did not erase Rabi'a's very different experiences of her son and her various interpretations of his behavior and its causes.

Rabi'a had clearly given much thought to the possible reasons for Ashiq's difficulties and had spent much time and energy during his childhood seeking a cure for him. Several times, in several different contexts over the course of our conversations, she told us about Ashiq and how he became ill. Each version was slightly different. Rabi'a struggled to understand Ashiq's fate from many different perspectives, each of which located him somewhat differently in her social world and was linked to whatever aspects of her own identity had primacy at the particular moment in our conversations.

Through a Western medical lens, Ashiq could be diagnosed by means of an array of symptoms that are discernible though not salient in Rabi'a's accounts. He often had "fits" at night, for instance, suggesting that he had suffered minor brain damage at some point that had produced epilepsy and some retardation. Explanations such as this would have been used in certain contexts by other members of Rabi'a's extended family, including her husband, Ashiq's father. But this objectification does not in any way capture who Ashiq was and how he affected the lives of others, which was, after all, the issue for those around him.

When Rabi'a's many stories about her son and her relationship to her son are examined, particularly when we also consider what Rabi'a communicated to me about her own identity and self-images, ambivalence about the status of her dead son emerges as a recurrent theme. Rabi'a's descriptions of her son's sainthood are at the same time a vehicle for articulating her ambivalences about her relationships with others. Further, they also illustrate how the *majzub* exposes the detailed texture of the social fabric and opens a window into the unknown.

Stories about Ashiq

Rabi'a told the first story of Ashiq during our first interview, following several tales about experiences in her natal family and something of her life in Lahore. It was in the context of talking about her own dreams, which often cause her to feel tension, that she first alluded to her son Ashiq:

RABI'A: I have had this illness, this problem of feeling burdened [*bojh*] in my dreams, since Ashiq was born. Then I got a *ta'wiz* [amulet] for this disease, after he was born.
ANWAR: Do you still have it with you?
RABI'A: No, it has disappeared. I don't know where it has gone.
ANWAR: How long were you sick after Ashiq's birth?
RABI'A: About six months. Then my illness fell on Ashiq. I took him and went wandering [i.e., to doctors, *pirs* – saints, healers, etc.] Some people said some things, others said others. Some said he is a *sa'in* [holy man, saint].

In this story, Rabi'a's focus was on her own distress, struggles, and dream experiences. She remembered having been afflicted with a feeling of tension, of being burdened, from the time of Ashiq's birth. She felt that she had somehow passed her tension on to Ashiq, as if she were responsible for his illness. She did not overtly attribute the cause of the illness to external influence of any kind, or suggest that anyone was sending her the dreams that caused the strain, though such ideas are available to her within her system of beliefs. Instead, this story stressed her own feelings of connectedness with Ashiq and responsibility for Ashiq's condition through a process consistent with a model of the person prevalent in South Asia in which interaction with another can shape the "substance" and wellbeing of a person (Marriott 1976).

A moment later, prompted by a question of mine, she described again and in more detail what happened to Ashiq at 6 months of age:

KATHY: Did you feel anything unusual or special about his birth?

RABI'A: No, he was completely fine for six months. Tariq's father [i.e. Rabi'a's husband; Tariq was the connecting link between us] went to the village to take me back [from her parent's village to his own village]. Ashiq was born there.[5] It was summertime, very hot. God knows, he got heatstroke. On the way on the train, someone cut his hair. I don't know. Some threads from my *piranda* [hair ornament] were cut, too. On the way to the house, he began to vomit. I just thought, "perhaps he got heatstroke." That was all. After that, he was continually sick. He didn't speak for five years. He was always in my lap.

ANWAR: He didn't ask for anything, like "I feel hungry?"

RABI'A: Nothing. I gave him something. He was always in my lap. Someone said to me, "Sit this baby in the sand." Vilait's father [a person unknown to me] said, take *kol, tabashir* [chalk, which she said was commonly used as a Yunani medicine to reduce sores on the tongue or inside body], for reducing excess heat, and *choti ilachi* [cardamom]. Mix them together. Give it to him, and then he will talk. I gave it to him for five days. After five days, Ashiq said "Mama." Then he began to talk.

This set of explanations is quite different from the first. Rabi'a this time gave a straightforward mechanical explanation of his illness, heatstroke. She immediately added an alternative explanation based on very different premises. The alternative idea that "someone cut off his hair" alludes to a common technique of black magic. She – very tentatively – attributed the cause of Ashiq's illness to the evil intentions of another. But the two explanations, heatstroke and magic, seem to have been presented interchangeably.

Her organizing train of thought[6] at that point was clearly her family's ailments or "complaints" (Wilce 1994). This theme continued:

RABI'A: Even now my fingers get rigid [her son interpolated that this was a "nerves" problem]. Now I am quite worried about my daughter. Because it has been fourteen years. My daughter has had no daughter.

KATHY: What did she do for the problem?

RABI'A: She went to *pir*s. One time the *pir* said, "Take an almond that has two pieces inside it and bring it to me. I will read something over it. After that give it to your daughter and son-in-law." But she did not go to that *pir* [i.e. Rabi'a herself had gone to the *pir* on behalf of her daughter, who did not follow up on the advice]. She went repeatedly to a *pir* in Kharian [a town about an hour north of Lahore] but not here. Now she doesn't want to go to any *pir* because she has become very worried, or rather, disappointed.

TARIQ: She says, "If I am to have a child, it can come only from God, not from any *pir*."

RABI‘A: When she began to get treatment from the Kharian *pir*, I went to Data Sahib [Lahore's most important Sufi shrine]. I told my dream to a *faqir* [a beggar-ascetic] there. [In the dream] I saw that someone closed a water pipe by filling it with dust. Baba [the *faqir*] said, "Your daughter's birth canal is closed . . . You should bring your daughter before me once."

Her husband [Rabi‘a's daughter's husband] doesn't believe this. He says, "We will see."

The core issue continued to be disease and possible cures. Ashiq's partial cure involved a Yunani (Greek) medicine[7] that corrected the problem of excessive heat in his body, which presumably had been caused by the heatstroke. She, Ashiq, and her daughter were all afflicted with diseases that may or may not have been caused by the malicious activities of others.

A subtext of this discussion is thus the question of whether black magic can cause disease and whether *pir*s can cure it. This became explicit in Rabi‘a's comment about her daughter's husband. Nevertheless, this issue, which is a crucial one for those who are concerned with being "modern" or with distinguishing "reality" from superstition within a modernist discourse, did not seem particularly salient for Rabi‘a, except to the extent that my presence as an American made it so. She seemed hesitant to commit herself to a position that she suspected I might think was foolish. Mention of her daughter's husband may reflect something of this dynamic in our first interview, especially her fear about whether I would respect her and her practices. Rabi‘a had also been reluctant to discuss black magic as a cause of Ashiq's disorder. She hesitated to invest herself in this explanation at this moment in our conversation, distancing herself from it by saying "I don't know" immediately after raising the possibility of such an explanation. She may have been uncertain about what I would think of this type of explanation. This was our first meeting, and she probably assumed that I would be more receptive to a medical "scientific" explanation.

Not much more salient is yet another description of Ashiq's condition, an alternative that shapes his very identity – the fact that he was a saint. From this discursive positioning, his peculiarities of behavior and speech were caused by his being *majzub*, i.e. so drawn to God that he was not fully of this world. In this conversation, she presented him as having an illness, with only a hint of his identity as a *sa'in* (saint). Ashiq was portrayed as a family member who had a disorder. The suggestion that he might be a *sa'in* was attributed to the anonymous people she encountered in her wanderings in search of a cure and was given no particular weight in the conversation.

A couple of weeks later when we met again, she once more told us of the onset of Ashiq's troubles, but this time the narrative context was quite different. She herself was not the topic of conversation, and we were not focused on disease. Anwar began our conversation by asking her to tell us about her "brother-in-law who is a *pir*," taking an initiative that reflected his status as a friend of the family by indicating his own pre-existing knowledge of this man, Sa'in Sahib. After Rabi'a gave us a lengthy description of Sa'in Sahib's practices as a *pir* and his position in the family,[8] our conversation (like our previous meeting's discussion about disease) eventually came around to Ashiq. She began to discuss who Sa'in Sahib's eventual successor would be. She described a boy, the son of another brother-in-law, who is regarded by all as the person who should "sit on the *gaddi*" (the honored seat; i.e. he will be the caretaker of the shrine):

> All say that after Sa'in Sahib, this boy should sit on the *gaddi*. His name is Achi. He is 12 or 13 years old. At first the *nazar* [gaze] was on Ashiq, but now, after his death, people's *nazar* is on Achi.

After some description of what Achi has done to gain this recognition, she continued, eventually shifting to a direct focus on Ashiq:

> because he [Achi] doesn't go to school, doesn't work, always sits near Sa'in Sahib. His parents sent him to work, but he also gave that up. He returned to the village.
>
> My own son was *sa'in*. When he was 6 months old, I was returning from my parents' village to my husband's village. On the way, a strange woman cut a bit of my little boy's hair and some threads of my *piranda*. After this, he became sick. For five years he did not speak a single word. Then he began to speak. That which he spoke to me came true. Usually he spoke little, but whatever he said was true. It has been twelve years since he died. But people still call me Ashiq's mother.

This story is similar to the story she told in our first meeting, but with some striking differences. This time, she only mentioned his illness rather than describing it, and she never mentioned heatstroke. She stated that he did not speak, just as she had during our previous conversation. This time, however, she used his mode of speaking as evidence for his sainthood, in contrast to our first meeting, when she went on to describe an ailment of her daughter. All this was preceded by a statement asserting that Ashiq was a *sa'in*, in contrast to the first story, when she merely stated that some people had said that he was a *sa'in* as a way of explaining his abnormality.

Like her first story, this one is constructed out of elements that seem to be inconsistent. In the first one, the explanations for Ashiq's abnormality seemed to be presented as an array of alternative possible "diagnoses" proffered by the many people she consulted as she sought a cure. This time the inconsistent elements are apparently being presented as a sequence of facts. They are not given as diagnoses but as facts that serve as explanations for why he was different from others. On the one hand, he was different because he was sick due to a form of black magic. On the other hand, he was different because he was a *sa'in*. The sequence and logic of her statements might appear to be that he was *sa'in* because of black magic (*kala 'ilm*) (see Ewing 1982): she began with the statement that he was a *sa'in*, and then immediately began to describe the act of black magic. Using a logic of diagnosis, one might infer from this that black magic caused him to be a *sa'in*. But she would have objected to this interpretation. Rather, her story asserts the significance of Ashiq's life in terms of inconsistent interpretive frames that are simply juxtaposed. These two explanatory models – that he was a *sa'in* and that he was ill – are tied to different historical moments in the evolution of her relationship with her son. She has not chosen one over the other as "reality," but rather experiences both as true. At this point in her life, with Ashiq already dead, she is not centrally concerned with what in particular caused his disorder. But she is concerned with his ongoing identity and is deeply ambivalent about it.

On the one hand, Ashiq was a difficult child and young adult who was sickly and often socially inappropriate. On the other hand, he was – is – a saint. He was a source of worry and embarrassment, a sign of her failure as a mother. In this role, he was a target of her anger and a source of guilt. These mixed feelings find voice in her many stories of Ashiq's life. Her stories of him during our first meeting expressed one aspect of this side of their relationship: her responsibility for his physical disorder, his connectedness to her through this disorder (her own disorder "fell" onto him), and her efforts, some of them successful, to cure his disorder. Even though the stories she told during our second meeting were all couched in the discursive context of his sainthood, they included many elements that suggested her impatience with his socially inappropriate behavior, behavior that reflected an illness or disorder. Again, her mixed feelings of guilt and anger found voice. Here is an example:

> One time in summer he went out early in the morning. I looked for him the whole day. His father had gone to the office. In the evening a neighbour woman said to me, "We should ask for an announcement in the mosque." I asked for an announcement [*elan*]. As it turned out, Ashiq had wandered to Samnabad [another Lahore neighborhood]. He was with the bear tamers. There, one bear tamer heard the announcement and asked Ashiq, "What is your name?" He answered "Ashiq Hussain." "There has been an announcement for you. Go back to your home." Then he came home. I asked him, "You didn't forget the road?" [He was probably 21 at the time.] "No, I didn't forget the road. Where I went, I saw fun [*shughal mela*]." He just stood there.
>
> He loved sweepers, puppies; he brought home four puppies. [It is unusual for Pakistanis to keep dogs as pets. They are regarded as dirty, polluting and promiscuous.] He kept them in the courtyard. He was only afraid of his father. No one else.

Taken out of context, it is the story of a socially inappropriate, childlike, probably cognitively deficient young man whose mother had difficulty managing him. But within the context of a conversation about sainthood, this story is also taken up into another net of meaning, another discourse, that gives both Ashiq and Rabi'a very different identities. Ashiq's death is commemorated every year. These commemorations enact Ashiq's identity as a saint. It was following Rabi'a's description of these commemorative activities that she told me the above story. She had already listed the several activities that were carried out as part of the rituals established by Sa'in Sahib and the family to commemorate Ashiq's death:

> After his death, Tariq started *bhangra* [a special kind of dance when someone beats the drum], because Ashiq liked *bhangra* very much. He didn't eat anything the whole day. He just wandered around. One time in summer . . . [and Rabi'a launched into the above story].

The connection between the prelude and the story was that Ashiq liked drums, dancing, and the like with such abandon that he forgot everything else. This is a quality of a *majzub*. Rabi'a's concerns as a mother were encompassed by a narrative of sainthood. Yet they were not erased. Both voices, both narratives, emerged simultaneously (Bakhtin 1981).

How did Ashiq's and Rabi'a's identities become articulated through a discourse of sainthood? Rabi'a did not describe the precise point in time when Ashiq was first described as a *sa'in*, but the process of Ashiq's interpellation vis-à-vis a discourse of sainthood can be discerned from her stories. During Ashiq's childhood, Sa'in Sahib, who is the elder brother of Rabi'a's husband, developed a relationship with the boy and let it be known that he intended to designate Ashiq as his successor. This had implications for the relationship between mother and son. Rabi'a's stories suggest that Sa'in Sahib often intervened in their relationship, forcing her to be more accommodating to Ashiq's wishes:

ANWAR: Did any special things in life please Ashiq?
RABI'A: No, he had no interest in eating.
ANWAR: Did any special kind of clothes please him?[9]
RABI'A: Yes, sometimes, he liked special kinds of cloth. One time when my eldest daughter was married, we went to the bazaar to shop. Sa'in Sahib and one of his *murid*s [disciples] were with me. When we were coming back, he began to demand, "I want to buy playboy cloth." I said, "I have no money." He lay on the ground. Sa'in Sahib said, "What is this?" I stayed silent. Ashiq said immediately, "Sa'inji, I have to buy that cloth." Sa'inji was angry with me. He said, "Rabi'a Bibi, he never demands anything. If he demands it, give it to him." He immediately said to the shopkeeper, "Give us cloth for one *kamiz* [shirt]." Sa'in Sahib still has that same *kamiz*.

Sa'in Sahib's power to intervene stemmed from two sources: he was Rabi'a's husband's elder brother and thus the authority and decision-maker for the extended family, and he had a special connection to God that was reflected in his status as *sa'in*. Sa'in Sahib had inserted himself between mother and son.

Sa'in Sahib's two distinct sources of authority reinforce each other but nevertheless co-exist in uneasy tension. This is because Sa'in Sahib is a man whose authority as eldest brother might well have been questioned had it not been for his status as *sa'in*. Rabi'a made it clear in her descriptions of Sa'in Sahib that he has not fulfilled the conventional social expectations that normally give a man respectability, power and authority: he has not held a proper job, he did not successfully fulfill the role of husband to the unfortunate woman selected to marry him, and he did not produce children of his own. Rabi'a accepts his authority over her in the management of extended family relationships, but she is ambivalent. She expresses this ambivalence in stories that position him both as a social oddity and as a saint.

Stories of Sa'in Sahib

Let us return now to the beginning of our second conversation, when Anwar asked Rabi'a to tell us about Sa'in Sahib:

ANWAR: Khalaji, tell us about your *jhet* [elder brother-in-law], who is a *pir*. Tell us about the events that he foretold that came true, and tell us about his attitudes towards his family members.

Rabi'a responded on a negative note, juxtaposing an ideology of sainthood with the tensions of family life:

RABI'A: For him all are equal; but in fact he loves his followers more than his family.
ANWAR: When you were married, you and your husband were cousins, and you already knew Sa'in Sahib?
RABI'A: Yes, but I felt shame [*sharm ati he*] anyway. Sa'in Sahib told me to put my *dupatta* [thin shawl, worn as a sign of modesty by virtually all Pakistani women either across the shoulders or on the head] on my head in front of him.

With this act of ordering Rabi'a to cover herself in front of him, Sa'in Sahib asserted his authority over her. At the time of her marriage, Rabi'a's husband was still living with his parents. In recounting this episode, she was describing how she moved into an extended family in which status relationships, including the age ranking of brothers, were clearly and explicitly marked by the deference behavior of their wives:

ANWAR: Was he a *sa'in* from the beginning? He never got married?
RABI'A: No, in the beginning he got married, because he was the eldest. His mother cried because he wasn't willing to get married. Then he married his *khala's* [mother's sister's] daughter. But he passed most of his time with his *dada* [father's father], who was also a *sa'in*. For this reason, he didn't like marriage.

ANWAR: How old was he when he got married?

RABI'A: About 25 or 26. After that he didn't go to his house.

ANWAR: Did Sa'in Sahib refuse to get married?

RABI'A: He neither refused nor accepted [*Na inkar na ikrar*]. He didn't return to the house for twelve years after his marriage. Instead, he sat in the *dere* [village meeting place] outside. After twelve years, his *khala* said, divorce my daughter. Sa'in Sahib wanted his wife to become *sa'in*, too. Because what is there to take from the world? Our Sa'in Sahib is a *langotia faqir* [i.e. has made a vow of celibacy never to remove his loin cloth].

The world is such that it does not give respect; on the contrary, he had to make a big sacrifice in order to gain respect ['*izzat*]. I fought with people, but once he asked me to sit down with him. He said, "Rabi'a Bibi, tell these people what they want you to tell them. If they don't call me a bad person, then we people will become proud. These people will in this way wash away even my smallest sins."

Some beautiful, fair-skinned women came to him once at night. And they were wearing quite a bit of gold. Sa'in Sahib told them to leave immediately.

One man named Muhammad Din gave up all his worldly things and came to stay forever with Sa'in Sahib, because he says "Peace is available from Sa'in Sahib. I have no need for land and home." Now he has become very aged. First Muhammad Din used to take *charas* [hashish] and *bhang* [an intoxicating drink], but when he came to Sa'in Sahib he gave it all up.

In this passage she positioned herself as a loyal member of the extended family *vis-à-vis* the outside world. She depicted Sa'in Sahib as a saintly figure, different from other men. Though she was not explicit about what the issues were that led her to fight with outsiders, her subsequent train of thought makes it clear enough: he was accused of being corrupt, of indulging in debauchery with women and drugs behind the cover of his spiritual claims. Muhammad Din, judging from this description, could be characterized as a *malang* [a religious mendicant who disregards aspects of Islamic law; see Ewing 1984], since he was known to have been corrupt. His presence thus threw Sa'in Sahib's respectability into question, as did visits from strange women. As a family member, Rabi'a described acting personally insulted when Sa'in Sahib's respectability was challenged. His admonishment to her was to adopt a strategy well known in the Sufi tradition, the *malamati* stance, drawing blame onto oneself as a way of removing self-conceit on the path of spiritual development (see Hujwiri 1976: 62–63). Sa'in Sahib's identity as a *sa'in* gives him status and authority, but his identity in many respects operates at the very edge of everyday respectability and even challenges the foundations of everyday life.

Anwar asked a question that refocused on the expectations of everyday life and his violation of them:

ANWAR: Tell me about the divorce.

RABI‛A: He went to his wife and told her, "Stay in this house like this if you want to be my wife," but she said, "Give me a divorce." His wife's family put a lot of pressure on him for a divorce. They wanted to marry her to someone else. Sa'in Sahib became angry. He wrote on a paper, "I give you a divorce."

ANWAR: Did he get it from the court?

RABI‛A: I don't know where he got it. But he spent a lot of money on it. It has been a long time since the divorce. The girl's parents remarried her, and then she became blind. When she became blind, her second husband took another wife. People began to say that it was because she was divorced from a *sa'in*.

ANWAR: Is she still alive?

RABI‛A: No, she died. He [Sa'in Sahib] had no interest in the world. People said that she received a *faqir*'s *bad-du‛a* [bad prayer, curse; i.e. that Sa'in Sahib had cursed her]. When this woman remarried, she had a son. But none from Sa'in Sahib. When she was alone in the house and Sa'in Sahib would come, he would run if he saw that his mother was not there.

[Anwar commented to me as we went over the tape of the interview together later: "I have seen him. He doesn't look like a man – he wears gold earrings, pink clothes. When I went to visit him and saw him from the back, I asked Tariq if a guest had come, because I thought it was a woman. Tariq said, 'No, that's my *taia* (father's elder brother).' I was embarrassed."]

ANWAR: Didn't he even come home for the evening meal?

RABI‛A: No, usually he ate in the *dhera* [men's gathering place in the centre of the village]. He prayed for other people for children, but no children were born in his house. All is Allah's work. Sa'in Sahib says, "I pray, but God's willingness is necessary."

ANWAR: Was he a *sa'in* from birth?

RABI‛A: He sat at the shrine and started to write *ta‛wiz*. He became a *sa'in*.

The story of the divorce and Anwar's aside about Sa'in Sahib's ambiguous gender status make clearer the extent to which Sa'in Sahib's behavior lies so close to the edge of respectability that his presence stimulates anxiety and hostility in others. Outsiders sometimes see him as a threatening presence who has the power to curse those around him. This was an explanation given for his ex-wife's blindness. Not only did he not fulfill his role as a husband; he is guilty of an even more basic violation of social order, dressing like a woman. He creates anxiety and calls attention to the constructedness of social order by disrupting its ordering principles. But this is precisely the quality that makes sainthood so powerful: it forces people to confront the arbitrariness and limited nature of their everyday lives, thereby opening a window for the perception of something beyond. This is what Sa'in Sahib himself had told Rabi‛a when she had felt her identity as a woman in a respectable family threatened.

Rabi‛a respects this position, but she also expresses an ambivalence in her

Plate 8.2 Sa'in Sahib

relationship with Sa'in Sahib. Rabi'a has been disappointed in Sa'in Sahib, both as eldest brother-in-law and head of the family and as a *pir*. But he is a brother-in-law to be obeyed. Because of his violation of everyday standards of respectability and the resulting social criticisms of Sa'in Sahib, she has felt her own sense of respectability and identity as a member of his family threatened. On top of that, she often feels that she does not benefit from his status as a *pir*. Because she is of the same family, he is not someone she could turn to in solace as an idealized other, as one would a *pir*. He produces cures and children for others, but he could not do so even for himself, much less for her.

The *sa'in* and the symbolic order

But the source of Rabi'a's frustration with Sa'in Sahib is in some respects more fundamental than simply that she cannot idealize him as a *pir* because she is close enough to see his flaws. An important component of the tension can be seen by returning to an examination of the process by which Ashiq became a saint, a process that involved Sa'in Sahib's insertion of himself between mother and son. Psychodynamically, this process can be understood in terms of a relationship involving four people: Ashiq, Rabi'a, Sa'in Sahib, and Ashiq's father, who is Sa'in Sahib's younger brother (and, of course, Rabi'a's husband).

Ashiq's father fulfills the role of husband and father in a far more conventional manner than Sa'in Sahib: he works at a government job, he provides his family with a house and necessities, and he is often away. He functions as a kind of absent presence in Rabi'a's stories. He is the ever-present threat of discipline:

> One day he [Ashiq] brought in a porcupine. It was injured. It was bleeding. I said, "You've gotten your clothes all dirty with blood." He said, "Ammiji, it will drink water, and then it will die. Let him drink the water." This very thing happened. After drinking the water, it died. People don't like to touch porcupines. When it died, he said, "Before my father comes home, I will make a coffin. Then you can wash my clothes."

Implicit in Ashiq's last two statements is that he will hide the evidence of his transgression before his father returns. Ashiq has done something socially inappropriate, for which he could be punished. He has polluted himself with blood and touched something disgusting. The same motif recurred at the conclusion of the story of the time he wandered off to watch the bear tamers (see above). Ashiq's father had "gone to the office" when the events of the story transpired. Only at the very end of the narrative does his name reappear, and then only in the abstract, in his role as disciplinarian: "He [Ashiq] loved sweepers, puppies; he brought home four puppies [again, a source of pollution]. He kept them in the courtyard. He was only afraid of his father. No one else."

This is a classic oedipal situation. To use Lacanian terminology, the father of these narratives[10] is the representative of the Law, the Symbolic Order, the Other who is never fully present but structures the unconscious of the oedipal child through the act of prohibition. The child adopts a subject position *vis-à-vis* this Symbolic Order, apparently accepts his gendered position as a successor to his father.

But these are stories of subversion: Ashiq outwardly submits to his father's discipline, but not by adopting a subject position that will lead to identification with his father. He asks his mother to collude with his transgressions. Rabi'a recognizes this subversion and attributes it to Sa'in Sahib. A saint may be simply an alternative representative of the Symbolic Order, as the *pir* often is. Rabi'a herself seeks out such *pir*s in her search for cures, *pir*s who represent God as the ultimate source of authority and power, the Other of the Symbolic Order *par excellence* (see Ewing 1997). But the true Sufi, as Sa'in Sahib suggests, undercuts this Symbolic Order, subverts it to open up the mystery of life. In his daily practice, Sa'in Sahib undercuts the authority of the Father, the Symbolic Order (while, paradoxically, maintaining his authority over the extended family, and even over Ashiq's father). This can be seen, for instance, in the story of the shirt, where Ashiq threw a tantrum because Rabi'a refused to buy him a shirt. Sa'in Sahib undercut her authority as representative of discipline and the Father, and bought him the cloth. The undercutting, however, goes beyond the control and discipline in a moment of tantrum. In his own behavior, Sa'in Sahib has refused even a gendered positioning. The story of the cloth suggests that he was encouraging that refusal in Ashiq as well.

The result is that Ashiq, too, has refused the Symbolic Order and has escaped its constraints (see Deleuze and Guattari 1983). He identifies with the abject, that which has been dismissed as impure, dangerous, and disgusting (see Kristeva 1982), and evades the discipline of everyday life. The power of this escape is recognized and revered by many of those who know him: people allow him to wander off with their goats; they give him gifts; shopkeepers call him to their shops for his blessing. This is the power of the *majzub*.

But it is painful for parents to see a child escape their efforts to position that child in the world. When Ashiq was alive, Rabi'a was pulled in several conflicting directions. She was torn between wanting to recognize the power that Ashiq represented and wanting to maintain her expectations of what a son should be in an ordered world in which she and her husband had the authority and responsibility for raising that son.

Ashiq's death

Rabi'a's story of Ashiq's death encapsulates all these themes. The sense of being rejected in favor of another shapes her perception of his death far more strongly than any idea of his sainthood. At the ultimate hour Ashiq turned away from his mother and chose to align himself with Sa'in Sahib. His father was away, off in the world of modern medicine, trying to buy something that would rescue him from death.

Rabi'a described many of Ashiq's utterances that came true as proof of his sainthood, but to her the most significant event he forecast was his own death. The ability to predict one's own death is generally recognized as a sign of great spirituality. It is an ability attributed to many saints.[11] Rabi'a's story of Ashiq's death includes many narrative elements that articulate the identity of a saint in a similar way. Nevertheless, it is shot through with expressions of the tension that characterized the relationship between mother and son and the relationship between Sa'in Sahib and Rabi'a as brother-in-law and sister-in-law. Rabi'a and Sa'in Sahib had clearly vied for the loyalty of her son, and it is evident that Sa'in Sahib had won:

RABI'A: Before Ashiq went to the village for the last time, he met with everybody. We people were all ready to go to the village. We were all worried about where Ashiq had gone. He said to everyone, "This is the last time I will see you. Now I won't return." It was December, just as it is now. I wanted to go to the village only a few days before the *mela* [the annual celebration at the family shrine], but he had been pushing me to go more quickly. Before we left for the village he disappeared. After three or four hours, he finally returned to the house. I asked him, "Ashiq, where did you go? You were very late. Now it will be night while we are traveling to the village." So he said, "I went to see all of my aunts, because I won't be coming back." I thought that he was talking nonsense [*fazul*]. But after he died, I realized that he had spoken the truth. I hadn't understood. He said, "I went to them to ask forgiveness because I won't return." As he was going to the village for the last time, he said to his eldest sister, "Apa, you should keep watering my trees." At that time there was one pomegranite tree and one grapevine. His sister replied, "Do it yourself." Then he said, "No, I won't return."

When my son left here he was fine. He was fine during the whole *mela*. After a few days, there was another *mela* in another village. After that he went to my parents' village. He took sugarcane with him. There was also sugarcane in that village. My sister-in-law started laughing and asked, "Why did you bring this sugarcane from that village? We have it in our village." He said that he had brought it for Ghazala [Tariq's future wife, a cousin]. He always said that "Ghazala is ours." I always insisted that the other cousins are also ours. Then he started to abuse me and said that only Ghazala is ours. When he returned to his *taia*'s [i.e. Sa'in Sahib's] village, I wanted to return to Lahore. I asked Ashiq, "Would you like to go with me to Lahore?" He refused, and I left him there with his *taia sa'in*.

He went with Sa'in Sahib to another *mela* in the next village. He got sick there. God knows better. He caught pneumonia [*sardi* – cold]. He was seriously ill. So Sa'in Sahib wrote me a letter. Meanwhile my elder daughter Souraya said to me, "Mother, you should go to the village. I saw a horrible dream [*khofnak*]." I said, "I will go tomorrow." That day Ashiq was seriously ill. I went quickly to the village. When I got off the bus, I asked people from the village, "Have you seen my Ashiq?" The people said, "He is better now. At first he was very sick." I was so upset [*parishan*] that I cannot tell it. When I arrived at the house, Ashiq was on the bed. Muhammad Din [Sa'in Sahib's disciple] was sitting near him. He said, "Now you have come, after so many days. Ashiq is very sick." I looked in my son's direction. He turned his face away. I went to that side. He turned his face the other way. I stayed six days there. My son didn't say anything to me. . . .

On the day he died, early in the morning, he said to Sa'inji, "Say to my mother, 'Go from here.' I want to talk with you." Sa'inji said to me, "Rabi'a Bibi, go outside." I stood outside the door and listened. He said, "You will collect a lot of money." [Rabi'a and her daughter began to cry intensely at this point during the narration.] He said to Sa'inji, "Mother should leave this place." Sa'inji was crying.

ANWAR: Why was Sa'inji crying?
RABI'A: He knew he was going to go before it happened. Ashiq said to Sa'in Sahib, "Seven people will come with drums. And many people will come.

Much money will come. And tie a turban on me when I die. And don't be nervous [*ghabrana*]. And fix the turban on my head right now." Sa'in Sahib said to me, "Rabi'a Bibi, give me the turban that is hanging on the wall." I got the turban. Ashiq began to say, "This turban – " Sa'inji said, "Tomorrow we will both go on a trip and get a new turban from there. Today, tie this one."

Sa'in Sahib tied the turban on Ashiq. And he cried as he did it. When he had tied it, Ashiq said, "I want to see a mirror. Now where is my mother. Call her." Then I sat in front of him.

ANWAR: Then did he say any *dil ki bat* [words from the heart]?
RABI'A: They weren't words from the heart. Yes, he began to talk. After he died, all his utterances came true. The drum beaters came. A lot of money was collected. . . .

After he died, a *sera* was tied on him [an ornament with gold threads that hang over the face, usually worn by a man at his wedding]. A turban was put on. Much money was collected. The whole village did not cook for sixteen hours.

First they collected the money in their shirt-tails. Later, there was so much money that they made a *jholungia* [a big cloth held up by four sticks].

His *mela* takes place every year. So Sa'in Sahib repeats all these things. Everything happens just as it was on the first day. They cook big pots of food. *Qawwal* [singers] come. There is *qawwali* [devotional singing] the whole night.

This is the story of the death of a saint. The death reshapes reality and transforms the ambiguities of Ashiq's strange actions and peculiar statements into the utterances of a *majzub* – prognostications that are fulfilled at the moment of his death. The story begins with Ashiq bidding a final farewell to all his friends and family in the city. But, like the prophet who is not recognized in his own land, Ashiq is mocked and criticized. His sister responds to his final request to her with the lack of respect typical of siblings the world over: "Do it yourself." His mother, like all mothers, chides him for being late. Through the eyes of those who cannot see, he is merely irresponsible and foolish.

This is a narrative of recognition, narrated with the voice of one who recognizes the identity of a saint. It is told by one who did not see but who has been transformed by the events she is narrating: "I thought that he was talking nonsense. But after he died, I realized that he had spoken the truth. I hadn't understood." In this plot, Rabi'a casts herself as one of those who failed to see the truth while he was alive. But with his death, her reality has been transformed, and her identity as the mother of a saint has been established. The moment of death is the transformative event.

But this speaker was precisely – and negatively – positioned during the transformative events. In the extended description of Ashiq's death, Rabi'a vividly communicates her positioning – her marginalization – with respect to the establishment of the sainthood of her son. We hear many of the events by listening

A *MAJZUB* AND HIS MOTHER

Plate 8.3 A *mela* at the family shrine

through a crack in the door, or sitting quietly facing the back of the saint's head. It is a story of connection refused, of a son who escaped an identity as her imperfect son. In the beginning of the narrative, before he becomes sick, all of their exchanges are of disagreement over the significance of Ashiq's utterances. Once he is ill, he refuses to recognize her or to allow her to recognize him: he keeps his face turned away. It is only after the turban has been tied – when he adopts the appearance of a saint – that he calls her in and requests that she look at him. She becomes his mirror. It is the moment at which he sheds finally and completely the image of the defective, foolish child that he saw in her gaze and identifies with the image of the saint as it is now reflected in the mirror of her eyes. He has forced even his mother to recognize him as a saint. This recognition comes only through the mediation of Sa'in Sahib, who once again has inserted himself between mother and son. From that moment, all of his "foolish" statements and actions are retroactively transformed into the acts of a *majzub*.

The narrative is not simply a story from the past. The moment of his death was a transformative event that is something to be relived and reaffirmed. It organizes present time for Rabi'a, her emotional space and the identity associated with her position as the mother of a saint. It also creates an explicit ritual structure for the present, a ritual structure that reaffirms Ashiq's identity as a saint and his relationship to the family and the community. The events of the death form the basis of a ritual that is repeated every year. The moment of his death marked the beginning of a liminal period – the suspension of everyday time[12] – when the whole village suspended its normal routines: "The whole village did not cook for sixteen hours." During this liminal time, Ashiq's identity as a saint was affirmed, marked by his power to suspend the routines of a whole village. This liminal time is recreated as an annual ritual: "Everything happens just as it was on the first day." This story, like other stories of the deaths of saints, creates a ritual time and space set apart from everyday life.

We, too, were drawn into that ritual time. As she began the story, she made the link between that "sacred" time and the moment of narration: "It was December, just as it is now." She drew her listeners into reliving the story as she told it, to the point that she and her daughter were crying intensely as she described the morning of his death. Time seemed to slow as she described the details of his last moments. Anwar and I were also drawn into the recreation of the story: a few days later, we, too, went to the village to participate in the *mela* that commemorates his death every year. We were also warned of its liminality, told that we could not be served like guests while we were there.

I have interpreted this story as the recognition of a saint and the creation of a ritual time and space in connection with that recognition. But the story is multivocal. Alongside the voice of a narrator who was transformed by the death into one who recognized the saint is the voice of a mother who could not do enough for her ailing son, the mother whose job it was to focus on the everyday needs of her son and to protect him. Perhaps if she had taken him with her back to Lahore, he would not have gotten sick; or if she had stayed with him in the village. . . . She failed to rush quickly enough back to the village after her daughter's warning dream, a feeling expressed overtly by a disciple: "Now you have come, after so many days." Not mentioned was her husband's failure to return in time with modern medicine. It was her daughter who brought that up in response to a question from Anwar. Her intense crying during the narration was that of a mother who has lost a son, and came at a moment in the story when she was separated from him, forced to wait outside the door. This is in contrast to the moment when she describes herself as the mother as mirror of a saint, who simply sat in front of him, looking at him. This mutual gaze was not a moment of connectedness, of words from the heart, but rather a moment of prognostication from a saint who was already other, whose identity was mediated by the recognition of the world.

Conclusion

So what does it mean to be *majzub*, to have one's mind "burned by God?" For me, for now, it means to be able to step outside of the confines of a restrictive social order, the confines of a Symbolic Order organized in terms of an array of hegemonic discourses, and to represent the opening up of infinite possibilities through the acknowledgement of that which in other circumstances is abjected,

A *MAJZUB* AND HIS MOTHER

dismissed as disgusting, polluted, childish, dangerous. Ashiq is one who escaped. Deleuze and Guattari (1983), in their radical critique of the world of Western psychiatry, have suggested that the conceptual apparatus and practices of psychiatry and psychoanalysis are a repressive structure that reproduces the constraints of a capitalist order. They criticize Lacan's suggestion that the only alternative to acceptance of the oedipalization of desire in terms of a repressive Symbolic Order is psychosis. Similarly, those who revere a *majzub* refuse to reduce such a person to the identity of one who is mentally defective or psychotic. The conceptual space that the *majzub* represents is analogous to the space for the flow of desire that Deleuze and Guattari also seek to open up through their work. They, too, were inspired by individuals who have been marginalized by those who, through their discipline and power, reinforce the authority of a hegemonic discourse and are blind to the possibilities that those individuals represent.

Notes

The field research on which this paper is based was conducted in 1984–1985 and was supported by a grant from the American Institute of Pakistan Studies. I have used pseudonyms to protect the privacy of the people who were willing to share their lives with me.

1. This idea is widespread in the Muslim world. Westermarck, in his study of ritual and belief in Morocco (1926), discussed several instances of people labelled *majzub*. One of the dead saints of Fez who was *majzub* was known to have gone about naked through the streets. In another case, Westermarck took note of a man eating openly on the street during Ramadan, the month of fasting, and was told, "The poor fellow does not know what he is doing, his mind is with God" (Westermarck 1926: I, 49).
2. The logical consequences of a cultural relativism based on general statements of difference have resulted in arguments by anthropologists suggesting that different cultural logics shape the emotional structures of human beings in such fundamental ways that we can gain only a cognitive understanding of these emotional structures through the vehicle of their culturally shaped verbal articulations of this experience (e.g. Rosaldo 1984; Lutz 1988).
3. See Wilce (1994) for the use of the term *pagal* as a way of dismissing the complaints of a troublesome family member so that he or she is rendered socially powerless, a strategy that has much in common with the experience of many Americans.
4. In Platts's Urdu–English dictionary (1983: 631), this word is transliterated *Sāhi* or *Sāñī*, and is a local term for a religious mendicant or *faqir*. I have chosen the transliteration *sa'in* (with a nazalized n) as a closer guide to the Punjabi pronunciation.
5. It was standard practice for a woman to return to her parents' village to give birth.
6. Or "schema," to use Strauss and Quinn's terminology (Strauss and Quinn 1997).
7. This is a system of medicine administered by local practitioners (*hakims*) that is based on early Greek ideas and techniques as these were transmitted through Arabic sources with the spread of Islam (see Beer 1980).
8. I will present this first portion of the conversation below, when I discuss Rabi'a's relationship with Sa'in Sahib.
9. This series of leading questions suggests that Anwar already knew this story and was trying to draw it out of her.
10. In keeping with Lacanian usage, I speak here not of the actual father in all of his

complexity, but of the father as signifier. In this story, we seem to see only this signifier, and not the nuanced portrayal of an actual father.

11 But it should also be noted that when describing a deceased parent, it is not uncommon for a person to attribute their parent with this ability and provide a detailed, idealized account of the parent's last day.

12 It is an instance of a ritual process described by Turner that functions to effect the social transition from one status or identity to another (Turner 1969).

References

Bakhtin, M.M. (1981) *The Dialogic Imagination: Four Essays*, ed. Michael Holquist, trans. Caryl Emerson and Michael Holquist, Austin: University of Texas Press.

Beer, David (1980) 'The Concept of Person in the Hellenic Intellectual Tradition in Islam', unpublished MA thesis, Department of Anthropology, University of Chicago.

Deleuze, Gilles and Felix Guattari (1983) *Anti-Oedipus: Capitalism and Schizophrenia*, trans. Robert Hurley, Mark Seem and Helen R. Lane, pref. Michel Foucault, Minneapolis: University of Minnesota Press.

Ewing, Katherine P. (1982) 'Sufis and Adepts: Islamic and Hindu Sources of Spiritual Power among Punjabi Muslims and Christian Sweepers', in Steven Pastner and Louis Flam (eds) *Anthropology in Pakistan*, Cornell University South Asia Monograph Series, Ithaca NY: Cornell University Press, pp. 74–102.

Ewing, Katherine, P. (1984) 'Malangs of the Punjab: Intoxication or *Adab* as the Path to God?', in Barbara Daly Metcalf (ed.) *Moral Conduct and Authority: The Place of Adab in South Asian Islam*, Berkeley: University of California Press, pp. 357–371.

Ewing, Katherine P. (1997) *Arguing Sainthood: Modernity, Psychoanalysis and Islam*, Durham NC: Duke University Press.

Foucault, Michel (1973) *Madness and Civilization: A History of Insanity in the Age of Reason*, New York: Vintage Books.

Hujwiri, Ali bin Uthman (1976) [1911] *The Kashf al-Mahjub: The Oldest Persian Treatise on Sufism*, trans. Reynold A. Nicholas, Lahore: Islamic Book Foundation.

Kristeva, Julia (1982) *Powers of Horror: Essays on Abjection*, trans. Leon S. Roudiez, New York: Columbia University Press.

Lacan, Jacques (1977) *Ecrits: A Selection*, trans. Alan Sheridan, New York: W.W. Norton.

Lutz, Catherine A. (1988) *Unnatural Emotions: Everyday Sentiments on a Micronesian Atoll and their Challenge to Western Theory*, Chicago; University of Chicago Press.

Malinowski, Bronislaw (1948) *Magic, Science, and Religion and Other Essays*, New York: Doubleday Anchor Books.

Marriott, McKim (1976) 'Hindu Transactions: Diversity without Dualism', in Bruce Kapferer (ed.) *Transaction and Meaning: Directions in the Anthropology of Exchange and Symbolic Behavior*, Philadelphia: ISHI, pp. 109–142.

Mudimbe, V.Y. (1988) *Invention of Africa: Gnosis, Philosophy, and the Order of Knowledge*, Bloomington: Indiana University Press.

Platts, John T. (1983) [1911] *A Dictionary of Urdu, Classical Hindi, and English*, Lahore: Sang-e-Meel Publications.

Rosaldo, Michelle (1984) 'Toward an Anthropology of Self and Feeling', in Richard A. Shweder and Robert A. LeVine (eds) *Culture Theory: Essays on Mind, Self, and Emotion*, Cambridge: Cambridge University Press, pp. 137–157.

Said, Edward W. (1979) *Orientalism*, New York: Vintage Press.

Strauss, Claudia and Naomi Quinn (1997) *A Cognitive Theory of Cultural Meaning*, Cambridge: Cambridge University Press.
Turner, Victor W. (1969) *The Ritual Process: Structure and Anti-Structure*, Chicago: Aldine.
Westermarck, Edward (1926) *Ritual and Belief in Morocco*, 2 vols, London: Macmillan.
Wilce, James (1994) 'Repressed Eloquence: Patients as Subjects and Objects of Complaints in Matlab, Bangladesh', PhD dissertation, University of California, Los Angeles.

Part 4

CHARISMA AND MODERNITY

9

THE LITERARY CRITIQUE OF ISLAMIC POPULAR RELIGION IN THE GUISE OF TRADITIONAL MYSTICISM, OR THE ABUSED WOMAN

Jamal Malik

Introduction: literary critiques of mysticism

The use of contemporary literature as a source for the reconstruction of religious and societal conditions and discourse has been neglected by orientalists thus far. It is only very recently that a change in this regard has been observed; even social anthropologists have increasingly begun to consider literary contributions in order to illuminate the social structure of Muslim societies and the cultural articulations of their intellectuals and activists. Indeed, modern Muslim literature is full of statements about society which implicitly or explicitly value the Islamic tradition, especially with regard to mystic culture and the popular piety connected with it. In an early and, it would appear, little noted contribution, Rotraud Wielandt drew upon modern Arabic literary texts for a valuation and assessment of Islamic folk piety (Wielandt 1984). Central concerns of that article were the veneration of holy men as the 'embodiment of an elevated wisdom', as well as postulates pertaining to modernisation and enlightenment. Ostensibly, contemporary literati and Muslim reformist activists do propagate reformist ideas; nevertheless, one may pose the question of whether these forces are not still bound up with norms and symbols which are rooted in a long tradition. Esoteric ideas and mystical organising principles are, for that matter, also observable in the religious political community of the Muslim Brethren and other similar organisations.

Apparently, the delineation of traditional poetic topoi has thus far been regarded as a feature of 'reform literature'. However, the situation seems to be more complex, and one may ask if this rather unilateral typology should not be abandoned.

In what follows I would like to show how mystical tradition and veneration of holy men – and in this context especially gender problematics – are perceived in contemporary literature and how old and handed-down ideal patterns and symbols lie hidden behind reformist–aesthetic perceptions. The specious contradiction between reform postulates and traditional discourse is especially evident in modern Urdu literature, which is most popular in India and Pakistan, but also enjoys considerable popularity in Great Britian and North America. Before I turn to this literature in detail, some words about the meaning of the veneration of holy men and shrine cults in South Asia, as well as about the development of the Urdu short story, are in order.

Shrine cults in South Asia

Much has been written about Sufi shrine cults, widespread in the Muslim world (Crapanzano 1973; Gellner 1979; Gilsenan 1973; von Schwerin 1981; Pfleiderer 1985; Troll 1989). In these shrines, the cult surrounding the personality of the Prophet Muhammad is elaborated in its perfection (Schimmel 1985). South Asia in particular seems to be imbued with this popular culture. Spencer Trimingham (1971: 22) comments: 'Indian Islam seems to have been essentially a holy-man Islam.' The cult of the holy man (*pîr*) and the associated folk piety is particularly evident in the countryside, where major landlords and large-scale land concentrations are crucial features, especially in Punjab and Sindh. In many cases, the local *pîr* represents the local landlord or is at least closely related to him. The *pîr* guarantees the local villagers' participation in divine blessing (*baraka*), which is tied to strict obedience (*itâ'a*) and self-sacrifice by followers of the *pîr* (*bai'a* means literally the buying of the soul of the adept or disciple by the saint). For the local population, the holy man thus represents moral authority. This moral authority creates distance and a certain fear among the followers, on the one hand, but can be realised through selflessness and devotion, on the other. Authority is regenerated and stabilised through cyclically repeated rituals which have an affirmative character for the local population, are based on a normative consensus, and convey a collective identity. The profane world of the followers is thus transcended, providing a sense of social security and collective identity while social differences are erased, at least ritually. Popular religious ideas mean that people seek and find a source of satisfaction in an organised associational life and 'fraternal certitude and security' in mystical institutions (Eickelman 1981: 228). The tombs of holy men and the ritual drama performed there afford refuge and experiential unity: 'For it was through its rituals that a shrine made Islam accessible to nonlettered masses, providing them with vivid and concrete manifestations of the divine order, and integrating them into its ritualized drama both as participants and as sponsors' (Eaton 1984: 334).

Of particular importance are the ritual periods when secular time is displaced by sacred time and when shrine visitors may be said to be transported into a 'liminal' state of oblivion during the annual feasts (Arabic: *'urs*; literally marriage, i.e. the soul's union with the beloved, God; cf. Turner 1979: 97; Gellner 1985: 80;

Currie 1989: 130 ff). The shrine is an institution which is simultaneously therapeutic, social, economic and political; and in contrast to mosques, it also provides an alternative source of communication and identity, especially in the rather monotonous lives of peasants generally and women in particular (for the significance of shrines for women, see, e.g., Jeffery 1979; Mernissi 1993: 49–66; Fernea and Fernea 1972: 385–401; Tapper 1990: 236–255). Here sick persons can be healed, destitutes find shelter and refuge, and, in political crises, sanctuaries can be used as catalysts for mobilisation. Since a variety of activities – including so-called 'un-Islamic activities' – takes place around these centres, and because shrines also often represent the last refuge of marginalised social groups, they can be regarded as microcosms of local Islam.

The holy man, the enlightened one and his descendants – the *sajjâdah-nashîn* and administrator (*mutawallî, mujâwir*) – exert absolute authority, and pious villagers, often illiterate, can come, with the passage of time, to be regarded by the shrineholders as servants, or even, indeed, as slaves. In fact, there is a significant contradiction between a postulated ritual equality and the practised hierarchy at the bigger shrines and lodges. These developments have given rise to considerable criticism from many quarters, from orthoprax and reformist scholars, as well as from the colonial sector. Muslim modernists like Muhammad Iqbal have referred to these developments in ideological terms as *pirism* (Schimmel 1975a: 43, 338, 572 f).

Criticism of the shrines

The peculiar forms of shrine cult were pilloried at a fairly early stage. One of its first outspoken critics was Ibn Taymiyya (1263–1328) (Memon 1973), who is even now often referred to as an authority on this subject. Reformist movements in the eighteenth century also condemned what they called the exploitative and parasitical shrine cult and the monopoly of landed property mostly stemming from the ideology of the 'feudal' system. The reformists demanded a purification of Islam from local ideas and rituals, and they postulated mystic reform (Ansari 1984; Baljon 1989; Puhlitî 1988). This reformism, however, appealed mostly to restricted urban groups that adhered to the tradition of the Prophet Muhammad (*sunna*) in a scripturalist sense. Their reformism was designed mainly to legitimise their new social status as traders, bankers and representatives of 'scribal groups', and to express an emancipatory world view (Gran 1979; Washbrook 1990). The prevalent syncretism reflected in popular Islam and in 'un-Islamic' practices could, however, not be crushed entirely, even if it was discussed critically in literary circles (see, for example, some of the verses of Saudâ and Mîr Taqî Mîr; Russell and Islam 1969; Ali 1973).

British colonialism adopted this critique and developed it further into a comprehensive attack on the 'Orient', with the objective of legitimising colonial power and pushing through its notion of modernisation. It perceived local Islam as a backward, fanatic and obscurantist religion characterised by superstition. To

Westerners, Islam had to be reformed and modernised: cults and 'strange' modes of belief were best abolished. This criticism seems to have had a decisive impact on those social groups which were directly exposed to the colonial system. The nineteenth-century urban reform movement in India and elsewhere in the Muslim world was very much connected with this colonial expansion and encroachment on the minds of Muslims (Hourani 1967).

A new literature

With colonialism came the emergence of new social classes that ostensibly found themselves caught between the polarities of 'tradition' and 'modernity'. These groups may be regarded as having some form of intermediary societal status (Malik 1996). Some of them gradually tried to find new ways to articulate their specific cultural concerns. Their reaction to both the colonial system and traditional values can be traced in several areas: besides Islamic education and economic transactions, literary production also witnessed a significant shift – similar tendencies can be observed in the Middle East. Thus, traditional styles and literary genres such as *dâstân* (story, fable, tale), poetry and elegies slowly gave way to new literary production. Accordingly, by the end of the nineteenth century, a growing prose element can be discerned, while realistic and sociopolitical writings were beginning to appear. The new urban literary culture included novels and autobiographical accounts which reflected upon, among other things, didacticism, political activism and psychoanalysis. The new writings also raised problems of gender and of bi-cultural issues. The only traditional mode of literary communication that really survived this aesthetic revolution was the *ghazal* (lyrical love poem, ode). In addition, the colonial printing press introduced in the nineteenth century had a decisive impact on Urdu literature (Azâd 1986; Hayy 1923; Jâlibî 1987; Tassy n.d.; 'Azîm 1966; Husainî 1990; Russell 1970, 1992; Sadiq 1984; Schimmel 1975a; Rothen-Dubs 1989; Sarûr 1951; Suhrawardy 1945; Samî'allâh 1988; Chandan 1992; Khân 1990). In this way, new themes and styles were popularised over large areas.

Against the background of a world economic crisis, emerging European and Japanese fascism and nationalist movements in colonial regions, another brand of literature emerged: social realism. Its young writers tried to enrich, to modify and to legitimise their own literary culture – which was a mixture of 'tradition' and 'modernity'. Of special importance in this context is the short story, which seems to have developed only in the first quarter of the twentieth century. Influenced by Western and Russian models, it quickly became one of the most popular literary genres in contemporary South Asia, as well as in the Arab and Persian world (Hafiz 1993; Brugman 1984; Wielandt 1983; Rypka 1959: 344 ff). This medium seemed to be the most suitable approach by which to display a new self-statement *vis-à-vis* the colonialists. It also reflected to some degree an intellectual confrontation with Europe in that it seemingly introduced nomenclatural changes in colonial ideas and concepts, created neologisms, and reinterpreted values important to the Indian environment.¹ Naturally, the literary reformers sharply attacked indigenous traditional structures as well. However, their criticism of their own culture required them to perceive an inherent oriental backwardness or non-development. Therefore, they propagated modernisation, usually rejected traditional norms and old-established patterns of order, and postulated an emancipatory world view, such as *al-hadm wa al-binâ'* (destruction and reconstruction), like their Egyptian counterparts (Hafiz 1993: 216). In the Indian tradition, the young social realists simultaneously regarded themselves as the 'inheritors of the best tradition of Indian civilization' (Coppola 1974: vol. 1, 7) and as reformers who could resist the spirit of reaction, in the forms of fascism, exploitative colonial power and the traditional establishment. Thus, the reformists had positive recourse to well-known traditions of literary discourse that were grounded in the Islamic world view. However, their definition of themselves as an *avant-garde* was based primarily on their having studied in Europe and on their claim to privileged agency *vis-à-vis* the masses.

For that period, at least two main currents can be delineated in South Asia. On the one hand, the *Bihishtî Zewar* (Heavenly Ornaments) written by the well-known Muslim scholar, Sufi and divine Ashraf 'Alî Thânawî (d. 1943) suggested conventional middle-class manners to the Muslim female (Metcalf 1991). On the other hand there were the so-called 'progressives'.

The rise of the Urdu short story is said to have begun with an anthology called *Angâre* (Burning Coals), although several Indian writers were already well known for their short stories. *Angâre* was published in 1932 in Lucknow by four young Urdu writers who had spent some time in England. In their short stories they dealt with current social and religious conditions in South Asia, particularly the position of women and the power of religious dignitaries. Their transgressive dismantling of prior taboos was designed to shock through the use of such literary devices as crude language, internal monologue, and stream-of-consciousness writing techniques. Their offensive approach caused strong and widespread protest from traditionalist quarters as well as from the British masters (Mahmûd 1972: 436 ff; Sadîd 1991: 484 ff; Coppola 1981). Consequently, some months later, the anthology was banned, and since then it has not been republished in Urdu.² But what is most important in this context is that these writers, together with others, spearheaded the establishment of the Progressive Writers' Association (PWA), which first came together in Aligarh and was soon constituted in London. It launched its first all-India meeting in 1936 under the chairmanship of Premchand (1880–1936), who was famous for his social-realist stories on rural India. As a result of internal ideological tensions, the movement split up after some years (A'zimî 1972; Coppola 1974; Ansari 1990; Pradhan 1985; *JSAL* 1986). But it had a most important impact, since its roots were in South Asian tradition, and it thus paved the way for a critical and realistic approach towards literature as a vehicle by which to bring social predicaments to light. Hence, it had a strong impact on Urdu. It is interesting to note that even the movement of *adab islâmî*³ and its predecessor, the *halqah-ye arbâb-ye dhauq* (Circle of Possessors of

Good Taste), which was established in 1939, developed in reaction to this new literature (Sadîd 1991: 554–617, 618–628; Mahmûd 1972: 399 ff).

It is not my purpose here to go into further details about this most interesting organisation, the PWA. Instead of providing a general overview of contemporary literature and the living tradition in it, I will concentrate in what follows on an early representative of the PWA, Ahmad Nadîm Qâsimî. Other important writers in this tradition are, for example, Sa'âdat Hasan Manto, Intizâr Husain and 'Ismat Chughtâ'î (Flemming 1985; Memon 1980, 1981, 1983, 1991; Chughtai 1990; Khalid 1972; Ansari 1990).

Following a biographical sketch of his life and his activities as a progressive writer, I would like to examine Qâsimî's literary expertise and his stand *vis-à-vis* traditional institutions and specifically shrines, by summarising one of his latest short stories, which illuminates elements of Islamic mystic culture veiled behind a critique of the shrine cult. Through this deconstructive approach I hope to make clear how far reformist writers are affiliated with popular Islamic traditions. At the same time the story exposes the abuse of women in popular Islam and the disturbed nature of the political emancipatory process.

Ahmad Nadîm Qâsimî

For analytical purposes, Qâsimî may be called a representative of the above-mentioned intermediary group, a label which may be derived from his biography. The tussle between 'modernity' and 'tradition', particularly in rural society, finds articulation in several of his short stories; because he makes rural society the prime object of his stories, he is called the Premchand of Pakistan (Shaikh 1981; *Afkâr* 1975; *Herald* 1987; Malik 1989, 1990a; Malik 1992).

Ahmad Nadîm was born in 1916, the son of the mystical leader of a village in the district of Sargodha in the Punjab, where Sufi shrine cults are extremely popular. As a *pîrzâdah* (son of a *pîr*) he experienced family quarrels which were directly connected with the tomb to which his ancestors were attached. He enjoyed traditional as well as formal education, and in 1934 finished his BA at Punjab University.

Before Partition, Qâsimî had already worked as a tax and excise subinspector and as a journalist, and was thus more or less drawn away from the so-called traditional sector of society. He established literary journals and supported the demand for the establishment of an independent Pakistan. After Partition he became general secretary of the PWA of Pakistan, a post he held until 1954, when the organisation was declared illegal by the Ayyub Khan regime.[4] It was only in 1987 that the PWA was formally re-established; due to internal fractiousness, however, it faded away very quickly. In 1963, Qâsimî began to establish himself as a national writer and was supported by the government of Pakistan. Since 1974, he has been chairman of the *majlis-e taraqqî-ye adab*, Lahore, an all-Pakistan literary institution.

Nadîm took up the progressives' tradition of criticising existing 'feudal', often

LITERARY CRITIQUE OF ISLAMIC POPULAR RELIGION

religiously legitimated structures. In his stories he showed how gender, social stratification, caste and ideological suppression work hand in hand in contemporary rural areas (Qâsimî 1953, 1955, 1959a, 1959b, 1980, 1985, 1989; Italiaander 1966). As a result, he is known for his strong condemnation of the existing, traditional order as an obstacle which hampers the development of democratic institutions; his stories and poems have been reprinted repeatedly; for example, the short story '*Bain*', ('dirge' or 'lament' but also 'separation'), written in 1983 apparently reflects his own traumatic experiences as a *pîrzâdah*. The story found some resonance due to its ostensible political message and it was translated into English and German (Qâsimî 1985; Malik 1990a: 56–62; Bhatti 1992). In '*Bain*' a shrine administrator who was on good terms with the ruler of Pakistan of the time, Zia ul-Haqq, is discredited. Thus, the story implies a critique of the political culture based on an authoritarian and quasi-military system. However, the story also elaborates upon the shrine cult in a literary-aesthetic way and reflects the inherent romantic mysticism of the author, who himself hailed from a mystical family tradition. It is this dimension of the story which has hitherto been neglected.

The sanctuary of Shâh Daulah

'Dirge' deals with the activities in and around the *dargâh* (court, shrine) of Shâh Daulah Daryâ'î in Gujrat. Before reproducing parts of the short story and analysing it, it seems important to provide some basic information about this Sufi tomb, which was taken over by the Pakistan Auqaf Department in the 1960s (on the Auqaf see Malik 1990c). I shall focus on the famous cult attached to it, a cult to which Nadîm's story does not, however, refer directly.

Plate 9.1 The shrine of Shâh Daulah

The information that follows is based on historical and biographical accounts as well as on *malfûzât* literature (namely, the imputed speeches and utterances of holy men) and it has been extracted from, among other works, Ibettson's *Glossary* and the work by Sharîf Kunjâhî (Ibbetson and Maclagan 1911–1919; Kunjâhî 1985: on the importance of *malfûzât* for the reconstruction of medieval social history see Nizâmî 1961; Askari 1981; Desai 1991; Lawrence 1979; Paul 1990). According to these sources, Shâh Daulah – whose birth name was Qâsim – lived in Mughal times and died at an advanced age around AH 1676 in Gujrat. His ancestors were Afghans, but it is also claimed that he was a *Sayyid* (descendant of the Prophet). After a turbulent childhood he became supervisor of the treasury of a local official, and also worked as a mendicant and an ordinary labourer for some time. He then spent twelve years at the feet of a Suhrawardi Sufi, but it is recorded too that he was initiated into the Qadiri order. Due to some disputes with the local people of Sialkot, he migrated from there and, after some years, moved to Gujrat 'in obedience to divine instructions ... During his life he devoted himself to works of public utility [hence his *laqab* or title 'Daulah', 'wealth'] and the constructions of religious buildings', especially bridges (hence his *laqab* 'Dargâ'î', 'one affiliated to water'). He was popular among 'Muslims as well as Hindus, became famous for his miracles and received large gifts' in kind, but refused to accept land grants. The colonial sources are of the view that through his charismatic or miraculous powers (*karâmât*) Shâh Daulah was able to control female infanticide, which was widespread in Jammu State at the time (Ibbetson and Maclagan 1911–1919: 631).

Shâh Daulah's shrine is particularly known for its *Chûhâ*s or Rat-children, who are without understanding or the power of speech. After some initial training they are passed on to a *faqîr* (religious mendicant) and made to beg in the name of Shâh Daulah. According to colonial sources, the story goes that:

> Shah Daulah, like other saints, could procure the birth of a child for a couple desiring one, but the first child born in response to his intercession would be a *Chūhā* – brainless, small-headed, long-eared and rat-faced. The custom used to be to leave the child, as soon as it was weaned, at Shah Daulah's *khanqah* [Sufi lodge], as an offering to him. After the saint's death the miracle continued, but in a modified way. Persons desiring children would go to the saint's shrine to pray for a child, and would make a vow either to present the child when born or make an offering to the shrine. In some cases, when the child was duly born in response to the prayer, the parents neglected to make the promised gift. Upon this, the spirit of the offended saint so worked on the parents that the next child was born a *Chūhā*, and all subsequent children as well, until the original vow was fulfilled.
>
> (Ibbetson and Maclagan 1911–1919: 630)

LITERARY CRITIQUE OF ISLAMIC POPULAR RELIGION

Several scholars have tried to explain the evolution of this tradition. Some argue that the bad conscience of parents, particularly mothers, set free certain chemical reactions that caused this peculiarity (Kunjâhî 1985). Others claim that the lack of regular income at the *dargâh*, since no land was attached to it, resulted in the holy men's total dependence on the alms and offering of the followers, while it was also suspected that the followers (*murîdûn*) were involved in traffic in women (Ibbetson and Maclagan 1911–1919: 630). However, in contemporary and even later *malfûzât* and biographical accounts there is no mention of the *Chûhâ* cult (Kunjâhî 1985). It therefore seems likely that this cult arose only later, by the end of the nineteenth century – after the shrine had been reconstructed (1898). The editor of *Indian Antiquary* points out that these were the extreme forms of the cult and 'that a band or order of *faqîrs* makes a living out of a certain class of local microcephalous idiots, and the convenient existence of an important shrine.' He goes on to say that:

> the absence of landed property in possession of the band, or any recognized right to succession to the leadership, and the entire dependence on the earnings, in turn dependent themselves on the gullibility of the 'faithful', all make it almost certain that Bháwan Sháh [a *murîd* of the Shâh] took the opportunity of the (then recent) decease of a well-known ancient and holy man to find a sacred origin for the unholy traffic of his followers ... But ... [there is] no ground for supposing that he [the Shâh] had anything to do personally with the poor idiots now exploited by the sect, band, or order of *faqîrs* that have fastened themselves on to his name.
> (Ibbetson and Maclagan 1911–1919: 636 ff)

Because of the economic needs of the shrineholders, it is also suspected that these children are 'artificially produced after their birth as ordinary infants' (Ibbetson and Maclagan 1911–1919: 637). The sanctuary of Shâh Daulah thus has a particular reputation – fertility, justice and punishment – which, however, does not keep people from regularly paying homage to the spirit of the holy man and his successors; even the nationalisation policy of the Auqaf Department since the 1960s could not totally change the perceptions deeply rooted in the minds of the rural population and the authority exercised by the shrine administrator, the *mujâwir*, who ideally represents state power.

Even if the cult of *Chûhâ*s is fascinating in itself, '*Bain*', to which I will turn immediately, hardly takes it into account. The author does not mention the *Chûhâ* cult explicitly, but uses the sanctuary as a means by which to point to the corruption of the shrineholders, in particular the *mujâwir*, to the myth created and perpetuated around hereditary holy men, to the rape and exploitation of women as well as to the decadence of the political establishment. The story, however, also reverts to complex mystical symbolism and the semantic connotations which seem to lie beyond grammatical speech and thus address the subconscious, in this way determining people's actions. And, as will be seen, fear plays an important role in tying the local population to the tomb.

'*Bain*' and Shâh Daulah

The content of '*Bain*', a frame story, is quickly narrated: by means of an internal monologue, a mother informs us about the feelings, pains and fears which she and her husband – a poor Punjabi peasant – went through during the preceding sixteen or seventeen years. The mother is overwhelmed by the birth of the first child, a daughter, Rano (a diminutive form for 'princess'), who is surrounded by a divine light. The father, however, is sceptical, because he knows the dangers involved in bringing up a beautiful girl – beautiful even though she falls on her forehead and damages it. At the age of 5, Rano – like most other children – is sent to *Bîbîjî* (the teacher), to learn to recite the Qur'an at her feet. Soon it becomes known that her voice is also of an extraordinary beauty, so that in a short while she becomes the leading reciter. Even the *mujâwir* of the shrine nearby is overwhelmed by the girl. The mother only becomes aware of Rano's maturity when the girl receives a proposal from some relatives. On this very day, however, the shrine administrator says that the girl Rano should be brought to the *dargâh* and should recite the holy Qur'an there for three days. This, he adds, Shâh Daulah had ordered in a dream.

It seems that different legends had developed around the shrine, and that it had become an institution of justice, symbolised by the holy hand of Shâh Daulah, which, in order to judge, would rise from the grave. Out of respect and fear of the punishment threatened by the holy man, the parents and the child at once embark for the sanctuary. The camel journey to that place becomes a wonderful cosmic experience. After reaching the *dargâh*, Rano remains there while her parents go back home. Returning to the holy place three days later they see Rano in a desperate state. She is waiting for the holy hand of Shâh Daulah. Only if the hand shows up and justice is done can she return, a litany she often repeats. It is said that she is possessed by a wicked ghost. In the course of the story Rano becomes weaker and finally dies. The story ends with a description of nature as it began, with Rano in the arms of her mother, under the tree of life. What has happened and how did the death of the girl come about?

Mystical dimensions of '*Bain*' and gender

In terms of its action, '*Bain*' draws a picture of the complex hierarchical world of shrines and their milieu as well as of the social stratification and stigmatisation of female children and their exploitation and evident rape by male authorities, even in a surrounding which is more or less a female domain, the shrine.[5] It also displays how aspects of folk religion work in South Asia, and how legends surrounding holy men and holy places develop and are perpetuated. '*Bain*' provides rich data about the complex hierarchical shrine world (*pîr*, *mujâwir*, etc.) and its background, and about the mystical tradition, as well as about the belief in the holiness of shrines, the institutions of collective identity, and above all 'justice'. It shows that the shrine cult has become a falsehood void of any mysticism, or, in other words, an expression of corrupt political power. Behind the story, however, lies mystical cosmology and symbolism, which I would like to illuminate by drawing on Sufic terminology.

The story can be divided into two main parts: while the first deals with the period of Rano's childhood and her esoteric experiences (see column 4 of Figure 9.1),[6] the second leads us into the dark world of the exploitative shrine cult that results from the girl's maturity and her initiation into the female world. The juncture of these two parts – childhood and maturity – is elaborated by the mystical journey, a climax of the story.

'*Bain*' acquaints the reader with the perceptions of *taraqqî* (the mystical ascent) and with its symbolic dynamism, which is taken advantage of by the enigmatic *mujâwir*. The idea of illumination (*ishrâq*) and of emanation are touched upon, however, without explicit mention. Both mystical elements stand in the tradition of Ibn 'Arabî (d. 1240), who further elaborated the idea of *wahdat al-wujûd* (the unity of being).

Even the damaging of Rano's forehead seems to point to her being chosen from amongst the villagers as a profound leader. The illuminated girl with supernatural qualities is imprinted (*dâghdâr*) with a crescent, initiated, as it were, and thereby dignified. Her beauty and her lovely voice are attributes of the enhanced position she has achieved on her own and which is gradually elaborated and refined, in the sense of spiritual degrees of the soul or the mystical ascent (see column 3 of Figure 9.1). The *wahdat al-wujûd* becomes evident when she submerges into the cosmos. Time stands still and space becomes sacred, while everybody and everything listens to her saintly voice. The shrine administrator also witnesses the divine gift when visiting the village. He identifies her voice – a kind of exclamation (*faryâd*) or a longing for blessing and for purification of her lower self (*al-nafs al-ammâra*; for the Sufic technical terms used in what follows see, e.g., Fâkhirî 1990; Schimmel 1975b), so to speak, with the fluttering (*pharpharâhat*)[7] of angels' wings. At this stage her recitation (*tilâwat*) may already be regarded as a kind of *dhikr*, which receives stronger meaning with incantation (*chhûh-mantar*), as an expression of inhaling and exhaling the holy words. In this way she purifies her blameworthy soul – *al-nafs al-lawwâma* – and thus sets out on her journey for the path of gnosis. Her soul is inspired – *al-nafs al-mulhama*. Hence Rano represents *baraka* and bestows life: 'Women used to come to [her] with their dishes and utensils filled with water' to be blessed by her. Here it also becomes clear that the *dargâh* is a female domain, at least in quantitative terms – in contrast to mosques, which are frequented by men.

By now Rano has left the stage of *sharî'a* – the exoteric revelation or the profane Islamic law – and is on the *tarîqa* – the mystical path. Exoteric – *sharî'a* – and esoteric – *tarîqa* – as well as *haqîqa* – the truth or reality – are three levels of the cosmic evolution which connect the different spheres of existence or nature (see columns 2 and 1 of Figure 9.1). Thus, she is able to act as a holy being by

Figure 9.1 Rano's mystical path

[1] Spheres of existence	[2] Stages of cosmic development	[3] Spiritual degree on the path	[4] Development in the text
The world of the Godhead ('*âlam al-lâhût*')	Haqîqa (essence)	Perfect soul (*al-nafs al-kâmila*)	Cosmic unity; end of journey
		Approved soul (*al-nafs al-mardîya*)	Camel journey; Qur'an recitation[a]
		Contented soul (*al-nafs al-râdiya*)	Experience of divine nature; camel journey
The world of power ('*âlam al-jabarût*')	Tarîqa (esoteric)	Tranquil soul (*al-nafs al-mutma'inna*)	Start of camel journey; maturity
		Inspired soul (*al-nafs al-mulhama*)	*Baraka* initiation through *mujâwir*'s dream
The angelic world ('*âlam al-malakût*')			
	Sharî'a (exoteric)	Blameworthy soul (*al-nafs al-lawwâma*)	Identified by *mujâwir*; incantations
The world of humanity ('*âlam al-nâsût*')		Unregenerated soul (*al-nafs al-ammâra*)	Qur'an recitation; early childhood

[a] Recitation of the Qur'an at this stage of mystical experience is, according to classical mystical ideas, additive and non-developmental. It 'spoils' the mystical ascent and makes development rather circular.

practising miracles (*karâmât*), again illuminated by divine light (*nûr*). But with her advancement to puberty, she gradually becomes subject to societal conventions – a totalitarian power which destroys the democratic process.

Accordingly, the girl's maturity or sexualisation and the marriage proposal coincide with the anniversary of the holy man's death, *'urs*, the unification of the *pîr* with God. It seems that she is going to be married to the spiritual authority, when already 'all you possessed you had given away in the name of the Lord' (*maulâ kî râh*). A dream – a popular way of conveying messages and legitimising actions (von Grunebaum and Caillois 1966; Azam 1992) – authorises the *mujâwir* to bind Rano to the sanctuary, 'otherwise', he added, 'Sân'în Daule Shâhjî would put all villagers to fire and ash' (*bhasam karnâ*). This is the factual mystical initiation, so to speak; she becomes a follower (*chelî*) or *murîd* of the *dargâh*. This initiation is, however, done in a kind of *Uwaisî* tradition (Uwais al-Qaranî was a prototype of piety who lived in Yemen at the time of the Prophet), or through the spirit of the legendary *Khidr*, (a guide of the mystics and patron of pious travellers), rather than in an act of a formal *bai'a* (Schimmel 1975b; Trimingham 1971;

Husaini 1967; Baldick 1993; Elboudrari 1992). But the gap is bridged by an immediate genealogical birth: no *silsila* (chain of spiritual descent) is referred to which would legitimise the spiritual position of the *murshid* (spiritual guide) and the *murîd*.

One also learns that fear is the prime motivational force inducing the villagers and adepts to be loyal to the moral authority emanating from the shrine. The affiliation with the shrine and its representative is deeply entrenched in their minds, and their identification with him seems to produce a strong fear of being punished if they do not obey. Because of this identification, the villagers must experience a feeling of destroying both themselves and the mystical leader in the event of disobedience. Thus, the personal union with the holy man is a crucial link between him as the unique authority and those who obey him, an identity which is established and perpetuated by means of myths, legends, miracles, and social as well as mystical affiliations. A precondition for that is that the actors belong to a common semantic household:

> The upper part [*sar bâne kî taraf se*] of the holy grave opened and the Pîr stretched out his holy hand [*dast-e mubârak*]. The culprit then was drawn to the shrine [*mazâr sharîf*] from wherever he was, laid his neck into the holy hand of the Sân'înjî [the *pîr*] and died on the spot [*dher honâ*]. Thereafter the holy hand disappeared into the holy grave and its fissures closed as if they had never been opened. Therefore, nobody dared to neglect Sân'în Daule Shâh's orders.

Fear also draws the parents and the daughter to the tomb. The climax of Rano's mystical experience is developed in the journey to the holy place, on the back of a camel, and the end of the journey symbolises the transition from the *unio mystica* (mystical union) to the institutionalised world of shrines. This part of the narration is reminiscent of the *rihla* of the *qasîda* (the second part of the classical Arabic ode, which consists of the poet's journey to the beloved) in ancient Arabic poetry, or of a classical divine and mystical journey in which the spiritual stations (*maqâmât*) are experienced by the soul of a novice, or of the ascent of the Prophet Muhammad (*mi'râj*).[8] This may be illustrated in the following passage:

> On the very next day we embarked for the *dargâh*. I sat on one side of the saddle, and you, my darling, on the the other, while your father sat in the centre ... As soon as the camel started to move, you began to recite the Holy Qur'an. My dear sweetheart, my pure girl, I saw with my own eyes that wherever the camel passed, people flocked to us from far. They accompanied us crying and saying 'Praise the Lord, praise the Lord.' Flocks of birds, swallows and pigeons approached the saddle. They dived down to the camel as if they were drinking the nectar [*sharbat*] of the voice of my little daughter, danced and then swam far away ...

Heaven came to my mind when your father, bending over the saddle, whispered into my ear: 'Look up, what luminous [*nûrânî*] birds are these flying along with us? I have never seen birds like these in this area, as if stars were sparkling on their feathers. They look like angels [*farishte*] coming from heaven!' And, my darling [*ânkhon kâ nûr*], even I, your illiterate mother, can swear upon my oath that these were really angels, as if little innocent children had wings and were fluttering through the air. They had come to listen to my purified [*pahaunchî hû'î*] daughter's holy recitation.

Rano had become mature, sitting on the same level as her mother. The family now left the material or human world, *'âlam al-nâsût*, and entered a divine atmosphere, the world of angels or of intelligible substances, *'âlam al-malakût*, which is perceived only through spiritual insight or a separation, *'Bain'*, from the material world. Here everything becomes united with spirituality. It seems that during the journey the girl also reaches the world of spiritual existence or power, *'âlam al-jabarût*, which lies beyond external forms and in which the divine orders and powers are located. This stage results from deeply experiencing divine nature. The soul flows into tranquility – *al-nafs al-mutma'inna* – and consequently becomes contented – *al-nafs al-râdiya*. One has the impression that, during the journey, Rano really witnesses the image of God or divine nature – *'âlam al-lâhût* – when the worlds unite with her and the all-embracing harmony calls up associations of paradise. Her soul is approved, so to speak – *al-nafs al-mardîya*; she experiences the stage of *haqîqa*, (the ultimate goal), in which her soul becomes illuminated in perfection – *al-nafs al-kâmila*, obviously before she has reached the shrine.

So far Rano is still a child, free and innocent, and has attained the highest mystical stages. The latter part of the narrative, however, deals with her physical and metaphysical exploitation, for her saintly experience is now seen in contrast to the dark world of shrines. The shrines can be interpreted as the traditional society at large, which grasps the maturing girl and binds her to narrow and suffocating societal claims. It is this institutionalised form of mysticism that casts gloom over and destroys her luminous life, in spite of her mystical perfection; or – in political terminology – the liberal democratic culture stands in contrast to the totalitarian military domination.[9]

Reaching the tomb we witness a kind of a bargain between the parents and the *mujâwir*, like the *mahr* (bridewealth): the parents are declared dwellers of paradise (*jannatî* – without intercession of any authority) by the shrine administrator. In response they leave the child – the present (*ni'mat*) – as a trust (*amânat*) at the *dargâh*. With this bargain Rano, the little princess, virtually becomes a slave, bound to the 'holy' place. During the *'urs* the girl falls victim to the corrupted society. Her chapped lips with their bloody scurfs, her tangled hair without the *châdar* (shawl), and her desperate wait for justice (*insâf*) and judgment (*faisala*) point to a forcible defloration and desecration. Her mouth and her voice, with which she established the unique connection with the mystical world, are now deformed and abused.

In her agony she is 'possessed' by ghosts (*jinn*, *bhût*), as the *dargâh* family opines, in a manner reminiscent of institutionalised witch-hunting. During her lonely struggle, a struggle to attain justice and purify her soul, she becomes extremely weak, similar to a kite (*patang*) whose cord has been cut and which drifts through the air without any destination.[10] This tussle reminds one of the *mujâhadat al-nafs* (fight against the carnal soul) or the concept of *tafriqa* and *jam'* – diversity or separation and unification – in the context of the emanation concept, and of the longing for salvation.

As an abused virgin Rano feels herself spoilt and guilty. Trusting in God she waits patiently for the hand of the holy man to redeem her from her stigma, purify her soul, and do her justice:

> You did not even think of covering your hair when you saw your father. Your colour became sandy and you began to cry and to shout when you recognized us: 'Don't come nearer to me, father, keep away from me, mother! I will stay here now, I will stay here as long as the shrine of Sân'în Daule Shâh does not open and his holy hand does not appear. I will stay here until a settlement [*faisala*] is made. I will stay here until justice [*insâf*] is done and the shrine opens. If it does not open today it will open tomorrow, after a month, after one year, after two years. The shrine will definitely open at some time and the holy hand will definitely appear. Then I will myself return to my father and mother and will arrange their shoes neatly my whole life long and will always wash their feet and drink the water. But now, now I will not come. I cannot come now. I am bound, tied up (*bandhî*: female slave). I am destroyed.'

Rano stays at the shrine day and night; before submitting to the final judgement, however, she tries to stand up against the *mujâwir*, the representative of malignity, in his own tradition: the stones the unfortunate (*bad nasîb*) daughter threatens to throw at him are those of Shâh Daulah, who is still the prime authority to her and who reflects the embodiment of the sacred.

The next stage of Rano's 'obsession' gradually displays her approaching death. It is symbolised by her flinging the skirt presented by her parents – as a last attempt to call her back from the shrine – into the burning coals of the public kitchen (*langar*). This skirt, this last connection with her lived mystical world, has, indeed, no proper place at the shrine. Later her father repeats a quite similar act: he indignantly throws the shroud (*kafan*) sent by the *mujâwir* into the burning coals of the fire heating the water for the great ablution (*ghusl*). The institutionalised mystic can merely present Rano with this skirt, the shroud. The action of the father, who also complained (*faryâd karnâ*) about the alleged obsession of his daughter, is a clear denouncement of the shrine cult.

The attempts of the parents to free their child fail. One night they are called to the *dargâh*, but now the world seems to be turned upside down: whereas in the beginning Rano was sitting at the top end of the grave, now she lies at its bottom end, at the feet of Shâh Daulah, in the candle-light (*chirâgh kî raushanî*). Her illuminated eyes have turned grey and stuck fast, the lips tremble slightly and she says in a feeble voice:

> My dear parents. Who knows why the grave does not open? Even though there was no justice, at least the case has been decided. I do not care if I am the culprit. Sân'în Daule Shâh, you made me wait too long, though. Now, when on the day of resurrection we will all assemble and be presented before God – before God – God!' Thereafter you became silent and since then you have remained silent.

She passes from freedom and liberty – or political self-development – into the compulsions and constraints of the society – or political suppression – that have not only deformed her individualism but destroyed her existence, her being found, *wujûd*:

> And now, my sweetheart, my pure and good, my clean and innocent daughter Rano, come and let me kiss the extinguished moon on your forehead one last time. See how the purple blossoms of the common bead-tree smell. And the squirrels are playing on the tree of life, running from its stalk up to its top. The wind blows gently as if young shoots were bursting forth even from the centuries-old dry wood. Everywhere around there is the hum of your recitation and the smell of the burning of the shroud sent by Sân'în Hazrat Shâhjî [the *mujâwir*] is spreading everywhere. And I am full of pain now, a pain which I experienced when I gave birth to you.

Hence, the 'separation' concludes tragically; it is a separation from the material and mystical world and also from the mother, under the tree of life, the leaves of which are used for funeral rites. Indeed, Rano did not even get the chance to grow into the role of a free woman; instead, she died into the role of a subject female; she died a societal death. Still, the blossoms, shoots and the smell all hint – although very subtly – at some kind of hope: the democratic principles may have survived, taking command of the political culture subliminally.

Conclusion

In Qâsimî's story, 'Dirge' or 'Separation', there is no discussion of using children for economic purposes; one does not find direct hints of the female infanticide which was supposedly prevalent at this shrine in former times; and the rat-cult is not mentioned. However, it is implicit that Rano was the first and only child born after a long time but was – obviously – not presented to the *dargâh*, although the parents must have paid homage (*salâm karnâ*) to the sanctuary and they must also have prayed for a child. There are also clear instances of traffic in women or girls and of societal infanticide, a phenomenon widespread not only in South Asia (for Egypt see, e.g., Qabbânî 1983: 575–640; Wild 1994: 200–209).

Thus, '*Bain*' stands in the reformist tradition. Mysticism as it was propagated by early Sufi masters like Hasan al-Basrî and al-Hallâj is accepted; the veneration of holy men, however, is repudiated as unlawful innovation, that is, *bidaʿ*. Cult mysticism – or the totalitarian system – should be abolished because it restricts individual – or democratic – freedom, calls for the radical submission of the novice (Rano) – or citizen – under the shaikh (*mujâwir*) – or ruler – and would therefore deviate from the right path – or the liberal polity. The story of a woman abused at a sanctuary points out this demand very clearly, though in allegorical terms. In a certain sense an abuse of mysticism may be observed as well.[11] Claims for this kind of radical dissolution of autochthonous structures or the modernisation of cult or tradition are also discernible in radical Islamic and 'progressive' movements, as well as in 'quietist' associations. All of them refer to the golden age of pristine Islam. Such demands, are, however, at the expense of the vast majority of the population, especially women, who find an alternative institutional and communicative framework in the shrine cult.

In this way the contradiction mentioned at the beginning becomes obvious: even if many contemporary literati publicly argue against this kind of mysticism or shrine cult, which displays feudal and undemocratic structures, they still use – as has been shown paradigmatically with '*Bain*' – traditionally known and accepted patterns of cultural articulation.[12] In this way they adhere to a common symbolic framework and a common semantics. In order to make discernible the latent and hidden meanings that lie behind the profane action, the stories must, however, be marked in their complexity. '*Bain*' offers this symbolism and thus reflects the wealth of mysticism. The theoretical placement of modern literature into a literary historical and sociological context, which still has to be elaborated, should take into consideration this dimension.

Acknowledgements

I am grateful to Christian Szyska, Nita Kumar, Ulrike Freitag, Kallé Amthauer, Charles Earle, F. Muhammad Malik and other dear friends for their most valuable comments on earlier drafts of this chapter.

Notes

1 The underlying orientalist approach may, however, be questioned; it seems problematic to maintain that these new social formations were unilaterally inspired by colonialism. It seems that they not only referred to a long indigenous tradition, but also inspired the colonial power.
2 Interestingly, the anthology was reprinted in Hindi only recently, but the controversial passages, such as those hinting at sexual and religious abuses, were omitted.

Moreover, several important Persian and Arabic words were replaced by Sanskrit idioms.

3 In *adab islâmî* individuals and their interaction with God are supposed to be of prime importance. The main aim of its critique was the agnosticism and obscenity propagated by the PWA.
4 It should be pointed out here that Ayyub Khan himself utilised holy men for his own political purposes: the pro-Ayyubian *malfûzāt-e khizarî* was most important in this context.
5 However, it should be pointed out that the power in shrines is usually held by men.
6 It should be made clear that Figure 9.1 illustrates this first part of the story only.
7 Only the words in parentheses from this point on are given in the original text of '*Bain*'.
8 For different concepts of journeys and travels in the Muslim context see, for example, Eickelman and Piscatori (1990).
9 The girl's age of 16–17 may call to mind the duration of the era between 1962 and 1979. The year 1962 witnessed the lifting of martial law under Ayyub Khan, when 'the basic democracies order was incorporated into the constitution, which now ideally provided for a federal system of government and an all-powerful president to be elected by the basic democrats', while in 1979 the military finally re-established its political authority (Jalal 1992: 302 ff).
10 In South Asia the tradition of kite flying or, better, kite fighting is very popular. The cord of the kite is produced in a sophisticated way and incorporates, among other things, fine pieces of glass. The aim of flying kites is to cut the cord of the other kite flyers, by complicated movements. See, for example, Sharar (1989:130 ff); Nadîm and Nayyar (1988).
11 In one sense one may also detect Qâsimî abusing Rano, for the sake of his supposedly political message.
12 For example, Intizâr Husain consciously quarries Islamic and especially Shiite topoi for his short stories.

References

Afkâr (1975) *Nadîm Nambar*, Karachi.
Ali, A. (1973) *The Golden Tradition*, New York and London: Columbia University Press.
Ali, A. (ed.) (1983) *Selected Short Stories from Pakistan*, Islamabad: Pakistan Academy of Letters.
Ansari, K.H. (1990) *The Emergence of Socialist Thought among North Indian Muslims (1917–1947)*, Lahore: Book Traders.
Ansari, M.A.H. (1984) 'Shah Wali Allah attempts to revise Wahdatu'l-Wujûd', *Islamic Quarterly* 28: 150–164.
Askari, S.H. (1981) *Maktub and Malfuz Literature as a Source of Socio-Political History*, Patna: Khuda Bakhsh Oriental Public Library.
Azâd, Muhammad Husain (1986) *Ab-e hayât*, Lakhna'û: Uttar Pradesh Urdû Akademî.
Azam, U. (1992) *Dreams in Islam*, Pittsburgh, PA: Dorrance.
'Azîm, W. (1966) *Dâstân sê afsânê tak*, Delhi: Sultâniya Bûk Depot.
A'zimî, K.R. (1972) *Urdû meñ taraqqî pasand adabî tahrîk*, 'Aligarh: Anjuman-e Taraqqî-ye Urdû.
Baldick, J. (1993) *Imaginary Muslims: The Uwaysi Sufis of Central Asia*, London: I.B. Tauris.
Baljon, J.M.S. (1989) 'Shah Waliullah and the Dargah', in Christian W. Troll (ed.) *Muslim Shrines in India*, New Delhi: Oxford University Press, pp. 189–197.
Bhatti, S.S. (1992) 'A Lament', *Pakistani Literature* 1, 1: 81–88, Islamabad: Pakistan Academy of Letters.

Brugman, J. (1984) *An Introduction to the History of Modern Arabic Literature in Egypt*, Leiden: Brill.
Chandan, G. (1992) *Jâm-e Jahân Numâ (Urdû sihâfat kî ibtidâ)*, Dehli : Maktabah-ye Jâmi'ah.
Chughtai, I. (1990) *The Quilt and Other Stories*, New Delhi: Kali for Women.
Coppola, C. (ed.) (1974) *Marxist Influences in South Asian Literature*, 2 vols., Michigan: East Lansing.
Coppola, C. (1981) 'The Angare Group: The Enfants Terribles of Urdu Literature', *Annual of Urdu Studies* 1 : 57–69.
Crapanzano, Vincent (1973) *The Hamadsa: A Study in Morrocan Ethnopsychiatry*, Berkeley: University of California Press.
Currie, P.M. (1989) *The Shrine and Cult of Mu'in al-Dîn Chishtî of Ajmer*, Delhi: Oxford University Press.
Desai, Z.A. (1991) *Malfuz Literature as Source of Political, Social and Cultural History of Gujarat and Rajasthan*, Patna: Khuda Bakhsh Oriental Public Library.
Eaton, R. (1984) 'The Political and Religious Authority of the Shrine of Bâbâ Farîd', in Barbara Daly Metcalf (ed.) *Moral Conduct and Authority: The Place of Adab in South Asian Islam*, Berkeley: University of California Press, pp. 333–356.
Eickelman, D. and J. Piscatori (eds) (1990) *Muslim Travellers: Pilgrimage, Migration, and the Religious Imagination*, London: Routledge.
Eickelman, D.F. (1981) *The Middle East: An Anthropological Approach*, Englewood Cliffs NJ: Prentice-Hall.
Elboudrari, H. (1992) 'Entre le symbolique et l'historique: Khadir immémorial', *Studia Islamica* LXXVI : 41–52.
Fâkhirî, S.K.M. (1990) *Istilâhât-e tasawwuf*, Karachi: Dâ'irat al-Musannifîn.
Fernea, R.A. and E.W. Fernea (1972) 'Variation in Religious Observance among Islamic Women', in N.R. Keddie (ed.) *Scholars, Saints and Sufis*, Berkeley: University of California Press, pp. 385–401.
Flemming, L.A. (1985) *Another Lonely Voice: The Life and Works of Saadat Hasan Manto*, Lahore: Vanguard.
Gellner, E. (1979) *Saints of the Atlas*, Chicago: University of Chicago Press.
Gellner, E. (1985) *Leben im Islam*, Stuttgart: Klett-Cotta.
Gilsenan, M. (1973) *Saint and Sufi in Modern Egypt*, Oxford: Clarendon Press.
Gran, P. (1979) *Islamic Roots of Capitalism: Egypt, 1760–1840*, Austin: University of Texas Press.
Hafiz, S. (1993) *The Genesis of Arabic Narrative Discourse: A Study in the Sociology of Modern Arabic Literature*, London: Saqi Books.
Hayy, S. 'Abd al- (1923) *Gul-e Ra'nâ*, Lahore: Ishrat.
Herald (1987) Karachi: Pakistan Herald.
Hourani, A. (1967) *Arabic Thought in the Liberal Age, 1798–1939*, Oxford: Oxford University Press.
Husainî, A.A. (1990) *Urdû Nâwal kî târîkh awr tanqîd*, Aligarh: Educational Book House.
Husaini, A.S. (1967) 'Uways al-Qaranî and the Uwaysî Sûfîs', *Muslim World* 57: 103–113.
Ibbetson, D. and E. Maclagan (1911–1919) *A Glossary of Tribes and Castes of the Punjab and the North West Frontier Provinces, Vols I–III*, Lahore: Government Press.
Italiaander, R. (ed.) (1966) *In der Palmschwenke, Pakistan in Erzählungen*, Herrenalb: Erdmann.
Jalal, A. (1992) *The State of Martial Law: The Origins of Pakistan's Political Economy of Defence*, Cambridge: Cambridge University Press.
Jâlibî, J. (1987) *Târîkh-e adab-e Urdû, II (athârwîn sadî)*, Lahore: Majlis-e Taraqqî-ye Urdû.

Jeffery, P. (1979) *Frogs in a Well: Indian Women in Purdah*, London: Zed Press.
Jeffery, P. (1985) 'Creating a Scene: The Disruption of Ceremonial in a Sufi Shrine', in I. Ahmad (ed.) *Ritual and Religion among Muslims of the Sub-continent*, Lahore: Vanguard, pp. 162–194.
JSAL (1986) *Journal of South Asian Literature: Essays on Premchand*.
Khalid, L. (1972) 'Ismat Chughtai – Personality Sketch', *Mahfil* 8, 2–3: 189–194.
Khân, N.A. (1990) *Hindûstânî Press, 1556–1900*, Lakhna'û: Uttar Pradesh Urdû Akademî.
Kunjâhî, S. (1985) *Hadrat Shâh Daulah Daryâ'î Gujrâtî: Hayât o ta'lîmât*, Lahore: Markaz Ma'ârif Awliyâ Mahkamah Awqâf Punjâb.
Lawrence, B.B. (1979) *Sufi Literature in the Sultanate Period*, Patna: Khuda Bakhsh Oriental Public Library.
Mahmûd, S.F. (ed.) (1972) *Tâ'rîkh-e Adabîyât-e Musalmân-e Pâkistân o Hind, X, 1914–1972*, Lahore: Punjab University.
Malik, F.M. (1992) *Ahmad Nadîm Qâsimî: Shâ'ir awr Afsânahnigâr*, Lahore: Sang-e Mîl.
Malik, J. (1989) 'Urdu Kurzgeschichten', in *Pakistan: Eine Dokumentation des Südasienbüros*, March: 86–91.
Malik, J. (1990a) 'Sultan', Kurzgeschichte aus Pakistan, *Südasien* 2–3: 60–65.
Malik, J. (1990b) 'Todesklage', Kurzgeschichte aus Pakistan, *Südasien* 10, 7–8: 56–62.
Malik, J. (1990c) 'Waqf in Pakistan: Change in Traditional Institutions', *Die Welt des Islams* 30 : 63–97.
Malik, J. (1996) *Colonialization of Islam*, Delhi: Manohar.
Memon, M.U. (1973) *Ibn Taimîya's Struggle against Popular Religion, with an Annotated Translation of his Kitâb iqtidâ' as-sirât al-mustaqîm mukhâlifat asbâb al-jahîm*, The Hague and Paris: Mouton.
Memon, M.U. (1980) 'Partition Literature: A Study of Intizâr Husain', *Modern Asian Studies* 14, 3: 377–410.
Memon, M.U. (1981) 'Reclamation of Memory, Fall, and the Death of the Creative Self: Three Months in the Fiction of Intizâr Husain', *International Journal of Middle Eastern Studies* 13, 1: 73–91.
Memon, M.U. (1983) 'The Writings of Intizâr Husain', *Journal of South Asian Languages* 18, 2.
Memon, M.U. (1991) 'Shi'ite Consciousness in a Recent Urdu Novel: Intizâr Husain's Bastî', in C. Shackle (ed.) *Urdu in Muslim South Asia: Studies in Honour of Ralph Russell*, Delhi: Oxford University Press, pp. 139–150.
Mernissi, F. (1993) *Die vergessene Macht: Frauen im Wandel der islamischen Welt*, Berlin: Orlanda.
Metcalf, B.D. (1991) *Perfecting Women: Maulânâ Ashraf 'Alî Thanawi's Bihishti Zewar: A Partial Translation with Comments*, Berkeley: University of California Press.
Nadîm, W. and A. Nayyar (1988) *Patang Bâzî*, Islâmâbâd: Lok Virâ.
Nizâmî, K.A. (1961) '*Malfûzât* kî târîkhî ahammiyat', in Mâlik Râm (ed.) *'Arshî Presentation Volume*, Delhi, pp. 3–15.
Paul, J. (1990) 'Hagiographische Texte als historische Quelle', *Saeculum* 41, 1 : 17–43.
Pfleiderer, B. (1985) 'Mira datar dargah: The Psychiatry of a Muslim Shrine', in Imtiaz Ahmad (ed.) *Ritual and Religion among Muslims of the Sub-continent*, Lahore: Vanguard, pp. 195–233.
Pradhan, S. (ed.) (1985) *Marxist Cultural Movements in India: Chronicles and Documents (1936–47)*, 3 vols, Calcutta: Mrs Santi Pradhan.
Puhlitî, Muhammad 'Ashiq (ed.) (1988) *Al-qawl al-jalî; malfûz Hadrat Shâh Walî Ullâh Muhaddith Dehlawî*, trans. and anno. Taqî Anwar 'Alawî, Lakhna'û: Nâmî Press.

Qabbânî, N. (1983) *Al-aʿmâl al-shiʿrîya al-kâmila: Yaumîyâtu imra'atin lâ mubâliya*, Beirut: Manshûrât Nizâr Qabbânî.
Qâsimî, A.N. (1953) *Ghar sê ghar tak*, Rawalpindi: Matbûʿât (reprint).
Qâsimî, A.N. (1955) *Bazâr-e Hayât*, Lahore: Matbûʿât (reprint).
Qâsimî, A.N. (1959a) *Berg-e Hennâ*, Lahore: Matbûʿât (reprint).
Qâsimî, A.N. (1959b) *Sannâta*, Lahore: Nayâ Idârah.
Qâsimî, A.N. (1980) *Nîlâ Patthar*, Lahore: Matbûʿât (reprint).
Qâsimî, A.N. (1984) *Kapâs kâ Phûl*, Lahore: Matbûʿât (reprint).
Qâsimî, A.N. (1985) 'Bain', in Muhammad Yâr (ed.) *Muntakhib afsânê, 1983–85*, Rawalpindi.
Rothen-Dubs, U. (1989) *Allahs indischer Garten*, Frauenfeld: Waldgut.
Russell, R. (1970) 'The Development of the Modern Novel in Urdu', in T.W. Clark (ed.) *The Novel in India: Its Birth and Development*, London: George Allen and Unwin, pp. 139–150.
Russell, R. (1992) *The Pursuit of Urdu Literature: A Select History*, London: Zed Press.
Russell, R. and K. Islam (1969) *Three Mughal Poets*, London: George Allen and Unwin.
Rypka, J. (1959) *Iranische Literaturgeschichte*, Leipzig: Harrassowitz.
Sadîd, A. (1991) *Urdû adab kî tahrîken: ibdetâ'î-ye Urdû se 1975 tak*, Karachi: Anjuman-e Taraqqî-ye Urdû.
Sadiq, M. (1984) *A History of Indian Literature*, London: Oxford University Press.
Samîʿallâh (1988) *Unîswîn Sadî men Urdû ke tasnîfî idâre*, Faidâbâd: Nishât Press.
Sarûr, A.A. (ed.) (1951) *Urdû Adab, Hasrat Nambar*, Aligarh: Anjuman-e Taraqqî-ye Urdû.
Schimmel, A. (1975a) *Classical Urdu Literature from the Beginning to Iqbal*, Wiesbaden: Harrasowitz.
Schimmel, A. (1975b) *Mystical Dimensions of Islam*, Chapel Hill: University of North Carolina Press.
Schimmel, A. (1985) *And Muhammad is His Messenger*, Chapel Hill: University of North Carolina Press.
Shaikh, S. (transl.) (1981) *Selected Short Stories of Ahmad Nadeem Qasimi*, Karachi: National Book Foundation.
Sharar, A.H. (1989) *Lucknow: The Last Phase of an Oriental Culture*, trans. and ed. E.S. Harcourt and Fakhir Hussain, Delhi: Oxford University Press.
Suhrawardy, S.A.B. (1945) *A Critical Survey of the Development of the Novel and Short Story*, New York: Longman.
Tapper, N. (1990) 'Ziyaret: Gender, Movement, and Exchange in a Turkish community', in Dale F. Eickelman and James Piscatori (eds) *Muslim Travellers: Pilgrimage, Migration and the Religious Imagination*, London: Routledge, pp. 236–255.
Tassy, G. de (n.d.) [1870–1871] *Histoire de la Littérature Hindouie et Hindoustani*, 3 vols, New York: Burt Franklin.
Trimingham, J.S. (1971) *The Sufi Orders in Islam*, Oxford: Oxford University Press.
Troll, Christian W. (ed.) (1989) *Muslim Shrines in India: Their Character, History and Significance*, New Delhi: Oxford University Press.
Turner, V. (1979) *Process, Performance and Pilgrimage*, New Delhi: Concept.
von Grunebaum, G. and R. Caillois (eds) (1966) *The Dream and Human Societies*, Berkeley: University of California Press.
von Schwerin, Kerrin (1981) 'Saint Worship in Indian Islam: The Legend of the Martyr Salar Masud Ghazi', in Imtiaz Ahmad (ed.) *Ritual and Religion among Muslims in India*, Delhi: Manohar, pp. 143–161. Reprinted Lahore: Vanguard.

Washbrook, D. (1990) 'South Asia, the World System, and World Capitalism', *Journal of Asian Studies* 49, 3: 479–508.
Wielandt, R. (1983) *Das erzählerische Frühwerk Mahmûd Taymûrs*, Beirut: Beiruter Textstudien.
Wielandt, R. (1984) 'Die Bewertung islamischen Volksglaubens in ägyptischer Erzählliteratur des 20. Jahrhunderts', *Die Welt des Islams*, 23: 244–258.
Wild, S. (1994) 'Nizâr Qabbânî's Autobiography: Images of Sexuality, Death and Poetry', in R. Allen *et al.* (eds) *Love and Sexuality in Modern Arabic Literature*, London: Saqi Books, pp. 200–209.

10

PROPHETS AND *PIR*S

Charismatic Islam in the Middle East and South Asia

Charles Lindholm

Introduction

This chapter will explore, admittedly in a preliminary and sketchy fashion, some of the reasons why charismatic Sufism first appeared in Islamic society, despite the fact that the message of Islam is overtly opposed to all forms of spiritual elitism. Having outlined this process, I will then venture some equally tentative hypotheses as to why Sufism has more or less vanished as an active force in the Middle East, yet has remained influential in South Asia. My contention, in brief, is that the rise and fall of Sufi influence in the Middle East is an historically conditioned reflection of fundamental tensions within the egalitarian Middle Eastern cultural ethos, the rise of modern ideals, and the heightened repressive power of the central state. In contrast, the relative success of Sufism in South Asia has its roots in a sociocultural context wherein hierarchical distinctions between human beings are taken for granted and where the local autonomy and moral authority of powerful Sufi brotherhoods have largely been retained.

Charisma in Islam: exemplars in an emissary religion

As George Makdisi writes, more than any other great religion, mainstream Islam is "characterized by the basic equality of all Muslims in the eyes of the law as God's submissive servants" (Makdisi 1983: 85). Sunni Muslims have no authoritative body to interpret doctrine, no ecclesiastical council, no synods or pope, as in Christianity, no gaon as in Judaism, no sanctified imam, as in Shi'ism. There are no formal priests, no official church, no church hierarchy. In principle, Sunni Islam is resolutely anti-authoritarian and denies all claims to special virtuoso religious status: anyone who is able to recite and who knows the ritual can lead the Friday prayer in the mosque, just as anyone capable of reading (or of hearing someone else read) can interpret the Qur'an. Any believer can choose to worship at any mosque, to follow any teacher, to accept any of the schools of interpretation of the divine law, including one different from that of his parents or friends.

So radical is the ideal of individualism and egalitarianism in Islam that Muhammad, the bearer of Allah's message to humankind, is never presented in the Qur'an as a God himself, or as God's companion, or even as supernaturally gifted. He is only an ordinary man whom God had mysteriously appointed as his spokesman, his "warner." Muhammad's sole task was to enunciate the Word of Allah – his only miracle was the recitation of the Qur'an. He was God's instrument, not his vessel.

In its eschatology and in the character of its Prophet, Sunni Islam is the purest case of what Max Weber called emissary religion;[1] that is, a religion in which God is utterly omnipotent and transcendent, but nonetheless active and moral, ordering humanity onto the right path. In this type of annunciation, any claim to union with the deity is an unforgivable sin. The prophet of the ethical God is not an ecstatic mystic, but a sober messenger bringing God's edicts and his promise of salvation to the world. Those who heed the emissary's message band together in the community of the righteous, where each person is personally responsible for obedience to the ethical commands of God, each is an active moral agent in the world, each is fated to be judged as an individual by the deity on the final day.

Weber contrasts emissary prophecy to exemplary prophecy, wherein the prophet is the living receptacle of a static, immanent, and abstract essence. Devotees are a spiritual elite who seek self-loss through merger with a spiritual force that is believed to lie beneath the surface of ordinary life. Technical disciplines, such as meditation and withdrawal from the world, over and above moral righteousness, are the road taken to reach this end. In popular understanding, the exemplary saint is a magical being; a God on earth who can intercede to help ordinary human beings escape their round of suffering and delusion.

Exemplary religion is the natural home of charisma, since it rests upon the recognition of a spiritually gifted individual's oneness with the sacred. In contrast, there would seem to be no room in the egalitarian religion of Islam for the advent of charismatic virtuosos with supernatural powers. Yet in practice this has not proven to be the case; in fact, Islam has provided a warm home for many charismatics who claim to be unified with God. Shi'ism is, of course, the sect that has made charisma central to its message, while Sufi saints have been part of the Middle Eastern Islamic scene from the earliest era, and continue to be so in many Islamic societies to this day. How can this seeming paradox be explained?

Partly the appearance and persistence of charismatic leaders in Islam is due to theological and pragmatic difficulties in implementing the Muslim vision of a complete and encompassing divine order that could be read in the holy text and enacted on earth. The Qur'an, being finite, does not and cannot explicitly cover all circumstances. There are many areas of behavior left out, some questions are not specifically answered, other precepts are ambiguous, and sometimes there are apparent contradictions or seeming impossibilities in the text. Also, since human beings are fallible, it is always possible that God's commands will be distorted or misconstrued even by the best of interpretations. Alternative explications of Qur'anic texts by respectable religious scholars give clear evidence of the difficulty of gaining absolute certainty of Allah's directives. These difficulties put Muslims into a state of indecision as to the proper way they should behave in order to stay on the right path, and opens the door not only for analogical reasoning but also for charismatics who claim a special capacity to intuit God's desires.[2]

Charisma was also awakened by the fact that in the Qur'an Allah proclaims himself to be utterly transcendent, unpredictable, and indeterminable, bound not even by His own Words. Furthermore, in Islam, as in Calvinism, only God knows the state of a human soul; the blasphemous drunkard may be saved while the pilgrim who piously prays, fasts, and gives alms to the poor may be damned. Suffering from a pervasive awareness of the dangers of sinfulness and hypocrisy, in fear of God's unpredictable wrath, and perplexed by ambiguities as to the interpretation of the holy word, early Muslims naturally sought other means to find salvation beyond the problematic and difficult study of the sacred text.

In particular, they turned their eyes toward the Prophet himself, since it seemed reasonable that he, of all Muslims, was certainly the most likely to be saved. This led to the collection of "reports" of the Prophet's life and sayings (*hadith*), and the customs (*Sunna*) he followed. By learning what Muhammad said and did, devotees could model their lives on his, thereby pleasing God.

Accompanying the compilation and imitation of the Prophet's words and deeds was a greater emphasis on his perfection (see Andrae 1936); increasingly, he was portrayed as pure, infallible, capable of foreseeing the future, of cursing his enemies, of splitting the moon in the sky, of ascending to heaven while still alive, and, above all, of interceding for the frightened faithful on the terrible day of judgment.[3] In consequence, some Muslims focused their hopes for salvation on Muhammad, and elevated him to near-divine status. The tendency toward the apotheosis of the Prophet reached its apogee in the poetry of the late nineteenth-century Indian Sufi and jurist Ahmad Riza Khan Barelwi, who wrote that "The two worlds seek to please Allah / God seeks to please Muhammad / Muhammad is the threshold to Allah / Allah is the threshold to Muhammad" (quoted in Sanyal 1995: 433). In the same fashion, Shi'ite Imams and Sufi saints were placed beneath Muhammad in a hierarchy of intercessors worthy of the veneration of the faithful.

Undoubtedly an evolving emphasis on Muhammad's sacred status as perfect man, and later Muslim adoration of charismatic saintly figures, was a response to the natural anxiety generated by the necessary ambiguity of the sacred word and by the Muslim premise of an absolutely transcendent God – but there is more to it than that. Muhammad's charisma was not solely a posthumous creation. By all accounts, Muhammad was indeed an individual who drew his followers to him by his exceptional character; he was loved first, then obeyed; submission to the emotional compulsion exercised by him as a person defined the Muslim faith for the devout; it was Muhammad himself who provided the emotional core for the community of faithful, the *umma*. Reverence for the Prophet gave believers the resolve to stand together against the corrupt world. Later Sufi saints offered the same benefit, providing mediation, peace, and personal contact with the divine in the midst of a society that unfortunately remained threatening and violent, despite the admonitions of Islam.

In sum, a felt charismatic bond with the Prophet drew Muslims into the community of believers and simultaneously gave them a sense of personal spiritual expansion that is the hallmark of charismatic discipleship. At the same time, as we have seen, the actual message carried by Muhammad modestly downplayed and even denied his own charismatic role. Charisma in Islam then is both a response to the anxieties aroused by its own austerity and a reflection of the potent and compelling character of the founder, which stands in many senses in contradiction with the egalitarian message he bore – a creative tension that has animated Islam ever since.

The maintenance of charisma: Shi'ites and Sufis

In the *umma*, under the authority of Muhammad, uncertainty was kept at bay as the Prophet served as the final arbiter of all disputes and offered his followers a real and immediate sense of their own salvation. But after his death the community of believers broke down into rancorous rivalry as leadership rapidly passed to purely secular commanders who governed by force rather than by virtue. In response to the corruption of the community of the faithful, some Muslims naturally attempted to reawaken the charismatic inspiration that had first given them their shared identity and sense of spiritual communion.

Among these were the partisans of Ali, the Shi'ites, who argued that the best candidate was Ali, the son of Abu Talib, Muhammad's father's elder brother and Muhammad's guardian; Ali had married Muhammad's eldest daughter, Fatima, and was his foster brother as well, since he had been raised alongside Muhammad as a child. If he was Muhammad's spiritual successor, then the Shi'ites reasoned that his charisma too could be inherited by his descendants, one of whom must always be the wearer of Muhammad's mantle. It was the duty of the true Muslim to discover this holy person, and then to adore him and obey him unconditionally (see Dabashi 1993).

Unhappily for the Shi'ite faithful, their search was prone to repeated splits, since in every generation there were a number of potential claimants to the imamate. Also, none of the proclaimed Imams were able to recapitulate Muhammad's feat and dominate the Islamic world. Certain Shi'ite regimes – Fatimid, Safavid and others – did challenge and frighten the secular Sunni kingdoms, but eventually they fell prey to the inevitable destroyers of all charismatic political movements: rationalization and demystification. Their followers melted away, and they crumbled into dust – until the most recent advent of political

Shi'ite fervor in modern Iran, which is seeking, against all odds, to escape a similar fate.

Meanwhile, other devout Muslims sought a non-political solution to the waning of the charismatic moment. As we have seen, the mainstream response was to undertake an intensive study of the life and sayings of the Prophet. According to Louis Massignon (1954), by the late eighth century a few of these early *hadith* transmitters had evolved into the pioneers of Sufism. What made these particular seekers unique was that they did not just recite the traditions, but believed they could achieve spiritual transformation through emulating the abstemious purity of the first Muslim community and the selfless habits of Muhammad. To do this, the more ardent and ascetic of them withdrew into remote regions where, like Muhammad, they preached to the rural people, who were drawn to the missionaries because of their austerity, dedication, and learning.[4]

These *wali*s or "friends of God" believed they were destined to renew the faith and stifle the evil practices of the day. In contrast to the learned (the *'ulama*) and the transmitters of hadith, they believed this goal could not be accomplished by mere book learning, but required an actual transformation of the devotee through strict discipline in channeling and controlling the passions (*nafs*) that otherwise would divert the seeker from his quest. The pursuit of enlightenment also required an ascetic detachment from the usual preoccupations of humanity and a high moral vision.

By the twelfth century, the individual pursuit of enlightenment had become well institutionalized. Inspired Sufi saints (*shaikh*s, *murshid*s or *pir*s) founded *tariqa*s (lodges – literally pathways) where they were surrounded by pupils (*murid*s – ones who have made it their[5] will to enter the path, also known as *salik*s, wayfarers). In their teachings, the Sufis said that God can only be known intuitively. As Massignon explains, the Muslim mystical journey does not seek any conclusive state, but requires "a general disposition of the heart to remain always malleable throughout the succession of these states . . . one must not spend time comparing their respective merits, nor become attached to one or another of these instruments of grace as an end in itself" (Massignon 1982, vol. III: 25).

This mystical doctrine meant that unlike the ordinary Muslim who had a corpus of laws and traditions to provide a baseline for behavior, the Sufi had no sure signposts for his quest. Even the holy texts were not a certain guide, since according to Sufi teachings what may seem wrong according to the letter of the law may actually be right for the Sufi saint who is beyond rules. Similarly, rituals have significance only insofar as they reflect the "heart" of the practitioner, and even acts of piety may be interpreted as obstacles in the path to enlightenment. In these circumstances, the quandary of the ordinary Muslim was multiplied exponentially: how could the *murid* be sure he was not deluding himself, mistaking his own desires for those of God, and allowing enthusiasm to lead him into heresy or insanity?

The uncertainty and potential for solipsism was countered (at least in part) by the student's immersion into the protective community of brothers, where he shared out all his worldly goods with his fellows, living with them in a communist community where distinctions of wealth, knowledge and strength ceased and the word "my" was anathema. The spiritual "band of brothers" imitated the communalism of the original *umma*, and like them they were united under the authority of a charismatic spiritual guide to whom the *muridin* submitted in a relationship of absolute love and trust (*tawakkul*).

Having submitted to his master's discipline, just as the *umma* submitted to the Prophet, the student then was ready to be emptied of his ego through *wajd*, or "finding"; this was conceptualized as a journey through stages of enlightenment to the depths of the soul, where the manifestation of God was waiting to be experienced, an experience defined for this reason by Schimmel (1975) as that of "instancy" rather than ecstacy. In Hegelian fashion, the journey of the *murid* was understood as reflecting the expansion and contraction of the soul as it moved spirally toward a final reconciliation; hope alternated with fear, intoxication with sobriety, presence with absence, unity with separation. Sufi pupils could be rated according to the number of these stages they had gone through. However, because of the subjectivity of the stages, there was great controversy over the weight to be given to each of them, or even their order.

The most important debate was over the way in which enlightenment should be expressed. Some masters, most famously al-Junayd (d. 910), emphasized sobriety (*sahw*) over intoxication (*sukhr*). The "sober" school retained its influence for many Sufis, but the ecstatic practice of *dhikr* (remembrance) soon became the central and defining "liturgical" ritual (Gilsenan 1973) of successful Sufi orders, as dramatic group performances of remembrance drew crowds of onlookers, who often became lay devotees of the brotherhoods, giving money and patronage to them.

In time the relationship between the Sufi master and disciple was elaborated into a complex hierarchical spiritual edifice. This began as disciples gathered together in a *khanaqa* (a Sufi lodge, *zawiya* in North Africa) to learn from their master, practice the discipline of the group, undertake collective rituals, and participate in the local community. After the founder's death, the tomb of a revered saint became the centre for the proliferation of new devotional cults around Sufi lodges (Trimingham 1971). Each new cult validated its authenticity by tracing a *silsila*, or spiritual genealogy, to the sacred founder (often Abdul-Qadir al-Jilani), who himself was linked back through to Ali or the first caliph, Abu Bakr, and if possible connected back to Muhammad himself. By placing themselves in a spiritual line to the founders of Islam, the *tariqas* validated their own present-day authenticity and perpetuated in attenuated and rationalized form the charismatic relationship between the founding *pir* and his devotees, which, in theory, was a reiteration of the bond between Muhammad and the enlightened *umma*.

Sufis were also hierarchically ordered in the present by means of a ranked structure of visible and invisible saints culminating in a mystical ruler at least as powerful as the Shi'ite Imam. The theory behind faith in the hidden administration of saints went as follows: Muhammad was not only the final Prophet, he was also a perfect man, sent by God to maintain the order of the universe. In esoteric language, he was the *qutb*, the cosmic pivot, who brings the world to perfection. According to the Sufis a *qutb* must exist for every generation, even though, as "God's bride" he was veiled from ordinary men, and discerned only by the purified elite.

Many Sufi authorities believed that the world pivot of the day had legal authority equal to that of Muhammad in his era, since the power of both came from the same source: God himself. In more esoteric doctrine, a prophet dispenses graces without being transformed, while the saint is transformed without dispensing graces. The saint is therefore superior since he is close to union with God, while the prophet is only God's vehicle. Of course, Muhammad was unique in taking both roles at once. In any case, the *qutb* filled the role of the imam in Shi'ite Islam, but without the necessity of being of Ali's line.

Revolving around the present-day pivot of the universe was an elaborate status order of his *khalifa* (deputies), characterized by Macdonald as "a saintly board of administration by which the invisible government of the world is carried on" (1909: 163). These lesser saints were thought to have superhuman powers, such as the ability to be in two or more places at once, see into the heart of the disciple and ferret out any hypocrisy, manifest objects at will, curse, and bless, and especially the crucial ability to intercede for their followers on Judgment Day. The invisible order of the "friends of God" became tangible in the local *tariqas*, where the resident *pir* was the *khalifa* of a greater *pir*, who was supposedly under the authority of a still greater hidden master, and so on, extending in the present to the hidden seal of the saints and back in time to Ali, Abu Bakr, and Muhammad himself; even the humblest *murid* beginning on the path was a part of this great chain of sanctity. The only problem was that the members of the secret sanctified order could only be recognized by their charismatic aura, since they had no objective credentials.

The notion of sacred power finding earthly expression in the institutionalized communities of the brotherhoods provided the popular imagination with a picture of an eternal and perfect holy order operating in secret that superseded (at least in imagination) the dissolute and by now crumbled hierarchy of secular power. This hidden order stood apart from the corruption of government and provided ordinary Muslims with intercessors who could state their case to a far-distant and impenetrable God. As Marshall Hodgson puts it: "There might no longer be a Caliph with power in the ordinary political sense. But there remained a true spiritual Caliph, the immediate representative of God, who had a far more basic sway than the outward Caliph" (Hodgson 1974: 228).

In its heyday in the twelfth century during the reign of the Seljuks, and for centuries afterwards, the network of Sufi brotherhoods exerted tremendous influence in the spreading but diffuse cultural universe of Muslim society. Because Sufi sects could introduce themselves into the moral margins between the tribes and had an affinity with the hierarchial structure of the guilds and clubs of the urban quarters, they provided the local coherence and sense of unity in an expanding and pluralistic universe that the legalistic, rigorously egalitarian and abstract textual scholarship of the *'ulama* could not. With their capacity to offer an actual experience of religious ecstasy, they gave the ordinary people an escape from the desanctified and fragmented world of the everyday. The Sufis were, Hodgson remarks, "the spiritual cement for the social order" (ibid.: 230). Yet, despite its great influence, by the twentieth century Sufism had ceased to be a moving force in the Middle East, though it still remained potent in South Asia, as the contributions to this book demonstrate. Why did this occur?

Sufism and modernity

Many commentators have seen the debunking influence of Western rationalism as the main culprit behind the decline of Middle Eastern Sufism. Swayed by the prestige and success of Western technology and science, Muslim reformers at the turn of the century saw the practices and beliefs of Sufism as primitive and pagan. They argued that in order to reach parity with the West Islam should cut away these "residues" and focus on "modern" aspects of Islam, such as consultation, personal liberty, rationality, and freedom of thought.

These modernist rationalistic puritans gave birth to later oppositional intellectual movements, such as salafism, which arose in the 1930s in North Africa as a response to French anti-Islamic propaganda. The Salafa reformers called for a return to what they believed to be an original Islam, and in the process vehemently repudiated Sufism as anti-Muslim, primitive, and collaborationist. Similar campaigns were launched in the Indian subcontinent as well, notably by the puritan *'ulama* of the Deobandi school and later by various reformist movements such as the Tablighi Jama'at and the Jama'at i-Islami.

In both the Middle East and South Asia, the factors favoring the rise of purist orthodoxy are the same. As Ernest Gellner has pointed out, it was no accident that the advent of these anti-Sufi movements coincided with the increased domination of the tribal and rural world by the new urban administrative and technical class. This growing and increasingly culturally dominant segment of society naturally found the universalistic and abstract Islam of the urban *'ulama* more attractive than personalized, charismatic Sufism. The Islamic practice of this powerful segment of society also fit well, Gellner argued, with modern conditions – particularly the need for a standardized educational system and a replicable workforce (Gellner 1983). According to Gellner, in contrast to the medieval character of the particularistic, closed, irrational, other-worldly, hierarchical, and personal world of Sufism, reformist Islam is universalistic, open, rational, this-worldly, egalitarian, and impersonal, and therefore has what Weber would call an elective affinity to the social conditions of modernity (Gellner 1983).

However, as Gellner himself has documented (1981: 99–113), it is not at all evident that charismatically structured organizations, such as Sufi *tariqa*s, are necessarily unable to adjust to modernity. On the contrary, because a charismatic leader can make unilateral decisions and quickly adapt to circumstances, paying little attention to the restrictions of traditional law, and because he can then immediately mobilize the labor of his dedicated followers, charismatic groups can, in principle, respond rapidly yet in a unified, organized fashion to opportunities arising in the fast-changing modern setting. The huge financial success of the South Asian Khojas, who are devoted to their spiritual leader, the Aga Khan, indicates the potential economic virtues of charismatic leadership – when the leader has a high degree of business acumen.

Furthermore, as the Khoja case amply indicates, Islamic mysticism does not necessarily require detachment from the world or a disdain for practical action or entrepreneurship (Rodinson 1973). Muhammad, the perfect man, was, after all, a highly successful entrepreneur, and Muslim doctrine has always been resolutely this-worldly. As a result, Sufi saints have never been able to withdraw completely into monastic isolation, but were often married men who raised children, worked as craftsmen, merchants, soldiers, bureaucrats, and so on, while simultaneously serving as the fountains of God's grace. Many of these exemplars advocated hard work, asceticism, and obedience to authority as disciplines leading to enlightenment, instilling in their devotees an almost Calvinist devotion to their daily duties in the workplace. And, as in Calvinism, the prosperity which sometimes followed as a result of these disciplinary practices was understood by the followers to be a sign of divine approval and a guarantee of salvation. Unlike the case in Calvinism, but with equal logic, worldly success could also be interpreted as proof of miraculous divine intervention on the part of the leader, thereby deepening the loyalty of the disciples to their saint.[6]

It seems quite clear, then, that the practice of charismatic Sufism – or any charismatic religion – is not precluded by the advent of capitalism or modern complexity. In fact, it is not unusual for Sufi followers to be successful as entrepreneurs, military men, and professionals, and Sufism in South Asia and elsewhere has shown a remarkable, resilient capacity to cope with modern conditions. But, despite the theoretical potential for entrepreneurial innovation – realized in South Asia – in the Middle East Sufism has lost almost all its cachet.

If capitalism and recent developments cannot be blamed for Sufism's decline in the Middle East, perhaps, as some commentators argue, its erosion has its roots in the eighteenth-century Wahhabi revival in Saudi Arabia, an ethically rigorous austerity movement which promulgated anti-Sufi doctrines such as the prohibition of all worship at tombs and the cessation of Sufi practices such as *dhikr*. But if Wahhabism succeeded in undermining Sufism in the Middle East, why did it not do so in South Asia, where the Wahhabis were also vigorously active? Moreover, Wahhabism is not necessarily opposed to certain forms of Sufism. In fact, some major Sufi orders, such as the Nasiriyya and the Sanusi, responded to the pressures of colonialism and Westernization by making Wahhabi-like purification of Islam and imitation of Muhammad their watchword. These neo-Sufi movements, as Fazlur Rahman has called them (Rahman 1982), required disciples to become involved in the world in order to transform it. In this context, it is no surprise to find that Hasan al-Banna, the founder of the Muslim Brotherhood, began his career as a Sufi, or that Allal al-Fassi, who began the Salafa movement, was a member of a famous family of Sufi *shaikh*s in Fez.

The generally assumed negative relationship between modern puritan reform and the downfall of Sufism in the Middle East is therefore far from obvious; nor can explanation be found in any systematic capitulation by Middle Eastern *tariqa*s to colonialism or to indigenous secular authority, as some authors seem to believe. Certainly a number of Middle Eastern Sufis, like the overwhelming majority of *'ulama*, accommodated themselves to colonialism and secular rule; but many others did not. The Sanusi of Libya, for example, headed the struggle against Italian domination, and were strong proponents of a return to original practice. Elsewhere, other Sufi orders, some reformist, others ecstatic, led their clients against the state, following in the footsteps of the righteous Sufi rebellions of the past, such as those that led to the rise of the great Safavid dynasty in Iran, and to the ascendance of the Almoravids and Almohads in North Africa and Spain. For instance, in Turkey Naqshbandi Sufis led a rebellion to free Kurdistan in 1925, while Sufi-led uprisings against unjust taxation and government interference in local affairs continued in North Africa throughout the early part of this century. In fact, unlike the urban learned, who were generally (with the exception of Iran) easily co-opted into the central administration, Sufis in the Middle East – especially those in the tribal regions – continued to act as spokesmen for their people and leaders of opposition right into modern times.

Indeed, it was just their history of speaking out against corruption and tyranny and leading the righteous in rebellion that gave Sufis a wide degree of support even among the populace who were not committed to the worship of saints. However, present-day Middle Eastern state regimes, notoriously authoritarian and undemocratic, have made it a policy to suppress all dangerous oppositional voices, and their newfound power, backed up by Western technology, vast armies, and networks of spies, has given them the capacity to do so. No longer protected in tribal enclaves or urban ghettos, Sufi preachers have been obliged to accommodate themselves to the realities of subordination under unprecedentedly omnipotent central states. In so doing, they have lost what remained of their popular authority, and have been succeeded by Islamist zealots, who now take the forefront in contemporary religious struggles against government domination.[7] However, it is also a fact that the state did not find it very difficult to root out loyalty to Sufis – the ground had already been laid by a widespread dissatisfaction with Sufi claims to exemplary charismatic status.

The exaggeration of saintly authority

I would argue then that while it is no doubt true that Western colonial influence and policies, along with greater state control over religion and the elective affinity of modern society with more universalistic and textual versions of Islam, all contributed to the twentieth-century delegitimization of Sufism, nonetheless the primary cause for its loss of importance in Middle Eastern society must be deeper. I hypothesize that this cause is to be discovered in the compulsive tendency of Sufi sects to exaggerate the powers of their founders, which led them to set themselves at irreconcilable odds with the ascetic and egalitarian principles that animate Middle Eastern society.

The Sufi tendency to braggadocio is found everywhere. For instance, even Abdul-Qadir al-Jilani (d. 1166), the modest and tolerant founder of the Qadiriyya, the largest Sufi order, is reported to have boasted that "my foot is on the neck of every saint" (quoted in Schimmel 1975: 247). The modern saint al-Tijani went even further when he proudly declared himself to be the *Qutb al-Aqtab* (the pole of poles) and the seal of the saints, with command not only over all living *pirs* but over all those who had gone before him as well (see Gilsenan 1973). Similarly, the Arab poet Ibn al-Farid (d.1235) ends his great ode on mystical love with these words to his readers: "I found the full-grown men of the tribe (of Sufis no wiser than) little babes. For my contemporaries drink only the dregs of what I left; and for those before me, their (vaunted) merits are my superfluity" (quoted in Nicholson 1921: 266).

In a classic essay, R.A. Nicholson explains the escalating arrogance of Sufi saints in this way: "As the Bedouin brags about himself in order to assert the dignity of his tribe, so when the Mohammedan saints boast of the unique endowments which God has bestowed upon them, it is not self-glorification, but thanksgiving to Him 'from whom all blessings flow'" (ibid.: 173). Of course the mystic's claim to a transpersonal union with a higher being everywhere carries with it an element of grandiosity. However, the characteristic arrogance of mystics is amplified in Islam, where the theology of an absolute, omnipresent, omnipotent God points toward complete merger – and incomparable powers for the one who is merged. Jalaluddin Rumi puts the argument this way: "The man who says "I am the servant of God" asserts that two exist, one himself and the other God. But he who says "I am God" has naughted himself and cast himself to the winds" (Rumi 1972: 55–56). For the Sufi saint, "naughted" in God, his thoughts now must be God's thoughts, his feelings are God's feelings, and whatever he does must be willed by God – a mighty sensation indeed, and one that is continually apostrophized in Sufi rhetoric.

Overstatement was also much encouraged by the triumph of the "drunken" school which emphasized precisely the devotional practices of *dhikr* and other mystical disciplines that pushed adepts to believe themselves merged in "naughted" unity with an absolute deity – and then to claim their natural due as God's earthly vessel. The first of these communicants was Bistami, who in the ninth century cried "Glory be to me" as he was transported in ecstasy; when his scandalized students attacked him, they found their blows miraculously turned back upon them, demonstrating that their *shaikh* had indeed become the pure mirror of Allah. Similarly, in the thirteenth century, Rumi exclaimed: "Wine is intoxicated with me, not I with it! The world takes its being from me, not I from it!" (Rumi 1975: 32–33). Most famously, the great Sufi saint Hallaj (d. 922) declared "I am the Truth" or "my I is God"! These ecstatic proclamations, though governed by a moral imperative, scandalized the orthodox, since they are in direct contradiction to the Muslim doctrine of the irreducible gap between an unknowable supreme God and his fallible human creatures, equal in submission to his judgment.

But despite orthodox condemnation, those who claimed an ecstatic unity with Allah appealed to a larger and larger audience during the medieval period. A populace living in a state of chronic anxiety were drawn to the Sufis by their dramatic performances of *dhikr* and by their promise of salvation in the here and now. Sufi sects such as the Qalandariyya, lacking a doctrine beyond the urgent quest for a transcendent state of consciousness, became ever more successful; in competition, the masters of established *tariqa* also had to appeal to a sensation-seeking public. By the thirteenth century, successful brotherhoods relied primarily upon emotional public preaching, redistribution of wealth in charity, spectacular presentations of *dhikr*, and the performance of miracles to gain the approval of the populace and endowments from lay brothers.

There was a parallel withdrawal from moral activism among mystically inclined Sufi intellectuals, who were increasingly drawn to the esoteric teachings of Ibn al-Arabi (d.1240). In place of the ascetic and ethical messages of the early Sufis, Arabi constructed a complex, hierarchical, pantheistic, and contemplative neo-Platonic mystical vision. Adepts of his school spent their time meditating on the forty stages of ascent toward, and descent from, the loving perfect man, and pondering the twenty-eight degrees of emanation from the ultimate divine name, each emanation flowering in its own multifarious archetypical forms, all reflecting the perfect love of God. Arabi's devotees lost themselves in the abstruse detail of this eternally ramifying spiritual universe; for them, only those capable of grasping the metaphysical abstractions of the archetypes and emanations could truly experience God; ordinary people were inferior "link animals" (Massignon 1952).

Both intellectual Sufism and popular Sufism thus moved away from the egalitarian asceticism and restraint of early faith and toward a more indulgent immersion in ecstatic devotion to a charismatic leader, a perfect man, an emanation of God who draws the sensitive follower to him in a manner that the devotees likened to romantic love. The saint symbolized his spiritual authority by acting in a manner that marked him off from ordinary men: most saints dressed in special clothing, had long beards, moved with solemn dignity, showed no overt interest in power, appeared chaste and demure, carried no weapons, and spoke with deliberation. Others, taking the role of dervish, had begging bowls and wore patched robes; they wandered without a home, transformed in drug-induced trance. In all instances, the mystic sought to present himself as beyond the pale of the average person, both physically and spiritually.

But because the spiritual status of a *pir* rested primarily on a supposed inner transformation merely symbolized by his outer appearance and actions, there was a great potential for charlatanism. As a Middle Eastern proverb says, a beard may hide the face of a hypocrite. In consequence, the devotees gathered around the *pir* were obliged to convince potential followers and reassure themselves that their leader actually deserved the absolute devotion he demanded. To accomplish this they assumed that every unusual event that happened to them was due to a miraculous intervention by their leader,[8] and that these miracles proved his sacred quality. The *muridin* also elevated their leader to ever more empyrean heights because of the great spiritual status they themselves gained through their personal association with a great saint.

Exaggeration of powers also had an institutional source. Since the authority of a *pir* was charismatic, it could not be rationally codified, and it was not automatically handed on within the saint's family. Instead, the mantle was inherited by the most spiritually qualified initiate – who could only be recognized by his own ineffable charisma. This ambiguity led candidates to make more and more extravagant claims for their sanctity, and to demonstrate their holiness in competitions with rival "friends of God" where each contestant displayed his spiritual strength by eating live coals, walking on water, and curing the sick. These miracle contests could escalate into supernatural battles that were analogous to the power struggles waged between warriors and kings. Although the weapons of combatants were intangible, they were believed to be just as deadly as spears and swords, and casualties among the *muridin* could be high.

Despite the dangers to them, disciples joined in the game, vituperatively deriding the virtue of their antagonists' leaders, while bragging about the spiritual powers of their own *shaikh*, who might be presented as the present *qutb*, or at least as one of the most elevated members of the hidden holy administration. As an eighteenth-century anti-Sufi poet, Al-Badr al-Hijazi, angrily writes:

> Would that we had not lived to see every demented madman held up by his fellows as a "Pole"! Their *ulema* take refuge in him; indeed, they have even adopted him as a Lord, instead of the Lord of the Throne. For they have forgotten God, saying "So-and-so provides deliverance from suffering for all mankind."
>
> (quoted in Arberry 1950: 128)

Overstatement of a saint's powers tended to occur even when spiritual leaders made absolutely no grandiose claims for themselves in life, but were elevated to sainthood after their deaths by devotees who had their own reasons for deifying their dead *pir* (for cases see Miller and Bowen 1993; Evans-Pritchard 1949).

Saintly authority in egalitarian society

We can see then that a number of circumstances, both theological and sociological, pressed toward more and more extravagant claims for the absolute spiritual authority of Sufi saints and for the ecstatic merger of disciples in the entourage of the miracle-working *pir*. As I have argued at length elsewhere (Lindholm 1996), such tendencies are in direct contradiction to the values of egalitarianism and individualism that are central to Islam and that are at the core of Middle Eastern society as well. These values can be discovered in any number of ethnographic and historical accounts of the region. Typical is Henry Rosenfeld's description of the Bedouin nomads, where "each kin group, not accepting exclusive control of resources, fundamentally considers itself the equal of others in regard to prestige, honor, status, and in rights" (Rosenfeld 1965: 174). And elsewhere, among Jordanian villagers, Richard Antoun writes that the average 15-year-old "regards himself now as no man's servant and only undertakes chores out of the generosity of his own heart for his friends, and out of a sense of obligation for his kinsmen" (Antoun 1967. 295).

It might be argued that these rural people are egalitarian because they are, in fact, all equal – equally impoverished. But what is remarkable is that in the Middle East, even in the face of distinctions in status and wealth, the same ideology holds. For instance, among the sedentarized Lur of western Persia, where a small elite own almost all the land and animals, Jacob Black reports that:

> All Lurs consider each other on a footing of intrinsic equality; that is to say, the status of any given individual at any given moment is seen as achieved. No-one is born politically superior to anyone else. All Lurs believe that individual industry is the key to personal achievement and that only ineptitude, sloth or bad luck can prevent a man from attaining the highest goals, or, alternatively, can bring a man of importance and standing into straitened circumstances.
>
> (Black 1972: 616)

Black's view that the ideology of equality is merely a form of false consciousness is highly debatable (Lindholm 1996). In urban Morocco, Paul Rabinow tells us that poverty "indicates only a lack of material goods at the present time, nothing more. Though regrettable, it does not reflect unfavourably on one's character" (Rabinow 1977: 116). This egalitarian attitude is in marked contrast to the European Mediterranean, where the poor are thought to have less honor than their superiors (Stewart 1994: 132).

The same egalitarian ethos is reflected in the absence of honorifics in the Muslim world. According to Bernard Lewis: "From the beginning to the present day, there are no hereditary titles, other than royal, in the Islamic lands, except on a very limited and local scale, and even there by courtesy rather than by law" (Lewis 1988: 64). This egalitarianism extended even to rulers. As Hodgson tells us, in the Middle East "everyone knew well enough that in fact the king was a mere man among others. In himself he was a mere six feet of flesh, with passions like any other man, by no means unassailable" (Hodgson 1974, Vol. I: 283).

In this environment all men (although not women: see Lindholm 1992, 1996), regardless of standing, could and did meet and interact without deference. Even today, it remains the case that there is usually no bowing and genuflecting when persons of different social rank meet. The handshake and the embrace, which are signs of equality and intimacy, are Middle Eastern institutions. Even the legitimacy of the king was traditionally marked by a simple handshake given to him by his advisors and the *'ulama*; this handshake affirmed the equivalence of the contracting parties at the very moment that power was officially conferred on the ruler. If the ruler was in theory equivalent to his entourage, who only ceded him power, the entourage also were fundamentally equal to one another in their pursuit of the ruler's personal commendation.

It is with this background in mind that Lewis writes: "This is a society which always in principle, and often, at least to some extent, in practice, rejects hierarchy and privilege, a society in which power and status depend primarily on nearness to the ruler and the enjoyment of his favour, rather than on birth or rank" (Lewis 1988: 23). Similarly, Hodgson states flatly that in the traditional Middle East "equality was the basic principle, above all among free adult males"; in this context "every free Muslim should be accorded that personal liberty and dignity which was expected by the Arabian tribesman – being bound to obey no man without his own assent . . . [therefore] all free Muslims ought to be treated on an essentially equal basis" (Hodgson 1974, Vol. I: 344, 253).[9]

Within this egalitarian, individualistic, and competitive ethos, the very characteristics of the *pir* that drew his disciples' love and inspired crowds to ecstatic states of inspired trance also aroused qualms in the general public, who regarded the "friends of God" with a mixture of awe and fear that sometimes verged on repulsion. This queasy mixture of feelings is evident in the popular images of Muslim saints, who were thought to be hungry for power, extremely jealous, and suffused with a potent but polymorphous sexuality that allowed them to seduce those who went to them for spiritual help. Saints also used magic to punish anyone who failed to pay proper respect to them. Even animals were not immune. It is said that a bird that flew over Jilani's head without making obeisance was immediately blasted out of the air, while goats eating pasture belonging to a saint were believed to die automatically (Hodgson 1974, Vol. II: 227; Serjeant 1981).

Other recorded miracles were rarely the kindly acts Westerners might expect. For example, train conductors who demanded a fare from a *shaikh* might find their trains suddenly immobilized, their watches stopped – but all came right again when abject apologies were made. In other cases, the God-intoxicated *pir* was more violent: Rumi's mentor Shams magically deafened a pious *murid*, and forced him to recite in public that "there is no God but God, and Shams-i Tabrizi is his Prophet." When the student was attacked for this blasphemy, Shams roared with such might that he killed one of the attackers, proving his miraculous powers (cited in Hodgson 1974, Vol. II: 245). In folklore the *pir* maintains respect much as a sultan might: through the use of brute force.

The truth or falsehood of the beliefs held by the common people in the Middle East about the "friends of God" is irrelevant for the argument made here; certainly some saints were of a peaceful and kindly character. What is important is that the Sufi *pir*, because of his assertion of a special sacredness that emanates from his transfigured person, was venerated and even deified because of what were believed to be his extraordinary powers, but along with respect was a marked degree of ambivalence, fear, and distaste, as testified in the Moroccan proverb that "God's mercy comes from visiting a saint and going away soon" (quoted in Westermarck 1926: 228). In the Middle East, the saint was always a dangerous and ambiguous figure, followed when he could offer spiritual influence, ecstatic experience, and a variety of worldly connections and services, but abandoned when other sources of leverage and power were available that were less perilous, ambivalent, and demanding.

It is no accident, then, that the zenith of Sufism in the central Muslim lands was during the Seljuk period, when the caliphate had fallen and a purely secular authority had begun to suborn and encapsulate the *'ulama*, leaving the populace with very little in the way of either spiritual resources or legitimate authority. In these circumstances the Sufi lodges with their cosmic hierarchy of charismatics offered Muslim masses the experience of moral unity under sanctified leadership, as well as an imaginary universal order overseeing the disrupted universe.

But when the Islamicate slowly knit itself together again, and when orthodox scholars asserted their control over religious learning in state-sponsored schools, Sufi brotherhoods were increasingly pressed to hold their audiences by emphasizing the miraculous powers of their *pir*s and the potent experiences of ecstatic trance. These ever more prevalent aspects of Sufism were disturbing to the ordinary Middle Easterner, steeped in the egalitarian and individualistic traditions of his society, who was both drawn to and repelled by Sufic demands for deification of a leader and the concomitant repudiation of the follower's capacity for independence.

In sum, the delegitimization of Sufism in the Middle East was accelerated by modern conditions and especially by the dominant power of the central state, but was also rooted in a deep and pervasive conflict between Sufism, with its apotheosis of saints and demand for absolute obedience from disciples, and the characteristic Middle Eastern and Islamic values of equality and autonomy. It is no surprise then to find that Sufis have slowly lost their essential role in Middle Eastern society, and now serve only as mediators in marginal tribal areas, or provide ecstatic performances in impoverished urban communities, or serve as guides for cultured elites seeking a less demanding, more aesthetic, intellectualized version of Islam. This is where Middle Eastern Sufism is today, and most likely will remain for the foreseeable future.[10]

Sufism in South Asia

As in the Middle East, in South Asia the movement against Sufism spread widely and rapidly. Puritan reformers influenced by Saudi Arabian Wahhabism, preachers instructed in the textualism of the Deobandi school (Metcalf 1982), and zealots inspired by the messages of self-taught scholars such as Maulana Maududi have all vigorously opposed what they consider to be the unIslamic and innovative features of Sufi practice. In so doing, they have often appealed to the same arguments I have outlined above, citing the egalitarianism of Islam and decrying Sufi pretensions to act as intercessors with God. As in the Middle East, these attacks on Sufism have resonated with the ideals of the expanding Muslim middle class, especially as many South Asian Muslims have ventured to Mecca and discovered the low estate of Sufism in the Islamic heartland. As Gardner writes, these experiences, and the circulation of anti-Sufi propaganda, have led a number of upwardly mobile South Asian Muslims to separate themselves "from the cults of charisma and miracles which are increasingly left to the poor and powerless" (Gardner 1995: 147).

Nonetheless, even though religious disputes in South Asia have been quite as heated as those in the Middle East, the reformists have not managed to dominate the debate. Instead, *pir*s have been staunchly supported by a number of friendly *'ulama*, who marshal scriptural arguments to support Sufi practices (for a similar argument see Werbner 1996a). Furthermore, many South Asian *shaikh*s are often also religious scholars, and have proven to be well able to defend themselves by citing holy texts.[11] As the material in this volume shows, despite potent attacks by various reformist schools, Sufism nonetheless remains an important force in South Asia among all social groups. In fact, according to some commentators, Sufi brotherhoods may actually have gained converts among South Asian immigrants to Europe, who join *tariqa*s in order to find moral and social support in their new, foreign environments (see Werbner 1996b).

Sufism is therefore holding its own and perhaps even growing in South Asia, while it has simultaneously been marginalized and delegitimized in the Middle East. The most obvious reason why this should be so is simply that South Asia is on the periphery of inexorable theological changes emanating from the central cultural core of Islamdom. From this perspective, the ascendance of Sufism in South Asia is a temporary phenomenon, since purist Islam will necessarily triumph everywhere as greater textual knowledge slowly permeates the Islamic world, obliterating unorthodox, local-level practices (Robinson 1983). Such a position has a degree of plausibility, but it also assumes that a standard reading of the sacred texts is both possible and likely – dubious assumptions at best. Furthermore, by focusing completely on textual dissemination and the universality of Islam, this approach ignores precisely the fundamental political and cultural divergences between South Asia and the Middle East that anthropologists and sociologists want to correlate with differences in religious attitudes.

However, making such a correlation is a difficult task, not only because cross-cultural comparisons are in themselves exceedingly problematic, but also because the South Asian cultural universe is so incredibly complex and internally differentiated. For instance, even at the most superficial level, it would seem very hard indeed to make any statements that hold true both for the Gangetic heartland of India and for the Indus Delta, or that are equally applicable to the Muslim nations of Pakistan and Bangladesh and to India, Sri Lanka, or Nepal, where Muslims are a distinct minority.

Nonetheless, I believe we can postulate a multiple set of plausible and interconnected reasons for the continued salience of Sufism in South Asia. Beginning with the political dimension, we can note that in South Asia the British colonial powers generally followed policies of indirect rule, and were more or less content to leave local matters alone, so long as peace was maintained and taxes paid. This meant that they interfered very little with the already existent Sufi lodges under their jurisdiction. These brotherhoods held substantial local power as a result of their early connections with the Mughal state, their large entitled land holdings, and their armies of loyal supporters. On their side, Sufis were usually equally content to maintain the peace as long as they were allowed to continue their religious routines and keep their estates and authority.[12] This *laissez-faire* relationship meant that the power of Sufi *pir*s was not greatly disrupted or compromised by colonial interference, in contrast to the case in the Middle East, where more interventionist Italian and French administrations often had adversarial relationships with Sufi saints and their followings.

If Sufis in South Asia had greater autonomy during the colonial period than did their counterparts in the Middle East, their power was augmented even more after the departure of the British, as the new South Asian states developed into relatively democratic and open societies. Secular aspirants to political power in South Asia were therefore obliged to make coalitions with and concessions to local power brokers, including the independent and powerful Sufi brotherhoods, who could offer voting blocs in return for state favouritism. The brotherhoods therefore had concrete advantages to distribute to followers, and could keep their loyalty. They also had the resources and independence to continue safely fulminating against the excesses and hypocrisies of the secular elite and the official *'ulama*, and to make the traditional Sufi claim to represent a pure and sacred type of power.

This is in stark contrast to the situation in the Middle East, where totalitarian dictatorships did not tolerate any alternative local forms of authority. As a result, brotherhoods there lost all political or economic independence, and had little to offer their disciples. Railing against government corruption was also no longer possible, and the Sufis' forced acquiescence to the central state further undercut their credibility. In other words, South Asian Sufi saints proved that it is possible to have one's cake and eat it too – more actual power coincides with a greater capacity to indulge in rhetoric against the evils of power. In comparison, the saints of the Middle East lost their moral sway along with their wealth and strength.

It is plausible then to suggest that a colonial policy of indirect rule, combined with the democratic character of the modern South Asian state, permitted Sufi brotherhoods in the region to retain considerable economic and social independence, while also allowing them a continued capacity to take the moral high ground. However, these cannot be the sole sources of Sufi authority in South Asia. In fact, colonial or state repression of a religious sect may lead not to the disintegration of the sect but to increased zeal on the part of believers and a rush of conversions – as was demonstrated in the Iranian revolution.

Similarly, as we have seen, a number of Sufi lodges in the Middle East were active participants and even leaders in liberation struggles against colonial authority, which gave them extraordinary prestige when the new states gained independence. This might, in principle, have provided them with greater popularity than the pacifist and accommodative lodges of South Asia ever achieved. But instead, these Sufi groups, along with all others, were delegitimized and broken, and their radical rhetoric has now become the property of Islamist movements, while South Asian brotherhoods continue to prosper.

Perhaps considering the characteristics of the period when Sufism flourished in the Middle East will help explain this anomaly. As we have seen, Sufism reached its zenith during the Seljuk era, when Muslims were threatened by the downfall of the caliphate and the fragmentation of the empire. In this tumultuous period, Sufi *pir*s offered their clients a cosmic order and a sense of personal connection with sacred power as a substitute for a dangerous and chaotic secular world.

In a parallel manner, South Asian Muslims have also been plagued by a deep and pervasive sense of insecurity, engendered this time by the regional dominance of Hinduism, a religion which stands in such radical contrast to Islam that the Arab traveller al-Baruni wrote nine centuries ago that "we believe in nothing in which they believe, and vice versa" (quoted in Gaborieau 1995: 222). Muslim anxiety was increased when the religiously neutral British colonial administration withdrew, so that Muslims either remained as minorities under the authority of encompassing Hindu states, or else fled to create all-Muslim nations that nevertheless were locked in a condition of permanent confrontation with Hindu might.

Within this radically oppositional context, the austere textualism of orthodoxy has not provided many Muslims with either sufficient comfort or the strength to allay their anxiety, and they have turned instead to inspirational personal *pir*s, who give their disciples immediate feelings of connection to God and of miraculous salvation. These are the same charismatic rewards that were offered by Sufi saints during earlier periods of crisis in the central Muslim lands, and they will continue to appeal as long as Muslims feel themselves to be threatened by their Hindu neighbors. Indeed, popular recourse to charismatic leadership is not unique to Islam, but occurs wherever the taken-for-granted world is subjected to doubt and pressure (Lindholm 1990).

But the continuing crisis of confidence among South Asian Muslims in the face of Hinduism also cannot be invoked as the primary reason for the enduring importance of Sufism there. After all, the Muslims of the Middle East, while still constituting the overwhelming majority within their own nations, have also had their beliefs threatened, and have undergone the humiliation of domination by Christian and Zionist Westerners. Yet, as we have seen, by and large they have not resorted to Sufism, but rather have found solace in reformism and Islamist radicalism.

This pattern reflects the political and historical differences I remarked upon above, but it also points toward deeper cultural distinctions between the two regions. As I have tried to show, the predominant Middle Eastern value system is one that strongly favors egalitarianism and independence – values that deeply permeate Islamic theology as well. Sufism, with its intrinsic tendency toward apotheosis of saintly leaders, is an outgrowth but also a repudiation of that value system; as such, it eventually awakened ambivalence and rejection by the general Middle Eastern public. But such ambivalence and rejection has not occurred in South Asia, where there has been no popular revulsion from Sufism.

It seems reasonable to assume that the South Asian acceptance of Sufi claims to sacred power is a reflection of a prevailing world view that valorizes precisely what the Middle Eastern world wishes to deny: rank and distinction within a unified community. This attitude is, of course, most starkly expressed in the Hindu caste system, which ascribes every individual a permanent position within a totalizing structure of hierarchical differences based on the degree of pollution incurred by work at the caste specialty or by other group characteristics. Within this universe, one's position in the caste scale is conceived to be a reward or punishment for spiritual attainments in past lives, and is therefore not to be escaped in this life. Instead, one is linked forever to one's *jati* (caste or sub-caste) mates, who are more or less elevated in the scale of caste purity.[13]

South Asian Islam, of course, totally disavows the Hindu caste hierarchy, reflecting its egalitarian and individualistic origins in the Middle East. It is, in fact, precisely Islam's affirmation of human dignity and equality that has made it so appealing to many low-caste members of Indian society, and that is often taken by Muslims themselves as the most essential mark of their own identities. For instance, as Marc Gaborieau shows, Nepali Muslims distinguish themselves from their Hindu neighbors primarily by their refusal to abase themselves before their betters. Instead, "a Muslim, when greeting superior people, will never bow: he will stand upright, raise his hand to his forehead, and say Salam" (Gaborieau 1995: 222).

However, even though the ideals of Islam run counter to the values of the ancient South Asian world, South Asian Muslims still accept, albeit without convincing religious or ideological foundations (Ahmad 1978: 11), essential distinctions between persons of differing castes. As T.N. Madan notes, Muslims in India have "two sets of representations, one stemming from ideological considerations and the other from the compulsions of living" (Madan 1981: 58). And Gaborieau writes that despite their refusal to bow before their superiors, Nepali Muslim bangle-makers nonetheless "acceptent au moins les principes concernant la pollution, base du système des castes" (Gaborieau 1966: 89; see also Werbner 1995b for an example of the continuance of caste distinctions among Pakistani immigrants in England). From this perspective, despite the egalitarian ideology of Islam, South Asian Muslims have retained the cultural models prevailing in the Indian environment, as they too recognize and, more importantly, accept the hierarchical distinctions of purity and pollution that divide their Hindu neighbors.

The acceptance of hierarchical distinctions carries over into the religious realm, where aspects of Islam which valorize the sanctity of the descendants of the Prophet and the purity and encompassing love of mystical saints have generally been very considerably elaborated in South Asian religious discourse (see Schimmel 1975). This is not to say that Middle Eastern Muslims lack such status distinctions. In fact, as I have shown above and elsewhere (Lindholm 1986b), sacred (and secular) rank has long been highly developed in the Middle Eastern setting. But in the Middle Eastern context saintly claims to special authority constitute attempts to validate distinctions within an egalitarian and individualistic environment overwhelmingly hostile to such efforts. This is the conflict between austere emissary religion and charismatic exemplary prophecy. In South Asia, in contrast, saintly claims to sacral authority stand in harmony with the wider cultural conceptualization of a moral universe commanded by saintly, world-renouncing figures of superhuman purity and universal love.

Sufi saints in South Asia therefore were and are the Muslim equivalents of sanctified Hindu gurus, and the acceptance of *pir*s in South Asia was and remains in large part a direct substitution of the former for the latter.[14] This is a heritage that reformers have repudiated, but the continuing power of Sufism in South Asia shows that the assertion of saintly purity still has a deep appeal to the public at large, who hope for salvation from the corrupt world through the personalized intervention of a charismatic redeemer. In the Middle East, in contrast, people tend to resent any assertion of authority over them – whether that authority is secular or saintly – making Sufi professions of spiritual power comparatively more difficult to maintain. In other words, in the Middle East claims to spiritual superiority are held suspect, while in South Asia the intercession of exemplary sacred figures is eagerly sought.

Conclusion

To restate, I have argued that the tensions implicit in Muhammad's charismatic enunciation of an emissary religion of unparalleled purity inevitably led to the rise of charismatic saints who could serve as embodied moral exemplars for ordinary people. In the Middle East, these figures had their heyday as alternative power sources in periods of cultural and political disruption, but were gradually pressed to make greater and greater claims for their own powers and more extreme demands on the devotion and self-sacrifice of their disciples. This tendency was in contradiction to the general cultural ethos of equality and autonomy, and eventually led to the delegitimization of the Sufi movement.

However, this same trajectory did not occur in South Asia, where Sufism has maintained its hold on the public. This is partly because Sufi saints retained more autonomy and wealth in South Asia, which allowed them to offer disciples concrete rewards and also to present themselves plausibly as moral alternatives to corrupt politicians. Furthermore, the oppositional character of South Asian Islam inevitably heightened the anxiety of the faithful, and pressed them to seek personalized charismatic leaders. Finally, the hierarchical and devotional traditions of South Asian culture favor saint worship, despite the egalitarian messages of orthodox Islam. Hence, while Sufism has almost died in the Middle East, it has retained and even improved its position in South Asia.

Notes

1 See the essays "Religious Rejections of the World and their Directions" and "The Social Psychology of the World Religions" in Weber (1946) for Weber's most succinct statements. The alternative values of Shi'ite and Sufi sects will be explored later.
2 Of course, legal scholarship in Islam is based on historical reconstruction and analogical reasoning to provide the faithful with proper codes of behavior in new circumstances. Even here, however, technical expertise never gains absolute dominance. For more on this, see Lindholm (1996).
3 The theory that saintly mediators are a psychological response to an absolutely omnipotent and transcendent God was first posed by David Hume (1976), and has been famously applied to Islam by Ernest Gellner (1981).
4 Some believe the uniform of the early saintly preacher-ascetics was a rough robe of wool (*suf*), hence the term "Sufi."
5 Sufis were overwhelmingly male, though some women have followed the pathway, and the imagery of women in esoteric Sufism is often very positive.
6 See Werbner (1995a, 1996b) for the history of one such pragmatic cult in Pakistan and the United Kingdom, Gilsenan (1973) for an Egyptian case, and Abun-Nasir (1965) for a North African sect which has had great financial and religious success in Africa.
7 The degree to which these new Islamist movements are, in fact, the moral and organizational successors of Sufi cults has been interestingly discussed by Roy (1994).
8 Gilsenan (1973) notes that the more educated, respectable and wealthy members of brotherhoods see *karāmāt* (miracles) as connected to learning and character, while lower-status members cite dreams and voices as evidence of their master's powers. See Gardner (1995) for a parallel phenomenon in Bangladesh among newly wealthy Muslims, who now seek to "sanctify" their ancestors by claiming them to have been extraordinarily pious and orthodox.
9 Of course, equality and competitive individualism do not stand alone, but co-exist and correspond with a high estimate of the importance of bravery, independence, and generosity; a personal honor code based upon self-help, hospitality, blood revenge, and sanctuary, and rigid sexual mores of female chastity and seclusion. It is also crucial to note that honor is inextricably located within clans and tribes. Important too is a shared ethos of mercantilism, social mobility, cosmopolitanism, and calculating rationality.
10 As in so much else, Turkey is an exception. This is partially because the orthodox *'ulama* were completely absorbed into the Ottoman state. When the Ottomans fell, the only source of religious legitimacy were the Sufi sects, which remained strong despite Ataturk's attempts to suppress them. There is as well a deep tradition of saint worship in rank-conscious Turkish society, especially in the military, where spiritual hierarchies date back to Central Asian shamanistic practices. For some of the differences between Turkey and the rest of the Middle East, see Lindholm (1986a).
11 For an example of a paradigmatic South Asian Sufi-cum-scholar, see Sanyal's essay on Ahmad Riza Khan Barelwi (1995). In uniting Sufism and textual study, men like Ahmed Riza Khan recapitulate the early history of Islam. For example, Ibn Taymiyya, the medieval Hanbalite scholar often cited by purists as the most rigorous of anti-Sufi theorists, was himself a member of the Qadiriyya order of Sufis (see Makdisi 1974).
12 Exceptions include the two Hur rebellions against the British in the Sind by the followers of *pir* Pagara, a landlord, political leader and hereditary head of a Sufi brotherhood

who still retains great authority in present-day Pakistan (see Lambrick 1972 for a fictionalized account). The numerous religiously led uprisings in the NWFP (North West Frontier Province) might also be included, but from my perspective the NWFP has more in common with the Middle East than with South Asia.

13 For the classic version of this image of caste, see Dumont (1970). However, much modern scholarship shows considerable social movement and entrepreneurship, even among spiritual virtuosos. For instance, religious renunciants can make claims to special holiness by showing extraordinary asceticism and purity, or, conversely, by engaging in cannibalism and self-degradation or indulging in intoxication and excess. See Parry (1982) and Lynch (1990) for examples. We also know that the Kshatriya, or warrior caste, who traditionally served as rulers, established competing axes of valuation for themselves to counterbalance the Brahman's claims to pre-eminence. See Inden (1990) and Heesterman (1985).

14 For example, as de Munck writes: "In Sufism, Sri Lankan (and Indian) Muslims found their religious parallels to popular Buddhism and Hindu forms of worship" (1995: 499).

References

Abun-Nasr, Jamil (1965) *The Tijaniyya: A Sufi Order in the Modern World*, London: Oxford University Press.

Ahmad, Imtiaz (1978) *Caste and Stratification among Muslims of India*, New Dehli: Manohar.

Andrae, Tor (1936) *Mohammed: The Man and his Faith*, London: Allen and Unwin.

Antoun, Richard (1967) "Social Organization and the Life Cycle in an Arab Village," *Ethnology* 6: 294–308.

Arberry A.J. (1950) *Sufism: The Religious Attitude and Life in Islam*, Chicago: University of Chicago Press.

Black, Jacob (1972) "Tyranny as a Strategy for Survival in an 'Egalitarian' Society: Luri Facts Versus an Anthropological Mystique," *Man* n.s. 7: 614–634.

Dabashi, Hamid (1993) *Authority in Islam: From the Rise of Muhammad to the Establishment of the Umayyads*, New Brunswick: Transaction.

de Munck, Victor (1995) "Sufi, Reformist and National Models of Identity: The History of a Muslim Village Festival in Sri Lanka," in T.N. Madan (ed.) *Muslim Communities of South Asia: Culture, Society, and Power*, New Dehli: Manohar, pp. 493–521.

Dumont, Louis (1970) *Homo Hierarchicus: An Essay on the Caste System*, Chicago: University of Chicago Press.

Evans-Pritchard, E.E. (1949) *The Sanusi of Cyrenaica*, Oxford: Oxford University Press.

Gaborieau, Marc (1966) "Les Curautes du Moyen Népal: place d'un groupe de Musulmans dans une société des castes," *L'Homme* 6: 81–91.

Gaborieau, Marc (1995) "Muslims in the Hindu Kingdom of Nepal," in T.N. Madan (ed.) *Muslim Communities of South Asia: Culture, Society, and Power*, New Dehli: Manohar, pp. 211–239.

Gardner, Katy (1995) "Mullahs, Migrants, Miracles: Travel and Transformation in Sylhet," in T.N. Madan (ed.) *Muslim Communities of South Asia: Culture, Society, and Power*, New Dehli: Manohar, pp. 145–176.

Gellner, Ernest (1981) *Muslim Society*, Cambridge: Cambridge University Press.

Gellner, Ernest (1983) *Nations and Nationalism*, Ithaca NY: Cornell University Press.

Gilsenan, Michael (1973) *Saint and Sufi in Modern Egypt: An Essay in Comparative Religion*, Oxford: Clarendon Press.

Heesterman, J.C. (1985) "Power, Priesthood, and Authority," in J.C. Heesterman (ed.) *The Inner Conflict of Tradition: Essays in Indian Ritual, Kingship and Society*, Chicago: University of Chicago Press.

Hodgson, Marshall G.S. (1974) *The Venture of Islam: Conscience and History in a World Civilization*, Vols I, II, III, Chicago: University of Chicago Press.

Hume, David (1976) *Natural History of Religion*, Oxford: Oxford University Press.

Inden, Ronald (1990) *Imagining India*, Oxford: Blackwell.

Lambrick, C. (1972) *The Terrorist*, Karachi: Oxford University Press.

Lewis, Bernard (1988) *The Political Language of Islam*, Chicago: University of Chicago Press.

Lindholm, Charles (1986a) "Kinship Structure and Political Authority: The Middle East and Central Asia," *Comparative Studies in Society and History* 28: 334–355. Reprinted in Charles Lindholm, *Frontier Perspectives: Essays in Comparative Anthropology* (1995), Karachi: Oxford University Press, pp. 147–171.

Lindholm, Charles (1986b) "Caste in Islam and the Problem of Deviant Systems: A Critique of Recent Theory," *Contributions to Indian Sociology* 20: 61–73. Reprinted in T.N. Madan (ed.) *Muslim Communities of South Asia: Culture, Society, and Power* (1995), New Dehli: Manohar, pp. 449–467.

Lindholm, Charles (1990) *Charisma*, Oxford: Blackwell.

Lindholm, Charles (1992) "Quandaries of Command in Egalitarian Societies: Examples from Swat and Morocco,", in J. Cole (ed.) *Comparing Muslim Societies*, Ann Arbor: University of Michigan Press. Reprinted in Charles Lindholm, *Frontier Perspectives: Essays in Comparative Anthropology* (1995), Karachi: Oxford University Press, pp. 206–233.

Lindholm, Charles (1996) *The Islamic Middle East: An Historical Anthropology*, Oxford: Blackwell.

Lynch, Owen M. (1990) "The Mastram: Emotion and Person among Mathura's Chaubes," in Owen M. Lynch (ed.) *Divine Passions: The Social Construction of Emotion in India*, Berkeley: University of California Press, pp. 91–115.

Macdonald, Duncan (1909) *The Religious Attitude and Life in Islam*, Chicago: University of Chicago Press.

Madan, T.N. (1981) "Religious Ideology and Social Structure," in: Imtiaz Ahmad (ed.) *Religion and Ritual among Muslims of India*, New Dehli: Manohar, pp. 21–64.

Makdisi, George (1974) "Ibn Taimiya: A Sufi of the Qadirya Order," *American Journal of Arabic Studies* 1: 118–129.

Makdisi, George (1983) "Institutionalized Learning as a Self-Image of Islam," in Speros Vryonis (ed.) *Islam's Understanding of Itself*, Los Angeles: UCLA Press.

Massignon, Louis (1952) "L'alternative de la pensée mystique en Islam: Monisme existentiel ou monisme testimonial," *Annuaire de Collège de France* 52: 189–191.

Massignon, Louis (1954) *Essai sur les Origines du Lexique Technique and de la Mystique Musulmane*, Paris: J. Vrin.

Massignon, Louis (1982) *The Passion of al-Hallaj: Mystic and Martyr of Islam*, trans. by Herbert Mason, vols I–IV, Princeton NJ: Princeton University Press.

Metcalf, Barbara Daly (1982) *Islamic Revival in British India: Deoband, 1860–1900*, Princeton NJ: Princeton University Press.

Miller, James and Donna Lee Bowen (1993) "The Nasiriyya Brotherhood of Southern Morocco," in Donna Lee Bowen and Evelyn Early (eds) *Everyday Life in the Muslim Middle East*, Bloomington: Indiana University Press.

Nicholson, Reynold Alleyne (1921) *Studies in Islamic Mysticism*, Cambridge: Cambridge University Press.

Parry, Jonathan (1982) "Sacrificial Death and the Necrophagous Ascetic," in M. Bloch and J. Parry (eds) *Death and the Regeneration of Life*, Cambridge: Cambridge University Press.

Rabinow, Paul (1977) *Reflections on Fieldwork in Morocco*, Berkeley: University of California Press.

Rahman, Fazlur (1982) *Islam and Modernity: Transformations of an Intellectual Tradition*, Chicago: Univerisity of Chicago Press.

Robinson, Francis (1983) "Islam and Muslim Society in South Asia," *Contributions to Indian Sociology* n.s. 17, 2: 185–203.

Rodinson, Maxime (1973) *Islam and Capitalism*, New York: Pantheon.

Rosenfeld, Henry (1965) "The Social Composition of the Military in the Process of State Formation in the Arabian Desert," *Journal of the Royal Anthropological Institute* 95: 75–86, 174–194.

Roy, Olivier (1994) *The Failure of Political Islam*, Cambridge MA: Harvard University Press.

Rumi, Jalaludin (1972) *Discourses of Rumi*, trans. A.J. Arberry, New York: Samuel Weiser.

Rumi, Jalaludin (1975) *Teachings of Rumi: The Masnavi*, trans. and abridged E.H. Whinfield, New York: Dutton.

Sanyal, Usha (1995) "Pir, Shaikh and Prophet: The Personalization of Religious Authority in Ahmad Riza Khan's Life," in: T.N. Madan (ed.) *Muslim Communities of South Asia: Culture, Society, and Power*, New Dehli: Manohar, pp. 405–448.

Schimmel, Annemarie (1975) *Mystical Dimensions of Islam*, Chapel Hill: University of North Carolina Press.

Serjeant, R.B. (1981) "Haram and Hawtah: The Sacred Enclave in Arabia," in R.B. Serjeant (ed.) *Studies in Arabian History and Civilization*, Aldershot: Variorum, pp. 41–58.

Stewart, Frank (1994) *Honor*, Chicago: University of Chicago Press.

Trimingham, J. S. (1971) *The Sufi Orders in Islam*, Oxford: Oxford University Press.

Weber, Max (1946) *From Max Weber: Essays in Sociology*, New York: Oxford University Press.

Werbner, Pnina (1995a) "Powerful Knowledge in a Global Sufi Cult: Reflections on the Poetics of Travelling Theories," in Wendy James (ed.) *The Pursuit of Certainty: Religious and Cultural Formulations*, London and New York: Routledge, pp. 134–160.

Werbner, Pnina (1995b) "The Ranking of Brotherhoods: The Dialectics of Muslim Caste Among Overseas Pakistanis," in T.N. Madan (ed.) *Muslim Communities of South Asia: Culture, Society, and Power*, New Dehli: Manohar, pp. 134–160.

Werbner, Pnina (1996a) "The Making of Muslim Dissent: Hybridized Discourses, Lay Preachers and Radical Rhetoric among British Pakistanis," *American Ethnologist* 23, 1: 102–122.

Werbner, Pnina (1996b) "Stamping the Earth with the Name of Allah: *Zikr* and the Sacralizing of Space among British Pakistanis," *Cultural Anthropology* 11, 3: 309–338.

Westermarck, Edward (1926) *Ritual and Belief in Morocco*, vol. 1, London: Macmillan.

NAME INDEX

Abdi, S.N.M. 55
Abu Bakr 214
Abu-Lughod, L. 8, 117
Abun-Nasr, J. 230
Ahmad, A. 17
Ahmad, I. 17–18, 19, 228
Ahmad, M. 5
Ahmad, S. 99–100
Al-Azmeh, A. 17
Al-Badr al-Hijazi 221
Ali, A. 189
Andrae, T. 211
Ansari, M.A.H. 189, 191, 192
Antoun, R. 222
Arberry, A.J. 221
Asad, T. 8, 22
Azad, M.H. 190
Azam, U. 198
Azim, W. 190
Azimi, K.R. 191

Babb, L. 43, 52
Bakhtin, M. 136, 170
Baldick, J. 4, 17, 199
Baljon, J.M.S. 189
Barelwi, Ahmad Riza Khan 211, 230
Bari, M. 144
Barth, F. 4, 90
Basak, J. 55
Bashir, H. 108
Basu, H. 119, 134, 136
Beck, B. 130
Beer, D. 181
Benz, E. 146, 157
Bhatti, Liaqat 'Ali 143
Bhatti, S.S. 193
Bhaumik, S.N. 55
Bilu, Y. 158

Black, J. 222
Bloch, M. 5
Boddy, J. 7, 8
Bourdieu, P. 32–3
Bowen, D.L. 221
Bowen, E.S. 157
Boyer, P. 33
Brisbarre, A. 101
Brugman, J. 190
Buddenberg, D. 17

Callois, R. 198
Chaudan, G. 190
Chaudrasekharan, T. 58
Chughtai, I. 192
Clancey-Smith, J. 4
Cohn, B.S. 15, 53
Comaroff, J. 8
Combs-Schilling, M.E. 47
Connerton, P. 7
Coppola, C. 191
Crapanzano, V. 188
Csordas, T.J. 9
Currie, P.M. 17, 20, 133, 189
Cyril, G. 61

Dabashi, H. 212
Davis, R.H. 5
de Heusch, L. 96
de Munck, V. 61, 231
Delaney, C. 99
Deleuze, G. 176, 181
Denny, F.M. 80
Desai, Z.A. 194
Devisch, R. 7, 155, 158
Digby, S. 9, 144, 157
Dinzellbacher, P. 90

NAME INDEX

Douglas, M. 6, 32
Dumont, L. 14, 20, 118, 231
Durkheim, E. 155

Eade, J. 12, 96, 111
Eaton, R. 9, 13, 18–19, 52, 84, 89, 188
Eck, D.L. 43, 53
Eickelman, D. 4, 96, 188, 204
Einzmann, H. 17, 142
Eisenstadt, S.N. 14
Elboudrari, H. 199
Eliade, M. 79, 115
Elias, N. 7
Evans-Pritchard, E.E. 4, 221
Ewing, K. 52, 116, 119, 131, 135, 168, 175

Fakhiri, S.K.M. 197
Feher, M. 155
Fernandez, J. 7
Fernea, R.A. 189
Fischer, Michael M.J. 150
Flemming, L.A. 192
Foucault, M. 14–15, 22, 33, 160
Frazer, J.G. 162
Freitag, S. 65
Frembgen, J.W. 144, 146, 148, 155, 157
Fruzetti, L.M. 17
Fuller, C. 12, 130

Gaborieau, M. 9, 34, 117, 227, 228
Gadgil, M. 55
Gardner, K. 225, 230
Geertz, C. 4, 8, 15, 18
Gellner, E. 4, 187, 188, 216, 230
Gilmartin, D. 13
Gilsenan, M. 4, 52, 187, 214, 219, 230
Gokalp, A. 101
Gold, A.G. 13
Gramlich, R. 144
Gran, P. 189
Guattari, F. 176, 181
Guthrie, S. 33

Habermas, J. 16
Hafiz, S.A. 190, 191
Hallaj 219
Handelman, D. 9
Haq, M.E. 34
Hayy, S.A. 190
Heesterman, J.C. 231
Hemingway, F.R. 56, 62
Hodgson, M.G.S. 215, 216, 222, 223

Hourani, A. 190
Hubert, H. 96
Hughes, T.P. 60
Hujwiri, A. 172
Hulbe, S.K. *et al.* 55
Hume, D. 230
Husaini, A.A. 199
Hussain, S.S. 58
Hussaini, A.A. 190

Ibbetson, D. 194, 195
Ibn al-Farid 219
Ibn Arabi 197
Inden, R. 231
Iqbal, Muhammad 189
Islam, K. 189
Italiaander, R. 193

Jalal, A. 204
Jalibi, J. 190
Jeffrey, P. 189
Junayd, al- 214

Kakar, S. 20, 116, 122, 129, 131
Kapferer, B. 7, 11, 122, 156
Katz, S.T. 47
Khalid, L. 192
Khan, N.A. 190
Kristeva, J. 176, 181
Kunjahi, S. 194, 195
Kurin, R. 7, 112, 118, 122, 133

Lacan, J. 175, 180–1
Lambrick, C. 230
Launay, R. 17
Lawrence, B.B. 194
Levinas, E. 33
Levi-Strauss, C. 7
Lewis, B. 222, 223
Lewis, I.M. 157
Lindholm, C. 16–17, 89, 116, 157, 221, 222, 227, 229, 230
Lings, M. 4
Loeffler, R. 146
Logan, P. 130
Lutz, C.A. 8, 117, 181
Lynch, O.M. 126, 231

Macdonald, D. 215
Maclagan, E. 194–5
Madan, T.N. 228
Mahmud, S.F. 191, 192

NAME INDEX

Makdisi, G. 209, 230
Malhotra, K.C. 55
Malik, J. 190, 192, 193
Malinowski, B. 161
Marriott, M. 7, 165
Marx, E. 88–9, 90
Massignon, L. 213, 220
Maududi 224
Mauss, M. 96, 135
Mayer, A.C. 119
McDaniel, J. 157
Melucci, A. 16
Memon, M.U. 189, 192
Mernissi, F. 189
Metcalf, B.D 5, 13, 191, 224
Meyerhoff, B. 95
Miller, J. 221
Misra, A.C. 17, 119
Moini, S.L.H. 17, 60, 61
More, J.B.P.L. 61
Mudimbe, V.Y. 161
Mujeeb, M. 17

Nadim, W. 204
Nanda, B.N. 8, 117
Nandy, A. 19
Nayyar, A. 204
Nicholson, R.A. 6, 219
Nizami, K.A. 194

O'Flaherty, W.D. 123, 130

Parry, J. 13, 96, 135, 136, 231
Paul, J. 194
Peters, F.E. 79
Pfleiderer, B. 120, 131, 188
Pinto, D. 8, 117, 118
pir Pagaro 230
Piscatori, J. 204
Platts, J.T. 160
Pradhan, S. 191
Premchand 191
Puhliti, M.A. 189

Qabbani, N. 203
Qadhiri, S.H.S. 58, 73
Qudussi, M.I. 58
Quinn, N. 181

Rabinow, P. 222
Rahim, M.A. 60
Rahman, F. 8, 117, 217

Raja, M. 60
Rao, S. 70
Ricoeur, P. 115
Robinson, F. 18, 225
Rodinson, M. 217
Rosaldo, M. 181
Rosenfeld, H. 222
Rothen-Dubs, U. 190
Roy, A. 34
Roy, O. 230
Russell, R. 189, 190
Rypka, J. 190

Sadid, A. 191, 192
Sadiq, M. 190
Said, E.W. 161
Sallnow, M.J. 12, 96, 111
Sami'allâh 190
Sanyal, U. 211
Sarur, A.A. 190
Sayyid, M. 58
Schimmel, A. 8, 90, 117, 188, 189, 197, 198, 214, 219, 229
Schutz, A. 158
Schwerin, K.G. 17, 18, 188
Sen, D.C. 17
Serjeant, R.B. 223
Shaikh, S. 192
Shapiro, A.K. 157
Sharar, A.H. 204
Shariff, J. 56, 60
Sharma, U. 22
Shaw, R. 19
Sherani, S.R. 5
Shilling, C. 6, 9, 155, 156
Shils, E. 15
Sivananda, V. 58
Smith, W.C. 140
Stewart, C. 19
Stewart, F. 222
Stoller, P. 8
Strauss, C. 181
Suhrawardy, S.A.B. 190

Tablighi Jama'at 216
Talib, M. 8, 117
Tambiah, S.J. 5, 13, 16, 53
Tapper, N. 189
Tassy, G. de 190
Taussig, M. 8
Taymiyya, Ibn 189, 230
Trimingham, J.S. 4, 134, 188, 198, 214

NAME INDEX

Troll, C.W. 188
Tsing, A.L. 11
Turner, B.S. 155, 158
Turner, V. 6, 7, 9, 11, 12, 86, 95, 114, 115, 151–2, 158, 182, 188
Tylor, E.B. 162

Valeri, V. 121
van der Veer, P. 19–20, 134, 135
Vartak, V.D. 55
Vikor, K.S. 4
von Grunebaum, G. 198

Waardenberg, J.D.J. 8

Waghorne, J.P. 51
Washbrook, D. 189
Weber, Max 14, 153, 156, 158, 210, 216, 230
Weingrod, A. 17, 115
Werbner, P. 15, 21, 49, 85, 90, 101, 103, 118, 123, 130, 134, 225, 228, 230
Werbner, R. 7, 11, 12, 13, 73, 95, 96, 113, 130
Westermarck, E. 181, 224
Wielandt, R. 187, 190
Wilce, J. 166, 181
Wild, S. 203
Wilson, B.R. 16

SUBJECT INDEX

Abdullah, Sufi 105, 113
adab islâmî 191–2
Adam's peak 73
adultery 128
aesthetic approach 7–8
aesthetics of devotion 45–7
aesthetics of embodiment 153–7
Aga Khan 217
Ali, son of Abu Talib 212
Almohads 218
Almoravids 218
Angâre (Burning Coals) 191
anger 169
animal sacrifice 101–3, 104
anonymous shrines 12, 77–91; liminal ethics 88–9; liminality embodied 85–8; *pirs* 79–82; saints and wilderness 83–5
anthropological approaches 7–8
anthropomorphic objects *see* Bangladeshi Sufism
Arabi, Ibn al- 220
Arafat 97, 99
Arfin, Sultanal, of Baudan 60
asceticism 213
Ashiq (son of Rabi'a) 163–5, 174–6; death 176–80; Rabi'a's stories about 165–71
Atroshi, *pir* of 10, 43; appearances of spiritual power 38–9, 40–1, 41–2; devotion 45–7; expansion and construction 48–9, 50
authority 37–8, 188, 189; egalitarian society and saintly 221–4; exaggeration of saintly authority 218–21; saint and family 170–1

Bachu (disciple of Atroshi) 40
bad faith economy 15–16, 108–11
'*Bain*' ('Dirge'/'Separation') (Qâsimî) 193, 196–203; mystical dimensions and gender 196–202; and Shâh Daulah 196, 198–202
bala/churel (female spirits) 83
Bangladeshi Sufism 12–13, 31–54; aesthetics of devotion 45–7; appearances of spiritual power 36–42; embodying the sacred 33–4; living *pirs* 34–6; *pirs* and their plans 47–50; refractions of place and person 44–5; sources of charisma 31–3; subject/object of identity 42–4
Banna, Hasan al- 217–18
Banwa *jamaa* 63–5
Barri Imam 141, 142, 148, 149, 153
al-Baruni 227
Bava Gor shrine 20, 118, 119–20, 123, 124, 127; divination through ordeal 128–9; emotional states 125; gender and the cosmic order 121–2; rites of exorcism 131; saintly regional hierarchies 133–4
Bava Habash shrine 119, 122, 123, 125; restoring virility 127, 130
belief: reifying 5–6
Bengal: Islamisation of 18–19, 34, 52
Bháwan Sháh 195
bhut (spirits) 122
Bihishtî Zewar (Heavenly Ornaments) 191
Bilal 118
Bistami (Bustami), Bayezid 144, 219
Barewli, Ahmad Riza Khan 211
Britain 105–6, 113
British colonialism 189–90, 226
Bukhari, Alam Shah 145

capitalism 217
caste system 80, 228

SUBJECT INDEX

Chan Aga Badshah 142
charisma 209–12; maintenance of 212–16; and modernity 14–17; sources of 31–3; transition from life to death 153–7
Chishti order 56
Chughtâ'î, 'Ismat 192
Chûhâ (Rat-children) cult 194–5
churel/bala (female spirits) 83
colonialism 189–90, 218, 226
communal harmony 19–20
community 213–14; Bava Gor shrine 132–3; Mama Ji Sarkar 155, 156; pilgrimage and 99–100, 114–15
construction activities 47–50
coolness 122–3, 124, 125
cosmic development: stages of 197–8
cosmic order: gender and 120–2; healing cosmic disorder 122–4
cultural relativism 161

danger 86
darbar (courts) 35
dargah 35, 55–6
Daulah Daryâ'î, Shah: '*Bain*' and 196, 198–202; sanctuary of 193–6
death of the saint: Ashiq 176–80; Mama Ji Sarkar 10, 151–3
democratic states 226
demons *see* spirits/demons
Deobandi school 216
devotion: aesthetics of 45–7; Bangladeshi shrines 37–8, 38–9, 45–7; Mama Ji Sarkar 149–51, 153–5
Dhannaka, Baba 155
dhikr (remembrance) 214, 219–20; *see also* *Zikr*
Din, Muhammad 172, 177
disciples/pupils 48–9, 213–14; relationship with *pir* 39–42, 43, 52, 111–14
disease 166–7
divination through ordeal 128–9
du'a (supplicatory prayer) 108, 110, 112, 114
dukh (sorrow, suffering) 125–6

ecstasy 219–20; *majzub* and 144–6
egalitarianism 16–17, 209–10; conflicting values in South Asia 227–9; saintly authority and 221–4
Egypt 17

eid sacrifice 97, 99, 104
embodiment 3–27; aesthetics of 153–7; anthropological study of ritual embodiment 7–8; emotions 8–11; liminality 85–8; sacred 3–5, 33–4
emissary religion 209–12
emotion 156; embodied emotions 8–11; emotional states 125–7; hierarchy and 117–39
Eneyetpur, *pir* of 48
enlightenment, pursuit of 213–14
entrepreneurship 217
Ershad, President 38, 48
exaggeration of saintly authority 218–21
exchange, sacred 13; Nagore-e-Sharif 62, 72–3, 73–4; pilgrimage and 13, 73–4, 95–100, 114–15; *see also langar*
exemplars 209–12; identifications with exemplary persons 98–9
exorcism, rites of 131
expansion plans 47–50
exploitation 200–1
eyes 144

Faqir *jama'as* (mendicant priests) 63–5, 67
faqirs: asceticism and giving 104–5; *Sidi* 119
Farid, Baba: spring of 84–5
Fassi, Alla al- 218
fear 199, 223–4
femininity 123
fertility 129–30
flag festivals 61–3; *see also* Nagore-e-Sharif
'folk-religion' 17–21
fun (*maja*) 125–6, 132–3

gaddivaras 127
gender: '*Bain*' 196–202; and the cosmic order 120–2, 123, 124
Gesudaraj of Gulbarga 60
Ghamkol Sharif 100–15
giving: hierarchical 103–7; hierarchy of shrines 134–5; Nagore-e-Sharif 72–3; *see also* exchange, *langar*, sacrifice
goma (music and dance) 126, 133, 135–6
good faith economy 102–3; encounter with bad faith economy 108–11; experiencing 111–15
guilt 169

SUBJECT INDEX

Gujarat black saints cult 10–11, 20, 117–39; emotional states 125–7; gender and cosmic order 120–2; healing cosmic disorder 122–4; hierarchy of saints' cults 117–20; joy and fun 132–3; reversal of status hierarchy 135–6; saintly regional hierarchies 133–5; sorrow and suffering 132; transformative power of rituals 127–31
Gwalior, Mohammad Ghouse 56

Hajara (Hagar) 98–9
hajj 60, 97–100
hajrivale (people in a trance) 131
Hallaj, Mansur al- 144, 219
halqah-ye arbâb-ye dhauq (Circle of Possessors of Good Taste) 191–2
harmony, communal 19–20
Hashmatullah, Muhammad *see* Atroshi
Hazrat Gul Warith Khan *see* Ji Sarkar, Mama
healing powers 72–3, 81, 155
heat 122–3, 124, 125, 130, 132
hierarchies 189, 214–15; and emotion 117–39; emotional reversal of the status hierarchy 135–6; giving 103–7; saintly rituals and worldly hierarchies 132; of saints' cults 117–20, 133–5; South Asia 16–17, 228–9
Hijazi, Al-Badr al- 221
Hinduism 227, 228; syncretism 18–21
Huichal Indians, Mexico 95
humans: saints, demons and 121–2
Husain, Intizâr 192

Ibn 'Arabî 197
Ibn al-Farid 219
Ibn Taimiya (Taymiyya) 80, 189
Ibrahim (Abraham) 98
identifications with exemplary persons 98–9
Ilahi, Mahbub 151
indirect rule 226
infanticide 194, 202–3
infertility 129–30
insecurity 224, 227
'installation of the *Pir*' ritual 67
Iqbal, Mohammad 151
Ishrat, *Sayyid* 141, 147, 148, 149, 153
Islam: charisma in 209–12; and Hinduism 19–21; levels of Muslim practice 17–18; *see also under different forms*
Islamisation 18–19, 34, 52
Ismail 97, 98–9
Israel 17

Jahlal, Shah 34, 39
Jalali *faqir* 63–5
Jama'at i-Islami 216
Ji Sarkar, Mama 10, 140–59; aesthetics of embodiment 153–7; biography 141–4; *darbar* in Rawalpindi 146–9; *dargah* in Nurpur 151–3; respected as true *majzub* 146; veneration of 149–51
Jilani (Gilani), Abdul Qadir al- 56, 61, 142, 214, 219, 223
jinns (evil spirits) 83
joy (*maja*) 125–6, 132–3
al-Junayd 214
justice 196, 201

Kalanga cult 95
Kallar Kahar 84–5
Kanduri festivals 61–5; *see also* Nagore-e-Sharif
Kanifnath, saint of 55
Khan, Ayyub 192, 204
Khawaja Garib Nawaz 56, 72
Khidmat (public service) 100, 103
Khidr (Khizr) 12, 198
Khojas 217
Korosani Baba 45

Lallon Shah 39, 46
langar 11, 95–116, 134; encounter between good faith and bad faith economies 108–11; experiencing the good faith economy 111–15; perpetual sacrifice 100–7; pilgrimage and sacred exchange 95–100
liminality 9, 188–9; death of Ashiq and liminal time 180; embodied at anonymous shrines 85–8; ethics of marginal shrines 88–9; living *pirs* 35–6
literary critiques 187–208; 'Bain' 196–202; of mysticism 187–8; new literature 190–2; Qâsimî 192–3; sanctuary of Shâh Daulah 193–6; shrine cults 189–90
locality 44–5; sacralising 65–7, 79–80; *see also* space
loss: sense of 10

love 15–16, 117, 118, 146
Lurs 222

madness 9, 126, 160–1; 'holy fool' 144–5; *see also majzub*
magaj (temperament) 125
magic: and illness 166–7, 168–9; and religion 5–6; use as punishment 223
Mahmud, Shaikh Khalid 151
Mai Mishra 119, 125; gender and the cosmic order 120–1, 122, 123, 124; rituals of motherhood 127, 129–30
Maishbandar shrine 44–5
maja (fun, joy) 125–6, 132–3
Majid, Sain 'Abdul 153, 154
majzub: category of 144–6, 157–8; Mama Ji Sarkar and his followers 10, 140–59; relationship to mother and family 9–10, 160–83
Makhan Devi 123–4
Malang *jamaa* 63–5, 67
Manto, Sa'âdat Hasan 192
mastans 9, 88, 135; Sidi *faqirs* 126–7; *see also majzub*
Mecca, pilgrimage to 60, 97–100
mendicant priests 63–5, 67
Middle East 16–17, 209, 216–24, 227–8, 229–30; exaggeration of saintly authority 218–21; saintly authority and egalitarianism 221–4
Mina 97–8
Mir Jani Shah 142
miracles 85, 143, 223; contests of 221; *see also* healing powers
Modaleb Shah, tomb of 41, 45, 46–7
modernity: charisma and 14–17; Sufism and 216–18
Mondal *faqir* 63–5
mortuary symbolism 35–6
mother: *majzub* and relationship with 9–10, 160–83
motherhood: rituals of 129–30
Motilala, Rahim Gul 142
Muhammad, Prophet 47, 51–2, 53, 210, 214–15; charisma 211–12
Mu'in al-din Chishti of Ajmer 20
Mujibur Rahman Chisti 50
murids see disciples/pupils
Muslim Brethren 187
mystical ascent 197–8
mysticism: '*Bain*' (Qâsimî) 196–202; literary critiques of 187–8

Nabi-Bamsa ('Family of the Prophet') 18–19
Nagore-e-Sharif 13, 16, 20–1, 55–76; complex and the basic elements of the universe 70, 71; daily and weekly rituals 72; healing powers of the shrine 72–3; Kanduri festival 61–5; legend of Sahul Hameed 56–8; period of Sahul Hameed 58–61; pilgrimage and sacred exchange 73–4; reception of Nagore Andavar's *rowla sharif chadar* 67–9; revitalising power of the shrine 70–2; ritual processing 65–7, 68–9
Naqshbandi-Mujaddidiya Tariqa 48
Naqshbandi Sufis 218
Nasiriyya order 217
Navnath, saint of 55
Nayaka, Achutappa 58
nazarbazi (playing with looks) 144
nazrana (tributary gifts) 104, 107, 134
neo-Sufi movements 217–18
new literature 190–2
niaz (consecrated food) 134
Nurpur 151–3

ordeals 11; divination through 128–9; sacrifice during the *hajj* 99–100

Pakistani village shrines *see* anonymous shrines
perpetual sacrifice 96, 100–7
peripherality, sacred 11–14, 16, 114
pilgrimage 11–12, 60–1; to Mecca (*hajj*) 60, 97–100; sacred exchange 13, 73–4, 95–100, 114–15
Pillai, Palaniandi 67–8
pir-disciple relationship 39–42, 43, 52, 111–14
place *see* locality, space
plans 47–50
politicians 108–10
politics 48
Premchand 191
processing, ritual 65–7, 68–9
processual approach 7
Progressive Writers' Association (PWA) 191–2, 192
psychiatry 181
pupils *see* disciples/pupils

Qabul Auliya, Shah 142
Qadiriya order 56
Qalandariyya (Sufi order) 220

Qasim, Baba 101
Qâsimî, Ahmad Nadîm 192–3, 202–3; '*Bain*' and Shâh Daulah 196; mystical dimensions of '*Bain*' and gender 196–202
Qur'an: as text 210–11
qurbáni (*eid* sacrifice) 97, 99, 104
qutb (cosmic pivot) 214–15

Rabi'a 162, 163–80; Ashiq's death 176–80; Sa'in Sahib 171–6; stories about Ashiq 165–71
Rafai *jamaa* 64–5
Ramzan Moti-Sarwar, Shah 55
Rashid, Abdul 147
Rat-children (*chūhā*) cult 194–5
Rawalpindi 142, 146–9, 156, 157
rebellions 218
reformism 189, 216–18, 224–5
regional shrine hierarchies 117–20, 133–5
religion: magic and 5–6
remembrance (*dhikr*) 214, 219–20
respectability: violation of standards of 172–4
revitalising power 70–2
Rifa'i, Ahmad Kabir 134
ritual processing 65–7, 68–9
'ritual saint' 67, 69
ritual slaughter 101–3
rituals: anthropological study of ritual embodiment 7–8; saintly and worldly hierarchies 132; transformative power 127–31
rowla sharif chadar (shawl) 67–9
royal courts 13
Rumi, Jalaluddin 219

sacralisation 102
sacred: embodying 3–5, 33–4
sacred exchange *see* exchange
sacred peripherality 11–14, 16, 114
sacrifice 96, 97–8, 99; perpetual 96, 100–7
sadaqa (gifts to the poor) 103, 104, 107, 134
Saddar Uddin Chisti 46–7
Safavid dynasty 218
Saheb, Yusef 58–60
Sahib, Sa'in 167–8, 170–1; and Rabi'a's relationship to Ashiq 170, 174–6, 176–8, 179; Rabi'a's stories of 171–4
Sahul Hameed Nagore Andavar *see* Nagore-e-Sharif
'saint who disappeared' 81–2, 83, 86–7

saintly regional hierarchies 117–20, 133–5
saints: demons, humans and 121–2
salafism 216
Sanusi 217, 218
Sarmad, Sa'id 145
satellite lodges 104–5
Sawab (merit) 107, 111
Sayedabad, *pir* of 39, 50
Sayyids 80, 87, 103–4, 111, 117–18, 118–19; *Sidi faqirs* and *goma* at *Sayyid* shrines 135–6
secular rule 218
self-fashioning 14–15
Seljuk period 224, 227
sexuality 123, 123–4
Shams-i Tabrizi 223
Sharif, Ahmad 114
Sharshina, *pir* of 48
Shi'ism 210, 212–13
short stories 190–2; *see also* '*Bain*'
Sidi cult 10–11, 20, 117–39; *goma* at *Sayyid* shrines 135–6; hierarchy of saints' cults 117–20, 133–5; *see also* Gujarat black saints cult
slaughter, ritual 101–3
social realism 190–1
soul 6
South Asia 16–17, 209, 216; shrine cults 188–90; Sufism's continuing power 224–9, 229–30
space 12, 44–5, 49–50; *see also* locality
spheres of existence 198, 200
spirits/demons 121–2, 131; myth of powerful demoness 123–4; stonings of devils 98; wilderness 83, 89; *see also* witches
spiritual power 33–4; appearances of 36–42
spirituality 198, 199–200
springs 84–5
state 15–16, 218, 226; *see also* politicians, politics
stonings of devils 98
subjectivity 42–4
substantive approach 7–8
subversion 175–6
Sufi lodges 55–6, 106–7, 214; Bangladesh 35; satellite lodges 104–5
Sufism: criticism of shrines 189–90; delegitimization in Middle East 217–24; maintenance of charisma 212–16; and modernity 216–18; shrine cults 3–5,

188–9; in South Asia 188–9, 224–9; tolerance 55–6
Sunni Islam 209–10
suspension, state of 35–6
symbolic order 174–6, 180–1
syncretism 17–21

tabarruk (thanksgiving) 104
Tablighi Jama'at 216
test of faith 99–100
texts, personal 115
Thânawî, Ashraf 'Alî 191
theft 128
al-Tijani 219
Tinthin village shrine 55
tolerance, Sufi 55–6
tombs 35, 43; mortuary symbolism 35–6; *see also dargah*
Tourette syndrome 157–8
trance dances 132–3
transformative power of saintly rituals 127–31
trees 83–4

'ulama: faqirs and 105
umra 98
unknown saints' shrines *see* anonymous shrines
Urdu: short stories 191–2

'urs rituals 39, 40, 41, 61, 188; Barri Imam 153; Ghamkol Sharif 100, 101, 103, 105, 111; Gujarat shrines 132–3; Mama Ji Sarkar 151–2
Uwars al-Qarani 198

value systems 221–4, 227–9
virility 123; restoring 130
voluntary labour 100–1, 111

wahdat al-wujûd (unity of being) 197
Wahhabism 217
Watto, Mian Muhammad Yasin Khan 109
wells 84–5
wilderness 86, 89; saints and 83–5, 145
Wirikuta 95
witches 83, 89, 90, 128
women 100–1, 111, 112, 152; *see also* gender

zabah 104
Zaker Party 48
Zia ul Haque (Haqq) 45, 193
Zikr 103, *see also dhikr*
Zindapir 100, 102, 106; and giving 104–5, 107, 110–11; and politicians 108–10; relation to supplicants and disciples 111–14